DRAFTING AND ANALYZING CONTRACTS

A Guide to the Practical Application of the Principles of Contract Law

Third Edition

IT TAKES TWO TO MAKE A CONTRACT.

HOW TO WRITE A CONTRACT.

Rule :—1. The parties to a Contract are taken in the order in which they are written and referred to as "the party of the first part," "the party of the second part," without repeating their names. It matters not which name is written first.

2. After writing the date, names of the parties and their places of residence, state fully all that the first party agrees to do, and then state all that the second party agrees to do.

3. Next state the penalties or forfeitures in case either party does not faithfully and fully perform, or offer to perform, his part of the agreement.

4. Finally, the closing clause, the signatures and seals, the signatures of witnesses are written. (A seal is simply the mark of a pen around the word " seal," written after the signature.)

Scott J. Burnham

Professor of Law
The University of Montana Schoool of Law

LexisNexis™

LCCCN#: 2003111179

ISBN#: 0-8205-5788-9

Editorial Offices
744 Broad Street, Newark, NJ 07102 (973) 820-2000
201 Mission St., San Francisco, CA 94105-1831 (415) 908-3200
701 East Water Street, Charlottesville, VA 22902-7587 (804) 972-7600
www.lexis.com

To my parents, whose New England minds always took a practical turn

ACKNOWLEDGMENTS

This work began to take shape as I taught Contracts at the University of Montana School of Law. Dean John O. Mudd gave particularly strong encouragement to curriculum development that emphasized application as well as doctrine. In the summer of 1984, I was assisted by a grant from the National Institute for Dispute Resolution, which recognized the preventive law value of good drafting.

Other than these two, specific acknowledgments seem out of place, for to list is to limit. I would have to acknowledge not only those individuals who helped directly with the work, but those who have helped me to see a need and to fill it. I am grateful to them, the many teachers and students I have profited from as a law student, practitioner, and professor.

Excerpts from the following materials appear with the kind permission of the copyright holders. Additional permissions appear in the text.

Am. Jur. Legal Forms (2nd ed.). Copyright © 2000 West Group. Reprinted with permission.

Material from Bender's Uniform Commercial Code Service is reprinted with permission from Forms and Procedures Under the Uniform Commercial Code by Frederick M. Hart and William F. Willier. Copyright © 2003 by Matthew Bender & Co., Inc. All rights reserved.

Corbin, Contracts. Copyright © 1962, 2001 Matthew Bender & Co., Inc. All rights reserved.

Restatement (Second) of Contracts. Copyright © 1981 The American Law Institute. Reprinted with the permission of The American Law Institute.

Uniform Laws Annotated. Copyright © 1995 West Group. Reprinted with permission.

West's Legal Forms. Copyright © 1998 West Group. Reprinted with permission.

White & Summers, Uniform Commercial Code (5th ed.). Copyright © 2000 West Group. Reprinted with permission.

SUMMARY TABLE OF CONTENTS

———

TABLE OF CONTENTS

PART I
How the Principles of Contract Law
Are Exemplified in Drafting

Page

PART II
How the Principles of Drafting Are Exemplified in Contracts

PART III
How to Read and Analyze a Contract

Page

UCC - governs the sale of goods

INTRODUCTION

Goals of the book.

Law professors often say that the purpose of law school is to teach a person to "think like a lawyer." No doubt this is a desirable goal, but what does it mean? Thinking like a lawyer undoubtedly means understanding legal principles. But it is more than that. It also means applying those principles to solve particular problems, developing the skills lawyers use to express their thinking, particularly skills in oral and written communication, and developing the perspective to think and act in an ethical and responsible manner.

This book starts with your understanding of the principles of contract law and puts that knowledge to use, the kind of use practitioners make of legal principles. Drafting is the skill I focus on, for as Robert C. Dick wrote, "Legal drafting is legal thinking made visible."[1] It is my belief that this kind of practical application will sharpen your ability to think like a lawyer. This book uses drafting (1) to exemplify the principles of contract law, (2) to illustrate the principles in a planning context, and (3) to develop the skills of a lawyer.

1. Exemplification of the principles of contract law. Every law student takes a course called Contracts, but many do not actually work with contracts.

At the beginning of my second year of law school, I obtained part-time employment on the legal staff of a major motion picture company. Part of my job was to reduce complex agreements to one-page summaries for the use of non-legal executives, detailing what we had to do and when we had to do it. I recall feeling uneasy as I enumerated our obligations under one agreement. A provision stated that on our paying a songwriter a sum of money, the songwriter would be bound to write songs for us. Studying the language, I finally realized what was troubling me — we had not promised to pay the songwriter. We would not obtain a return performance from her if we didn't do it, but we didn't have to do it.

Only then, five months after successful completion of my Contracts class, did I fully realize the difference between a promise and a condition. I had studied cases in which I followed the analysis of judges and I had manipulated the concepts in an exam. My understanding of the principles was incomplete, however, until I saw how they were applied in a concrete situation. By demonstrating the application of the principles in drafting and by asking you to interact with the material in an active manner, this book should help you to understand the principles and to use them more effectively.

---

[1] ROBERT C. DICK, LEGAL DRAFTING 1 (Carswell 2nd ed. 1985).

2. Illustration of the principles of contract law in a planning context. When you use contract principles in drafting, you see them from a different perspective. This is the perspective of a planner. Contracts cases begin at a point after the parties have entered an agreement and the agreement process has broken down. The focus is on how courts resolve problems. As Jackson and Bollinger state, most cases "are examples of what a contract should not be. Once the lawyer learns the pitfalls, he should have the expertise to avoid them."[2] This message is implicit in case analysis; this book makes it explicit. It asks how the drafter can use the principles at the time the agreement is planned to prevent a breakdown later.

I believe that lawyers can make a contribution to preventive law through drafting. The lawyer as planner must understand the role of the legal principle in a particular agreement as it applies to a particular client in a particular situation. This process requires the drafter to articulate and reflect on the principles, a process which may prevent future disputes. The book constantly emphasizes what I call the three P's of drafting:

> *Predict* what may happen;
> *Provide* for that contingency; and
> *Protect* your client with a remedy.

Of course, it is not always possible to prevent a dispute from arising or to resolve it short of litigation. But thoughtful drafting can help the parties reach an agreement that is suitable for them and that is artfully expressed.

3. Development of the skills of a lawyer. This book looks at contracts from a perspective that will assist lawyers and future lawyers to develop the skills required in the practice of law. Charles A. Beardsley, past President of the American Bar Association, wrote:

> Learning draftsmanship in the school of experience exclusively is costly to clients; it is costly to the public, and it is costly to the lawyer. It is like learning surgery by experience — it is possible, but it is tough on the patient and tough on the reputation of the surgeon.[3]

Through the course in Contracts, lawyers gain knowledge of substantive law and develop analytical skills. As you know from the classroom experience, Contracts is far richer than that. It is also an introduction to voluntary interpersonal relationships, to the use of private law to increase personal autonomy, and to the crucial importance of language. Working with drafting not only reviews the substantive law but also develops additional skills and enriches the lawyer's perspective.

Lawyers spend most of their time neither in court nor in the library, but in their offices and at meetings. There they engage in activities requiring skills in oral and written communication, such as interviewing, counseling, and negotiating. Drafting is one form of communication. Through the

---

[2] JACKSON & BOLLINGER, CONTRACT LAW IN MODERN SOCIETY 1003 (West 2nd ed. 1980).

[3] Charles A. Beardsley, *Beware of, Eschew and Avoid Pompous Prolixity and Platitudinous Epistles!,* 16 CAL. ST. B.J. 65 (1941).

agreement the lawyers draft, the parties communicate with each other and, when necessary, with a court. Drafting as planning is often negotiation. The draft must be acceptable to both parties. Even when drafting a one-sided agreement, such as a contract of adhesion, the drafter must talk back to the draft, asking what to include and exclude.

It has often struck me that we learn lawyering principally by reading cases — and lawyers do not appear in the cases! Drafting brings lawyers into the picture, and when lawyers practice their craft, ethical issues inevitably arise. It is impossible to look at an aspect of the practice of law without an appreciation of the ethical considerations that permeate it. Nevertheless, ethical aspects of planning have been neglected in the literature of legal ethics. This book integrates ethical considerations into the discussion of substantive concepts.

Organization of the book.

The book is divided into three main parts.

Part I: How the Principles of Contract Law Are Exemplified in Drafting

Part I deals with the substantive law of contracts. Each chapter is keyed to the topics traditionally encountered in Contracts courses; for example, Offer and Acceptance, Consideration, Parol Evidence, Promise and Condition. Each chapter contains three parts: (1) Introduction, (2) Drafting considerations, and (3) Exercises.

1. Introduction. An essay explains the applicability of the principles of contract law to the drafting of agreements. For example, casebooks generally examine parol evidence from the point of view of an appellate court deciding whether the proffered evidence should have been admitted. This book reverses the process, encouraging the drafter as planner to ask before the signatures are applied to an agreement: Does this instrument contain all the understandings between the parties? Have I taken precautions to attain as much security for my client as is desirable? How can I accomplish these goals through drafting?

I hasten to add that the book is not another treatise on contract law. Many points of contract doctrine are omitted, and others covered only sketchily. The book focuses on principles that can be exemplified through drafting. For example, many of the traditional principles of offer and acceptance concern the process leading up to the drafting of the agreement. I examine those principles of offer and acceptance that can be demonstrated through drafting, such as the problem that arises under U.C.C. § 2-207 when each party claims to be bound by a different contract.

The book often points out the applicable law, for the drafter must consider legal requirements and prohibitions. For example, the laws of the jurisdiction with respect to consequential damages for breach of warranty are an important consideration in drafting a warranty. As a maximum, you are encouraged to research the law of your own jurisdiction; some of the Exercises are research questions. As a minimum, you should appreciate restrictions on the parties' freedom to establish "private law" in their agreement. You should also consider the policy questions and ethical considerations involved in drafting provisions contrary to law.

2. Drafting considerations. Brown and Dauer point out that the legal reasoning process used in planning is the reverse of that used in the case method. In cases, the facts are a given and their legal significance is a variable. In planning, the desired outcome is a given and the facts that will best produce it are a variable. The requisite lawyers' skills include determining the client's goals, developing the facts, using rules of law to attain the outcome, and predicting the consequences of a chosen course of action.[4]

We learn from the case method that the outcome of a particular case is a function of both the facts and the rules. The outcome will probably change when the facts change. The application to drafting is evident. In drafting, the facts are the language you employ in your contract. For example, in casebook materials on Mistake you study how courts have applied the doctrine to releases. In this book, you are asked to plan the transaction: What will happen if you use certain language? What consequences should you provide for? What language will best serve your client's needs?

The book presents and discusses language customarily used to serve a desired purpose. The drafter usually begins with a model, either formbook language or an agreement used in the past. Drafting from scratch is rare. Forms have utility; what they should not have is sanctity. When you understand the purpose of a provision, you are better able to determine whether the form language is appropriate and how to alter it. Drafting requires you to think about language, not to appropriate forms mechanically.

While I have included many examples of contract language and some forms, the purpose of these examples is to illustrate the process of thinking. The reader who wishes to incorporate this language in a document has missed the point. The language illustrates how the principle may be expressed for a particular client with a particular need. You must give similar thought to the document you are drafting and the client you are serving. One of David Mellinkoff's Rules of Legal Writing states:

> Some day someone will read what you have written, trying to find something wrong with it. This is the special burden of legal writing, and the special incentive to be as precise as you can.[5]

3. Exercises. Each chapter illustrates the concepts through exercises in which you are asked to work with a contract. For example, in the chapter on Indefiniteness, you are presented with an executed Buy-Sell agreement and asked to detect those provisions that may be too indefinite to be

---

[4] BROWN & DAUER, PLANNING BY LAWYERS 270 (Foundation 1978).

[5] DAVID MELLINKOFF, LEGAL DRAFTING: SENSE & NONSENSE 15 (West 1982).

enforceable. You may then evaluate the language in light of the principles of contract law and make suggestions for revision.

Part II: How the Principles of Drafting Are Exemplified in Contracts

Part I demonstrates how the substantive understandings find expression in individual provisions. Part II deals with the art of drafting, demonstrating how the individual provisions work together in a document. In drafting a document, you must synthesize the individual parts and express them with clarity. Part II contains some suggestions for doing so.

A well-planned agreement gains force from both its content and its style. There are many fine works on legal drafting that help the reader develop a better writing style. A number of those works are listed in the Bibliography. While this book often emphasizes the importance of clarity in drafting documents, its primary purpose is to show the connection between the substantive law of contracts and the expression of that substance in a contract. Only if you know what you want to say, and why you are saying it, can you write with the clarity that comes from conceptual understanding.

At some point research must stop and a decision must be made. Either you make a particular business decision or you don't; either you use particular language or you don't; either you sign a negotiated agreement or you don't. These decisions make us uneasy: if only we knew all the facts; if only we knew all the law; if only we knew what was going to happen. We must recognize these limits and go on. Knowing how to think like lawyers, we must have the courage to act like lawyers, to commit the product of our thinking to paper.

In the second edition, I added a chapter called "Drafting with a Computer." In this edition, I have added exercises to several chapters that involve the use of a computer in drafting and have explored contracts that are formed over the Internet.

The ease with which documents can be generated on the computer is an argument for greater understanding of contract law as applied to drafting. It is now possible to purchase software containing reams of legal forms, so that with the push of a few buttons out will pop a contract. An attorney who used a "hard copy" form as a model at least had to read through it when adapting it to a new transaction. The attorney who uses a computer must do the same. The advantage of the computer is that the time saved in drudgery can be devoted to the work the attorney is best suited for — the legal analysis of the document. This book will prepare you to meet that challenge.

Part III: How to Read and Analyze a Contract

As I conducted seminars on how to draft contracts, I frequently reminded the audience, as I state in Chapter 15, that you rarely start to draft on a blank slate. More often, you start with an existing contract or form. It slowly dawned on me that it would be helpful to know how to read the existing contract in order to draft changes to it. And then I realized that nothing prepares us for reading contracts.

Reading theory tells us that we use different techniques, called "protocols," to read different kinds of texts. My approach is simple. I assume that the main reason you don't read contracts is because you don't know how to read contracts, and you don't know how to read contracts because you have never been taught how to read contracts. Using the process known as "think through," I worked out the steps that I use to read contracts and teach you that method.

How to use the book.

The purpose of this book is to apply your knowledge of contract law to the drafting of agreements. Each chapter discusses the substance of contracts as applied to drafting and suggests language that may be employed to accomplish the purpose. Using the techniques in Part II, you can then assemble the various sections of the contract into a completed whole.

If you are using the book in conjunction with a Contracts class, I suggest reading each chapter of the book after you have studied the substantive topic discussed in that chapter. Because I sketch some of the applicable substance and because many of the topics are related, you may wish to read the book straight through. The book should be especially valuable after you have completed your substantive study, to review it, demonstrate its application, and synthesize the various parts. It could also be consulted before you begin a drafting assignment, either for a class or in practice.

You can study each chapter of Part I to better understand the application of a principle in practice and pull it all together in Part II.

If you are using the book in conjunction with a drafting or planning class, I suggest that you start with Part II, with reference back to each chapter of Part I when you require a better understanding of the substantive underpinnings of each part of the document. The organization is intended to be flexible, reflecting drafting as a lawyering skill. Development of the skill is not linear, but is part of a process, with various steps interrelated. This is seen in the related forms of organization: by topic and by the architecture of the agreement. The bibliography should be consulted for additional materials.

Part III, "How to Read and Analyze a Contract," might make a good starting place because it is written for a lay audience. If you don't understand the substantive law of contracts being discussed at a particular point, I have provided footnotes indicating the section of the book where discussion of that substance can be found. Alternatively, you could read Part III after you have finished the rest of the book, for you may find it helpful to see the material synthesized and organized in another way.

An invitation to the reader.

I have developed this book because I believe teachers and law students will find it useful in the classroom to integrate theory and practice. In writing it, I have often ventured into uncharted waters. In further developing this approach, I invite your assistance. If you have comments about the work, or suggestions for materials to incorporate in it, I would be glad to hear from you.

Part I

How the Principles of Contract Law Are Exemplified in Drafting

Chapter 1

OFFER AND ACCEPTANCE

§ 1.1 Introduction.

How does an agreement come about? The parties voluntarily enter into a contract because each considers the exchange to be in his or her best interest. Drafting is the private law-making whereby the parties bargain for the incorporation of terms in the contract. This bargaining process can take a number of different forms. Written agreements signed by both parties are usually formed in one of three ways:

1. One party presents the other with a prepared document for signature. This type of agreement is often known as a "contract of adhesion," for the party in the weaker bargaining position is unable meaningfully to bargain for better terms. Under the objective view of assent, a party who neither reads nor understands the agreement is nevertheless bound by it.

In this situation, the drafter for the party in the stronger bargaining position appears to be free to impose terms on the other party. Nevertheless, when planning the transaction, the drafter still faces a form of negotiation — the possibility that the law will not enforce the contract. Chapter 4, Enforceability, examines the constraints on the lawyer drafting such a one-sided agreement.

2. Each party sends the other its own prepared document. The documents state the same basic terms such as quantity and price, but differ on other terms. In spite of the differences in the documents, the parties ship the goods and pay for them. This type of agreement may give rise to "The Battle of the Forms," discussed in this chapter.

In preparing this document, the drafter must be aware of the rules of war governing this battle, and must plan for them. The task of the drafter is not only to incorporate favorable terms, but to assure that those terms will survive the resolution of the conflict between the forms.

3. The parties reach consensus on terms through a process of negotiation and then sign the agreement. The signatures of both parties on the document indicate that they have accepted the terms. The form of a negotiated agreement may vary considerably. It may be a letter drafted by one party and signed by the other. Or it may contain a web of tightly-drafted clauses crafted by careful negotiators.

Recall, however, that an offer is a promise to perform conditional on receiving acceptance. Often, a party does not intend that its offer be accepted without further negotiation. In that event, the drafter of the offer must take precautions to prevent a contract from being formed prematurely.

This book is concerned largely with negotiated agreements signed by both parties. When both parties execute the same agreement, the drafter rarely needs to demonstrate the occurrence of offer and acceptance. Therefore, the traditional rules of offer and acceptance, premised on a party making an offer that the other party either accepts or rejects, are often inapplicable to negotiated agreements.

This chapter looks at issues involving offer and acceptance that arise outside negotiated agreements. These issues include (1) drafting a firm offer and a letter of intent, (2) drafting an agreement in which acceptance is implied in fact, and (3) preparing for the "Battle of the Forms."

§ 1.2 Firm offers — U.C.C. § 2-205.   *Merchant buyers/sellers*

An option is a contract in which the offeree pays the offeror a consideration to keep the offer open. Under U.C.C. § 2-205, however, a merchant who makes a "firm offer" is unable to revoke the offer even if there is no consideration flowing from the offeree. The section states:

> An offer by a merchant to buy or sell goods in a signed writing which by its terms gives assurance that it will be held open is not revocable, for lack of consideration, during the time stated or if no time is stated for a reasonable time, but in no event may such period of irrevocability exceed three months; but any such term of assurance on a form supplied by the offeree must be separately signed by the offeror.

The drafter must be careful to create a firm offer only where one is intended. Because the statute appears in Article 2, it applies only to transactions in goods. It is also one of the few provisions in Article 2 that states a "merchant rule," making it applicable only when made by merchant buyers or sellers. Most importantly, it applies only to "an offer." *Offer* is not defined in the Code; we therefore look to the common law definition, which generally excludes an advertisement.

Putting together this substantive knowledge of the Code, we are now in a position to draft a firm offer. Compare these communications to determine which is a firm offer under the statute:

---

1. Sale! For the next ten days, all widgets are priced at $50 each. Hurry while supplies last!

Stop here

→ Pg. 14

> 2.   We are pleased to offer widgets at $50 each. Thank you very much for this opportunity to quote. s/ Merchant.

> 3.   This offer will remain open for two months from the date of this letter. s/ Merchant.

> 4.   This offer will remain open for six months from the date of this letter. s/ Merchant.

> 5.   We are pleased to offer widgets at $50 each. This offer is firm. s/ Merchant.

> 6.   Merchant writes: We are pleased to offer widgets at $50 each. Thank you very much for this opportunity to quote. s/ Merchant. In response, Customer writes: Your offer is firm and we may accept it at any time during the next thirty days. s/ Customer.

Example 1 is probably an advertisement rather than an offer; therefore, it can't be a firm offer. Example 2 is probably an offer, but it is not a firm offer, for it contains no terms giving assurance that it will be held open, as required by the statute. The language of Example 3 probably expresses a firm offer that may not be revoked for two months. In Example 4, the period during which the offer may not be revoked is limited by the statute to three months. The firm offer in Example 5 may not be revoked for a reasonable time, not to exceed three months. Example 6 would not constitute a firm offer unless signed by the merchant.

§ 1.3   Did negotiating parties intend an agreement?

Often one party submits a proposal or offer to the other party. There is a danger that the offeree will indicate acceptance before detailed terms are worked out. To prevent this from happening, an offeror may designate its preliminary proposal an "invitation to negotiate" rather than an offer. When making a proposal, the offeror could state orally or in writing:

> This letter [or proposal] is only a part of preliminary negotiations. We intend to be bound only upon the execution of a contract in writing.

Parties negotiating an agreement are not always successful. Unable to agree on terms, they may terminate their discussions. In that situation, are they bound by an oral agreement they reached even though no writing was signed? This issue must be resolved by examining the intent of the parties. They may have intended that the writing would merely memorialize an enforceable oral agreement. Or they may have intended to have no enforceable agreement without a signed writing.

Parties who do not intend an agreement until a writing is signed should make that understanding express. They often do so in a "letter of intent." A "letter of intent" must state exactly what that intent is. For example, during negotiations the parties could agree orally or in writing:

> The parties do not intend to be bound except by a written agreement signed by both parties containing mutually acceptable terms of the transaction.

§ 1.4 Objective manifestation of assent.

Contract law requires an objective manifestation of assent. In spite of the commonly heard phrase, we don't form contracts through a "meeting of the minds" (unless we are on the planet Vulcan). In written contracts, the usual manifestation of assent is a signature. In oral contracts, it might be a handshake, the words "It's a deal," or the like. In an auction, assent might be manifested by a gesture or by lifting a paddle with a number on it. These actions all say, "I intend to be bound."

A few years ago, we began seeing "shrink-wrap" transactions. The language of the contract was printed on a box that contained computer software. The box was then wrapped with clear plastic through which the language could be read. The language informed the offeree that the act of unsealing the wrapping constituted acceptance of the terms. For example:

> YOU SHOULD CAREFULLY READ THE FOLLOWING TERMS AND CONDITIONS BEFORE OPENING THIS DISKETTE PACKAGE. OPENING THIS DISKETTE PACKAGE INDICATES YOUR ACCEPTANCE OF THESE TERMS AND CONDITIONS. IF YOU DO NOT AGREE WITH THEM, YOU SHOULD PROMPTLY RETURN THE PACKAGE UNOPENED; AND YOUR MONEY WILL BE REFUNDED.

Now we see "click-wrap" transactions on the internet. Moving the mouse over a button and clicking is probably an appropriate manner of indicating assent. Nevertheless, the drafter should take steps to insure that the agreement is stated in such a way that assent is clearly expressed. The user should have the opportunity to view the terms before indicating assent. The terms should be clear and readable. Terms that might be beyond the user's reasonable expectations should be conspicuously called to the user's attention. The words of assent should be clear and unambiguous.

For example, the following image shows the buttons the user may click following the terms and conditions:

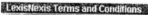

LexisNexis Terms and Conditions
NOTICE: By selecting the "ACCEPT" button, you are indicating that you understand, accept and agree to the General Terms and Conditions for use of the LexisNexis services set forth below, and that you are authorized to make this selection.

Accept   Decline

Copyright © 2003 LexisNexis, a division of Reed Elsevier Inc. All rights reserved. Your use of this service is governed by Terms & Conditions . Please review them.

§ 1.5 The Battle of the Forms — U.C.C. § 2-207.

Section 2-207 is used to resolve the "Battle of the Forms" between a buyer and seller of goods. The relationship begins peacefully enough. An offeror sends its prepared form to an offeree; e.g., Buyer sends a Purchase Order to Seller. The offeree checks the material terms: price, quantity, date of delivery, and payment terms. If it agrees with those terms, offeree responds with its prepared form; e.g., Seller sends an Acknowledgment to Buyer. There is agreement on the material or "dickered" terms in the offering document and the accepting document. The boilerplate terms differ, however, for each party has prepared those terms in advance of the transaction and without reference to the other's form. Even if a party notices differences, it is not economically efficient to hold up the transaction to resolve them. The result is a disparity between the offering document and the accepting document.

In most cases, peace reigns. The parties generally perform by shipping the goods and paying for them. But something may later go wrong; for example, Buyer claims a breach of warranty. Each party pulls the documents from its files and discovers the conflicting terms; for example, Buyer's form contains generous warranty terms while Seller's form contains a limitation of remedies for breach of warranty. The battle is on to determine whether there is a contract and, if so, whose terms prevail.

Section 2-207 provides:

Additional Terms in Acceptance or Confirmation

(1) A definite and seasonable expression of acceptance or a written confirmation which is sent within a reasonable time operates as an acceptance even though it states terms additional to or different from those offered or agreed upon, unless acceptance is expressly made conditional on assent to the additional or different terms.

(2) The additional terms are to be construed as proposals for addition to the contract. Between merchants such terms become part of the contract unless:

(a) the offer expressly limits acceptance to the terms of the offer;

(b) they materially alter it; or

(c) notification of objection to them has already been given or is given within a reasonable time after notice of them is received.

(3) Conduct by both parties which recognizes the existence of a contract is sufficient to establish a contract for sale although the writings of the parties do not otherwise establish a contract. In such case the terms of the particular contract consist of those terms on which the writings of the parties agree, together with any supplementary terms incorporated under any other provisions of this Act.

Many authorities have suggested that § 2-207 is inadequately drafted. One problem is that the statute reaches a number of logical decision points (i.e., forks in the road) and only pursues one of the alternatives. For example, subsection (1) tells us that an expression of acceptance operates as an acceptance even though it states additional or different terms; subsection (2) tells us what to do with additional terms, but not different terms. Within subsection (2), we are told that between merchants the additional terms become part of the contract; we are not told the rule for agreements when both parties are not merchants.

Revised Article 2 substantially simplifies the issues. It defers to §§ 2-204 and 2-206 to determine whether a contract is formed. Once it has been determined that a contract has been formed, § 2-207 determines what terms the contract contains. It provides:

§ 2-207. Terms of Contract; Effect of Confirmation.

If (i) conduct by both parties recognizes the existence of a contract although their records do not otherwise establish a contract, (ii) a contract is formed by an offer and acceptance, or (iii) a contract formed in any manner is confirmed by a record that contains terms additional to or different from those in the contract being confirmed, the terms of the contract, subject to Section 2-202, are:

   (a) terms that appear in the records of both parties;

   (b) terms, whether in a record or not, to which both parties agree; and

   (c) terms supplied or incorporated under any provision of this Act.

Under the Revised § 2-207, if the terms are not agreed upon by both parties, they are knocked out and the default rule is supplied.

The following flow chart is designed to supply the missing alternatives to original § 2-207:

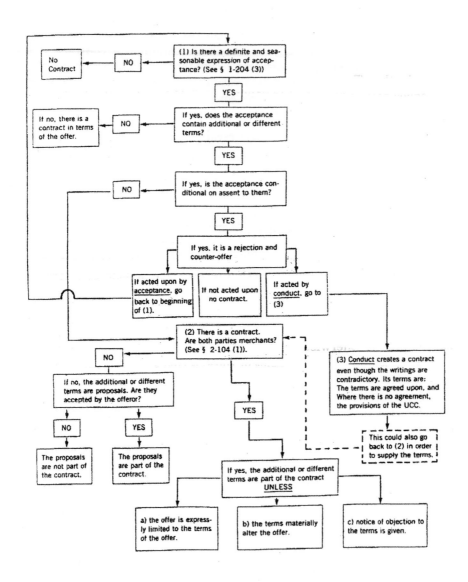

The goal of this discussion is not to resolve all the problems that arise under § 2-207, but merely to suggest points where drafting may help achieve the best result. A number of difficulties arise in drafting under the statute. The language of subsection (1) to the comma provides:

> A definite and seasonable expression of acceptance or a written confirmation which is sent within a reasonable time operates as an acceptance even though it states terms additional to or different from those offered or agreed upon

The purpose of this provision is to change the common law "mirror-image" rule, which provided that a response containing terms not in the offer was not an acceptance but a counteroffer. Under the Code, a response that does not conform to the offer may be an acceptance. But to operate as an acceptance, the expression must be "definite." If the material terms (i.e., price, quantity, date of delivery, payment terms) differ, is there a contract? For example, the offer requests "1000 widgets @ $1 each" and the response acknowledges sale of "1 widget @ $1000 each." Although authority is split on this issue, the better rule seems to be that a document containing significantly different material terms is not an acceptance. The statute is aimed at resolving conflicts in the boilerplate terms, not the dickered terms. If this is the case, then problems with material terms cannot be resolved through drafting. The client must examine each deal to insure that the material terms coincide.

Assuming that when the material terms do not coincide there is no acceptance, then there is no contract. Either party may refuse to perform if performance has not begun. Often, however, the parties have performed; e.g., the seller has shipped the widget and the buyer has accepted it. It is then necessary to resolve the conflicting terms. This is done by reference to subsection (3) of the statute:

> Conduct by both parties which recognizes the existence of a contract is sufficient to establish a contract for sale although the writings of the parties do not otherwise establish a contract. In such case the terms of the particular contract consist of those terms on which the writings of the parties agree, together with any supplementary terms incorporated under any other provisions of this Act.

For example, if the price terms did not coincide, then the term would be established under the U.C.C. default rules. With respect to price, the rule would be § 2-305, which provides for a reasonable price if nothing is said as to price.

Let us assume now that the material terms coincide but the boilerplate terms do not. The language after the comma in § 2-207(1) creates an exception to the rule that a response containing additional or different terms operates as an acceptance. Under the language after the comma, the offeree's response is an acceptance "unless acceptance is expressly made conditional on assent to the additional or different terms." This is a drafting point. Apparently either party could include this language. For example, Buyer as offeror might state:

Acceptance. Acceptance of this offer must be made on its exact terms and if additional or different terms are proposed by Seller, its response will constitute a counteroffer, and no contract will come into existence without offeror's assent to the counteroffer.

Assume Buyer does not include this language. What language by the Seller as offeree would suffice to prevent the Seller's response from becoming an acceptance of Buyer's terms? Consider these alternatives:

> 1. *Additional or Different Terms.* This acceptance is expressly made conditional on assent by Buyer to any terms additional to or different from those contained in Buyer's offer. If Buyer does not assent, there is no acceptance.

> 2. Buyer agrees that this acknowledgment is posterior to and supersedes any conflicting oral or written terms or conditions of purchase.

> 3. Subject to conditions printed on the reverse side of this form.

The language in Example 1 would probably be effective, for it tracks the language of the statute to avoid any question of whether it suffices as expressly conditional. Examples 2 and 3 probably fall short of express language that would satisfy the statutory requirement. If the response is not expressly conditional, there is an acceptance. Whether executory or performed, the agreement is enforceable, with the terms determined under subsection (2), which we will shortly examine.

What is the consequence of including language effective to satisfy the statutory requirement in subsection (1) following the comma? When a response satisfies the statutory requirement, there is no acceptance. Without an acceptance, there is no contract. If the contract is executory, there is no remedy for nonperformance. If the parties have performed, then we must drop down into subsection (3) to determine the terms of the contract. Therefore, by including language effective under subsection (1) after the comma, a party may prevent the other party's terms from prevailing, but does not obtain its own terms. The terms will be the default provisions of the Code. This result could be detrimental to one party. For example, the U.C.C. warranty and limitations provisions are more likely to favor a buyer. Therefore, a seller must be careful not to invoke subsection (3).

Let us now return to consideration of subsection (1) before the comma, assuming neither party has added language that satisfies the exception after the comma. We have agreement on the material terms but not on the boilerplate terms. Subsection (1) tells us there is an acceptance, so we have a contract. To determine its terms, we must drop down to subsection (2):

> The additional terms are to be construed as proposals for addition to the contract. Between merchants such terms become part of the contract unless:

> (a) the offer expressly limits acceptance to the terms of the offer;

(b) they materially alter it; or

(c) notification of objection to them has already been given or is given within a reasonable time after notice of them is received.

Under subsection (2), the offeree is seen as proposing the additional terms to the offeror. Between merchants, the additional terms become part of the contract except in three circumstances. One of those circumstances arises when "the offeror expressly limits acceptance to the terms of the offer." This is a drafting point. What language by the offeror would suffice to prevent the additional terms in the response from becoming part of the contract? Consider these alternatives:

---

1. Subject to the conditions on the reverse side.

---

2. *Acceptance — Different Terms.* Buyer expressly limits acceptance to the terms of this offer. Buyer objects to the inclusion of any different or additional terms proposed by Seller in its acceptance of this offer, and if they are included in Seller's acceptance, a contract for sale will result upon Buyer's terms stated herein.

---

3. *Acceptance.* Acceptance of this offer must be made on its exact terms and if additional or different terms are proposed by Seller, its response will constitute a counteroffer, and no contract shall come into existence without offeror's assent to the counteroffer.

The language in Example 1 does not appear strong enough to satisfy the statutory requirement that "the offer expressly limits acceptance to the terms of the offer." This language appears merely to say that the terms on the reverse side are part of the offer.

When a drafter wishes to comply with a statutory provision, the drafter should track carefully the language of the statute. Here, subsection (2)(a) of the statute states, "the offer expressly limits acceptance to the terms of the offer." The drafter of Example 2 provides, "Buyer expressly limits acceptance to the terms of this offer." By using in the contract the same language used in the statute, the drafter has left little doubt that the contract satisfies the statutory requirement.

While the language of Example 2 states that the parties have a contract on Buyer's terms, Example 3 states that they do not have a contract. Section 2-207 provides no instruction on dealing with the language of Example 3.

If a contract were then created by conduct, the terms would be determined under subsection (3). As discussed above, this result could be detrimental to the offeror, for the terms supplied by the U.C.C. could be less advantageous than the terms in offeror's form. Therefore, an offeror probably obtains the greatest advantage with a provision such as Example 2.

Subsection (2) provides for the treatment of additional terms, but what becomes of the different terms? One view holds that the different terms are considered rejected because the fact that they conflict with offeror's terms constitutes "notice of objection" under (2)(c). This rule is more easily stated than applied. For example, is a term in the response that differs from a term that is not expressly in the offer but is implied by the Code an additional or a different term? Many cases simply eliminate any distinction by reading subsection (2) as though it refers to "additional *or different* terms. . . ."

What happens when the parties are not both merchants? The statute states only that between merchants the terms become part of the contract. To determine the rule in other circumstances, we can apply the interpretive rule *expressio unius est exclusio alterius,* the expression of one excludes another. Under this interpretation, in transactions *not* between merchants the terms do *not* become part of the contract. If the non-merchant is the offeror, then the conflicting terms of the merchant may be excluded from the contract.

Recall, however, that an offeror who uses language that satisfies subsection (2) will not necessarily get its terms. If the offeror included the language of subsection (2)(a) and the offeree included the language of subsection (1) after the comma, it could be argued that the language of the acceptance was a different term. This analysis is incorrect. To have a different term in an agreement, there first has to be an acceptance. Under the exception to subsection (1), the language of express condition prevents offeree's response from being an acceptance. Therefore, the analysis would drop down to subsection (3), not subsection (2).

To complicate matters further, subsection (3) states that terms are found in "any other provision of this Act." Some authorities view this language as including subsection (2). The approach then becomes circular. Even if you were thrown into subsection (3), you would use the subsection (2) analysis. For example, between merchants, if a buyer offeror used the language after the comma in subsection (1), the offeree's terms could become part of the agreement unless the buyer fit one of exceptions in subsection (2). Under exception (b), proposed terms are rejected if they materially alter the terms of the offer. Courts often focus on this provision, which keeps an unusual term out of a contract.

Emerging from the fog of § 2-207 is this important principle: drafters who want unusual terms must negotiate for their acceptance. This is the approach used in the United Nations Convention on Contracts for the International Sale of Goods. Article 19(2) provides:

However, a reply to an offer which purports to be an acceptance but contains additional or different terms which do not materially alter the terms of the offer constitute an acceptance, unless the offeror, without undue delay, objects orally to the discrepancy or dispatches a notice to that effect. If he does not so object, the terms of the contract are the terms of the offer with the modifications contained in the acceptance.

§ 1.6   Ethics in offer and acceptance.

As we have seen, contract formation requires "objective manifestation of assent." A contract is formed by what the parties do externally, not by what goes on internally in their heads. If you manifest assent, you are bound whether you have read the contract or not, and whether you understand the terms of the contract or not.

A drafter may be tempted to take advantage of this principle. If the other party is bound whether they have read the contract or not, there may be a temptation to load the contract with favorable terms. *See* Chapter 4, Enforceability. Sometimes the advantage may arise because the party does not know the language in which the contract is written, or the party is illiterate and does not read at all. The general rule is that the party who remains silent and does not ask for assistance in this situation is negligent and bears the risk of entering the contract. There may be exceptions, however, if advantage was knowingly taken.

Sometimes an offeree is tempted to take advantage of this principle by neglecting to inform the offeror that she has changed the terms of the offered contract. The offeree will take the contract and say that she needs to think about it before signing. She will then make changes in the text. These changes could be accomplished by crossing out terms or by inserting language between the lines. The offeree might even redo the contract using similar word processing defaults, so it looks the same. She will then sign it and return it to the offeror. The offeror will then sign it and file it away.

When a problem arises, the offeror will react with surprise to the changed text. The offeree will remind the offeror of the rule of objective manifestation of assent — the parties are bound by the contract they signed. The offeror has supposedly learned a valuable lesson, to read the contract before signing it. Fortunately, the decided cases have not let offerees get away with this practice. Although it is wise to read a contract before signing it, as a practical matter, people do not read it when they assume the offered language has not changed. Courts have therefore held that an offeree has committed fraud if the offeree does not call the changes to the attention of the offeror. As one court said in response to the offeree's argument that the offeror was negligent in not reading the contract:

> Where it appears that one party has been guilty of an intentional and deliberate fraud, by which, to his knowledge, the other party has been misled, or influenced in his action, he cannot escape the legal consequences of his fraudulent conduct by saying that the fraud might have

been discovered had the party whom he deceived exercised reasonable diligence and care.

Furthermore, an attorney who engages in this practice probably violates the Rules of Professional Conduct. When the attorney for the other party gives you a contract for your consideration, if you wish to make changes in it, always point out the changes or enumerate them in a cover letter.

§ 1.7 Exercises.

1. The Click-Wrap Agreement. At its web site, Company has an agreement to be completed when the user pays for the goods that he or she has selected. It looks like this:

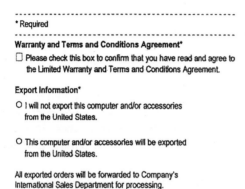

When the user clicks on the Terms and Conditions, the user sees terms that begin as follows:

STANDARD TERMS OF SALE AND LIMITED WARRANTY AGREEMENT

This Agreement applies to any order, purchase, receipt, delivery or use of any products and services (collectively, "purchase") from Company, Inc., or any of its subsidiaries or affiliates ("Company") or a Company authorized reseller ("Reseller"), unless you enter into a separate written agreement with Company. **THIS AGREEMENT APPLIES TO YOUR PURCHASE UNLESS YOU NOTIFY COMPANY IN WRITING THAT YOU DO NOT AGREE TO THIS AGREEMENT WITHIN 15 DAYS AFTER YOU RECEIVE THIS AGREEMENT AND YOU RETURN YOUR PRODUCT OR CANCEL SERVICES UNDER COMPANY'S REFUND POLICY. THIS AGREEMENT CONTAINS A DISPUTE RESOLUTION CLAUSE. PLEASE SEE SECTION 8 BELOW.**

How could Company better demonstrate that the user had assented to the terms, including the bold print provisions?

2. The "Battle of the Forms." In this transaction, a buyer sent its Purchase Order on one form and the seller sent its Sales Confirmation on another form.[1] Because the forms stated the same essential or "dickered" terms, the parties filed the forms away without close examination. Is the governing contract provision found in buyer's form, seller's form, or neither form when the following disputes arise:

    a. Seller claims it can't fully perform because of a fire.

    b. Buyer claims the delivered goods are not merchantable.

    c. Twenty days after receipt of the goods, Buyer gives Seller notice that the goods are not merchantable.

    d. Buyer returns the goods to Seller.

    e. Buyer seeks to have the dispute resolved in arbitration.

    f. Buyer asks that New York law be applied to resolve the dispute.

Suggested approach: First, determine whether there is language sufficient under § 2-207(1) after the comma to prevent an acceptance from arising. Then, assuming there is not sufficient language to prevent an acceptance, find the relevant language in Buyer's form and Seller's form with respect to each issue. Use § 2-207(2) to determine which provision becomes part of the contract.

Query: How would this problem be resolved under Revised § 2-207? Has your jurisdiction enacted the revised version?

PURCHASE ORDER
ABC Inc.

60 West 28th Street
New York, New York 10028

Seller's Name	Eager Beavers, Inc.
Address	Missoula, Montana
Our Order No.	B-12345
Date	September 1, 2003
Delivery Date	September 15, 2003
Terms	30 days cash
F.O.B.	Buyer's office
Shipping Instructions	Via Smith Trucking

Description of Goods:

  100 adult beaver skins suitable for hats @ $150 each

---

[1] MANDEL, THE PREPARATION OF COMMERCIAL AGREEMENTS. Copyright © 1972, The Practising Law Institute. Reprinted with permission.

ABC Inc.
By /s/ John J. Astor

Accepted on Behalf of Seller:

_____

TERMS AND CONDITIONS

1. Time of delivery and description of goods are of the essence of this contract. Buyer reserves the right to refuse any goods and to cancel all or any part of this order if Seller fails to deliver any part of the goods in accordance with the terms of this order.

2. Delivery shall not be deemed to be complete until goods have been actually received and accepted by Buyer, notwithstanding any agreement to pay freight, express or other transportation charges, and the risk of loss or damage in transit shall be upon Seller.

3. By accepting this order Seller acknowledges that the goods covered by this order are intended for the manufacture and sale of wearing apparel, and any defect in such goods may occasion special damage to Buyer.

4. Seller warrants that the goods covered by this order are of merchantable quality and fit and safe for consumer use. Acceptance of this order shall constitute an agreement upon Seller's part to indemnify Buyer against all liability, loss and damage, including reasonable counsel fees, sustained by Buyer by reason of failure of goods to conform to such warranties or to any requirement of law. Such indemnity shall be in addition to any other remedies afforded by law.

5. If any of the goods covered by this order are subject to the Wool Products Labeling Act, the Fur Products Labeling Act, the Textile Fiber Products Identification Act, the Flammable Fabrics Act, or any similar legislation, Seller's acceptance of this order shall constitute a continuing warranty that the goods delivered under this order conform to the requirements of all such legislation and applicable rules and regulations promulgated thereunder.

6. Any controversy or claim arising out of or relating to this contract or the breach thereof, shall be settled by arbitration held in New York, New York, in accordance with the rules of the American Arbitration Association, and judgment upon any award rendered in such proceedings may be entered in any court having jurisdiction thereof.

7. This contract contains the entire agreement of the parties. It may not be modified or terminated orally, and no claimed modification, rescission or waiver shall be binding on Buyer unless in writing signed by a duly authorized representative of Buyer.

8. This contract shall be governed by the laws of the State of New York.

SALES CONFIRMATION
Eager Beavers, Inc.
Water Supply Road
Missoula, Montana 59802

Sold to: ABC Inc.

                                 60 West 28th Street

                                 New York, New York 10028

Date: September 5, 2003

Our Ref. No.:   S-6789

Cust. Order No.:   B-12345

We hereby confirm receipt of your order as set forth below:

100 adult beaver skins @ $150/skin delivered 9/15/03 via Smith Trucking FOB your office terms 30 days cash.

                                 Eager Beavers, Inc.

                                 By /s/ Theodore Cleaver

                                 Seller

Accepted:

_____

Buyer

TERMS AND CONDITIONS OF SALE

1. This order is accepted on and subject to the following terms and conditions, which may not be modified except by a writing signed by Seller's duly authorized representative.

2. SELLER WARRANTS THAT ALL GOODS WILL CONFORM TO CONTRACT SPECIFICATIONS. ALL OTHER WARRANTIES, INCLUDING WITHOUT LIMITATION THE WARRANTIES OF MERCHANTABILITY AND FITNESS FOR A PARTICULAR PURPOSE, ARE EXCLUDED.

3. Seller shall not be liable for any delays in delivery or any failure to deliver due to causes beyond Seller's control, including but not limited to acts of God, war, mobilization, civil commotion, riots, embargoes, domestic or foreign governmental regulations or orders, fires, floods, strikes, lockouts or other labor difficulties, machinery breakdowns, or shortages of or inability to obtain shipping space or transportation. In such circumstances, unless otherwise agreed, the time for delivery shall be deemed extended for a period of sixty (60) days (and if payment is to be made by Letter of Credit, Buyer shall cause the Letter of Credit to be extended for a similar period). If delivery is not

made within such extended period, the contract shall be deemed cancelled by mutual consent without liability to either party.

4. Except as otherwise provided herein, Seller shall not be responsible for freight, transportation, insurance, shipping, storage, handling, demurrage or similar charges. If such charges are by the terms of sale included in the price, any increase in rates becoming effective after the date hereof shall be for the account of the Buyer.

5. Seller shall not be liable for normal variations in tolerance, dimensions, weights and quantity. Weights, sizes and quantities as determined at Seller's source of supply shall be conclusive.

6. Buyer is required to give written notice to Seller of any claim promptly upon receipt of the goods and in any event within fifteen (15) days thereafter, and Seller shall thereupon be afforded a reasonable opportunity to inspect the goods.

7. If any portion of the goods delivered to Buyer are defective or otherwise not in accordance with contract specifications, Seller shall have the right in its discretion either to replace such defective goods or to refund the portion of the purchase price applicable thereto. No goods shall be returned to Seller without Seller's written consent. In no event shall Seller be liable for the cost of processing, lost profits, injury to good will or any other special or consequential damages.

8. If by the terms of sale credit is extended to Buyer, Seller reserves the right to revoke credit if Buyer fails to pay for any goods previously delivered when due or if in the judgment of Seller there has been a material adverse change in Buyer's financial condition and thereupon Seller shall have the right to demand payment or other assurance which it deems adequate before shipment of any further goods.

9. Interest will be charged on all past-due accounts at Seller's prevailing rates, not in excess of rates permitted by law.

10. Any controversy or claim arising out of or relating to this contract, or the breach thereof, shall be resolved solely by recourse to the courts and not by arbitration.

11. This contract shall be governed by and construed according to the laws of the State of Montana.

3. Ethics. Buyer and Seller, two businessmen, come to see you. They have drafted a contract based on a form that they downloaded from the Internet. They have agreed on all the terms and just want you "to look it over to make sure everything is legal." Can you do so?

Chapter 2

CONSIDERATION

§ 2.1 Introduction.

Restatement (Second) of Contracts § 17 states:

> (1) Except as stated in Subsection (2), the formation of a contract requires a bargain in which there is a manifestation of mutual assent to the exchange and a consideration.

> (2) Whether or not there is a bargain a contract may be formed under special rules applicable to formal contracts or under the rules stated in §§ 82–94.

In the usual case, as described in § 17(1), a contract is a two-way street. To focus on the exchange, the attorney might find it helpful to draw a diagram, indicating the consideration that each party is receiving. For example, if Anne promises to pay Bill $500 in exchange for Bill's promise to sell her his automobile, the agreement may be diagrammed as follows:

$500

Anne $\rightleftarrows$ Bill

Automobile

Subject to the exceptions described in § 17(2), an agreement that does not include a two-way exchange will be unenforceable. For example, a father promises half of his farm to his daughter. The agreement may be diagrammed as follows:

1/2 **Farm**

Father ⟶ Daughter

Without some return promise or performance by the daughter, the agreement would lack consideration. Without a consideration for it, the father's promise would be labelled a *gift promise*. As a gift promise, it would not be enforceable.

What if the daughter promised her father her undying gratitude in exchange for half of the farm? There is an exchange, as indicated in this diagram:

1/2 **Farm**

Father ⇄ ⟶ Daughter

Undying Gratitude

The father may not have bargained for this return promise. In addition, the daughter's return promise has no economic value.

§ 2.2 Statutes dispensing with consideration.

At common law, a promise under seal was enforceable under the action of *covenant*. The original seals were wax impressions, but as literacy spread, the seal became less formal. Remnants of seals are found on legal documents today. The initials *L.S.* (*locus sigilli,* the place of the seal) may be found on the signature line. A document may state "signed and sealed" or "witness my hand and seal." These statements are meaningless. In most jurisdictions today, there is no distinction between sealed and unsealed instruments. U.C.C. § 2-203 states:

> The affixing of a seal to a writing evidencing a contract for sale or an offer to buy or sell goods does not constitute the writing a sealed instrument and the law with respect to sealed instruments does not apply to such a contract or offer.

In many jurisdictions, statutes have done away with the requirement of consideration in particular transactions. The drafter must take care that the contemplated transaction is within the statute and must follow carefully the statutory requirements. For example, U.C.C. § 2-209(1) provides:

> An agreement modifying a contract within this Article needs no consideration to be binding.

This statute applies only to transactions "within this Article," that is, transactions involving the sale of goods. Furthermore, although the statute appears to stand by itself, it must be read in light of the § 1-203 obligation of good faith. To better assure enforceability, parties drafting a modification might include an explanation of the commercial reason for the modification. *See* § 11.3.

Sometimes the statute dispensing with consideration requires a signed writing. For example, § 2 of the Uniform Premarital Agreement Act provides:

> A premarital agreement must be in writing and signed by both parties. It is enforceable without consideration.

§ 2.3 Recital of consideration.

To constitute consideration, a performance does not require the payment of money or the delivery of material goods. Restatement (Second) of Contracts § 71 states that the performance may consist of (a) an act, (b) a forbearance, or (c) the creation, modification or destruction of a legal relation. For example, a separation agreement between husband and wife may not provide for the payment of money. Nevertheless, the destruction of the legal relation, marriage, is a sufficient consideration. Each party is releasing the other from the claims inherent in that relationship.

A contract often consists of a number of exchanges. As long as each party exchanges something of value, it is not necessary that each promise by one party has a particular corresponding promise by the other. For example, assuming a widget is worth $10, the father could promise to sell half of the farm and a widget to his daughter for $10. On occasion, where the exchange may appear to be unbalanced or a particular provision may seem onerous, it may be wise to recite consideration for that particular provision in order to better protect the agreement from a charge of unconscionability. The recital of consideration, like the recitals that often precede agreements, may communicate to the court the reasons for the apparently unfair provision. For example, in a franchise agreement, the recitals might explain why there are so many controls on the franchisee's operation.

§ 2.4 The adequacy of consideration.

What if the father agreed to accept his daughter's promise of $1.00 in exchange for his promise of half of the farm? This exchange is illustrated in this diagram:

1/2 **Farm**

Father ⇄ Daughter

$1.00

In this exchange, the daughter has promised the father something that has economic value. In a free economy in which private parties may generally make their own bargains, it is often said that the law does not inquire into the adequacy of consideration. That is, as long as the requirement of consideration is met, it does not matter if the values exchanged are not equivalent.

The principle often finds expression in agreements that state:

> For $1.00 and other good and valuable consideration, receipt of which is hereby acknowledged, I agree as follows . . . .

This form might be used when the parties to the agreement do not want to reveal to third parties the amount of the sale price. It is also used by parties who do not actually pay the consideration but hope that the recitation will make the agreement "legal." For example, an agreement may recite: "In exchange for your promise to _____, I have paid the sum of _____." Some states have statutory presumptions that "[a] written instrument is presumptive evidence of a consideration," or "[t]here was good and sufficient consideration for a written contract."

The drafter cannot rely on these statutory presumptions, but must anticipate that the imbalance in the values exchanged may raise many questions. For example, the return promise may not be enforceable if the money is not actually paid, or, even if it is paid, if the promise was not bargained for. The $1.00 may indicate a sham transaction in which the parties agreed to this token in an attempt to turn a gift promise into an enforceable agreement. Knowing that it is hard to *promise* to make a gift, the attorney should advise the client to make the gift outright or through a will.

The problem of gift promises is particularly acute with respect to charitable pledges. On occasion, a donor makes a pledge to a charity and then fails to tender the money. Is an agreement reciting a promise to make a charitable contribution (donation) enforceable? Restatement (Second) of Contracts § 90(2) suggests that a charitable subscription may be binding without proof of reliance. Nevertheless, because there are cases to the contrary, the drafter of a pledge ought to include a real consideration and the recipient should be prepared to demonstrate actual reliance. For example, the drafter might state "In consideration of the hospital affixing a plaque in donor's memory in a prominent place in the hospital. . ." or "To assist in the establishment of a cancer research facility. . . ." The hospital should then prepare to demonstrate that it had mounted the plaque or undertaken work on the facility.

§ 2.5 Drafting the recital of consideration.

In drafting, the recital of consideration should demonstrate the exchange of something of value. For example:

> In consideration of the sum of _____ Dollars ($_____) paid to _____ [seller] by _____ [buyer], the receipt of which is hereby acknowledged, _____ [seller] agrees as follows:
>
> _____

Often an agreement will contain language such as:

> In consideration of the mutual promises and agreements herein contained, the parties agree as follows . . .

This flowery language is surplusage. A court will look at what you do, not at what you say. What matters substantively is that the agreement actually contains mutual promises, not that it recites consideration. The standard practice is simply to express the mutual obligations without using the word *consideration*. For example:

> 1. Seller shall transfer and deliver to Buyer, and Buyer shall accept and pay for the following goods: _____.
> 2. Buyer shall pay Seller $_____ for the goods on delivery.

Sometimes an agreement does not expressly contain the mutual promises. For example, consider the following agreement, signed by Buyer and Seller:

> Buyer agrees to pay Seller $1,000 to purchase Seller's 1980 Buick Skylark.

This agreement does not recite the consideration flowing from Seller to Buyer. Buyer expressly promises to pay Seller $1000. Seller, however, does not expressly promise to sell the car. Under these facts, a court would nevertheless find that the consideration requirement was satisfied. In a U.S. Supreme Court case involving the sale of land, the seller promised to sell the land but the buyer did not expressly promise to buy it. The Court held that "[t]he tenor of the 'agreement' throughout imports mutual undertakings."

§ 2.6   Illusory contracts.

An agreement may not be enforceable if one party has an alternative that will not exchange something of value. For example, if the father promises his daughter half of the farm in return for her promise that "either I will pay you $100,000 or I won't," there is an alternative which would not result in an exchange. This kind of agreement has been variously described:

- It is *illusory,* because in reality it promises nothing.

- It lacks *consideration,* because something of value does not necessarily flow one way.

- It lacks *mutuality,* because both parties are not bound to exchange something of value.

- It lacks *commitment,* because one element of a promise is that the promisee understands that a commitment has been made.

In the classic case of *Wood v. Lucy, Lady Duff-Gordon,*[1] Lady Duff-Gordon promised Wood the exclusive right to place her endorsement on products. The agreement also provided that Wood would collect all profits from the endorsements and share them with Lady Duff-Gordon. However, Wood never promised to obtain the endorsements. Lady Duff-Gordon claimed that the agreement was illusory, that is, lacking consideration for her promise, because Wood was not required to do anything. The New York Court of Appeals held that given the commercial context and the parties' business interests, the agreement contained obligations, albeit "imperfectly expressed." Having decided that there was an obligation on Wood's part, the court then had to determine the extent of that obligation. It determined that Wood was required to make "reasonable efforts" to perform. The concept has been codified in U.C.C. § 2-306(2) with respect to exclusive dealings in goods:

> A lawful agreement by either the seller or the buyer for exclusive dealing in the kind of goods concerned imposes unless otherwise agreed an obligation by the seller to use best efforts to supply the goods and by the buyer to use best efforts to promote their sale.

§ 2.7   Distributorship agreements.

Issues often arise as to whether distributorship or franchise agreements are illusory. Consider, for example, this agreement:

A and *B* agree that *B* may distribute *A*'s products in the State of Illinois for a period of ten years from the date of this agreement.

There are two problems with this provision. First, *A* has not promised to do anything. As we have seen, it would probably be implied that *A* has promised to use best efforts to make the products available. Second, *B* has not promised to do anything. The word *may* is permissive, allowing *B* to perform or not. The intent of the parties is probably not to say that *B* may

---

[1] 222 N.Y. 88, 118 N.E. 214 (1917).

or may not perform, but that *A* is permitting *B* to distribute its products. An interpretation is favored that upholds an agreement. *See* § 7.1.

A redraft that makes the obligations express might look like this:

> *A* and *B* agree as follows. *A* shall make its products available to *B*. *B* shall distribute *A*'s products in the State of Illinois for a period of ten years from the date of this agreement.

Parties usually express the "term" of their agreement, that is, the time of its duration. In the distributorship agreement, for example, the term is ten years. Sometimes one or both parties wish to reserve the right to terminate the agreement. For example:

> *A* and *B* agree that *B* shall distribute *A*'s products in the State of Illinois for a period of ten years from the date of this agreement. *A* may terminate this agreement at any time.

It could be argued that this agreement is illusory, for it appears that *A* is not bound to do anything. After the agreement is signed, *A* could turn around and terminate. If the agreement is illusory, *B* is not bound either, for unless both parties are bound, neither is bound. There are various ways to draft around this problem. We will look at:

- Criteria for termination
- Time when both are bound
- Silence as to term
- The U.C.C. approach

a. Criteria for termination. If a party's power to terminate is conditional on the occurrence of events beyond the party's control, then the agreement may not be illusory. For example:

> *A* and *B* agree that *B* shall distribute *A*'s products in the State of Illinois for a period of ten years from the date of this agreement. *A* may terminate this agreement at any time that *B* becomes insolvent.

Under this clause, *A*'s power to terminate is limited. *A* may not exercise the power at will, but only when objective criteria are met.

b. Time when both are bound. If it contains a stated period of time before termination is effective, then the agreement may not be illusory. For example:

> *A* and *B* agree that *B* shall distribute *A*'s products in the State of Illinois
> for a period of ten years from the date of this agreement. *A* may
> terminate this agreement on ten days' written notice to *B*.

Under this termination provision, both parties are bound for at least ten
days. While this agreement is not illusory, it may be subject to scrutiny.
A court may find that it is unconscionable for *A* to pull the rug out from
under *B* so quickly, particularly if *B* has made a substantial investment
in reliance on the agreement.

   c. Silence as to term. Sometimes an agreement is silent as to both term
and termination. For example:

> *A* and *B* agree that *B* shall distribute *A*'s products in the State of
> Illinois.

In the absence of a termination provision, clearly the parties are not bound
forever. Some courts hold that the agreement is illusory. Others permit a
distributorship agreement to be terminated at will by either party; reasonable notice may or may not be required. Others provide that the agreement
is terminable at will only after a reasonable time and on reasonable notice.
Other courts have provided that the agreement may not be terminated in
bad faith. One of the principal reasons for allowing termination after a
reasonable time is the substantial reliance of the distributor. The measure
of a reasonable time might be a sufficient time to recover the reliance costs.

   d. The U.C.C. approach. U.C.C. § 2-309(3) resolves the termination
problem with respect to contracts for the sale of goods. It provides:

> Termination of a contract by one party except on the happening of
> an agreed event requires that reasonable notification be received by the
> other party and an agreement dispensing with notification is invalid
> if its operation would be unconscionable.

Pursuant to this approach, the parties could provide for reasonable notice.
Of course, the notice must in fact be reasonable. Particularly in a contract
of adhesion, the drafter may wish to use recitals to explain the reasonableness of the provision.

§ 2.8 Output and requirements contracts.

   Contracts that did not state a specific quantity to be sold or purchased,
but stated quantity in terms of the output of the seller or the requirements
of the buyer, posed problems at common law. For example, consider this
agreement:

> Seller shall sell to Buyer and Buyer shall purchase from Seller all bread crumbs produced by Seller in its factory at 115 Thames Street, Brooklyn, New York, during the period commencing June 19, 2004, and terminating June 18, 2005, at a price of 6 cents per pound.

This is an "output" contract. While Buyer has agreed to buy the entire output of Seller, Seller has not agreed to have an output. Therefore, it can be argued that there is no consideration, for Seller is not obligated to do anything. U.C.C. § 2-306(1), however, expressly recognizes output and requirements contracts, making the quantity subject to the obligation of good faith:

> A term which measures the quantity by the output of the seller or the requirements of the buyer means such actual output or requirements as may occur in good faith, except that no quantity unreasonably disproportionate to any stated estimate or in the absence of a stated estimate to any normal or otherwise comparable prior output or requirements may be tendered or demanded.

An example of a requirements contract would be Buyer's promise to purchase from Seller "all the bread crumbs Buyer requires."

§ 2.9 Satisfaction clauses.

Satisfaction clauses are a form of express condition. *See* § 10.3. A party may provide that she is not bound "unless I am satisfied with *X*" or "unless *X* is satisfactory." If the event — lack of satisfaction — occurs, then the party is not bound. If a buyer's obligation to go through with the purchase is conditional on buyer's "satisfaction," however, it appears that the decision to be bound or not is entirely within buyer's control. All buyer has to do is say, "I'm not satisfied," and the deal is off. If one party has the option of performing or not performing, the agreement is illusory. Note that even though buyer is the one who has this option, seller may use this principle to escape from the deal. Seller may do so because an agreement that lacks consideration is not enforceable. To put it another way, if both parties are not bound, neither party is bound.

Under the modern view, however, satisfaction clauses do not necessarily make an agreement unenforceable. Satisfaction clauses are of two types: objective and subjective. Objective satisfaction clauses relate to quality, operative fitness, or mechanical utility. A clause in a house purchase that made the purchase subject to buyer's satisfaction with an Inspection Report would probably be of this type. Courts apply a reasonable person standard: Would a reasonable person standing in the shoes of the contracting party be satisfied if objective criteria are applied? It is not enough that buyer is not personally satisfied. The buyer would have to demonstrate that a reasonable person would not be satisfied.

Subjective satisfaction clauses relate to fancy, taste, or judgment. A clause in a contract with a portrait studio stating that payment is subject to buyer's satisfaction with the portrait would probably be of this type. Courts do not look at whether a reasonable person would be satisfied but whether the party who may exercise the satisfaction clause is satisfied. However, that party must use good faith in exercising his or her judgment. When this standard is applied, the exercise is no longer a matter of whim. It is open to objective examination of the honesty of the party.

Of course, as a practical matter, it may be hard to prove that a party is not honestly satisfied when the subjective standard is applied. To avoid this problem, the drafter might provide for the satisfaction of a third party. For example, a contract between an owner and a builder could provide that the owner's obligation to pay is conditional on his or her satisfaction with the results. Alternatively, the contract could leave the decision up to a third party, such as an architect. An American Institute of Architects agreement provides in part:[2]

> The issuance of a Certificate for Payment will constitute a representation by the Architect to the Owner, based on the Architect's observations at the site and the data comprising the Application for Payment, that the Work has progressed to the point indicated and that, to the best of the Architect's knowledge, information and belief, quality of the Work is in accordance with the Contract Documents . . . . The issuance of a Certificate for Payment will further constitute a representation that the Contractor is entitled to payment in the amount certified.

The expression of satisfaction of the third party is similarly restricted by a requirement of good faith.

§ 2.10 Exercises.

1. Research. Research the law of your jurisdiction to determine the effect of seals. You will find a useful table in the Restatement (Second) of Contracts, Chapter 4, topic 3. Also, see if you can find statutes in your jurisdiction that dispense with consideration. Note any requirements the drafter must comply with.

2. Recital of consideration. In the following contract, is there consideration for the painting and the car?

---

[2] AIA Document A101. Copyright © 1987 by The American Institute of Architects.

> July 7, 2004
>
> Seller hereby agrees to sell to Buyer the following items:
>
> 1. black Bic ball-point pen
>
> 2. Seller's Picasso painting "La Reve"
>
> 3. Seller's 2001 Jaguar automobile
>
> Buyer hereby agrees to pay Seller the amount of 89 cents.
>
> [Signed] Seller [Signed] Buyer

3. Recital of consideration. A separation agreement between Husband and Wife contains, among others, the following provisions:

> 5. Neither party shall pay support to the other.
>
> 6. There are no children of the marriage.
>
> 7. Each party shall keep the property that is in his or her name. There is no property of the marriage.
>
> 8. Each party renounces all rights he or she has as the spouse of the other, including but not limited to estates rights.

Is there consideration to support the contract?

4. The family dispute. Under the following facts, the plaintiffs contend that the agreement between the defendants and their mother is enforceable, while the defendants contend that the agreement is unenforceable. What theories support each point of view?

> Defendants, a brother and sister, were tenants in common of certain real estate. In 1958, defendants, at the request of their mother, entered into a written agreement with her whereby "in consideration of the sum of One ($1.00) Dollar to them paid by Julia A. Allen [the mother], the receipt whereof is hereby acknowledged," they promised that if they sold the property during their lifetime, they would divide the proceeds equally among themselves and their three brothers. The agreement recited that the parties "have hereunto set their hands and seals." The $1.00 was never paid.
>
> The mother died in 1981. In 1983 the defendants sold the property and refused to share the proceeds with the brothers, who brought suit. The original 1958 agreement had either been lost or misplaced, but a copy was received in evidence. The copy did not disclose anything purporting to be a seal after the signatures of the parties.

The plaintiffs made the following arguments. Which arguments best support their claim that the agreement is enforceable:

a. The agreement stated that it was under seal.

b. The adequacy of the consideration recited in the agreement may not be questioned.

c. There was consideration for the defendants' promise because the agreement recited the receipt of one dollar.

5. The charitable subscription. Is an agreement reciting a promise to make a charitable contribution (donation) enforceable? For example, consider the following pledge:

Mount Sinai Hospital Development Fund of Mount Sinai Hospital of Greater Miami, Inc.

In consideration of and to induce the subscriptions of others, I (we) promise to pay to Mount Sinai Hospital of Greater Miami, Inc., or order the sum of <u>Fifty Thousand and no/100 dollars: $5,000.00</u> payable herewith, balance in nine equal annual installments commencing on <u>July 1, 2005</u>.

Signature	<u>s/ Daniel Donor</u>
Date	<u>July 1, 2004</u>

Consider the following questions:

a. What promise does Donor make?

b. What is the consideration supplied by the Hospital? In what way is "to induce the subscriptions of others" a consideration exchanged for Donor's promise?

c. Would this pledge be enforceable in your jurisdiction? Rewrite the pledge so that it would be enforceable in your jurisdiction.

6. The buy-sell agreement. Peter Seller and Oscar Buyer entered into an agreement for the sale of Peter's house to Oscar. As often happens, each party signed the agreement in the presence of a broker without consulting an attorney. In addition to the usual provisions, the buy-sell agreement contained the following Special Provisions:

---

1. Buyer may have an engineer inspect the premises for structural soundness and deliver a report within thirty days. If Buyer is not satisfied with the report, he shall not be obligated to purchase the property.

2. Seller shall complete the remodelling of the living room, including installing drapes that match the rug, within thirty days. If Buyer is not satisfied with the remodelling, he shall not be obligated to purchase the property.

Consider the following questions:

a. Assume you are the attorney for Seller. He tells you that he has been offered a higher price and wants to get out of the deal with Buyer. What legal arguments are available in support of Seller's position? Will these arguments succeed?

b. Alternatively, assume you are the attorney for Buyer. He wants to get out of the deal with Seller. He says, "Here's a copy of the engineer's report. I am not satisfied. Furthermore, the drapes Seller put in the living room don't match the rug. I am not satisfied." What legal arguments are available in support of Buyer's position? Will these arguments succeed?

c. How could an attorney have drafted the Special Provisions to better assure the enforceability of the agreement?

Chapter 3

INDEFINITENESS

§ 3.1 Introduction.

A contract usually consists of an exchange of promises. According to Restatement (Second) of Contracts § 2, a promise must be sufficiently definite "to justify a promisee in understanding that a commitment has been made." This chapter asks you to determine whether the language is so indefinite as to fail to qualify as promissory. The stakes are high — if the language is indefinite, there is no contract.

Why do contracts contain indefinite language? At worst, the drafters may be hasty or careless. More likely, in a routine transaction they may not want to take the time or trouble to hammer out all the details. Or they may not foresee future possibilities. Or they may foresee them and not wish to raise them for fear of jeopardizing the deal.

Furthermore, people often enter agreements without consulting a lawyer. This is true even for major purchases such as an automobile or a house. The terms for purchase of a house are usually set forth in an agreement provided by a broker known as a Buy-Sell Agreement or Earnest Money Receipt. After filling in the blanks to reflect the bargain they have struck, the buyer and seller sign the agreement. They have committed themselves to a deal. They are not concerned about breach, for each expects to perform.

One of the parties may later wish to escape from the bargain. The buyer may find property that is more desirable or the seller may get a better offer. The other party, unwilling to renegotiate the bargain, may demand performance. Each may consult an attorney. To the party seeking enforcement of the deal, the attorney is a hero who will give meaning to the sanctity of the contract. To the party seeking escape from the deal, the attorney is a trickster who will demonstrate that the apparently black and white agreement contains shades of gray.

The attorneys are neither heroes nor tricksters. They are concerned with the meaning of *words,* the medium in which lawyers function. When attorneys scrutinize the words of a document, they look for language that indicates whether the document is enforceable. The party who refuses to perform may be able to defend by claiming: you can't recover for my failure to honor our contract because we never had a contract! In addition to indefiniteness, the attorney will look for:

> • *Lack of mutuality.* One party may have made either no promise at all or a promise that will permit that party to decline to perform. An agreement in which one party is not under any obligation is often described as "illusory" or lacking mutuality. *See* § 2.6.

43

- *Lack of clarity.* The language used by the parties may be so vague or ambiguous that it is not possible to determine their intent. *See* § 7.4.

In examining agreements for indefiniteness, it is important to distinguish among three different cases:

1. The parties do not intend to enter into a contract.

2. The parties intend to enter into a contract.

3. The parties intend to enter into a contract with some provisions to be agreed upon at a later time.

§ 3.2 The parties do not intend to enter into a contract.

Negotiating the agreement. Suppose *A* says to B, "I'll buy your business for $100,000," and *B* responds, "It's a deal. We'll have the lawyers write it up." The lawyers, however, cannot agree on all the terms of the deal. *A* might assume the deal is off while *B* insists that it is on. This situation raises a question of intent. One party may have understood, "We don't have a deal until we have a final signed writing." The other party may have understood, "We have an enforceable oral agreement which will be memorialized in written form."

Often the party who attempts to enforce the oral agreement will be frustrated by the Statute of Frauds. Or a court may deny enforcement on grounds that the agreement was indefinite if it required too many further points of agreement. But sometimes the oral agreement will be enforced. A party who desires not to be bound without a final signed writing should make that desire clear. *See* § 1.3. For example:

- A proposal that might otherwise be construed as an offer could be marked "Letter of Intent."

- A written offer might state, "The validity of the proposed agreement is conditional on the parties reducing the agreement to writing and signing it."

- During negotiations, one party might state, "It should be understood that no agreement is effective without a signed writing."

Providing flexibility. Business persons who have long-term relationships often do not expect to be held to every term in an agreement. Because they do not intend an enforceable agreement, their relationship cannot be described as contractual. They want to have a flexible agreement that can change as circumstances change. Not only do they often use authority other than the rules of contract law, but they find other ways to resolve their disputes. Even a cursory glance at reported contracts cases indicates that established businesses which contract frequently with each other do not take their disputes to court. Arthur Rosett contrasts the American theory with the Japanese view:[1]

---

[1] ROSETT, CONTRACT LAW AND ITS APPLICATION 61 (4th ed. 1988). Copyright © 1988 by The Foundation Press, Inc. Reprinted with permission.

Accepting the indeterminacy of the future, the Japanese are said to conceive of a contract as establishing a relationship and a commitment mutually to pursue solutions to problems as they arise. It is useless, they think, to try to make words do what people cannot; what is unknowable will remain so no matter how detailed the contract. What is written should have sufficient leeway to suggest the nature of the relationship, and what is unwritten should be supplemented with sensible elements of good will and a mutual desire to resolve problems when they arise by a process of harmonious accommodation.

Outside of the business area, parties may not intend their agreements to be enforceable contracts. Their agreements may be casual, such as social commitments, or they may facilitate discussion. For example, a group called SADD (Students Against Driving Drunk) has promulgated a "Contract for Life" between parent and teenager:[2]

---

[2] SADD, *Contract for Life*. Reprinted with permission.

CONTRACT FOR LIFE

A Foundation for Trust and Caring

This contract is designed to facilitate communication between young people and their parents about potentially destructive decisions related to alcohol, drugs, peer pressure and behavior. The issues facing young people today are often too difficult to address alone. SADD believes that effective parent child communication is critically important in helping young adults make healthy decisions.

Young Person

I recognize that there are many potentially destructive decisions I face every day and commit to you that I will do everything in my power to avoid making decisions that will jeopardize my health, my safety and overall well being, or your trust in me. I understand the dangers associated with the use of alcohol and drugs and the destructive behaviors often associated with impairment.

By signing below, I pledge my best effort to remain alcohol and drug free, I agree that I will never drive under the influence of either, or accept a ride from someone who is impaired, and I will always wear a seat belt.

Finally, I agree to call you if I am ever in a situation that threatens my safety and to communicate with you regularly about issues of importance to us both.

_____

Young Person

Parent (or Caring Adult)

I am committed to you, and to your health and safety. By signing below, I pledge to do everything in my power to understand and communicate with you about the many difficult and potentially destructive decisions you face.

Further I agree to provide for you safe, sober transportation home if you are ever in a situation that threatens your safety and to defer discussion about that situation until a time when we can both discuss the issues in a calm and caring manner.

I also pledge to you that I will not drive under the influence of alcohol or drugs, I will always seek safe, sober transportation home, and I will always remember to wear a seatbelt.

_____

Parent/Caring Adult

SADD and all SADD logos are registered with the United Stated Patent and Trademark Office and other jurisdictions. All rights reserved by SADD, Inc. a Massachusetts non-profit corporation. Copying of this material is prohibited unless written permission is received. SADD, Inc. sponsors Students Against Driving Drunk, Students Against Destructive Decisions and other health and safety programs.

Students Against Destructive Decisions
SADD, Inc. PO Box 800 Marlborough, MA 01752 Tel. 508-481-3568 Toll Free 1-877-SADD-INC

§ 3.3 The parties intend to enter into a contract.

The parties may intend a contract, but after negotiations they may be unable to agree on a particular term. They may fudge the terms they can't agree on, hoping that the circumstances not provided for will never arise.

David Mellinkoff offers this example of "calculated ambiguity":[3]

> Labor and management negotiators have hammered out agreement, except on *cost of living*. The sticking point is whether the negotiated wage shall be adjusted up and down, or only up. A strike deadline is imminent. Weary negotiators settle for a calculated ambiguity — *subject to a cost of living adjustment*. The problem of interpretation may never arise. If it does, one side will insist that clearly it means up *and* down, the other as vehemently, obviously only *up*. The controversy will be settled under circumstances different from those when the contract was negotiated. In the meantime, there has been labor peace.

Alternatively, the parties may intend a contract but lack sufficient information to make their agreement definite. Unwilling to take a chance on future conditions, they may not wish to commit themselves to a particular price or quantity. The seller of goods may be unwilling to take the risk that the contract price will be lower than the market price at the time of delivery while the buyer may be unwilling to take the risk that the contract price will be higher.

For example, an agreement between the buyer and seller of a citrus crop might provide:

Seller shall sell and transfer to the Buyer all the fruit that meets the standards for the use specified in this contract at the time of picking the fruit. . . . Price of fruit and harvesting and delivery charges will be the market price and charges at the time the fruit is harvested.

---

§ 3.4   The parties intend to enter into a contract with some provisions to be agreed upon at a later time.

Courts are often asked to decide whether an agreement is an enforceable contract or merely "an agreement to agree." For example, an agreement between the buyer and seller of a citrus crop might provide:

Seller shall sell and transfer to the Buyer all the fruit that meets the standards for the use to be agreed upon at the time of picking the fruit. . . . Price of fruit, harvesting and delivery charges, and harvesting dates shall be agreed upon between the Buyer and Seller before the fruit is harvested.

What result did the parties intend if they could not reach agreement? If a court determines that the parties did not intend to be bound if they could

---

[3] DAVID MELLINKOFF, LEGAL WRITING: SENSE & NONSENSE. Copyright © 1982. Reprinted with permission of the West Group.

not agree, it will not enforce the agreement. But if it determines that the parties intended to be bound, or if the term is relatively unimportant, the court may scrutinize the agreement to determine whether the means are available to determine for the parties the terms they did not express.

§ 3.5 The resources of the law: The U.C.C.

The common law premise that parties who "agree to agree" do not form a contract has been changed by U.C.C. § 2-204(3), which states:

> Even though one or more terms are left open a contract for sale does not fail for indefiniteness if the parties have intended to make a contract and there is a reasonably certain basis for giving an appropriate remedy.

The purpose of the change is stated in the Official Comment to § 2-204:

> Subsection (3) states the principle as to "open terms" underlying later sections of the Article. If the parties intend to enter into a binding agreement, this subsection recognizes that agreement as valid in law, despite missing terms, if there is any reasonably certain basis for granting a remedy. The test is not certainty as to what the parties were to do nor as to the exact amount of damages due the plaintiff. Nor is the fact that one or more terms are left to be agreed upon enough of itself to defeat an otherwise adequate agreement. Rather, commercial standards on the point of "indefiniteness" are intended to be applied, this Act making provision elsewhere for missing terms needed for performance, open price, remedies and the like.

Because the U.C.C. provides that only those agreements in which the parties intended a contract do not fail for indefiniteness, the drafter might include a clause stating that intent. For example:

Although one or more terms is left open in this agreement, the parties intend this agreement to be a present contract. Open terms are to be determined as stated in this agreement or, in absence of the manner stated or a failure of the manner stated, by applicable provisions of the Uniform Commercial Code.

The open term may be supplied from a number of sources. For example:

a. One of the parties. *See* § 2-311(1). The determination is constrained by the standards of good faith and commercial reasonableness as stated in §§ 1-102(3), 1-203, and 2-103(1)(b). For example:

> Buyer shall pay as a price the unit cost of each item sold hereunder as it appears on Seller's price list on the date of shipment multiplied by the number of units shipped.

b. A third party. *See* §§ 1-103 and 2-305. This device may be useful to bring about agreement between parties who are unable to deal constructively with each other. For example:

> Within 5 days from the signing of this agreement, Seller shall secure an appraisal of the goods by the American Livestock Association. The price of the goods will be the value found by this appraiser. Seller shall bear the cost of appraisal.

c. An external standard or event, such as a market price or the terms set by other parties. *See* § 2-305. For example:

> Buyer shall pay as a price for the goods the Cash Price of the goods on the day of delivery as reported in the Wall Street Journal.

d. Gap fillers. If the parties do not provide a source to make a term definite, or if the source fails, then the term may be supplied by the "gap filler" provisions of the U.C.C., including:

price	§ 2-305
quantity	§ 2-306
delivery	§§ 2-307, 2-308
time	§ 2-309
payment	§ 2-310

§ 3.6   Other resources to make an agreement definite.

A number of resources are available to a court seeking to find a commitment between the parties in spite of indefinite language. These resources include statutes and case law, custom and usage, extrinsic evidence, and objective methods of determination.

a. Statutes and case law. An agreement does not exist in isolation nor, unfortunately, are drafting problems uncommon. An analogous statute or the decisions of courts in like cases are a good resource. Ideally, the drafter versed in preventive law techniques will become aware of these resources and draft with a view to avoiding the problem. If the planning opportunity is foregone, the resources are available in the adversary proceeding to demonstrate how courts have aided those who did not correct the mistakes of the past.

For example, a city agreed to pay "all costs of construction and subsequent operation, maintenance and repair of said sewage system with the house connections thereof" but the agreement did not specify the term of the city's obligation. The court held that "where the parties have not clearly expressed the duration of a contract, the courts will imply that they intended performance to continue for a reasonable time."

b. Custom and usage. Course of performance, course of dealing, and usage of trade are important tools of interpretation under the U.C.C. *See* §§ 1-205 and 2-208. These resources are available outside the U.C.C. as well.

For example, an agreement between a beet grower and a sugar company provided that "Seller shall personally grow, on suitable land in Santa Maria Valley, and deliver to Buyer 239 acres of beets during the year 1949." The court held that where the parties entered the agreement with knowledge of the custom and usage in the industry, those terms would be applicable to them.

c. Extrinsic evidence. The purpose of the parol evidence rule is to exclude extrinsic evidence once it has been determined that the writing represents the final and complete agreement of the parties. *See* § 6.1. If, however, the agreement is missing terms, then it cannot be fully integrated and may be supplemented with evidence of additional terms. For example, an agreement between the buyer and seller of a truck referred many times to delivery but did not contain a delivery date. The court held that the agreement may be supplemented by an oral conversation between the parties in which the seller agreed to deliver within 10 weeks.

d. Objective methods of determination. The drafter may refer to an objective source, such as a market. For example, a lease provided that "At any time during the original term of this lease or any extension thereof or any tenancy thereafter, lessee shall have the option to purchase the premises for the then prevailing market price." The court held that "This provision, in our opinion means fair market value and meets the necessary standards required by law with respect to the certainty of the purchase price. . . ."

On the other hand, a provision in a buy-sell agreement that "This agreement is contingent upon purchaser obtaining approval of a conventional mortgage loan of $29,000" was held indefinite when it did not "set forth the term of the mortgage and at what interest rate the mortgage shall be."

§ 3.7 Ethics in drafting.

Suppose A is not sure it wants to be bound by a contemplated agreement with B. A wants its attorney to employ indefinite language in the agreement as an "escape clause." Assuming the language goes unnoticed by B, the parties will begin to perform the agreement. But A could at any time claim benefit of the "escape clause" to permit it to withdraw from the bargain.

Would it be ethical for an attorney to draft such a clause for *A* in the expectation that *B* would not notice it? If *A*'s attorney noticed in the draft proposed by *B* a clause that could be invoked by *A* to withdraw from the bargain, would it be ethical to refrain from pointing it out to *B*?

It is difficult to find applicable Rules of Professional Conduct, for the Rules are generally oriented toward regulating attorneys as combatants in the adversary system. Perhaps the most applicable is Rule 1.2(d):

> A lawyer shall not counsel a client to engage, or assist a client, in conduct that the lawyer knows is criminal or fraudulent, but a lawyer may discuss the legal consequences of any proposed course of conduct with a client and may counsel or assist a client to make a good faith effort to determine the validity, scope, meaning or application of the law.

A Comment on this rule states:

> A lawyer is required to give an honest opinion about the actual consequences that appear likely to result from a client's conduct. The fact that a client uses advice in a course of action that is criminal or fraudulent does not, of itself, make a lawyer a party to the course of action. However, a lawyer may not knowingly assist a client in criminal or fraudulent conduct.

In this case, the attorney has concluded that the agreement may be unenforceable. The issue then becomes whether failure to disclose this conclusion to *B* is fraudulent? As a practical matter, *A*'s attorney should inform *A* that there is a danger that the "escape clause" intended for *A*'s escape could be used by *B* to escape. Recall the rule of "mutuality of obligation": unless both parties are bound, neither party is bound. There is also a risk that a court could determine that the "escape clause" is enforceable. Note the resources available to a court in finding a commitment between the parties in spite of indefinite language. These possibilities suggest that the attorney's role in the transaction is not to counsel fraud but to determine the application of the law.

§ 3.8 Exercises.

1. Applying the U.C.C. gap-fillers. Which of the following written agreements is enforceable?

a. *A* and *B* agree that *A* will buy tomatoes from *B* for $5/bushel when the crop is ripe.

b. *A* and *B* agree that *A* will buy *B*'s entire tomato crop for $5/bushel when the crop is ripe.

c. *A* and *B* agree that *A* will buy 1000 bushels of tomatoes from *B* when the crop is ripe.

d. *A* agrees to buy *B*'s house. They agree on all the terms except price.

2. Commitment. Is the following agreement enforceable?

March 1, 2004

Company agrees to sell 100 Type A widgets subject to the approval of Company's Board of Directors and Customer agrees to buy if Customer is satisfied with the widgets.

Signed [authenticated] by   Signed [authenticated] by
Company   Customer

---

3. Ethics in drafting. The United States Supreme Court has held that it may be a violation of antitrust law for a franchisor to impose tie-in sales on a franchisee. A prospective franchisee brings an agreement to an attorney. The attorney concludes that the agreement contains an illegal tie-in provision. The Supreme Court has also held that the parties to such an illegal agreement are not *in pari delicto,* so the franchisee can sue the franchisor — and possibly recover treble damages — despite its knowing acceptance of the illegal term. May the attorney advise the client to take advantage of this situation?

4. The buy-sell agreement. The agreement that follows is typical of those used in real estate transactions. A broker acting on behalf of the seller shows a prospective purchaser the property. If the purchaser makes an offer, the broker reduces the offer to writing on this form. The broker then presents the offer to the seller. The seller may accept by signing the agreement or may tender a counteroffer which the broker presents to the purchaser. The process may continue until the agreement is signed by both parties.

It would appear from the circumstances that the parties intended a binding agreement. Certainly the broker thinks so, for the broker's agreement usually provides that the broker becomes entitled to a commission on execution of the agreement, whether or not there is a closing.

You are attorney for one of the parties who wishes to escape from the bargain. Look over the agreement to detect those terms that may be too indefinite to qualify as contractual obligations. Are these terms capable of being made more definite? If so, what resources or authority can be used?

What are the consequences if a party is successful in escaping from the deal? Does the seller get to keep the money paid into escrow? Does the broker earn a commission?

EARNEST MONEY RECEIPT AND AGREEMENT TO SELL AND PURCHASE

_____Missoula_____, Montana ___October 1___, 20_03_

RECEIVED FROM_____ Bright Buyer _____ hereinafter called Purchaser the sum of (check, cash, note)__ five hundred dollars __ ($_600_) paid to Agent as earnest money in part payment of the purchase of the following described Real Estate in _____ County, State of Montana, to-wit: _____

(hereinafter "Property") commonly known as _____ Smith Ranch _____.
Together with the following described property: all irrigation fixtures and equipment, including stoker and oil tanks, water heaters and burners, electric light fixtures, bathroom fixtures, roller shades, curtain rods and fixtures. Venetian blinds, window and door screens, storm doors and windows, linoleum, attached television antenna, all shrubs and trees and all other fixtures attached thereto, except: _____ Venetian blinds _____ are to be left upon the premises as part of the property purchased. The following additional personal property is also to be left upon the premises as a part of the property purchased: _____.
The total purchase price of __ 10% over VA appraised value __ ($_____) is payable as follows:
__ $20,000 VA loan __
__ balance on purchase money mortgage payable at one-third (1/3) gross crop per year __
__ Special Provisions: This agreement is contingent upon Purchaser obtaining a zoning permit for a Trailer Park on 10 acres of the property. __

1. Purchaser agrees that earnest money placed with Agent is to be deposited in Agent's trust account within 3 business days of Seller's Acceptance of this Agreement unless otherwise provided for herein.

2. It is further agreed that Seller shall at his expense furnish Purchaser a title insurance policy as evidenced by a title commitment in an amount equal to the purchase price, insuring merchantable title thereto vested in Purchaser, free and clear of all liens and encumbrances except: encumbrances hereinabove mentioned, zoning ordinances, building and use restriction reservations in federal patents, utility easements of record, others: _____

It is agreed that the Agent assumes no responsibility in regard to the title and the Agent recommends the Purchaser have the title to the property examined by an attorney.

3. The real property is to be conveyed by a warranty deed and the personal property, if any, by Bill of Sale, both shall be free and clear of all encumbrances except those described in Section #2.

4. If Seller's title is not merchantable or insurable and cannot be made so within a reasonable time after written notice containing statement of defects is delivered to Seller, then said earnest money herein receipted for shall be returned to the Purchaser on demand, and all rights of Purchaser terminated unless Purchaser waives said defects and elects to purchase.

5. If said sale is approved by the Seller and Seller's said title is merchantable or insurable and Purchaser neglects or refuses to complete the purchase or shall fail to pay the balance of the purchase price as hereinabove provided, then said earnest money may be forfeited to the Seller at Seller's election as liquidated damages and not as a penalty and this Agreement thereupon shall be of no further force or effect unless the Seller elects to enforce this Agreement by requiring the buyer to specifically perform in accordance with the terms of this contract.

6. The Purchaser agrees that this contract does authorize the Seller to enforce the remedy of specific performance. The Seller agrees that this contract does authorize the Purchaser to enforce the remedy of specific performance.

7. Seller and Purchaser agree to pro-rate the taxes, special improvement assessments, interest, and other matters as of the date of closing. (See Section 8), unless otherwise stated, except for perpetual special improvement district taxes, if any, which will be assumed by the Purchaser as of date of closing. All other special improvement taxes will be: (check one)

( ) paid off by the Seller at time of closing   ( ) assumed by the Purchaser ( ) not applicable in this transaction.

8. The closing date of this sale shall be within 30 days after the county gives the permit for the trailer park or 30 days beyond said date shall be allowed for completion of third party financing or assumption approval if they are called for herein, which shall be the termination date unless otherwise agreed. The Purchaser and Seller will, on demand, deposit in trust with the closing Agent, all instruments and monies necessary to complete the purchase in accordance with this Agreement.

9. Possession shall be delivered to Purchaser on or before the date of closing. (See Section 8).

10. Purchaser enters into this Agreement in full reliance upon his independent investigation and judgment and there are no verbal or other Agreements which modify or affect this Agreement. Purchaser agrees to accept property and appliances in "as is" condition unless otherwise provided for.

11. Time is of the essence in this Agreement. This Agreement is binding upon the heirs, personal representatives, receivers, trustees, successors and assigns and each of the parties hereto. Purchaser's rights herein are not assignable without Seller's written consent.

12. The parties agree that earnest money may be used for an appraisal and credit report required to secure financing. If financing is called for, Purchaser agrees to make immediate application for such financing, and to exert best efforts to procure such financing. If Purchaser fails to use his best effort, he will be in breach of this Agreement and Seller may exercise the right provided Seller, for Purchaser's breach under Sections 5 and 6 above. If financing or assumption approval is necessary and cannot be obtained, it is agreed that the unexpended earnest money will be returned to Purchaser.

APPLICABLE ONLY FOR V.A. PURCHASER

13. "It is expressly agreed that, notwithstanding any other provisions of this contract, the Purchaser shall not incur any penalty by forfeiture of earnest money or otherwise be obligated to complete the purchase of the property described herein, if the contract purchase price or cost exceeds the reasonable value of the property established by the Veteran's Administration. The Purchaser shall, however, have the privilege and option of proceeding with the consummation of this contract without regard to the amount of the reasonable value established by the Veteran's Administration.

APPLICABLE ONLY FOR F.H.A. PURCHASER:

14. In event funds for this transaction are to be derived from an F.H.A. insured loans, "it is expressly agreed that, notwithstanding any other provisions of this contract, the Purchaser shall not be obligated to complete the purchase of the property described herein or to incur any penalty by forfeiture of earnest money deposits or otherwise unless the Seller has delivered to the Purchaser a written statement issued by the Federal Housing Commissioner setting forth the appraised value of the property for mortgage insurance purposes of not less than $_____ which statement the Seller hereby agrees to deliver to the Purchaser promptly after such appraised value statement is made available to the Seller. The Purchaser shall, however, have the privilege and option of proceeding with the consummation of this contract without regard to the amount of the appraised valuation made by the Federal Housing Commissioner."

15. The Seller agrees to pay a mortgage discount or origination fee not to exceed (_____%) of the Purchaser's proposed mortgage amount.

16. All loss or damage to any of the above described real or personal property by any cause is assumed by Seller through date of closing.

Agent __s/_____   By __s/_____
        REAL ESTATE FIRM   SALES REPRESENTATIVE

I/We hereby agree to purchase the above described Real Estate property at the firm price and/or the terms and conditions as set forth in the above offer and grant to said sales representative _____ days hereafter to secure Seller's acceptance hereof. I hereby authorize Agent to release pertinent financial information concerning my credit, ability to pay and employment to either Seller or potential lender to this Agreement. I/We hereby acknowledge receipt of a copy of this Receipt and Agreement to Sell and Purchase, bearing the Agent's and my/our signatures.

__s/ Bright Buyer_____ Purchasers
Purchaser's Address _____
Phone _____

For valuable consideration I/we agree to sell and convey to the Purchaser the above described property on the terms and conditions hereinabove stated and agree to pay the commission provided for in the listing Agreement for services rendered in this transaction. In the event of a forfeiture of the deposit as above provided, the said deposit shall be used first to pay the Agent's incurred expenses related to this sale and the balance shall be apportioned to the Seller and Agent equally, provided the amount to the Agent shall not exceed the agreed commission. I/We acknowledge receipt of a copy of this Receipt and Agreement bearing my/our signature and that of the Purchaser named above.

5. Negotiation Exercise. Pair up as Buyer and Seller. Assume there has been an auction on a website such as eBay with the Buyer the high bidder on the Seller's "mint condition" copy of *Air Pirates* comic book #1 with a bid of $80.

At this point, the auction site leaves the parties to conclude their deal. Each pair of students will now get together to work out the remaining terms of their contract. Although you are negotiating face-to-face for the sake of convenience, assume the Buyer is in a jurisdiction thousands of miles from the Seller and the parties are contacting each other by telephone or email. If you are familiar with the assistance an auction site may offer to buyers and sellers, you are free to incorporate this knowledge into your contract, but such procedures are not "rules" that have to be followed.

Did you reach an agreement? If not, is there a contract? If yes, did you memorialize the agreement in writing? What are the terms?

Chapter 4

ENFORCEABILITY

§ 4.1 Introduction.

A contract establishes *private law,* the law that will govern the parties' relationship under the agreement. In many instances the parties are free to determine their rights and duties and to express them as they please. But there are limits. This chapter explores the parameters of the parties' freedom to make their agreement: when may they dictate the substance and form of the agreement and when will the law dictate the substance and form?

There are various sources of law that an agreement may contravene. The law may be statutory, it may have developed through case law, or it may be found in a declaration of "public policy." The effect of violating the law may vary as well:

a. It may be illegal to make the bargain. For example, a statute may prohibit one who is not a lawyer from rendering legal advice. Or a statute may prohibit contractors from conspiring on bids. In these cases, there is often a sanction imposed for entering the contract.

b. It may be unlawful to render or promise a performance. For example, a residential lease contains an exculpatory clause, exculpating the landlord from the landlord's own negligence. Courts may have determined that such an agreement is not enforceable. Sometimes this kind of agreement is referred to as "illegal." It is not illegal in the sense that a penalty may be imposed on one of the parties. Often the only effect of the clause is that it is unenforceable.

c. It may be lawful to make the bargain and to perform it, but the bargain is unenforceable. For example, many contracts with minors are not enforceable against the minor. Or a contract may be unenforceable because of the Statute of Frauds.

It is important to distinguish which type of illegality may be involved in the agreement you are drafting. While you would not want your client to enter into an illegal contract, your client may want to take a chance on entering one that may be held unenforceable.

§ 4.2 Regulation of form.

Very often, legislation and sometimes case law regulates not what is said, but the way it is said. The law may require "plain language," prohibit certain language in agreements, require specific language, or require type size or format. For example, Plain Language (or Plain English) laws have been adopted in a number of states. *See* § 18.1. Plain language affects not only form, but also substance. Often, a drafter taking the trouble to rewrite a contract in plain language changes not only the style but also the content. In particular, unenforceable provisions may be detected and eliminated.

§ 4.3 Regulation of substance.

When drafting an agreement in a particular substantive area, the drafter must be familiar with the applicable law, both statutory and common law. Checklists, forms, and previously drafted documents can be of value. These aids should always be supplemented by research into the latest developments in the area.

As we have seen in Chapter 3, if the parties intend an agreement but fail to express it completely, the law will usually complete the agreement for them. These terms are read into the agreement as "default" provisions when the parties fail to specify otherwise. It is important for the drafter to be aware of what the default provisions will be. If the drafter is unhappy with the default provision, freedom of contract usually permits the parties to contract around it.

For example, U.C.C. § 1-102(3) permits parties to vary the U.C.C. by agreement "except as otherwise provided in this Act and except that the obligations of good faith, diligence, reasonableness and care . . . may not be disclaimed. . . ." A drafter who is familiar with the default provisions of the Code may wish to use freedom of contract to stipulate a different outcome. Consider whether these variations on the default provisions would be enforceable:

1. U.C.C. § 2-509(3) provides:

> In any case not within subsection (1) or (2), the risk of loss passes to the buyer on his receipt of the goods if the seller is a merchant; otherwise the risk passes to the buyer on tender of delivery.

The drafter includes this provision in a contract between merchants:

Risk of loss. The risk of loss of the goods passes to the Buyer as soon as the goods are identified to the contract.

---

2. U.C.C. § 2-719(3) provides:

> Consequential damages may be limited or excluded unless the limitation or exclusion is unconscionable. Limitation of consequential damages for injury to the person in the case of consumer goods is prima facie unconscionable but limitation of damages where the loss is commercial is not.

The drafter includes this provision in a contract for the sale of consumer goods:

Consequential Damages. In the event of breach of this contract by Seller, Buyer shall not be entitled to any consequential damages in excess of $1000.

---

3. U.C.C. § 1-102(3) provides:

> The effect of provisions of this Act may be varied by agreement, except as otherwise provided in this Act and except that the obligations of good faith, diligence, reasonableness and care prescribed by this Act may not be disclaimed by agreement but the parties may by agreement determine the standards by which the performance of such obligation is to be measured if such standards are not manifestly unreasonable.

The drafter includes this provision in a sales contract:

Diligence. Dates of delivery set forth in this agreement are estimates only. Seller shall inform Buyer 10 days before the actual dates.

In Example 1, the parties have effectively varied the risk of loss provision of § 2-509. In Example 2, because the goods are consumer goods, the parties' variation is probably not effective, for § 2-719(3) expressly states that the limitation is unconscionable. In Example 3, the parties have set forth standards for measuring diligence. This expression is permissible unless the standards are unreasonable.

§ 4.4　Surrendering a right.

If the law provides one party with a right, privilege, or defense, you may want to draft an agreement in which that party surrenders the right, privilege, or defense. Can you do so? It can be difficult to determine whether the parties have the freedom of contract to change the default rule. A maxim of equity states:

> Anyone may waive the advantage of a law intended solely for his benefit. But a law established for a public reason cannot be contravened by a private agreement.

The public interest apparently allows some benefits to be surrendered by private agreement while others cannot be surrendered. The drafter must determine whether the law is intended for personal or public benefit. Laws, however, do not come with flags attached indicating whether they are established for private or public benefit. It is therefore difficult to determine which rights can be waived. For example, which of these contract terms is enforceable under this test:

> 1. No action may be commenced on this contract unless brought within two months after accrual of the cause of action on which suit is based.

> 2. If I am now indebted to the Company on any prior leases, bills or accounts, it is agreed that the amount of each periodical installment payment to be made by me to the Company under this present lease shall be inclusive of and not in addition to the amount of each installment payment to be made by me under such prior leases, bills or accounts; and all payments now and hereafter made by me shall be credited pro rata on all outstanding leases, bills and accounts due the Company by me at the time such payment is made.

Example 1 is an agreement to limit the statute of limitations. As a general rule, parties are free to shorten the statute of limitations by agreement, but as a matter of policy it may not be unreasonably short. The issue is whether under the facts and circumstances of this case, the statute was unreasonably short. If it was, then the provision would be unenforceable. Example 2 is the notorious "cross-collateralization" clause from *Williams v. Walker-Thomas Furniture Co.* The lower court held that the provision was not prohibited by statute, but the appellate court remanded for a determination as to whether the clause was unconscionable at common law in a consumer contract. If it were found to be unconscionable, then it would offend public policy and would be unenforceable. In a negotiated agreement between commercial parties, however, the provision would probably be inoffensive.

§ 4.5   Unconscionability.

U.C.C. § 2-302 allows a court to strike a provision or an entire agreement that it finds to be unconscionable. The concept has been applied at common law as well. In general, courts have found agreements to be unconscionable if the party with the superior bargaining power used that power to exact unfair terms. If you are in a position to draft an agreement for a party with superior bargaining power, it would be wise to research the kinds of provisions that have been held to be unconscionable in that substantive area. The cost of incorporating unconscionable provisions may be high. Not only may the transaction be avoided, but because unconscionable provisions are often found in standardized agreements, an adverse decision could affect a series of transactions. It may be prudent in those circumstances to exercise restraint.

If you must include a potentially unconscionable provision, consider the following drafting techniques:

• Explain the reason for what appears to be a harsh term. Recitals at the beginning of the agreement may be appropriate for this purpose. For example, courts sometimes find the terms of franchise agreements unconscionable. Recitals could explain the reasons for the terms. For example:

> The franchise fee and royalty that are established in Section Eighteen herein constitute the sole consideration to franchisor for exploitation of its system and trademark. The restrictions and controls on franchisee's operation and acquisition of supplies established herein are intended solely to protect franchisor's rights to its trademark and to discharge franchisor's obligation to other franchisees to maintain a high level of quality of trademarked products.

● State provisions in a form that makes clear that the other party knew of the provisions and agreed to them. Courts are often hostile to provisions written in fine print or on the back of agreements. Use a different color of ink, use bold type, or provide for the individual's initials. The provision should also be spelled out in plain language. For example, the cross-collateralization clause from the *Williams* case might be rewritten as:

If you fail to make a payment on time, we may repossess everything we have ever sold you on credit. Initial here: _____

---

§ 4.6 Severability.

A severability clause purports to answer the question, "If a court refuses to enforce part of our agreement, will it give effect to the remainder?" In the severability clause, the parties urge the court not to throw the baby out with the bathwater, but to salvage what it can of the agreement after excising the illegal part. The provision may not be very meaningful, for it seems to state the default rule. *See* Restatement (Second) of Contracts § 184. Similarly, if a court determines that a term in the agreement may be unconscionable, the court will generally make up its own mind up as to whether the offensive provision goes to the essence of the agreement. *See* U.C.C. § 2-302. The language might look like this:

> The invalidity, in whole or in part, of any term of this agreement does not affect the validity of the remainder of the agreement.

§ 4.7 Consumer Protection Acts.

In most jurisdictions, Consumer Protection Acts forbid "unfair or deceptive acts or practices." Often, these statutes apply not only to consumer transactions but to commercial transactions as well. Unlike common law claims, claims arising under these acts can be easily proven, for fraudulent intent and reliance are not issues. Minimum damages, punitive damages, and attorneys' fees may also be granted to a successful plaintiff.

Claims under these Acts will probably become more frequent as attorneys become more aware of their broad scope. For example, many Acts provide that the following is a violation:

> Representing that a consumer transaction confers or involves rights, remedies or obligations that it does not have or involve or which are prohibited by law.

Illegal and unenforceable provisions are often found in consumer credit contracts. Drafters may include them unintentionally, perhaps because they have traditionally been included, or intentionally for their *in terrorem* value. Language is called *in terrorem* (by way of threat) when it is not legally enforceable but may scare the reader into compliance. The efficacy of *in terrorem* language may be demonstrated by the number of consumers who have left attached to their pillows tags that state DO NOT REMOVE THIS TAG UNDER PENALTY OF LAW. The drafter who inserts an unenforceable provision for its *in terrorem* effect, expecting that a court will at worst determine that it is not enforceable, may find that the provision creates a liability under a Consumer Protection Act.

Under these circumstances, is it prudent to include illegal or unenforceable provisions in agreements? What are the ethical considerations?

§ 4.8 Ethics in drafting.

Ethical responsibilities in drafting agreements have received little consideration from the bar, for ethical standards generally address the adversarial context. We will examine the available resources, including:

- The Code of Professional Responsibility
- The Model Rules of Professional Conduct
- Ethics Committee decisions

a. The Code of Professional Responsibility. The Code of Professional Responsibility does not address the issue. DR 7-102(A)(7) provides:

> In his representation of a client, a lawyer shall not: . . . Counsel or assist his client in conduct that the lawyer knows to be illegal or fraudulent.

b. The Model Rules of Professional Conduct. The drafters of the Model Rules of Professional Conduct began by addressing drafting issues more squarely. The Discussion Draft of Rule 4.3 (January, 1980) stated:

> A lawyer shall not conclude an agreement, or assist a client in concluding an agreement, that the lawyer knows or reasonably should know is illegal, contains legally prohibited terms, would work a fraud, or would be held to be unconscionable as a matter of law.

Comment:

Moreover, a lawyer is not absolved of responsibilities for a legally offensive transaction simply because the client takes the final step in carrying it out. For example, a lawyer who prepared a form contract containing legally prohibited terms is involved in a transaction in which the form is used, even though the lawyer does not participate in the specific transaction.

The Final Proposed Draft of Rule 1.2, *Scope of Representation,* paragraph (d), however, stated:

> A lawyer shall not counsel or assist a client in conduct that the lawyer knows or reasonably should know is criminal or fraudulent, or in the preparation of a written instrument containing terms the lawyer knows or reasonably should know are legally prohibited, but a lawyer may counsel or assist a client in a good faith effort to determine the validity, scope, meaning or application of the law.

Comment:

> Law in many jurisdictions prohibits various provisions in contracts and other written instruments. Such proscriptions include usury laws, statutes prohibiting provisions that purport to waive certain legally conferred rights and contracts provisions that have been held unconscionable as a matter of law in the controlling jurisdiction. A lawyer may not employ these terms. On the other hand, there are legal rules that simply make certain contractual provisions unenforceable, allowing one or both parties to avoid the obligation. Inclusion of the latter kind of provision in a contract may be unwise but it is not ethically improper, nor is it improper to include provisions whose legality is subject to reasonable argument.

Rule 1.2(d), as adopted by the American Bar Association on August 2, 1983, provides:

> A lawyer shall not counsel a client to engage, or assist a client, in conduct that the lawyer knows is criminal or fraudulent, but a lawyer may discuss the legal consequences of any proposed course of conduct with a client and may counsel or assist a client to make a good faith effort to determine the validity, scope, meaning or application of the law.

Comment:

> Paragraph (d) applies whether or not the defrauded party is party to the transaction. Hence, a lawyer should not participate in a sham transaction; for example, a transaction to effectuate criminal or fraudulent escape of tax liability. Paragraph (d) does not preclude undertaking a criminal defense incident to a general retainer for legal services to a lawful enterprise. The last clause of paragraph (d) recognizes that determining the validity or interpretation of a statute or regulation may require a course of action involving disobedience of the statute or

regulation or of the interpretation placed upon it by governmental authorities.

It is apparent that Model Rule 1.2(d) as adopted is considerably watered-down from earlier drafts. It could be argued that the deletion of the reference in the Final Proposed Draft to "the preparation of a written instrument containing terms the lawyer knows or should know are legally prohibited" indicates an intent to exclude drafting from the scope of the rule. There remains a proscription against "criminal or fraudulent" conduct. Inclusion of an unenforceable clause is not criminal. Is it fraudulent? The fact that the drafters enumerated "the preparation of a written instrument" as something additional to criminal or fraudulent conduct suggests that they did not regard the practice as fraudulent.

c. Ethics Committee decisions. Two ethics committees have issued opinions on the applicability of the rules to particular drafting situations: drafting of a void waiver and drafting of a surrogate mother contract. We will examine these opinions and explore the application of these guidelines to the drafting of an exculpatory clause.

With respect to a drafter's including a waiver that is void as a matter of public policy, the Association of the Bar of the City of New York and the New York County Lawyers' Association rendered this opinion:[1]

> You inquire if it is ethical for a lawyer to insert in a contract a waiver of right, which waiver is void "as against public policy."
>
> You state that the right in question is a tenant's right to a sixty-day period to reconsider and cancel an agreed-upon increase of rent under the Emergency Rent Laws. You further state that many times a layman does not know his rights and could be deceived into compliance by such an illegal clause.
>
> In the opinion of our Committee it is not within the proper standards of ethics for a lawyer to insert such a waiver in a contract if the lawyer knows that such a waiver is against public policy and void as a matter of law.
>
> A lawyer must himself observe and advise his client to observe the statute law (Canon 32).[2] If a waiver in a contract has been held by a court of last resort to be void as against public policy as a matter of law, he should so advise his client. If the client should nevertheless insist on its incorporation in the contract, the lawyer should refuse to do so, for if he should comply with his client's request he would thereby become a party to possible deception of the other party to the contract.

---

[1] Opinion 722, December 6, 1948, Reprinted with permission of The Association of the Bar of the City of New York, Committee on Professional and Judicial Ethics.

[2] Canon 32 of the 1908 Canons of Professional Ethics, as amended, stated in pertinent part:

> He must also observe and advise his client to observe the statute law, though until a statute shall have been construed and interpreted by competent adjudication, he is free and is entitled to advise as to its validity and as to what he conscientiously believes to be its just meaning and extent.

In the language of Canon 29 as to the lawyer's duty to uphold the honor of the profession, "He should strive at all times to uphold the honor and to maintain the dignity of the profession and to improve not only the law but the administration of justice."

In the second example, a law firm was retained to prepare a contract between a client and a surrogate mother, pursuant to which a surrogate mother would be artificially inseminated with the client's semen, and if a baby resulted, the surrogate mother would surrender the child to the client and his wife. The firm requested an opinion as to the ethical propriety of the proposed contract. The Committee on Professional and Judicial Ethics of the Association of the Bar of the City of New York replied as follows: [3]

> A law firm has been retained by a client to prepare a contract between the client and a third party. Under the terms of the proposed contract, the third party (a "surrogate mother") would be artificially inseminated with the client's semen; if pregnancy and birth ensued, the surrogate mother would deliver the child to the client and his spouse, and would forfeit all rights with respect to the child. The law firm has advised the client that the contemplated contract may not be enforceable in the courts, but the client has indicated his desire to proceed with the contract nevertheless.

> The law firm asks whether it is ethically proper to prepare a contract in these circumstances. Assuming the proposed contract is not illegal, we conclude that no ethical rule prohibits a lawyer from preparing such an agreement.

> We offer no opinion on the legality or enforceability of the contemplated contract for that is a question of law outside this Committee's jurisdiction. It is, of course, incumbent upon the inquiring law firm to determine whether the contract is illegal. If the law firm determines that it is illegal, then the lawyer must refuse to draft the contract. DR 7-102(A)(7) states that a lawyer shall not "counsel or assist his client in conduct that the lawyer knows to be illegal." If, however, the firm concludes (as it apparently has) that the contract is merely voidable or unenforceable, then nothing in Canon 7 or elsewhere in the Code of Professional Responsibility prohibits the firm from drafting such a contract as long as the firm advises the client of the risks that the contract might not be enforced or may be voided by the other party.

> We note that the law firm should advise the third party to seek separate counsel for it appears that the surrogate mother may have an actually, or potentially, adverse interest to the firm's client. [Text of DR 7-104 omitted.]

---

[3] Opinion 81-67. Reprinted with permission of The Association of the Bar of the City of New York, Committee on Professional and Judicial Ethics.

§ 4.9 Application: Exculpatory clauses.

The two ethics opinions draw a distinction between provisions that are "illegal" and those that are "merely voidable or unenforceable." This issue often arises with respect to an exculpatory clause in a residential lease. The effect of the provision is to excuse the landlord from liability for the landlord's willful, reckless, or negligent conduct.

Is it illegal to insert an exculpatory clause in a lease? If it is not illegal, will a court find it unlawful? If the only consequence of including the clause in the lease is that a court would find it unenforceable, would it be an ethical violation for you to draft the clause in the agreement?

Inclusion of the exculpatory clause is illegal under Uniform Residential Landlord and Tenant Act § 1.403, which has been adopted in several jurisdictions. This is a rare case in which it may be illegal to include the language in the agreement. Clauses exculpating landlords from negligence in residential premises have been held unenforceable in many jurisdictions.

In preparing the lease, the attorney is probably assisting the client in evading laws making persons responsible for their negligent acts. It could be argued that this law is not enacted for a public reason and therefore can be contravened by private agreement. Many jurisdictions have adopted standards for determining the extent of public interest, usually concluding that residential apartments are within its sphere.

If a court finds the term unenforceable, but the only sanction is refusal to enforce it, there may be little impact on drafting. The attorney should advise the client not to rely on the provision; i.e., the landlord should obtain insurance. The attorney might also suggest that the client may obtain better results by settling for less. In some cases, inclusion of illegal terms may lead to the unenforceability of the entire contract.

It can also be argued from a rule-oriented ethical perspective that the rule permitting the lawyer to make "a good faith effort to determine the validity, scope, meaning or application of the law" allows the lawyer to distinguish a particular case. For example, if case law held that an exculpatory clause was unenforceable because the tenant lacked equal bargaining power in an area where housing was scarce, this policy consideration may not apply to another tenant or another area. Finally, while the effect of the client's conduct is to deceive tenants, the elements of fraud are probably absent. Intent is probably lacking where inclusion of the exculpatory clause merely makes the agreement unenforceable. The attorney may believe that a court will not enforce it, but the attorney does not know it.

Consider, however, the potential impact on tenants. Tenants may understandably believe that what is written in a contract is binding. Even if unenforceable, the clause may have an *in terrorem* effect. The purpose of including the provision, then, seems only to mislead tenants into thinking that they do not have a right that they have. This practice may be unfair or deceptive under Consumer Protection Acts.

Even if the conduct is not unethical based on analysis of the Code or Rules, an attorney may still refuse to draft the clause. The Comment to Rule 1.16 states that "The lawyer also may withdraw where the client insists on a repugnant or imprudent objective." More positively, it may be possible to engage in an ethical dialogue with the client. The attorney working with the client may be able to mitigate the harsh effects of a contract while meeting the legitimate business needs of the client. Professor Justin Sweet states:[4]

> For better or worse, the average American lawyer is competitive enough to try to do better than the [Uniform Commercial] Code if he has the bargaining power. In doing so, he often deludes himself by being oblivious of the possibility that such exercise of power may not be judicially enforceable and by forgetting that good will and fair dealing may be very essential to his business client's interest.

§ 4.10 Exercises.

1. Research. Check the law of your state to discover statutes which affect the substance or form of agreements. Statutes affecting form may:

  a. Require "plain language";

  b. Prohibit certain language in agreements;

  c. Require specific language; or

  d. Require type size or format.

Statutes affecting substance may:

  a. Prohibit certain agreements;

  b. Prohibit certain terms in agreements; or

  c. Supply terms in agreements.

Note any sanctions for including prohibited language or terms.

2. Representing an unsavory client. Assume that your client has inserted an exculpatory clause in the rental agreement. He brings you the following letter, which a tenant has written to him:

Dear Mr. Landlord:

Ten days ago I informed you that the light on my landing is not functioning. You did not repair it. Three days later I tripped over a large piece of plaster that fell from the wall on that landing and broke my leg. I spent $1000 on doctor's bills and nursing care, which I expect you to pay.

Sincerely,
Elderly Widow

He wants you to send this reply:

---

[4] Justin Sweet, *The Lawyer's Role in Contract Drafting*, 43 CAL. ST. B.J. 362, 367 n.7 (1968).

Dear Elderly Widow:

I call your attention to paragraph 20 of our lease, which clearly states that I am not responsible for your unfortunate loss. Since you agreed to this provision (which was in our mutual interest, as it saved me the expense of obtaining insurance, a savings I was able to pass on to you), I regret that I can do nothing for you. I am, however, sending a bouquet of flowers by way of wishing you a speedy recovery.

Have a nice day,
Mr. Landlord

What would you advise the client? Suppose you approve the sending of the letter and it results in a loss to Elderly Widow; for example, she forgoes her claim until after the statute of limitations has run. Would she have any claim against the landlord? Against you?

3. Thinking like a lawyer. In 1955, the New Jersey Superior Court in *Kuzmiak v. Brookchester, Inc.,* held that exculpatory clauses in residential leases are unenforceable due in part to the unequal bargaining positions of landlord and tenant.

Shortly thereafter, a case came to the Superior Court on the following facts:

Plaintiff Gustavo Cardona, a tenant in a tenement house owned by defendant Eden Realty Company, Inc., was injured as a result of a fall allegedly caused by a loose metal nosing on a stair of the common stairway located in said building. His suit for damages asserts negligent maintenance of the stairway and maintenance of a nuisance. The court granted defendant's motion for summary judgment upon the basis that the lease signed by the parties exculpated defendant from responsibility.

The rental agreement, which was typed in both English and Spanish, provided for a month-to-month tenancy at the rate of $52 a month. It required the tenant to furnish his own painting, stove, heat, heating equipment, hot water, refrigerator, shades, screens, storm windows, toilet seat, door locks, and all fixtures needed in the occupation of the premises.

The lease contained an exculpatory clause which recited that in consideration of the reduced rental provided for, the tenant covenanted not to sue the landlord and the landlord would not be liable to the tenant for any damage, loss or injury to property or person by reason of any existing or future defect in the premises, including acts, omissions, negligence or nuisance of other persons or tenants or of the landlord or his agent, and including that arising from falling plaster, leaking roofs — or faulty or inadequately lighted or repaired sidewalks, stairs, halls, alleys, yards or cellars.

In addition to this purported exculpation of defendant from its acts of negligence, the lease also contained a novel provision in which the landlord recited that it had no public liability insurance and if the tenant desired to eliminate the exculpatory clause, written notice thereof should be given the landlord, in which event the rent would be increased $2 a month. The agreement went on to say that following termination of the exculpatory clause by the tenant, the landlord's liability "shall be that provided by the general laws of the State. The landlord *shall not* become an insurer by virtue of such termination."

The lower court concluded that this so-called option provision, coupled with the consideration received by the tenant for the exculpatory clause in the form of a reduced rental, removed defendant from the line of cases, and more particularly, *Kuzmiak v. Brookchester,* 33 N.J. Super. 575, 111 A.2d 425, holding that it is against public policy for a landlord to exculpate himself from his own acts of negligence when dealing with residential properties since the parties are in an unequal bargaining position. It found that this distinguishing feature vitiated the unequal bargaining position philosophy of *Kuzmiak.*

Has the drafter of Eden Realty Company's lease successfully overcome the deficiency of the lease in *Kuzmiak?* If not, has the attorney violated the Code of Professional Responsibility or the Model Rules of Professional Conduct?

Chapter 5
CAPACITY

§ 5.1 Introduction.

Formation of a contract requires the free assent of the parties. Assent may be lacking if (1) the behavior of one party induces the other to enter the contract, or (2) the status of a party impairs his or her ability to contract. Behavior includes acts which constitute defenses to contract formation: fraud, duress, undue influence, and unconscionability. The principal characteristics that may affect a person's status to contract today are mental capacity, age, and lack of authority.

§ 5.2 Behavior.

"I made him an offer he couldn't refuse." Everyone is familiar with the Godfather's way of saying that he compelled the other party to enter a contract. Suppose that party sought to avoid the contract with the Godfather on grounds of duress. In court, the Godfather's *consiglieri* might point to a provision in the agreement that states, "I am entering this agreement of my own free will. I mean it. I mean it. I mean it." He would argue that this provision bars the other party from claiming duress. Is the argument persuasive?

The argument is obviously not a good one, for it is black letter law that duress prevents a contract from being formed. Whether the contract was entered under duress is a question of fact. The relevant facts are the circumstances surrounding the making of the contract. The provisions of the agreement itself have little probative value on this issue. For example, the Godfather might have held a gun to his head while he signed the agreement containing those words. Because it proves so little, language characterizing the behavior of the parties is often omitted in drafting the contract.

Sometimes, however, language in the agreement may help make clear that one party did not take advantage of the other party's circumstances. A party may wish to show that the other party was represented by an attorney or had the opportunity to do so but declined. For example:

This agreement is voluntary and each of the parties has been represented by separate counsel, Husband by Mary Smith, Esq., and Wife by John Zilch, Esq. Each of the parties has read and approved the agreement upon the advice of counsel.

or

Husband has retained and been represented by Mary Smith, Esq., in connection with the negotiations for the drafting of this agreement. Wife has not been represented by counsel although she understands her right to be so represented, and has knowingly waived the services of counsel.

§ 5.3 Fraud.

Fraud, or misrepresentation, as it is often called in the context of contracts, is another form of behavior that one party may engage in to induce the other party to enter a contract. The statements that give rise to an allegation of misrepresentation may or may not be found in the contract. As a matter of preventive law, the attorney should tell the client to "get it in writing." The same admonition applies to the attorney, who must ask the client if any representations were made by the other party and then include them when drafting the contract.

If a representation is not found in the contract, an issue of parol evidence may be raised as to the admissibility of the statement. *See* Chapter 6, Parol Evidence. While it is often said that fraud is an exception to the parol evidence rule, the exception may not apply if the subject of the misrepresentation is found in the contract. The reason for the exception is evident from the nature of a fraud claim. A party claiming fraud must allege that a false representation was made. The written contract, however, may state in the merger clause that no representations were made. If a party claims that a representation was made, was it not incumbent upon that party to have either insisted upon putting the representation in the contract, or refused to agree to the merger clause? Unlike the party claiming duress, the party claiming fraud presumably had a choice.

The argument is not a good one. Evidence of misrepresentations should be admitted even if the contract states that there are no representations. The fact that a contract states that there are no representations certainly does not mean that none were in fact made. Although the fact that representations were made contrary to the language of the contract is not itself fraud, the language should not bar a showing of fraud. As a New York judge wrote in dissent, quoting Judge Augustus Hand:

"the ingenuity of draftsmen is sure to keep pace with the demands of wrongdoers, and if a deliberate fraud may be shielded by a clause in a contract that the writing contains every representation made by way of inducement, or that utterances shown to be untrue were not an inducement to the agreement," a fraudulent seller would have a simple method of obtaining immunity for his misconduct.

While drafters should not assist wrongdoers, it is apparent that a drafter who may have to persuade a court not to admit evidence of extrinsic representations should make the merger clause as detailed as possible, specifically enumerating areas where representations might have been made.

§ 5.4 Mental capacity.

The mental capacity of the party who executes an instrument is a significant issue in the law of Estates. Wills usually contain a statement that the testator is "of sound mind and memory." Just as assertions that the contract was not entered under duress are usually omitted in drafting, so are assertions that the person had the mental capacity to contract. In a situation where mental capacity may be in issue, the drafter might include the statement. The fact that these assertions are not self-proving is demonstrated by this cartoon:[1]

"I, EMPEROR DUANE VI OF NEBRASKA,
BEING OF SOUND MIND . . ."

§ 5.5 Minority.

A minor generally has the capacity to enter only voidable contracts. The minor's power to avoid the contract may terminate, however, if the minor

---

[1] Cartoon by Nick Hobart. Copyright © 1981 by West Group. Reprinted with permission.

misrepresents his or her age. Therefore, the drafter of a contract may wish to include a party's assertion that he or she was of age to contract. The statement could then be used as proof that the minor represented that he or she was of lawful age to contract. Unlike a provision stating that there has been no duress or misrepresentation, this provision is not used to prove that the assertion is true. It is used to prove that the minor engaged in a misrepresentation.

§ 5.6 Authority.

Capacity to contract may also be important when dealing with a business. You may want to know whether the individual with whom you are contracting has authority to act for the business. If the business repudiates the acts of the individual, recall from the law of agency that you must prove that the individual had actual or apparent authority. As a matter of preventive law, however, if you establish the individual's authority at the time of the transaction, you will not have to litigate the issue later.

You can establish the individual's authority by having the business execute a power of attorney indicating that the individual is authorized to enter the particular transaction. For example, the following power of attorney authorizes an individual to enter purchasing contracts on behalf of a corporation:

ABC Company, a corporation organized and existing under the laws of the State of Missouri, and having its principal office at 123 Monticello St. in the City of Jefferson City, State of Missouri, does hereby constitute and appoint John Adams, of the City of Boston, County of Suffolk, Commonwealth of Massachusetts, its true and lawful attorney in fact, for the following purposes:

To execute contracts for the purchase of building materials, and to sign, indorse, and execute bills of lading and other shipping documents required for the transport of building materials in the United States or elsewhere, made out in the name of and payable by principal, and to perform all other acts necessary and desirable relating to such contracts, bills of lading, and other documents.

In witness whereof, ABC Company has caused this instrument to be sealed with its corporate seal, duly attested by the signature of its Secretary October 1, 2004.

> ABC Company
> By Thomas Jefferson
> Secretary

---

§ 5.7 Exercise.

1. Dealing with a minor. A merchant asks you to draft contract language that will protect him if he sells to a minor who misrepresents his or her age. In your research, you find this form language for a contractual representation of age:

> [Name or designation of declarant] declares that he is over the age of majority, being _____ years of age, and is not subject to any known disability to enter this agreement. He has read, understands, and accepts all the terms of this agreement, as recited herein.

a. Redraft the form in plain language. *See* Chapter 18, Plain Language.

b. Anticipate the issues that may arise if a minor who makes this representation later seeks to disaffirm the contract.

c. What advice would you give to a merchant who regularly deals with minors?

Chapter 6

PAROL EVIDENCE

§ 6.1 Introduction.

There are competing interests in the application of the parol evidence rule. On the one hand, we honor those who keep their word. The compliment, "His word is as good as his bond," loses its power if limited only to his written word. On the other hand, we seek certainty and stability, especially in commercial dealings. If a party could rely on a written agreement without concern that the other party might claim it was supplemented by oral understandings, the world of contract law would certainly turn more smoothly. Incidentally, *oral* means "spoken" and *verbal* means "using words." Try to use the terms with precision and avoid the habit of referring to agreements not reduced to writing as "verbal agreements."

While it is important that parties (and their assignees) be able to rely on the express terms of a contract, implicitly there must first be a determination of what the express terms are. In other words, before a contract can be enforced, it is first necessary to *find the contract*. To find the contract, we must start with the proposition that, in general, there is nothing wrong with contracts being oral. There may be problems of proof, so we may want to discourage them, but we do not deny them legal enforcement, with the few exceptions collectively known as the Statute of Frauds.

There is also, of course, nothing wrong with contracts being written. It follows that there is nothing wrong with a contract being partly written and partly oral — with one major exception. There is something wrong with a contract that is partly written and partly oral *if the parties intend the contract to be entirely written.* That is what the parol evidence rule is all about. It is best seen as a tool used in the process of finding the contract. When evidence is offered of terms extrinsic to a writing, application of the rule requires a determination of whether the parties intended their writing to be an "integration" of the entire agreement.

We are accustomed to seeing how this issue arises in court. As a trial lawyer, it is important to develop the instinct to pop out of your seat at the appropriate moment and say, "Objection — parol evidence rule." In appellate cases, the court must decide whether the trial court properly ruled on the admissibility of the evidence. This chapter asks you to step back to the beginning of the process. As a planner, the lawyer must be aware of the parol evidence rule at the time the contract is signed. The lawyer should practice preventive law so that this issue never reaches a court. The lawyer as drafter can help attain that goal by asking these questions at the time the contract is signed:

- Does this writing contain the final and complete statement of the agreement?

- How can I protect my client against a later offer of parol evidence to supplement or contradict the agreement?

- What customs and usages of trade may be assumed to be part of the parties' agreement?

§ 6.2 Is the agreement final?

Where is the agreement of the parties found? The parol evidence rule applies only when the agreement is found in a final and complete form, usually a writing. In a negotiated agreement, the process of negotiation is the process of determining which provisions will be included in the final agreement. A final draft is then hammered out for signature. Usually the parties intend the writing to be their final agreement. After the final draft is signed, all proposals, discussions, drafts, and the like are of no effect. In the vocabulary of parol evidence, the final agreement is an *integration* of the parties' understandings.

The drafter should read the agreement to detect any language that indicates it is not an integrated agreement. The face of the document is probably not conclusive on the question of whether the document is a final agreement, but drafting can make the answer clearer. For example, a buy-sell agreement (such as the one set forth in § 3.8, Exercise 4) may indicate that the parties intend to execute later documents, such as a purchase money mortgage, a deed, and a bill of sale. Or the parties may intend to replace a "letter of intent" initialed by them with a more formal agreement supplemented by stock transfers, security agreements, and the like. On their face, these agreements are not final.

On the other hand, an attorney may circulate a draft agreement on colored paper with the word "DRAFT" conspicuously written in the upper right hand corner. Impatient clients may then sign this draft. While on its face this document indicates that it is not the final agreement, the actions of the parties have probably made it a final agreement.

§ 6.3 Is the agreement complete?

A final agreement may not be the *complete* agreement of the parties; it may be only partially integrated. If it is partially integrated, then evidence may be offered to supplement but not to contradict the terms it contains.

For example, the following provision appeared in a contract for the sale of a medical instrument:

> The equipment supplied will be generally in accordance with the written Specifications, as provided by Seller to Purchaser, subject to reasonable deviations. . . . Seller shall not be responsible for performance figures given in any source other than the above mentioned specifications.

The reference in this provision to "specifications" shows that the agreement is only partially integrated. The complete agreement includes the terms of the specifications.

In another case, an agreement between the lessor and lessee of a gas station stated:

> The lessee may elect to pay for the gasoline upon such terms and conditions as the parties may mutually agree.

On its face, this agreement is not complete as to the payment term. Therefore parol evidence may be admitted to show the parties' agreement as to payment. Suppose, however, the agreement stated:

> The lessee shall pay for the gasoline weekly.

If the lessee wants to introduce evidence to prove that the parties agreed to monthly payments, this evidence would not be admissible under the parol evidence rule because it *contradicts* the final agreement.

§ 6.4 Merger clause.

To show that an agreement is completely integrated, that is, that the writing expresses the final and complete agreement of the parties, drafters often include a *merger clause*. This is an example of a merger clause:

> This agreement signed by both parties and so initialed by both parties in the margin opposite this paragraph constitutes a final written expression of all the terms of this agreement and is a complete and exclusive statement of those terms.

A merger clause will not bar all extrinsic evidence. The clause indicates that the agreement is final and complete. But if it is clear from the face of the agreement that some terms have been omitted, courts will generally allow evidence of those terms. For example, an agreement contained a provision stating:

> The front and back hereof comprise the entire agreement affecting this order and no other agreement or understanding of any nature concerning same has been made or entered into.

The agreement referred numerous times to delivery but contained no delivery date. The court allowed evidence of the seller's representation as to the delivery date. Note that the offered evidence supplemented but did not contradict the agreement. If the agreement had stated, "Delivery date 10 days from date of this agreement," a court would probably not allow evidence to contradict the provision. For example, a franchise agreement stated:

> This agreement may be terminated by either party at the end of any term by a 90-day written notice of intent to terminate.

The franchisee claimed that the franchisor's agents had assured him that the franchisor would terminate the agreement only for cause. The court found that because the offered evidence contradicted an integrated agreement, it was not admissible.

A seller who relies on salespersons to negotiate agreements may want to include language to protect the seller in the event the buyer claims that the salesperson made an additional representation. For example:

> MERGER CLAUSE. The seller's salespersons may have made oral statements about the merchandise described in this contract. Such statements do not constitute warranties, shall not be relied on by the buyer, and are not part of the contract for sale. The entire contract is embodied in this writing. This writing constitutes the final expression of the parties' agreement, and it is a complete and exclusive statement of the terms of that agreement.

§ 6.5 Exception: Formation issues.

An exception to the rule prohibiting extrinsic evidence arises when the evidence is offered not for the purpose of supplementing or contradicting the writing, but for the purpose of raising a defense to the formation of the contract itself, such as fraud, duress, or mistake. Recall that the purpose of the parol evidence rule is to find the contract. Under this exception, the evidence is offered not for that purpose, but to prove that a valid contract was never formed. Nor does the merger clause generally bar evidence offered for this purpose. *See* § 5.3. The merger clause, as part of the contract, evidences that it is integrated. But if the contract of which the merger clause is a part is not a valid agreement, then the merger clause itself is not enforceable. A clear example of this exception is duress. If a written contract states, "I enter this contract of my own free will. I mean it. I mean it. I mean it," this fact will not bar a party from presenting evidence that she signed it because the other party held a gun to her head.

§ 6.6 Adhesion contracts.

While it is imperative that the drafter include a merger clause to indicate completeness, the merger clause creates only a rebuttable presumption that the agreement is fully integrated. A court is more likely to give weight to a merger clause in a negotiated agreement than in an informal contract or in a contract of adhesion. Therefore, the drafter of a contract of adhesion should use devices that keep the merger clause from being just more boilerplate that the other party is unaware of.

For example, the disclosures of the Federal Trade Commission Used Car Trade Regulation Rule, 16 C.F.R. § 455, are intended to make clear that representations outside of the written contract are of no effect. *See* § 12.10, Exercise 5. The Used Car Buyers Guide states at the top:

> IMPORTANT: Spoken promises are difficult to enforce. Ask the dealer to put all promises in writing. Keep this form.

To explain the meaning of the "AS IS" disclaimer of warranty, the Guide states:

> YOU WILL PAY ALL COSTS FOR ANY REPAIRS. The dealer assumes no responsibility for any repairs, regardless of any oral statements about the vehicle.

Although intended to protect purchasers, the Buyers Guide will probably protect used car sellers as well, for it will be difficult for a court to admit extrinsic evidence in the face of such clear language stating that the agreement is complete. A consumer misled by an oral representation might still make a claim under a state Consumer Protection Act, however, for the issue under an Act is whether the statement was made, not whether it was part of the contract. *See* § 4.7.

§ 6.7 The U.C.C. parol evidence rule.

U.C.C. § 2-202 states:

> Terms with respect to which the confirmatory memoranda of the parties agree or which are otherwise set forth in a writing intended by the parties as a final expression of their agreement with respect to such terms as are included therein may not be contradicted by evidence of any prior agreement or of a contemporaneous oral agreement but may be explained or supplemented
>
> (a) by course of dealing or usage of trade (section 1-205) or by a course of performance (section 2-208); and
>
> (b) by evidence of consistent additional terms unless the court finds the writing to have been intended also as a complete and exclusive statement of the terms of the agreement.

Under this statute, course of dealing, usage of trade, or course of performance may be offered to explain or supplement an agreement even if the language is not ambiguous. For example, *A* sold steel slabs to *B* under an agreement that specified *B* was to make payment within fifteen days of receipt of the goods. When *A* sought interest on late payments, *B* argued that a course of dealing between *A* and *B* established *A* would not charge *B* interest on late payments. The court did not allow evidence of the course of dealing, for it was offered to *contradict* the express term of the agreement requiring payment within fifteen days. On the other hand, where a seller claimed that trade custom permitted it to add its higher costs to an express price provision, the court admitted the evidence on the grounds that it did not contradict but *supplemented* the price term.

In view of the unpredictable application of the rule, the drafter may wish to address the problem squarely. The drafter could include a provision specifically excluding the evidence. For example:

> No course of prior dealings between the parties and no usage of the trade shall be relevant to supplement or explain any term used in this agreement.

The use of such a broad prohibition could be dangerous, for the drafter may not be familiar enough with the client's business to know which terms should not be supplemented with reference to prior dealings or trade usage. Another alternative would be to specifically identify the particular usage. For example:

> The parties have at times in the past allowed a "grace period" for the delivery of materials. The parties specifically agree that in this agreement, delivery dates exclude any "grace period."

or

> In this agreement, *ton* means a weight of 2000 pounds.

§ 6.8 Collateral agreement.

Even if the writing is completely integrated, the parties may have made a side agreement. This side agreement, called a collateral agreement, may be enforceable if it satisfies the requirements of a contract (such as consideration) and if it does not contradict the integrated agreement. For example, *A* and *B* enter a buy-sell agreement for the sale of *A*'s house to *B*. The agreement states:

> The following personal property is also to be left upon the premises as a part of the property purchased: *none*.

B later claims that *A* agreed to leave the refrigerator behind. *B*'s attempt to offer evidence of this agreement would probably be barred. The buy-sell agreement is integrated and the extrinsic evidence contradicts the provision in the buy-sell agreement.

Suppose, however, *B* offered to prove that the parties orally agreed that *B* would purchase *A*'s refrigerator for $400. This agreement standing alone is enforceable. It does not contradict the buy-sell agreement, for that agreement recites that no personal property is sold as part of the house purchase, while the collateral agreement recites a separate consideration.

Most alleged collateral agreements do not stand by themselves. The attempt to prove a collateral agreement is often the same as an attempt to show that an agreement is not integrated. For example, the buyer of land attempted to show that the seller had agreed to remove a nearby eyesore. The court did not allow the evidence where the agreement was full and complete. The drafter must be watchful for any terms that are not part of the final agreement and must insist on their inclusion.

§ 6.9 Interpretation.

The parol evidence rule assists in determining where the agreement of the parties is found. Once the agreement has been found, an additional question may arise: what does it mean? Just as in a parol evidence issue, this fact question is not necessarily reached. For before evidence can be offered on the meaning of a word or term, the court must first determine that it is ambiguous. As with parol evidence, there is debate about what kind of evidence is permitted to assist the court in making this determination. Because most courts determine whether a word is ambiguous based on whether a reasonable person would think it had more than one meaning in the circumstances, rather than based on the "four corners" of the instrument, extrinsic evidence is usually allowed on questions of interpretation.

§ 6.10 Modification.

The parol evidence rule operates to exclude evidence of negotiations conducted *prior* to or contemporaneous with (if that is possible) the final agreement. Often, a party claims that after the final agreement was entered, the parties modified it. This is not a question of parol evidence. First, find the original agreement. Then, determine whether there have been any modifications. The policy limiting modifications to those made in writing is similar to the policy behind the parol evidence rule — to encourage parties to put all their agreements in writing, whether made before or after the written agreement. *See* Chapter 11, Modification and Discharge.

§ 6.11 Exercises.

1. Separation agreement. You represent the Wife in the negotiation of a separation agreement between Husband and Wife. After the terms of the agreement have been hammered out, the parties and the attorneys meet for the signing. Just before the Wife signs, the Husband says, "I realize, honey, that you aren't getting an awful lot of money. I wanted to give you more, but I felt I had to go along with the deal the lawyers worked out. I want you to know that any time things are tight and you need more money, just ask and I'll give it to you."

What should you do?

2. Sale of goods. Sarah is selling her car to Barney. During the negotiations, Sarah says, "This car will get at least 25 miles per gallon around town." After they agree on a price, Sarah gets a form contract from a stationery store and offers it to Barney for signature. The agreement states:

September 20, 2002. Sarah Seller and Barney Buyer agree as follows:

1. Seller shall transfer and deliver to Buyer and Buyer shall accept and pay for a 1982 Buick Skylark.

2. Seller shall deliver the goods to Buyer on October 1, 2002.

3. Buyer shall pay Seller $2000 cash for the goods on delivery.

4. The goods are sold AS IS without any warranty.

5. This writing is intended by the parties as a final expression of their agreement and is intended as a complete and exclusive statement of the terms of their agreement.

———————————   ———————————
        Seller   Buyer

Barney brings the agreement to you for your advice. What would you advise him?

3. Distribution agreement. A brewer and distributor enter the following agreement:

It is hereby agreed between Beck & Co., of BREMEN/GERMANY, brewers of BECK'S BEER, and _____, distributor of said beer that the said distributor is authorized to distribute BECK'S BEER under its California License(s) number _____ in the [County of] _____. Distributor's authority hereunder is non-exclusive. This agreement will continue in effect unless and until terminated at any time after January 1, 1973 by thirty days written notice by either party to the other.

May the distributor offer evidence to show that the agreement is not integrated?

If a court finds that the agreement is not integrated, may the distributor offer evidence to show that it is an industry-wide custom for a brewer to terminate only for cause?

How could the agreement have been drafted to prevent the introduction of such evidence?

4. Settlement agreement. An author and his new publisher enter this agreement.

Agreement made this 21 day of October, 1979, between Western Publishing Co., Inc., a Wisconsin Corporation, its successors and assigns (referred to as "Western"), and Herbert S. Zim of Miami, Florida, who is a citizen of the United States and resident of Florida (referred to as the "Author").

Background. The Author has written a series of books known as the "Golden Guides." The "Golden Guides" have been published by various publishers which have been acquired by Western. Western intends to continue publication of the existing "Golden Guides" under either the imprint of the original publisher or the imprint of Western. Western also intends to publish additional "Golden Guides" under the imprint of Western.

The parties agree:

1. Definitions.

1.1. "Golden Guides" or "Guides" as used herein means all books published or to be published or distributed by Western in the *Golden Guide* series.

1.2. "Individual Contract" as used herein means a contract between Western (including Western's predecessors in interest) and the Author.

2. The Author agrees to write 15 new Guides for Western. The Author shall deliver two complete copies of each manuscript in the English language of approximately 10,000 words in length, in content and form satisfactory to Western, together with any permission required and all photographs, illustrations, drawings, charts, maps and indexes suitable for reproduction and necessary to the completion of the manuscript not later than every 3 months from the date of this agreement until 15 Guides have been delivered.

3. The Author grants to Western during the term of copyright, including renewals and extensions thereof the exclusive right in the English language, in the United States of America, the Philippine Republic, and Canada, and non-exclusive right in all other countries except the British Commonwealth (other than Canada), the Republic of South Africa, and the Irish Republic, to print, publish and sell the Guides in book form.

4. If the Author incorporates in the Guides any copyrighted material, he shall procure, at his expense, written permission to reprint it.

5. The Author warrants that he is the sole author of the Guides; that he is the sole owner of all the rights granted to Western; that he has not previously assigned, pledged or otherwise encumbered the same; that he has full power to enter into this agreement; that except for the material obtained pursuant to Paragraph 4 the Guides are original,

have not been published before, and are not in the public domain; that they do not violate any right of privacy; that they are not libelous or obscene and that they do not infringe upon any statutory or common-law copyright.

6. The Author agrees that during the term of this agreement he will not, without the written permission of Western, publish or permit to be published any material, in book or pamphlet form, based on material in the Guides.

7. Western shall copyright the Guides in the name of the Author.

8. Western shall pay to the Author with respect to each Guide published or to be published or distributed by Western, a royalty on the retail price of every copy sold, less returns, of ten percent (10%). For example, if under an Individual Contract the Author was entitled to a royalty of 7%, Western shall pay an additional 3%, so that the total royalty is 10%.

9. In addition to the foregoing, Western shall pay the Author a bonus of $10,000 for each Guide published by Western.

10. This agreement shall be interpreted according to the law of the State of Wisconsin.

11. This agreement shall be binding upon the heirs, executors, administrators and assigns of the Author, and upon the successors and assigns of Western, but no assignment shall be binding on either of the parties without the written consent of the other.

12. This agreement constitutes the complete understanding of the parties. No modification or waiver of any provision shall be valid unless in writing and signed by both parties.

IN WITNESS WHEREOF the parties have duly executed this agreement the day and year first above written.

In the presence of   Western Publishing Co., Inc.

_____   _____
                                                       The Publisher

In the presence of

_____   _____
                                                       The Author

Assume that one of the Guides, *Insect Pests,* was originally published by Eastern, under a contract that called for the publisher to pay the author a 6% royalty. Eastern was acquired by Western. Western re-issues the Guide under the imprint of Eastern. Western does not pay the author a bonus and pays him a royalty of 6%. The author claims he is entitled to a $10,000 bonus and a royalty of 10%.

What is the basis for each party's position?

Should parol evidence be admitted to help resolve the question? What would that evidence be?

How could the agreement have been drafted to prevent the problem from arising?

Chapter 7

INTERPRETATION

§ 7.1 Introduction.

Interpretation is the process of ascertaining the meaning of the language of the contract in order to determine its legal effect. Many disputes involve the interpretation of the language used by the drafters. One authority stated:[1]

> In 1941 an unpublished study of 500 contracts cases decided in the year 1940 was made under my supervision. Among other things, we wanted to find out what contract problems were involved in "run-of-the-mine" litigation. We noted that about 25 per cent of litigated cases covered by the study and reaching appellate courts revolved about problems of interpretation of language. A good part of the difficulty, we concluded, was traceable directly to incomplete negotiation by the parties and poor draftsmanship either by the parties or their counsel. In many of the cases the courts bluntly said so.

Drafters have probably not changed their habits since Professor Shepherd conducted his study. It should be noted, however, that problems of interpretation are not always the *cause* of the dispute. Often a party who wants to avoid performance of a contract will enlist the aid of an attorney to examine the document for any assistance the language offers. During that careful scrutiny, problems of interpretation may be raised.

Ideally, drafters would obey the advice given to Alice by the March Hare: "Then you should say what you mean." It is probably impossible to attain this ideal, however. Problems of interpretation arise for a number of reasons:

- The drafter may have acted hastily or with inadequate preparation.
- Communications between lawyer and client may have been inadequate.
- The parties may not have foreseen the problem.
- The parties may have been intentionally indefinite. *See* § 3.3.

When drafting a contract, the drafter should keep in mind Professor David Mellinkoff's warning:[2]

---

[1] Shepherd, Book Review, 1 J. LEGAL EDUC. 151, 154 (1948) (reviewing LON L. FULLER, BASIC CONTRACT LAW (1947)).

[2] DAVID MELLINKOFF, LEGAL WRITING: SENSE & NONSENSE. Copyright © 1982. Reprinted with permission of the West Group.

Some day someone will read what you have written, trying to find something wrong with it. This is the special burden of legal writing, and the special incentive to be as precise as you can.

Mellinkoff is absolutely right — and the prospect is scary. How can you improve your drafting skills to avoid problems of interpretation? When you read a case involving interpretation, you see how a judge dealt with the problem. To apply the knowledge gained from studying the case, consider what the drafter might have done at the time the document was prepared. This is the practice of preventive law, office practice that prevents problems from arising and ending up in court. When you draft, engage in a dialogue with the contract language, constantly asking:

- What am I trying to say?
- Could it be interpreted in more than one way?
- How could I say it better?

The "Rules of Interpretation" employed by courts to resolve interpretation issues are helpful in suggesting the kinds of problems the vigilant drafter must detect. Here is one statement of those rules:[3]

The three primary rules of interpretation are:

1. Words are to be given their plain and normal meaning; except

   (a) Usage may vary the normal meaning of words.

   (b) Technical words are to be given their technical meaning.

   (c) Where possible, words will be given the meaning which best effectuates the intention of the parties.

2. Every part of a contract is to be interpreted, if possible, so as to carry out its general purpose.

3. The circumstances under which the contract was made may always be shown.

If after applying the primary rules the meaning of the contract is yet not clear, there are secondary rules tending to the same end — to ascertain and effectuate the intention of the parties. They are:

1. Obvious mistakes of writing, grammar or punctuation will be corrected.

2. The meaning of general words or terms will be restricted by more specific descriptions of the subject matter or terms of performance.

3. A contract susceptible of two meanings will be given the meaning which will render it valid.

4. Between repugnant clauses, a possible interpretation which removes the conflict will be adopted.

5. A contract will, if possible, be interpreted so as to render it reasonable rather than unreasonable.

---

[3] SIMPSON, THE LAW OF CONTRACTS (2nd ed. 1965). Copyright © 1965. Reprinted with permission of the West Group.

6. Words will generally be construed most strongly against the party using them.

7. In case of doubt, the interpretation given by the parties is the best evidence of their intention.

8. Where conflict between printed and written words, the writing governs.

As indicated by the rules of interpretation, the principal purpose of the rules is to "ascertain and effectuate the intention of the parties." This task can be accomplished more easily if the parties are clear about their intentions. In this chapter, we will examine some of the devices drafters may employ to clarify the parties' intentions. They can set forth the intentions at the beginning of the document in the form of *recitals*. They can clarify their use of *general and particular* expression. Most importantly, drafters must be alert for problems with English language that give rise to *ambiguity and vagueness*. We will examine some of the causes of ambiguity and some cures. We will also see how vagueness can be used intentionally. The use of these techniques is further examined in Part II, How the Principles of Drafting Are Exemplified in Contracts.

§ 7.2 Recitals.

The parties may wish to begin the agreement with a statement of their intentions. Often they do this through recitals, which were traditionally introduced by "whereas," but can simply state background without this formality. For example, a shareholders' agreement might begin:

RECITALS

WHEREAS, the Shareholders own all shares of the common Stock ("shares") of the Corporation; and

WHEREAS, the Shareholders and the Corporation desire to restrict the transferability of shares in order that the Corporation remain closely held and in order to avoid incompatible owners; and

WHEREAS, the Shareholders desire to create a market for the shares owned by deceased Shareholders.

THEREFORE, the parties agree as follows:

---

or

BACKGROUND

1. The Shareholders own all shares of the common stock of the Corporation.

2. The Shareholders and the Corporation desire to restrict the transferability of shares in order that the Corporation remain closely held and in order to avoid incompatible owners.

3. The Shareholders desire to create a market for the shares owned by deceased Shareholders.

The parties agree as follows:

Additional information on recitals is found in § 15.4.4.

§ 7.3 General and particular.

One of the most perplexing problems for the drafter is deciding how many particulars to enumerate. On the one hand, the drafter may provide a general description of a series of items. The drafter worries about whether it is clear that all particulars are included in that general description. On the other hand, the drafter may enumerate the particulars that are included in the general description. But the drafter worries about whether anything was omitted from the list of particulars.

For example, an attorney drafting a separation agreement between husband and wife drafts this provision:

Husband shall maintain hospital and major medical insurance for the minor children of the parties, with coverage equivalent to that currently available through his employment. Wife shall pay all uninsured medical expenses incurred on behalf of the minor children.

The drafter is concerned that a dispute may arise about whether a particular is included in "uninsured medical expenses." The general description may be filled out with a list of particulars:

Wife shall pay all uninsured medical, hospital, dental, ocular, orthodontic, and prescription drug expenses incurred on behalf of the minor children.

The drafter then wonders: What if a child is treated by a psychologist or an optometrist and the treatment is not covered by insurance? Must the wife pay the bill?

These problems are often resolved through the rules of interpretation known by their Latin names, *expressio unius est exclusio alterius* and *ejusdem generis.* Under the principle of *expressio unius est exclusio alterius* (the expression of one thing is the exclusion of another), the list of particulars is treated as exhaustive. Because the parties did not include psychological or optometrical expenses in the list, they must have meant to exclude them.

Caught on the horns of the dilemma of using language that is either overly general or overly particular, the drafter can resolve the problem by retaining the general description and preceding the list of particulars with the words "including but not limited to." This makes clear that the list of particulars is not exhaustive. For example:

> Wife shall pay all uninsured medical expenses, *including but not limited to* hospital, dental, ocular, orthodontic, and prescription drug expenses, incurred on behalf of the minor children.

The issue now is whether the particulars — psychological or optometrical expenses — come within the general description "medical expenses." Under the principle of *ejusdem generis* (of the same kind), the particulars that are not enumerated must be similar to the particulars that are enumerated. The wife could argue that expenses of a psychologist or an optometrist are not of the same kind because they are not rendered by one with a medical degree. However, the presence of hospital and drug expenses on the list would seem to broaden the meaning of the general description.

There may be other solutions to the problem. *Expenses* has two modifiers: *uninsured* and *medical.* It is easy to determine whether an expense is uninsured. The argument concerns whether it is medical. The vague modifier could be dropped: "Wife shall pay all expenses not covered by the insurance." If there are exceptions to this general statement, the exceptions could be particularized.

§ 7.4 Ambiguity.

The drafter strives for clarity and precision, goals which are often frustrated by vague and ambiguous language. A number of writers have pointed out a useful distinction between "vagueness" and "ambiguity." Vagueness is a matter of degree, a shading of meaning. Ambiguity is a matter of choice among different connotations; the meaning must be one thing or another. For example, A orders ten red shirts from B. The word "red" is vague, for the color red covers a wide spectrum. As another example, A orders ten red ball-point pens from B. The word "red" is ambiguous. Did A mean pens colored red or pens that write with red ink?

We will examine the intentional use of vague language in § 7.6. Unlike vagueness, ambiguity should never be used intentionally. Ambiguity often arises from the use of the English language. A useful distinction can be made between ambiguity in *semantics,* the meaning of words, and ambiguity in *syntax,* the way words are put together to form sentences. For example, the word "ton" may create a semantic ambiguity, for "ton" can mean different weights in different businesses. The sentence, "Ann told Barbara to order a horse to be shipped to her," contains an ambiguity in syntax: is the horse to be shipped to Ann or to Barbara? English syntax often produces different meanings depending on how you look at the sentence. Consider Zero's confusion about the sign in this cartoon:[4]

The drafter must be particularly vigilant to spot ambiguity, for it can be difficult to see. Ambiguity is like this drawing:

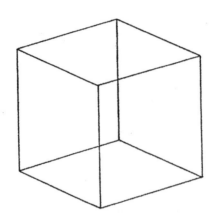

If you stare at it, you will see that it can have two different orientations. But if you don't look carefully, you will not see all the possibilities.

We will first examine some frequently-encountered areas of ambiguity and then look at some devices for avoiding them. The problem areas include:

---

[4] Cartoon by Mort Walker. Copyright © 1992 by King Features Syndicate, Inc. Reprinted with special permission of King Features Syndicate.

1. Connectives;
2. And/or;
3. Describing characteristics or classes;
4. Listing conditions or criteria; and
5. Modifiers.

§ 7.4.1   Connectives.

The connectives *and* and *or* must be used with care, for every use involves some risk of ambiguity. In mathematics, different symbols are used for different purposes. Not so in English. Some vocabulary may be helpful to explain the different senses in which *and* and *or* may be used. The word *and* is generally conjunctive, uniting things, while *or* is generally disjunctive, separating things. The problems arise because *and* has both a *several* and a *joint* sense, and *or* has both an *inclusive* and an *exclusive* sense:

- the *several and:*   A and B, jointly or severally
- the *joint and:*   A and B, jointly but not severally
- the *inclusive or:*   A or B, or both
- the *exclusive or:*   A or B, but not both

The meaning of *and* is usually *several*. For example, in the sentence "contributions to organizations that are educational and cultural are deductible," the usual interpretation is that the organization may be educational, cultural, or both. There are, of course, exceptions. In the sentence "the University shall have exclusive use of gold and silver as school colors," the *and* is probably joint, the sensible interpretation being that the University has exclusive use only of the combination of colors.

The meaning of *or* is usually *inclusive*. The Bankruptcy Code, 11 U.S.C. § 102(5), even codifies this interpretation, providing that "'or' is not exclusive." Because the inclusive *or* is similar to the several *and,* they may be used interchangeably, as in the sentence "contributions to organizations that are educational or cultural are deductible." Again, there are exceptions. Criminal statutes are narrowly construed. It is possible that the *or* in a criminal statute providing that a convicted person "shall be fined up to $100 or confined to jail for up to 60 days" could be interpreted to mean fined or imprisoned but not both.

Do not attempt to cure an ambiguity by changing a mandatory obligation to a permissive one. Consider this provision, introduced by the mandatory *shall*:

```
A shall ship apples and oranges
```

In this provision, *and* is probably joint. *A* performs by shipping both apples and oranges. *A* has not performed if *A* ships apples and not oranges, or oranges and not apples. Consider the change to a permissive provision:

```
A may ship apples and oranges
```

The drafter may have intended to permit *A* to ship either apples or oranges, for we tend to read the *and* in this provision as full sentence connecting: *A* may ship apples and *A* may ship oranges. If the *and* is several (apples or oranges or both), then the inclusive *or* may be substituted:

```
A may ship apples or oranges
```

In changing to the permissive form, however, the drafter has created another ambiguity, for the discretion may relate not to the choice between apples and oranges but between shipping and not shipping. Let us return to the mandatory *shall*:

```
A shall ship apples or oranges
```

Here, the *or* is probably exclusive. *A* performs if *A* ships apples or if *A* ships oranges. *A* has not performed if *A* ships both apples and oranges. In this context, it appears that a drafter who wants *or* to mean something other than *either* must expressly say so.

It seems impossible to state hard and fast rules for the use of *and* and *or,* for the result will often depend on the context. Because the meaning of *and* is usually *several* and the meaning of *or* is usually *inclusive,* the drafter must take precautions when the other meaning is intended. The goal is not to learn rules, however, but to learn vigilance: be aware that every use of *and* and *or* may signal a problem. The best advice is to:

- Identify all uses of *and* and *or,* treating each as creating a potential ambiguity.
- Ask whether *and* is identifying two classes or two characteristics of one class.
- Ask whether *and* and *or* include both of the classes or characteristics.
- Revise appropriately, asking whether tabulation would help clarify the meaning.

§ 7.4.2   And/or.

Sometimes to state that *and* is several or that *or* is inclusive, a drafter uses the phrase *and/or* as a shorthand way of saying, "A or B, or both." For example, if a seller would comply by shipping apples or oranges or both, a drafter may state, "Seller shall ship apples and/or oranges." Although it accurately conveys this meaning, drafters should avoid *and/or,* for its use in other contexts will cause ambiguity or absurdity. For example, in a will, a testator leaves a bequest to "A and/or B." Who gets the bequest?

A number of commercial cases have arisen in which the agreement specified that one party would deliver "A, B, and/or C," or "A and/or B and/or C." The possible combinations are so boggling that it is difficult to tell what was intended. On the other hand, a provision limiting liability "in the event of destruction in the Atlantic and/or Pacific," states an impossibility when read with the conjunctive *and.* These provisions should be rewritten for clarity.

In addition to the strong possibility of creating confusion, use of *and/or* may incur the wrath of the reader or judge. The bottom line on *and/or*? Its use is usually sloppy and careless. When you must clarify a several *and* or an inclusive *or*, spell it out. *Don't use and/or.*

§ 7.4.3   Describing characteristics or classes.

Often, syntactical ambiguity arises when it is not clear whether the drafter intended to enumerate two classes or two characteristics of one class. For example, in the sentence "The corporation shall pay a bonus to directors and shareholders," is the bonus to be paid to two classes of individuals or is it to be paid to one class of individuals with two characteristics?

The distinction between *and* as "full-sentence connecting" and "sentence-part connecting" is a useful way to describe this problem arising from the several and joint sense of *and.* If two classes are intended, the *and* is joining what could otherwise be two full sentences. If two characteristics are intended, the *and* is joining two parts of a sentence. After the ambiguity is detected, the drafter can redraft the sentence to better express the intended meaning. For example, when *and* is full-sentence connecting, the provision "The corporation shall pay a bonus to directors and shareholders" may be rewritten as "The corporation shall pay a bonus to directors" and "The corporation shall pay a bonus to shareholders." When *and* is sentence-part connecting, the provision may be rewritten as "The corporation shall pay a bonus to persons who are both directors and shareholders."

§ 7.4.4   Listing conditions or criteria.

Often a provision contains conditions that must occur, or criteria that must be satisfied, to achieve a result. Often *and* or *or* connect the conditions or criteria. The issue is whether only the occurrence of *all* of the conditions or criteria satisfies the provision (*cumulative* conditions or criteria) or whether the occurrence of *one* is sufficient (*alternative* conditions or criteria). To clarify these provisions, the drafter should:

- Reword the sentence from the adjective-noun form to a noun-subordinate clause form.

- Choose the appropriate connective. If the intention is that only the occurrence of all of the conditions or criteria satisfies the provision, then the correct connective is *and.* If the intention is that the occurrence of any one of the conditions or criteria satisfies the provision, then the correct connective is *or.*

- Enumerate the conditions or criteria in a tabular structure.

When listing alternative conditions or criteria, if the intention is to use the exclusive *or,* providing that "one or the other but not both" of the conditions or criteria must be present, that restriction must be clarified. For example:

The corporation shall make a contribution to an organization that is:

1) educational;

2) charitable; or

3) fraternal.

In this example, the *or* is read inclusively: the contribution could be made to an organization that possesses one or more of the characteristics. To state the exclusive *or,* restricting the contribution to an organization with one characteristic only, the drafter could provide:

The corporation shall make a contribution to an organization that has not more than one of the following characteristics:

1) educational;

2) charitable; or

3) fraternal.

Often, drafters are concerned that tabular structure looks awkward on the page or takes up too much space. There are a number of ways to resolve this concern. Tabular structure can be used only at those places in the agreement where the utmost clarity, particularly in a consumer transaction, may be required. Alternatively, once the drafter has used tabular structure to clarify ambiguities in a provision, the provision can be back-formed into a sentence with clearer syntax.

§ 7.4.5 Modifiers.

Sometimes it is difficult to determine whether a single adjective modifies only one noun or a series of nouns. In Dr. Seuss' famous book, *Green Eggs and Ham,* are both the eggs and the ham green or just the eggs? The same problem arises when a contractual provision states, "Seller shall ship frozen vegetables or fruit." If the seller ships fresh fruit, has it breached? The issue is whether "frozen" modifies both "vegetables" and "fruit," or "vegetables" alone. The drafter can resolve this ambiguity by employing the adjective before every noun it modifies: "Seller shall ship frozen vegetables or frozen fruit." The alternative meaning could be clarified by rearranging the words: "Seller shall ship fruit or frozen vegetables." Enumeration may also be employed:

Seller shall ship frozen
    1)   vegetables; or
    2)   fruit.

---

or

Seller shall ship
    1)   frozen vegetables; or
    2)   fruit.

Wordiness generally plagues legal writing. Clarity, however, is the ultimate goal, and the drafter should not hesitate to use additional words to clarify a meaning. Often additional words clarify a meaning by filling in the shorthand language we unconsciously use. For example, in one case, an insurance policy excluded coverage for any "disease of organs of the body not common to both sexes." The insured contracted a fibroid tumor of the uterus. The issue was whether "not common to both sexes" modifies "disease" or "organs of the body." The provision could be rewritten by eliminating the shorthand in the modifying phrase. To modify *disease*: "disease of organs of the body *that is* not common to both sexes." To modify *organs of the body*: "disease of organs of the body *that are* not common to both sexes."

§ 7.5 Cures for ambiguity.

It is difficult to advise on drafting to avoid ambiguity, for the problem cannot be cured until you discover it. The main goal, therefore, is to achieve sensitivity to the problem. With heightened awareness, the drafter should be better able to identify potential problem spots. In reviewing your draft:

- Detect any vagueness or ambiguity. In particular:
  Note vague language.
  Note each *and* and *or* employed.
  Note each modifier.

Note each definition.

Note each list.

- Use word processing search functions to assist you. For example, search for *and* and *or*. Create a macro that will search for vague terms. If you have defined a term, search for the other uses of the definition to make sure the term is consistently used. If you find a variation of the defined word, search for other uses of the variation.

- Determine whether the vagueness is intentional. If it is, leave it. If it is not, clarify it.

- Resolve the ambiguity through the use of clarifying language.

- Where appropriate, use tabulation or normalization.

We will look at some of these techniques in depth, including:

1. Definition;

2. Tabulation;

3. Application of tabulation; and

4. Normalized drafting.

§ 7.5.1 Definition.

Definitions can be helpful in eliminating both semantic and syntactic ambiguity. The drafter who is aware that a word may have more than one meaning can indicate the intended meaning in the contract. For example:

> In this agreement, *ton* means a unit of weight equal to 2000 pounds.

or

> In this agreement, *ton* means "long ton."

Sometimes *or* is used to state that words are synonymous or explanatory. The drafter who writes "*A* or *B*" may mean "*A*, that is, *B*." For example, "Seller shall ship young chickens or fryers." Here, the relationship of "fryers" to "young chickens" is synonymous. Synonyms should not be used in drafting. If the same thing can be referred to by two names, use one of them. The fact that a second word is used may suggest that a second meaning was intended. To make clear that a word has multiple meanings, the drafter might consider including a definitional section in the document. In the definitions, the drafter can explain that the two words mean the same thing. For example:

> As used in this agreement, *chickens* means fryers.

Definitions are also useful to replace a string of words with either a synonym or a more inclusive term. For example, a shareholders' agreement states:

> Shareholders may not sell, transfer, assign, pledge, encumber or otherwise dispose of or convey (by operation of law or otherwise) any or all of the shares of the Corporation. Exception: Shareholders may sell, transfer, assign, pledge, encumber, or otherwise dispose of or convey (by operation of law or otherwise) any or all of the shares if they comply with the following provisions.

The drafter has strung together all these words to make sure every possibility is covered. It is awkward to use the string throughout the agreement. But the drafter is insecure about reducing this string to a single word, for each word in the string may have a slightly different legal connotation. The drafter can resolve this problem by placing the string in a definition:

> As used in this agreement, *transfer* means to sell, transfer, assign, pledge, encumber or otherwise dispose of or convey (by operation of law or otherwise).

In the text, the defined term replaces the string:

> Shareholders may not *transfer* any or all of the shares of the Corporation. Exception: Shareholders may *transfer* any or all of the shares if they comply with the following provisions.

Make sure your use of definitions helps to achieve clarity. For example, a construction contract stated:

> In consideration of the performance by the said contractor of all of the covenants and conditions contained in this agreement and contained in the plans and specifications the owners agree to pay to the contractor an amount equal to the amount of all material furnished by the contractor and the labor furnished by the contractor together with payroll taxes and Insurance, also together with the sum total of the

> net amount due the subcontractors performing work or furnishing work for said construction. The Owners also agree to pay to the contractor, in addition to the amount specified hereinabove, a fee equal to 10% of the actual cost of the said residence, said fee to be paid after completion of said residence and acceptance thereof by the Owners. It is specifically agreed by and between the parties that notwithstanding the agreement hereinabove the owners shall not be required, under the terms of this agreement, to pay to the contractor any amount in excess of the sum of Thirty-Four Thousand, Five Hundred Dollars ($34,500.00) which is the estimated cost of construction, plus the fee provided for herein.

The contract uses various terms to indicate price, including *amount, sum total, actual cost, sum,* and *cost of construction.* There are only two concepts that need defining: the cost and the fee. These concepts could have been defined when they appeared in the first sentence and the second sentence and then combined to make the last sentence meaningful (we will clean up the garbage as well):

> If *the cost plus the fee* exceeds $34,500.00, the owners shall be liable to the contractor only for the amount of $34,500.00.

or

> If *the cost* exceeds $34,500.00, the owners shall be liable to the contractor only for the amount of $34,500.00 for the cost. The owners shall also pay the contractor a fee of 10% of the cost.

Now that we have cleared up that ambiguity, another becomes apparent: if the cost exceeds $34,500.00, did the parties intend that the fee not exceed $3450.00?

Among the pitfalls of users of definitions are:

- "Elegant variation," where the defined word is used in the agreement in a different sense.
- "Humpty-Dumptyism," where a term is defined to mean anything the parties want it to mean.
- "One-shot" definition, where a term is defined to be used only once.
- Failure to remember the Golden Rule of Drafting:

  Never change your language unless you wish to change your meaning, and always change your language if you wish to change your meaning.

Technology can help the drafter become aware of changes in language. When a concept is used more than once, use a compare feature to make sure the text is the same. Or block the text and insert the blocked text each time the same term is used. When a single word replaces a string, search for words in the string to determine whether there are uses that have not been replaced with the definition. Also, search for the defined term to insure that every use of the definition is consistent. After you have achieved consistency, plug the defined term in every place where the definition occurs to determine whether its use is appropriate.

For example, in the Buy-Sell agreement in § 3.8, Exercise 4, the definition "hereinafter 'Property'" follows the legal description of the real estate. The agreement goes on to use *property* in a dazzling variety of contexts, sometimes meaning real property, sometimes personal property, sometimes both, and sometimes in variations including "property and appliances," "property described herein," and "Real Estate property." When the drafter searches the document for the defined term, these misuses become apparent.

§ 7.5.2   Tabulation.

Writing in tabular form will help a drafter detect problems of syntactic ambiguity and will suggest how to resolve the problems. To create a tabulation, follow these Rules for Tabulation:[5]

1.   All items in an enumeration must belong to the same class.

2.   Each item in an enumeration must respond in substance and in form to the words that introduce the enumeration.

3.   If the sentence of which an enumeration forms a part continues beyond the last item of the enumeration, the part of the sentence that follows the enumeration must be appropriate to each item of the enumeration.

4.   An enumeration must be entirely indented from the material immediately preceding or following the enumeration.

5.   The next-to-last item of an enumeration usually ends with "and" or "or."

6.   If an enumeration takes the form of a single list following a sentence that is otherwise complete, no "and" or "or" follows the next-to-last enumerated item. For example, the Supreme Court of Texas had to decide whether a judge was eligible to serve under this statute:

> No person shall be eligible to serve in the office of Chief Justice or Justice of the Supreme Court unless the person is licensed to practice law in this state and is, at the time of election, a citizen of the United

---

[5] ROBERT DICK, LEGAL DRAFTING 117–18 (2nd ed. 1985). Copyright 1985 The Carswell Co. Ltd. Reprinted with permission.

> States and of this state, and has attained the age of thirty-five years, and has been a practicing lawyer, or a lawyer and judge of a court of record together at least ten years.

At the time of election, the judge was several days short of having been a practicing lawyer for ten years. The issue was whether the phrase "at the time of election" modified all three criteria that followed it or just the first one. Tabulation could easily have solved this problem:

> 1. No person shall be eligible to serve in the office of Chief Justice or Justice of the Supreme Court unless the person:
>
> is licensed to practice law in this state;
>
> is, at the time of election, a citizen of the United States and of this state;
>
> has attained the age of thirty-five years; and
>
> has been a practicing lawyer, or a lawyer and judge of a court of record together at least ten years.

or

> 2. No person shall be eligible to serve in the office of Chief Justice or Justice of the Supreme Court unless the person is licensed to practice law in this state and at the time of election:
>
> is a citizen of the United States and of this state;
>
> has attained the age of thirty-five years; and
>
> has been a practicing lawyer, or a lawyer and judge of a court of record together at least ten years.

Both Example 1 and Example 2 follow Rules 1 and 2. The items in the enumeration all describe the qualifications of the person who is the subject of the words that introduce the enumeration. Rule 3 is not applicable as the sentence does not continue after the last enumerated item. Rule 4 is followed by indenting the enumerated material. Rule 5 is followed by ending the next-to-last item with *and* to indicate that the criteria are cumulative. Rule 6 is not applicable, although we could have rewritten the provision so that the enumeration was preceded by a complete sentence. The tabulation achieves clarity lacking in the statute by making clear in Example 1 that the phrase "at the time of election" modifies only the second enumerated item; in Example 2, it modifies all the enumerated items.

§ 7.5.3   Application of tabulation.

To analyze a draft, follow these steps:

- Step 1. Highlight each *and* and each *or*.
- Step 2. Bracket the modifiers, conditions, and criteria.
- Step 3. Determine whether the referent (the thing referred to) of each modifier is clear.
- Step 4. Link words with the proper connective. Determine whether, in the particular context, *and* or *or* is appropriate.
- Step 5. Enumerate the conditions and criteria with the proper connective. The proper connective is *and* if the conditions or criteria are cumulative; *or* if they are alternative. If the *or* is exclusive, precede the list with "not more than one of the following."

Let us apply this analysis to the Magnuson-Moss Warranty Act, 15 U.S.C. § 2301(6), which defines a "written warranty" as:

(A) any written affirmation of fact or written promise made in connection with the sale of a consumer product by a supplier to a buyer which relates to the nature of the material or workmanship and affirms or promises that such material or workmanship is defect free or will meet a specified level of performance over a specified period of time, or

(B) any undertaking in writing in connection with the sale by a supplier of a consumer product to refund, repair, replace, or take other remedial action with respect to such product in the event that such product fails to meet the specifications set forth in the undertaking, which written affirmation, promise, or undertaking becomes part of the basis of the bargain between a supplier and a buyer for purposes other than resale of such product.

Paragraph (A) may be analyzed as follows:

The term "written warranty" means —

(A) any written affirmation of fact *or* written promise

(made in connection with the sale of a consumer product by a supplier to a buyer)

(which relates to the nature of the material *or* workmanship)

and

(affirms *or* promises that such material *or* workmanship is

(defect free *or* will meet a specified level of performance))

(over a specified period of time),

or

Analysis of this passage:

- *Modifiers.* It is unclear whether the modifiers that follow "written promise" modify only "written promise" or also "written affirmation of fact." It is also unclear what "over a specified period of time" modifies.

- *"And" and "or." Or* is a disjunctive between "affirmation of fact" and "written promise," between "material" and "workmanship," between "affirms" and "promises," and between Paragraphs A and B.

- *Conditions and criteria.* The phrases beginning with *made, which,* and *affirms* are all criteria relating to "written affirmation of fact or promise." Because the criteria are cumulative, the proper connective is *and.* Within the last enumerated criterion, "defect free" and "will meet a specified level of performance" are criteria relating to "material or workmanship." Because they are alternative, the proper connective is *or.*

We can now arrange the passage in tabular form. Following the Rules for Tabulation, we might arrive at the following:

The term "written warranty" means —

(A) any written

   1. affirmation of fact; or

   2. promise

which

     1.   is made in connection with the sale of a consumer product by a supplier to a buyer;

     2.   relates to the nature of the material *or* workmanship; *and*

     3.   affirms *or* promises that such material *or* workmanship

         a.   is defect free; *or*

         b.   will meet a specified level of performance over a specified period of time;

or

Note that the next-to-last item in the first and third enumerations ends with *or;* this list is alternative — the language that follows applies to either item. The next-to-last item in the second enumeration ends with *and;* this list is cumulative — the items that are modified must satisfy all three items.

The original lacked clarity in specifying what the phrase "over a specified period of time" modifies. The tabulation above follows the interpretation given by the Regulations: "a written affirmation of fact or a written promise of a specified level of performance must relate to a specified period of time." An alternative (and more reasonable) interpretation is that "over a specified period of time" modifies only "level of performance." That interpretation could be expressed as follows:

> 3. affirms *or* promises that such material *or* workmanship
>   a. is defect free; *or*
>   b. will meet a specified level of performance over a specified period of time;

This example illustrates Rule 3. In the first interpretation, the part of the sentence that follows the enumeration modifies both items of the enumeration, while here it modifies only one.

Tabulation is found more often in legislative drafting than in contract drafting. However, it may be seen in a number of consumer contracts. One of the goals of drafting in plain language is to reduce sentence length. Because the Flesch test of reading ease counts semicolons as ending a sentence, the drafter can achieve a better score by using tabulation. In the above example, Paragraph (A) of the Magnuson-Moss definition scored a 0 while the tabulated version scored a 56.733. A score of 40 or higher indicates plain language. *See* § 18.3.

Furthermore, even if tabulation is not included in the final draft of the agreement, the thought process is useful for determining when additional explanation is necessary. Tabulation may help the drafter see when to spell out that "*A and B*" means "*A or B or both*" or when to clarify the referent of a modifier. For example, Paragraph (A) of the Magnuson-Moss definition could be back-formed from the tabular form as follows:

> The term "written warranty" means (A) any *written* affirmation of fact or *written* promise, *either of which* 1) is made in connection with the sale of a consumer product by a supplier to a buyer; 2) relates to the nature of the material or workmanship; and 3) affirms or promises that such material or workmanship is defect free *over a specified period of time* or will meet a specified level of performance *over a specified period of time;* or (B) . . .

In this example:

- *written* was used twice to clarify that it modifies both *affirmation of fact* and *promise*
- *either of which* was added to clarify that the three criteria refer to both affirmation of fact and promise
- the three criteria were numbered for clarity
- *over a specified period of time* was used twice to clarify that it modifies both *defect free* and *specified period of time*

Under the Flesch test of reading ease, this redraft scored a just-above passing 41.97. The three drafts of Magnuson-Moss (original statute, tabulation, and draft back-formed from tabulation) received almost identical scores on syllables per word. The divergence in scores is entirely due to the sentence length. The original statute consists of one sentence. In the tabulation, the use of semicolons broke it down into five sentences. The back-formed draft retained some of the semicolons and, hence, counted as three sentences.

§ 7.5.4 Normalized drafting.

Normalized drafting represents an attempt to bring the certainty of symbolic logic to the drafting process. Layman Allen, the father of normalized legal drafting, explains that "[n]ormalized legal drafting is a mode of expressing ideas in statutes, regulations, contracts, and other legal documents in such a way that the syntax that relates the constituent propositions is simplified and standardized."

In normalized drafting, each provision is stated as a rule and the relationship between the conditions and the results in the rule is conveyed unambiguously. Just as there are many logical systems and many ways to express the relationship between conditions and results, there are many variations on normalized drafting. In the following discussion, normalized drafting is signaled by the following characteristics:

    1.   A set of standard syntax terms that connect propositions:

AND

OR

IF. . ., THEN. . . .

IF AND ONLY IF. . ., THEN. . . .

The capital letters cue the reader to the consistent use of the terms. Therefore, when the standard syntax terms connect propositions, they are written in capitals; when they are used within propositions, they are written in lower case letters.

    2.   A standard sequence of condition and result propositions: Conditions are stated before results.

    3.   Grammatical completeness: Each proposition is a grammatically complete sentence.

    4.   An outline format: Each full sentence is outlined with labels for each proposition.

For example, consider this contract term in non-normalized form:

> When this policy is renewable, it will be in force for the full premium period upon a renewal premium being paid not more than thirty days after the due date.

The normalized version of the term might read:

IF

(1) This policy is renewable, AND

(2) The renewal premium is paid not more than thirty days after the due date,

THEN

(3) The policy will be in force for the full premium period.

When using IF to introduce the proposition, the drafter is saying that the expressed condition is a legally sufficient way to reach the result. IF does not say that the expressed condition is the *only* way to bring about the result. If legal results arise only upon satisfaction of the specified conditions, the conditions are introduced by IF AND ONLY IF. The legal result can then be reached only if those conditions are present. The conditions are both necessary and sufficient to the result.

If an insurance company wanted to provide that an applicant for insurance must pay a premium of $100 and be insurable as the only conditions under which it would have the legal obligation to provide insurance coverage of the applicant, the company might draft the provision in normalized form as follows:

IF AND ONLY IF

(1) The applicant pays a premium of $100, AND

(2) The applicant is insurable,

THEN

(3) The company will insure the applicant.

Drafting is rarely so simple. Often, clients impose more complex conditions for reaching a result, or they may want more than one result to flow from satisfaction of a condition or a set of conditions. Cumulative conditions that are expressly required for a result are joined by AND. Alternate conditions for reaching results are joined to one another by OR. In normalized syntax, OR means that the result follows if any one or more of the OR-connected conditions are satisfied (the inclusive "or"). OR does not mean that one of the OR-connected conditions cannot be satisfied if another is (the exclusive "or").

Thus, if the company wants its obligation to provide insurance to arise only when (1) the applicant either pays a premium of $100 or signs a note for $100 payable to the company and (2) a licensed physician determines that the applicant is insurable, it might draft the normalized term to read:

IF AND ONLY IF

   (1) (A) The applicant pays a premium of $100, OR

   (B) The applicant signs a promissory note for $100 payable to the company, AND

   (2) A licensed physician determines that the applicant is insurable,

THEN

   (3) The company will insure the applicant.

If more than one result follows, the results are joined by AND in the same way the conditions were joined in the example, thereby saying that all the results are available if the conditions are satisfied. To avoid any confusion about the availability of the results, OR does not connect results. Where the results are intended to be equally available but not available together, there is at least one additional condition for each result that is not simultaneously available. These conditions must be expressed in the interest of accuracy.

For example, consider a criminal statute that lists conditions for conviction and then states the result:

The person may be fined up to $100 or confined in jail for up to 60 days.

The statute is ambiguous. Is the *or* inclusive (fine or imprisonment or both) or exclusive (fine or imprisonment, but not both)? This ambiguity would be resolved in normalized drafting as follows. To show that all the results are available (the equivalent of the inclusive *or*):

THEN

   (4)   The person is subject to a fine up to $100, AND

   (5)   The person is subject to confinement in jail for up to 60 days.

To show that the results are not simultaneously available (the equivalent of the exclusive *or*):

THEN

(4)   The person is subject to a fine up to $100, AND

(5)   The person is subject to confinement in jail for up to 60 days, AND

(6)   IF

     (A)   The court imposes a fine on the person under item (4), THEN

     (B)   The court may not confine the person under item (5) AND

(7)   IF

     (A)   The court confines the person under item (5), THEN

     (B)   The court may not fine the person under item (4).

This solution seems to achieve clarity at the expense of simplicity. Rather than decline to use OR to join results, the drafter could consistently use OR as inclusive, perhaps defining it as such. Or the drafter could always add "or both" when using the inclusive *or*.

Normalization has a number of strengths and weaknesses. Users of it have been better able correctly to analyze complex documents. Because of its consistent, mathematics-like use of logical propositions, normalized writing enables attorneys to build computerized expert systems quickly from the normalized rules. Normalized drafting has been criticized by Flesch for the "shredded" appearance of its text, which may impair reading ease, and by Dickerson for being overly rigid and complex. That is, it treats every connective as ambiguous when in fact most potential ambiguities can be resolved within their context. Even if the drafter does not express an agreement in normalized form, it can be an extremely useful diagnostic tool. The drafter could express a complex provision in normalized form in order to discover its ambiguities. After consulting with the client to ascertain the intended meaning, the drafter could then rewrite the provision unambiguously without using normalized form.

§ 7.6   Vagueness.

The drafter should be watchful for vague language. When ordering "red shirts," for example, the buyer may consider clarifying the desired color by including a sample. On some occasions, however, drafters intentionally use vague language. If the parties do not want to agree on precise standards for performance, they may use language that allows for flexibility. For example, a term stating that "Seller is excused if its nonperformance is caused by any damage to its plant due to circumstances beyond its control" could allow Seller to take advantage of a situation where there is minor damage to its plant. Instead, the parties might state that "Seller is excused if its nonperformance is caused by any material damage to its plant." The word material provides flexibility. The common law provides some guidance for its meaning; if the parties want more precision, they can define it themselves. For example:

> "material damage" means the inability of Seller to resume production at all or any portion of its plant because of damage to plant production facilities resulting from circumstances beyond its control.

The Uniform Commercial Code is notorious for its vague terms, such as "seasonable," "reasonable" and "commercially reasonable," and "good faith." Other vague terms include "workmanlike manner," "prompt," and "best efforts" or "reasonable efforts." When you encounter vague language, ask whether the vagueness serves a useful purpose or whether it should be made more precise. Do you want a party to have a "reasonable" time to act, or do you want them to act within 30 days? Sometimes you can use a vague term to negotiate a resolution to a dispute. For example, one party wants a term in a contract forbidding delegation of duties (*see* § 14.6):

> No duty under this contract may be delegated without the written permission of the other party.

The other party wants to permit free delegation. A solution to this stalemate may be to add vague language that allows some delegations but not others:

> No duty under this contract may be delegated without the written permission of the other party. Permission shall not be unreasonably withheld.

§ 7.7 Exercises.

1. Research. Find examples of judicial application of the Rules of Interpretation in your jurisdiction. What could the parties have done when drafting the contract to eliminate the need for judicial interpretation?

2. Ambiguity. Identify the ambiguity and redraft these provisions to eliminate it:

a. . . . . in trust for the maintenance and education of my son.

b. Husband shall pay the tuition of the children at any school, college, or university in the state system.

c. Never include a provision in a contract which you do not understand.

d. Employee shall receive severance benefits on termination of her employment by the Company. [Assume the employee quits. Does she receive severance benefits?]

e. Company shall renegotiate the Agreement with Customer if its expenses are greater than predicted.

3. Tabulation. Rewrite the following provisions in tabular form:

a. This passage from a homeowner's insurance policy:

> This coverage excludes: . . . 2. motorized vehicles, except such vehicles pertaining to the service of the premises and not licensed for road use.

The homeowners lost an antique car that was not licensed. What is the ambiguity in the provision? Analyze it and suggest how to remove the ambiguity by (1) using full sentences and (2) listing conditions or criteria.

b. This passage from an IRS Publication:

> A person is permanently and totally disabled when the person cannot engage in any substantial gainful activity because of a physical or mental condition, and a physician determines that the disability has lasted or can be expected to last continuously for at least a year, or can be expected to lead to death.

c. This provision from a contract:

> If Company does not have another use at the site for such facilities to serve other Company customers, and the Customer makes an offer to purchase such facilities for the unamortized investment in the facilities as determined pursuant to Exhibit F plus the appraised value of the property on which the facilities are located, and Company rejects the offer, then the Customer shall not be required to reimburse Company for any unrecoverable costs pursuant to Exhibit F.

4. Definition. Determine what is wrong with these uses of definition and correct them:

a. The following definition appears in a separation agreement between Husband and Wife:

> *Cost of living increase.* "Base alimony" is defined as $100 per week. In the first calendar year, Husband shall pay Wife the base alimony. In each subsequent calendar year, Husband shall pay Wife the base alimony plus a cost of living increase. The cost of living increase is the base alimony multiplied by the inflation rate for the prior year as determined by the Department of Labor.

Assume that in each year after the first year of the agreement, the inflation rate is 10%.

b. The definition of *Property* in the Buy-Sell Agreement in § 3.8, Exercise 4

5. General and particular. Rewrite the following provision to avoid the problem of listing too many particulars:

> If either trustee is at any time unable to act by reason of death, disability, or absence from the country, the other may act alone.

6. Vagueness. What terms in the following provision are vague? Do you think the flexibility is useful or would you rewrite the terms for greater precision?

> Each System or Additional Equipment will be installed at the "Installation Site" by Seller according to the manufacturer's installation specifications and the standard practices of the telecommunications industry. Customer shall allow Seller's employees, representatives and subcontractors reasonable access to the necessary premises for installation. Before and during installation, Customer is responsible to ensure the timely and adequate delivery, installation and functioning of the electrical and telecommunications connections and other environmental requirements.

7. Connectives. In each of the following examples there are three events, A, B, and C. Revise each sentence to carry out the intent:

> a. The intention is that the happening of <u>one or more</u> of the events will satisfy the condition:
>
> The Company may terminate this Agreement upon 7 days' notice to Customer if the following events occur: A, B, or C.
>
> b. The intention is that the happening of <u>only one</u> of the events will satisfy the condition:
>
> The Company may terminate this Agreement upon 7 days' notice to Customer if the following events occur: A, B, or C.
>
> c. The intention is that only the happening of <u>all</u> the events will satisfy the condition:
>
> The Company may terminate this Agreement upon 7 days' notice to Customer if the following events occur: A, B, or C.

8. Ethics. Can a lawyer leave an ambiguous term in a negotiated contract? Consider these facts:

> The inventor of a board game is attempting to sell it to a company that produces and markets games. The draft contract binds the company not to market any "competitive" games. L, the company's lawyer, is aware

that it intends to market a game that is somewhat similar to the inventor's game, but believes that, in the event of litigation, nonfrivolous arguments could be made either way as to whether the game is "competitive."

Does the lawyer have an obligation to warn the client that there may be litigation over the ambiguous term? Does the lawyer have an obligation to warn the inventor?

Chapter 8

MISTAKE

§ 8.1 Introduction.

The term *mistake* is used in many different contexts. It is defined in Restatement (Second) of Contracts § 151 as "a belief that is not in accord with the facts." In general, a mistaken assumption by one party is not sufficient to avoid the contract. But if both parties share a mistaken assumption about a material fact existing at the time the contract was made, the contract may be voidable unless the party seeking avoidance assumed the risk.

Parties to a contract often do not articulate their basic assumptions. The lawyer as planner can assist clients by discussing with them their goals in entering the contract. This discussion should help a client articulate the assumptions he or she may have made about the transaction. In negotiating the contract, it may then become clear whether the other party shares the same assumptions. Often the parties do not state their assumptions in the contract because they know they do not share them. In that case, raising the issue might jeopardize formation of the contract. The client must then decide which is the greater risk: jeopardizing formation of the contract now or facing a challenge to its enforceability later.

As a drafting matter, the best way to avoid problems with mistake is to state in the contract the assumptions that have been recognized. For example, a broker shows Buyer a plot of undeveloped land. After purchasing the land, Buyer discovers that the plot is not suitable for building because of an inadequate water source. Buyer may claim the defense of mistake, alleging that the parties assumed that the land was suitable for development. But if that assumption was not stated in the contract, Buyer may have bargained to purchase the land, whether suitable for building or not.

§ 8.2 Putting the assumptions in the contract.

Once the parties have articulated their assumptions, the drafter can incorporate them in the contract in a number of different ways, including (a) recitals and (b) representations and warranties. See Chapter 16, Operative Language, for a discussion of the consequences of the different approaches.

a. Recitals. Recitals may state the assumptions of the parties in entering the agreement. For example:

117

PREMISES. Buyer intends to use the property to build a primary residence. Seller intends to meet Buyer's needs by selling property that is suitable in all respects for that purpose.

b. Representations and warranties. A party who articulates an assumption may require the other party to indicate that it shares the assumption by making a representation of fact. For example, the purchaser of undeveloped land may require the seller to represent that there is an adequate supply of water. The parties should also provide a remedy — what do they intend to have happen if the representation is false? For example:

REPRESENTATIONS. Seller represents that the property is suitable in all respects as the location of a primary residence. Buyer may rescind the transaction if any representation contained in this agreement is substantially false.

or

WARRANTIES. Seller warrants that the property is suitable in all respects as the location of a primary residence. Seller shall indemnify Buyer if any fact is not as warranted.

§ 8.3 Assuming the risk.

A contract is not voidable on grounds of mistake if the party seeking avoidance has assumed the risk of a mistake. Parties desiring the security that an agreement will not be disturbed by a claim of mistake can indicate in the contract that a party has assumed the risk that certain facts are not in accord with its belief. Devices to accomplish this objective include:

a. A merger clause. The parties can provide that the document represents their entire agreement and that there are no other representations. For example:

This contract contains the entire agreement between the parties. Buyer affirms that neither Seller nor any agent of the Seller has made any representations or promises with respect to or affecting the property described in this contract not expressly contained herein. Buyer affirms that he relies upon his own personal observation and examination of the property herein described.

Note, however, that the defense of mutual mistake may be asserted in spite of a merger clause. *See* § 6.5.

b. An inspection clause. A contract may provide that a party has inspected and takes the risk of things not being in the condition he or she believes them to be. For example:

> Buyer has inspected and is familiar with the premises and the physical condition of all the furniture, fixtures and equipment and improvements thereon and therein, and enters into this Agreement on Buyer's own independent investigation.

c. A warranty. If a party warrants that certain facts are true, that party has agreed to bear the loss in the event that the facts are not as represented. For example, if *S* sells property to *B* and the contract contains a legal description of the property but no mention of its size, each party bears the risk of assuming that it measures a certain size. But if *S* warrants that the property contains ten acres, *S* must indemnify *B* if the property turns out to be smaller.

d. An absolute promise to perform irrespective of the actual conditions existing. A party may promise to perform in spite of existing conditions. *See* § 9.3. For example, in one case, the court held that a contractor accepted the risk where "[t]he elaborate contract provisions on 'Site Investigation and Representations,' [footnote omitted] together with the omission of the usual changed conditions clause, show that the risks of mistakes as to subsurface materials were deliberately placed on plaintiff;. . . ."

§ 8.4   Releases.

Releases provide a fruitful source of problems involving mistake. A release comes about in this way. *A* has a claim against *B,* say for personal injury. After negotiation, the parties enter into an agreement that *A* will give up the claim against *B* in return for a consideration paid by *B*. The contract they sign is the release. *A* may later discover that the agreement was improvident. Because of later discovered injuries or because of later consequences of the known injuries, the consideration paid may turn out to be inadequate. *A* sues *B* and *B* raises the release as an affirmative defense. In order to pursue the claim, *A* must avoid the release.

A may seek avoidance on a number of grounds, many of them related to drafting. *A* may seek to have the release interpreted favorably. Often the release is prepared by an insurance company representing the party against whom the claim was made. *A* may invoke the rule that an ambiguous agreement should be interpreted against the drafter. *A* may also seek to have the release reformed on the ground that it does not correctly express the agreement of the parties. Courts are particularly sensitive to the fairness of a release and may avoid it if it contains obscure or misleading language that would make enforcement unconscionable. For example, if the release looks like a receipt for money paid, it could be avoided on grounds that the releasing party lacked assent to the formation of the contract.

Compare the following sections introducing a release:

---

1. In consideration of _____ Dollars ($_____), receipt of which from releasee is acknowledged, [*or state other consideration*], releasor voluntarily and knowingly executes this release with the express intention of effecting the extinguishment of obligations as herein designated.

---

2. Releasor understands that he may have suffered injuries that are unknown to him at the present time and that unknown complications may arise in the future from injuries of which he is presently unaware. Releasor acknowledges that the possibility of such unknown injuries and complications was discussed in the course of negotiations leading to agreement on the terms of this release, and the sum to be paid by releasee hereunder was determined with due regard for such possibility.

---

3. I know that this paper is much more than a receipt. **It is a release. I am giving up every right I have.**

Example 1 is from a traditional form release. It is difficult to read and contains no explanation of the transaction. Example 2 provides some background to let the releasor know what risks are taken by entering the agreement. Example 3 uses everyday language to make clear the scope and effect of the document.

Another ground for avoidance, mutual mistake of the parties, turns on the basic assumptions of the parties at the time they entered the release. These assumptions are often recited in the agreement. For example, releases commonly recite that the release covers all injuries, known or unknown and of whatever nature or extent. These recitations may provide grounds for avoidance if they do not accurately reflect the assumptions of the parties at the time the contract was entered into.

§ 8.5　Ethical issues.

Whether a contract can be avoided on grounds of mistake depends on the facts known to the parties at the time they entered the contract. Mistake therefore raises a number of ethical concerns, including (a) disclosure of knowledge and (b) taking advantage of a mistake.

a. Disclosure of knowledge. One of the reasons there are exchanges is that one party overvalues an item and the other party undervalues it. One party may later regard the transaction as a bad deal and will say, "I made a BIG mistake!" Mistake in business judgment is usually a unilateral mistake and is not in itself grounds for avoidance.

Often, however, one of the parties knows more than the other and the one lacking knowledge may have made a mistake of which the other was aware. During the negotiation of a contract, when does one party owe the other an obligation to disclose information that it possesses? Consider Comment *d* to Restatement (Second) of Contracts § 161:

> In many situations, if one party knows that the other is mistaken as to a basic assumption, he is expected to disclose the fact that would correct the mistake. A seller of real or personal property is, for example, ordinarily expected to disclose a known latent defect of quality or title that is of such a character as would probably prevent the buyer from buying at the contract price. An owner is ordinarily expected to disclose a known error in a bid that he has received from a contractor. . . . Nevertheless, a party need not correct all mistakes of the other and is expected only to act in good faith and in accordance with reasonable standards of fair dealing, as reflected in prevailing business ethics. A party may, therefore, reasonably expect the other to take normal steps to inform himself and to draw his own conclusions. If the other is indolent, inexperienced or ignorant, or if his judgment is bad or he lacks access to adequate information, his adversary is not generally expected to compensate for these deficiencies. A buyer of property, for example, is not ordinarily expected to disclose circumstances that make the property more valuable than the seller supposes.

The following case illustrates the ethical dilemma. *S,* a minor, is injured in an automobile accident caused by *Z. S'* s doctors diagnose his injuries as rib fractures, concussion, and fractures of the clavicles. *S's* lawyer demands $6,500 from *Z. Z's* doctor examines *S* and discovers, in addition to the other injuries, an aneurysm (blood clot on the brain) which could endanger *S's* life if not treated. The doctor submits his report to *Z'* s lawyer, who does not disclose the findings to *S's* lawyer. *Z* accepts the $6,500 settlement and *S* executes a release. When a doctor examining *S* later discovers the aneurysm, should the release be set aside? Did *Z's* lawyer act ethically?

The court's decision was made easier by the fact that a settlement on behalf of a minor must be approved by the court. Because the court approved the settlement without full knowledge of the facts, it could vacate the settlement. If the settlement had been made by an adult, it could be attacked on grounds that the mistake stemmed from unknown injuries rather than from unknown consequences of known injuries. Even if the mistake was unilateral, the settlement might be vacated on grounds that the party with knowledge unconscionably took advantage of the other's lack of knowledge.

The court was clear that Z's lawyer did not violate any ethical obligation. While probably correct under the Model Rules, results such as this suggest the need for lawyer's ethics to go beyond the codified requirements. On a pragmatic level, Z's lawyer might have contrasted the present cost of a settlement based on full disclosure with the future cost of litigation to set aside the settlement in the event of discovery of the mistake, which might have occurred on the occasion of S's death.

b. Taking advantage of a mistake. Often a written agreement does not represent the parties' understanding. In that case, the writing can be reformed to reflect accurately the agreement. As Calamari and Perillo succinctly put it, "Contracts are not reformed for mistake; writings are." Sometimes, however, one party's mistake will slip into an agreement and the other may be tempted to agree on the basis of the mistaken proposal.

In one case, attorneys for a husband and wife were negotiating a separation agreement that required the parties to put a value on various properties that they would split 50-50. The wife's attorney sent the husband's attorney a proposal which contained this calculation:

Property X:	Value	$550,000
	Less mortgage	$300,000
	Net value	$150,000
	Wife's share	$75,000

The husband agreed to settle on the basis of this proposal. After the ink was dry, the husband sent the wife a letter pointing out the error in the calculation and saying, in effect, "Ha Ha!"

The wife asked the court to reform the agreement to give her what she would have had without the math error, another $50,000. The husband asked to start negotiating over again, for in accepting that proposal, he had accepted without question the wife's estimate of the value of other properties. Furthermore, he claimed the true value of Property X was only $450,000 anyway, so the "mistake" simply led to a correct result. What is the role of the attorneys in this case? If the attorney for the husband spotted the mistake, did he have an ethical obligation to point it out to the other attorney?

The court had little difficulty finding that because the husband knew that the wife intended a net value of $250,000, the agreement should be reformed to express that intention, giving the wife an additional $50,000. The court was silent on the attorney's conduct. No doubt one attorney is not obligated to educate another who has greater knowledge. If the attorney here knew of the mistake, however, then he also knew that the wife was signing a writing that did not contain the agreement she thought the parties had reached. By enforcing the agreement on which the minds of the parties had met, the court subtly penalized the husband for taking advantage of the mistake. Had he called the wife's attention to it and negotiated, the husband might have gotten a better settlement and would have avoided the later litigation.

§ 8.6 Exercises.

1. Disclosure. *S* is negotiating to sell *B* a hamburger stand on Main Street. *S* makes full disclosure of all sales records and answers all of *B*'s questions. *B* agrees to buy the stand. At the closing, *B* says, "I'm glad there's no competition for a hamburger stand in this area. You don't know of plans for any, do you?"

S looks at her lawyer, who says nothing. *S* says, "You will have to judge that for yourself." They sign the papers. A few days later, *B* learns that a national chain plans to open a hamburger stand across the street, and that *S* knew it.

Did *S* have an affirmative duty to disclose this fact to *B*? Did *S* have an obligation to tell what she knew in response to *B*'s question? If *S*'s lawyer knew of the chain's plans, did the lawyer act ethically? Can *B* get out of the deal? What could *B*'s lawyer have done to protect *B*?

2. Taking advantage of a mistake. *A* and *B,* with the help of their lawyers, negotiate a commercial contract. At the end of negotiations, *A* agrees to a provision that had been in dispute and without which *B* would not have agreed to the contract. However, the final version of the contract, which was typed in the office of *B*'s lawyer, does not contain this provision. What is the ethical duty of *A*'s lawyer?

3. Drafting a release. Andy Kraft was in his car waiting at a stoplight when a pickup driven by Grady Turner ran into him. The force of the collision caused Andy's neck to snap and left him with some minor pain. When Andy saw his doctor the next day, she gave him some painkillers and told him his injuries were "relatively mild" and that he "should recover in a short time." The expenses for the doctor and for a new tail light for Andy's car came to $46.

Grady is insured by Benevolent Gigantic, your client. Benevolent's agent, Bill Malone, wants to run over to Andy's house and get him to sign the standard release form, which he has already filled out. Malone shows you the form:

I, <u>Andrew H. Kraft,</u> residing at <u>1131 E. 38th St., Two Dot, Montana,</u> being of lawful age, for the sole consideration of <u>$46.00,</u> receipt whereof is hereby acknowledged, have remised, released, and forever discharged, and for my heirs, executors, administrators, and assigns do hereby remise, release and forever discharge <u>Grady Turner,</u> and his, her, their, and its successors and assigns, heirs, executors, administrators, and all other persons, firms, and corporations, of and from any and all claims, demands, rights, and causes of action of whatsoever kind and nature, arising from, and by reasons of any and all known and unknown, foreseen and unforeseen neck injuries and damage to my automobile resulting and to result, from a certain accident which happened on or about the <u>7th day of August, 2004</u> for which I have claimed <u>Grady Turner</u> to be liable, which liability is hereby expressly denied.

a. Recall the factors courts consider in deciding cases involving releases. Draft revisions in the release that Benevolent wants Andy to sign in order to better insure that a court will enforce it. Support your revisions with arguments based on the cases.

b. Are there any stylistic changes you would make in the form?

Chapter 9

FORCE MAJEURE

§ 9.1 Introduction.

One role of a lawyer is to predict what may happen during performance of a contract and to provide for those possibilities while drafting the contract in order to protect the client. These are the three P's of drafting:

PREDICT what may happen;

PROVIDE for that contingency; and

PROTECT your client with a remedy.

The drafter reading over a contract must determine whether the promisor has unconditionally promised to perform or whether contingencies that arise during performance will excuse the promisor. For example:

> Seller shall deliver 500 widgets on October 1, 2003. Buyer shall pay Seller $100 per widget on delivery.

On their face, these promises appear to be unconditional. But what will be the effect of future events? For example, Seller may have difficulty performing because of a natural catastrophe such as fire or flood. Government regulation may impede production. Seller's plant may have mechanical problems or labor problems. Seller may have difficulty getting required parts from suppliers or may face transportation problems. The contract price might become unfavorable if events such as war or embargo drive up the cost of materials. Inflation or other domestic events might similarly affect the price.

Buyer's obligation is limited to payment. This performance may not be affected directly by events. But events might lessen the value of Seller's performance to Buyer. Buyer may not want the goods if it has experienced a natural catastrophe. Government regulation might affect a resale market. Buyer's use of the goods might be affected by problems with equipment or labor. Events may cause the market price to fall so that the contract price becomes unfavorable.

Which of these events will excuse nonperformance and which will not? Looking at the common law default rules on impossibility and frustration, and the U.C.C. provisions on impracticability, a court will answer these questions if the contract is silent. The parties may, however, wish to expressly provide for these contingencies in their contract. In that manner, they can address circumstances in which it would be difficult to predict the result a court would reach. In addition, on the occurrence of those circumstances, they may use the private law of their contract to state a result different from the result a court would reach.

§ 9.2 Qualifying an obligation.

An attorney has available a number of techniques to qualify a client's obligations so that nonperformance will not be breach. Several of these techniques have been described in other chapters. For example:

a. An option contract. A party who pays a consideration in order to have an offer kept open is not bound to perform. If the party does not accept within the term of the option, the opportunity may be lost but the party is not in breach. The attorney may consider drafting an option when the party needs additional time to consider whether he or she wishes to be bound.

b. An obligation qualified by "best efforts." A party who promises "best efforts" or "reasonable efforts" does not promise to do the thing itself but only to use best efforts to bring it about. For example, an agreement between Broker and Seller may provide:

Broker agrees to use reasonable efforts to procure a ready, willing and able Buyer of the property. . . .

Broker has not promised to find a buyer, but to use reasonable efforts to find one. Therefore, if Broker does not find a buyer, Broker is not in breach as long as Broker used reasonable efforts.

c. An obligation that depends on output or requirements. Under an output or requirements contract, the buyer or seller is not locked in to a certain quantity. The quantity is flexible, within the confines of "good faith." For example:

Seller shall sell to Buyer and Buyer shall purchase from Seller all bread crumbs produced by Seller in its factory at 115 Thames Street, Brooklyn, New York, during the period commencing June 19, 2004, and terminating June 18, 2005, at a price of 6 cents per pound.

Under U.C.C. § 2-306, the quantity of output by the Seller is subject to the obligation of good faith.

d. A power to terminate. A contract may be illusory if there is no obligation to perform. But absent public policy considerations, a party who has an obligation to perform may provide for the power to terminate the obligation. For example:

> A and B agree that B shall distribute A's products in the State of Illinois for a period of ten years from the date of this agreement. A may terminate this agreement on 10 days' written notice.

A may relieve itself of the obligation to perform by giving notice to B.

e. A limitation of remedies. By limiting remedies, a party does not relieve itself of the obligation to perform, but restricts its liability for breach in the event of nonperformance. For example:

> *Consequential Damages.* In the event of a breach or repudiation of this contract by Seller, Buyer is not entitled to any consequential damages in excess of $1,000.

Under this provision, the Buyer has a remedy for the Seller's nonperformance. Because the parties agreed to a limitation of the remedy, the obligation of the Seller is qualified.

§ 9.3　Absolute performance.

A party to a contract expects the other party to perform its obligations. However, when extraordinary circumstances arise, courts may grant parties relief from their obligations. Restatement (Second) of Contracts § 261 states:

> **Discharge by Supervening Impracticability.** Where, after a contract is made, a party's performance is made impracticable without his fault by the occurrence of an event the non-occurrence of which was a basic assumption on which the contract was made, his duty to render that performance is discharged, unless the language or the circumstances indicate the contrary.

Similarly, U.C.C. § 2-615(a) provides:

> **Excuse by failure of presupposed conditions.** Except so far as a seller may have assumed a greater obligation and subject to the preceding section on substituted performance:
>
> (a) Delay in delivery or nondelivery in whole or in part by a seller who complies with paragraphs (b) and (c) is not a breach of his duty under a contract for sale if performance as agreed has been made impracticable by the occurrence of a contingency the non-occurrence of which was a basic assumption on which the contract was made or by compliance in good faith with any applicable foreign or domestic governmental regulation or order whether or not it later proves to be invalid.

While courts may excuse nonperformance of an obligation because of circumstances, the parties may use language that promises absolute performance. Usually the promise of absolute performance is expressly stated. For example, U.C.C. § 2-613 allows the parties to avoid the contract if goods identified when the contract was made are destroyed before the risk of loss passes to the buyer. The parties could draft around this provision with the following language:

> DESTRUCTION OF GOODS: Seller shall not be excused from performing its obligations under this contract if the goods identified are destroyed. Seller shall tender substitute goods of equal quantity and quality.

In a number of cases, the promise of absolute performance has arisen from apparently careless drafting. In one case, the contract stated:

> Seller warrants and agrees that there will be provided under the terms and provisions of this Agreement a [specified] quantity of gas. . . .

Seller sought to be excused when the specified quantity was not available. The court held that "[b]y warranting, rather than merely promising, the availability of sufficient quantities of gas, [Seller] assumed for itself the entire risk that future conditions would raise the cost of gas."

The court seems to have reasoned as follows. In order for nonperformance to be excused on account of supervening events, the parties must have assumed that a certain event would not occur.

Therefore, if Seller had promised to perform, nonperformance would be excused. But when a party makes a warranty, it assures the other party that a fact is true and that it will indemnify the other party if the fact turns out not to be true. A warranty is a promise to pay damages if the event does not occur. Thus Seller could not ask to be excused if the event — availability of the gas — did not occur.

In another case, Seller promised to deliver lumber within 45 days. The contract had two provisions specifying the remedies available to Buyer if Seller failed to perform on time:

> If the contractor *** fails to make deliveries of the materials or supplies within the time specified, or any extension thereof, the Government may by written notice terminate the right of the contractor to proceed with deliveries. In such event the Government may purchase similar materials or supplies in the open market *** and the contractor *** shall be liable to the Government for any excess cost occasioned the

Government thereby: *Provided,* that the contractor shall not be charged with any excess cost occasioned the Government by the purchase of materials or supplies in the open market *** when the delay of the contractor in making deliveries is due to unforeseeable causes beyond the control and without the fault or negligence of the contractor, including, but not restricted to acts of God *** floods *** unusually severe weather ***, if the contractor shall notify the contracting officer in writing of the cause of any such delay, within ten days from the beginning thereof, or within such further period as the contracting officer shall *** grant for the giving of such notice.

After award is made to the bidder, if he fails to make delivery at destination within the time specified by him, there will be deducted from payment to him, as a liquidated damage, not as a penalty, an amount equal to 1% of the bid price of the undelivered portion of the order for each calendar day of delay, including Sundays and holidays.***

When Seller was late, Buyer deducted an amount from the payment. Seller claimed benefit of *force majeure.* The court held that while the first provision contains a *force majeure* clause, the second does not. Buyer elected a remedy under the second provision. Because the second provision contained an unqualified promise to perform, nonperformance was not excused by events. The case suggests an application of the Golden Rule of Drafting: Never change your language unless you wish to change your meaning, and always change your language if you wish to change your meaning. *See* § 15.4.5.

§ 9.4 Force majeure.

Whether a party has promised absolute performance depends on the assumptions the parties made at the time of contracting about the future state of affairs. They may make their assumptions express by stating the events that they agree will excuse nonperformance. A clause in a contract that lists the circumstances that will excuse nonperformance is known variously as a *force majeure, vis majeure,* or act of God clause. The following are examples of *force majeure* clauses:

1. *Force majeure.* Deliveries may be suspended by either party in case of acts of God, war, riots, fire, explosion, flood, strike, lockout, injunction, inability to obtain fuel, power, raw materials, labor, containers, or transportation facilities, accident, breakage of machinery or apparatus, national defense requirements, or any cause beyond the control of such party, preventing the manufacture, shipment, acceptance, or consumption of a shipment of the goods or of a material upon which the manufacture of the goods is dependent.

---

2. *Force majeure.* Neither party shall be held responsible if the fulfillment of any terms or provisions of this contract are delayed or prevented by revolutions or other disorders, wars, acts of enemies, strikes, fires, floods, acts of God, or without limiting the foregoing, by any other cause not within the control of the party whose performance is interfered with, and which by the exercise of reasonable diligence, the party is unable to prevent, whether of the class of causes hereinbefore enumerated or not.

It is impossible for the drafter to contemplate every event that could interfere with performance. The drafter of a *force majeure* clause must decide how broadly or narrowly to draft the clause. This requires a careful balancing of specific enumerated events and general language. For example, under the above examples, would the seller be excused if a machine broke down? If a quarantine prohibited shipment?

Example 1 enumerates the event "breakage of machinery." It uses the general language "or any cause beyond the control of such party." Under the rule of interpretation known as *ejusdem generis* (of the same kind), it is assumed that the parties intended to include only events similar to the ones enumerated. It could be argued that an act of government, such as a quarantine, is not like these other events. Example 2 does not enumerate either of these events. It uses as general language "any other cause not within the control of the party whose performance is interfered with, and which by the exercise of reasonable diligence, the party is unable to prevent, whether of the class of causes hereinbefore enumerated or not." The last clause seems designed to get around the rule of *ejusdem generis* by referring to other classes of causes. Thus, Example 1 achieves its purpose with more specific enumeration and Example 2 with more general language.

§ 9.5 Drafting for specific situations.

It is important for the drafter to tailor the *force majeure* clause to the particular needs of a client. No clause should be copied from a formbook without thought. For example, the client might be concerned about a shift in market conditions that will cause the price to rise or fall. Courts have generally held that a change in the market price does not excuse nonperformance. Nor would the above examples of *force majeure* clauses cover this situation. The parties might resolve this problem by agreeing to set the price in the future, to peg the price to an external standard, or to modify the price in certain circumstances.

For example, a price escalation clause tailored to the needs of the gas business reads:

> If . . . Buyer shall enter into a contract providing for the purchase by it of gas produced from a field or fields located, and delivered to Buyer, within a radius of fifty (50) miles of any point of delivery provided hereunder, Buyer shall forthwith notify Seller of such fact, and if the price per one thousand (1000) cubic feet at any time payable under such other contract is higher than the price payable hereunder, each price payable hereunder which is less than the price payable at the same time under such other contract shall be immediately increased so that it will equal the price payable under such other contract.

Other provisions used in this particular industry to excuse nonperformance by Buyer include the tender of inadequate quantities, the tender of gas at insufficient pressure, failure of Seller to meet quality specifications, fire or other casualty, and violation of law. Provisions that excuse nonperformance by Seller include actions of government, and operation by Seller at a loss.

The drafter who includes a *force majeure* clause should also consider the consequences of excused performance. Did the parties contemplate that the agreement would be terminated or that it would be modified to address the unexpected event? A court might determine that because the contract does not address the case, the court can supply a reasonable term. *See* § 3.6.

Instead of providing for particular events that excuse nonperformance, the drafter might provide that the parties agree to renegotiate in the event of "hardship" or "gross inequity." Because the parties may not agree on whether there is in fact hardship and what a reasonable adjustment should be, the provision should be coupled with an arbitration clause in which the parties agree to turn such disputes over to an arbitrator for resolution. *See* § 13.5. For example, a "Fair Clause" used in international sales contracts contains these provisions:

> § 15.1 In entering into this long-term Agreement the parties hereto recognize that it is impracticable to make provision for every contingency which may arise during the term of this Agreement and the parties declare it to be their intention that this Agreement shall operate between them with fairness.
>
> § 15.2 Based on the foregoing principle the provisions of this Article 15 shall apply if during the term of this Agreement a new situation arises which is beyond the reasonable control of either party and which is not covered by any of the provisions of this Agreement and if such situation results in (a) a material disadvantage to one party and a corresponding material advantage to the other or (b) severe hardship to one party without an advantage to the other party.

* * *

§ 15.4(a) In situations described under § 15.2(a) a solution shall be found in order to restore a fair balance of advantages and disadvantages as between the parties.

(b) In situations described under § 15.2(b) a solution shall be found in order to remove the severe hardship for the party affected; provided, however, that the provisions of this Agreement, as changed or modified by such solution and considered as a whole, shall remain commensurate with those of other international contracts between copper mines and independent smelters/refineries at the time of such change or modification and

(i) in case [buyer] invokes the Fair Clause, shall be no less favorable to [seller] than the provisions of any other comparable international contract between [buyer] and any independent copper mine other than [seller]; and

(ii) in case [seller] invokes the Fair Clause, shall be no less favorable to [buyer] than the provisions of any other comparable international contract between [seller] and any independent copper smelter/refinery other than [buyer].

The comparison of provisions as aforesaid shall serve as a valuation basis for the adjustment of the particular provisions of this Agreement which are involved, for instance the smelting/refining charge, but shall not result in replacing the provisions of this Agreement by the provisions of any compared contract unless agreed upon between [seller] and [buyer].

(c) In arriving at solutions for either of the situations described in § 15.2, due consideration shall be given to such benefits as may have been obtained by each party as a result of a prior invocation of this Article 15.

§ 15.5 If either party hereto shall believe that a new situation described in § 15.2 shall have arisen, then, at the request of either party hereto, the parties shall promptly consult with a view toward reaching a mutually acceptable agreement dealing with such situation. In the event that within six months after the date of such request the parties shall not reach agreement with respect to such situation, either party shall have the right, exercisable within three months after the expiration of such six-month period, to refer the matter to arbitration pursuant to § 19.1. The arbitrator or arbitrators shall determine whether the particular situation is a "new situation" described in § 15.2(a) or in § 15.2(b) and, if so, shall, in any award entered, specify the section involved and unless the parties come to a prompt solution themselves, thereafter on the request of either party also establish a solution in conformity with § 15.4. Such arbitrator or arbitrators may obtain, for the purpose of establishing such solution, the opinion of an impartial expert of recognized standing in the international copper business, who shall not be domiciled in either the United States or Germany unless the parties hereto shall otherwise consent. Promptly after the entering of such award the parties hereto shall enter into a written agreement incorporating the terms of such award and making such changes or modifications in this Agreement as may be required in order to give effect to such award.

§ 9.6 Exercises.

1. Technological change. A contractor agrees to deliver a technological component built to its own specifications. The contract provides:

> The Contractor shall not be liable for any excess costs if any failure to perform the contract arises out of causes beyond the control and without the fault or negligence of the Contractor. Such causes include, but are not restricted to, acts of God or of the public enemy, acts of the Government, fires, floods, epidemics, quarantine restrictions, strikes, freight embargoes, unusually severe weather, and defaults of subcontractors due to any of such causes. . . .

The contractor is unable to perform because it proves technologically impossible to build the component. Is the nonperformance excused?

2. Endorsement contract. A sportswear corporation (Company) and a tennis star (Consultant) enter into an agreement in which the Company pays for the Consultant's endorsement of its products. The agreement provides in part:

> 8. *Annual Compensation.* For the rights and benefits granted to Company pursuant to this Agreement, Company agrees to pay to Consultant, as Annual Compensation, the amount of $100,000 in each Contract Year.
>
> 16. *Special Right of Termination by Company.* Consultant agrees that Company shall have the right to terminate this Agreement at the conclusion of any Contract Year, upon thirty (30) days prior written notice to Consultant or his legal representatives, upon the occurrence of either of the following conditions:
>
> (a) In the event of Consultant's death during the Contract Period; or
>
> (b) In the event Consultant is unable to play, by reason of illness, injury or other physical disability (or otherwise fails to compete) in international competitive tennis on a regular basis (herein defined

> as participation in a minimum of eight (8) major tournaments offering prize money of $50,000 or more in each Contract Year).

Questions:

a. If Consultant suffers an injury during the next tournament and is unable to play tennis for two years, what does Company have to pay him?

b. If Consultant is convicted on drug charges shortly after signing the agreement and Company determines that using his name on its products will damage its image, can it terminate the contract?

c. If Consultant grants a magazine interview in which he reveals that he is a member of the Ku Klux Klan and in which he makes several racist statements, can Company terminate the contract? Does it have to pay Consultant his Annual Compensation for the balance of the Contract Period?

d. A drafter who worries about everything that can possibly go wrong during the performance of a contract would never get a contract drafted. Are the fact situations in these questions things that the drafter shouldn't take the time to worry about?

e. Draft a *force majeure* clause with enumeration and general language appropriate for this contract.

3. Fair clause. Redraft the "Fair Clause" in § 9.5, applying the principles found in Chapters 16 and 17 of this book. For example, use recitals. Draft in the present tense. Avoid the passive voice. Avoid archaic and windy terms. Use tabulation.

Chapter 10

PROMISE AND CONDITION

§ 10.1 Introduction.

Parties entering an agreement contemplate performance. A lawyer, however, is the grouch at the party. The lawyer must always look down the road and foresee all the things that may go wrong. When a lawyer reads a contract, the lawyer must ask:

- What has each party promised to do?

- What has to happen before a party has to do what it promised?

- What happens if a party doesn't do what it promised to do?

After this analysis is completed, the law of promise and condition provides the tools the lawyer as drafter will use to build a stronger contract. The drafter can use these tools to build into the contract the means to induce the other party to perform its obligations. If the inducements are unsuccessful, the drafter can also protect the client by providing for the consequences of breach. *See* Chapter 13, Damages.

For example, an agreement provides:

A shall deliver her horse "Black Beauty" to B on October 1, 2003. The horse shall be in good health. B shall pay A $2000 on October 1, 2003.

A lawyer reading this agreement might ask these questions:

A promises to deliver a certain horse. What happens if A doesn't? The agreement states that B promises to pay $2000. Does B have to pay if A doesn't deliver the horse? Does A have to deliver the horse if B doesn't pay? The agreement states that the parties will perform on October 1. What if A performs but on October 2? Does B still have to perform? What if A performs on December 1? October 1, 2004?

The statement "The horse shall be in good health" is difficult to characterize. A has apparently undertaken no act. It does not make sense to say that A has the duty to deliver the horse in good health, for if the horse is not healthy, there may be nothing A can do to make it so. Does it mean that A promises to pay B damages if the horse is not in good health? Does it mean that B does not have to purchase the horse if it is not in good health? If B does not have to purchase the horse, can B also recover damages from A ? Do the answers to these questions depend on the meaning of "good health" and how close to that state the horse is?

In the event of a dispute, a court will provide answers to these questions. The drafter, however, is in a position to clarify the contract for the parties. Louis M. Brown has said that "a contract which does not specify remedies is analogous to intestacy." By thinking about these questions and determining whether to build some of the answers into the contract, the drafter is in a position to practice preventive law.

§ 10.2 Promise.

Recall the definition of *promise* in Restatement (Second) of Contracts § 2(1):

> A promise is a manifestation of intention to act or refrain from acting in a specified way, so made as to justify a promisee in understanding that a commitment has been made.

A promise in a legally enforceable agreement communicates that the promisor is under a duty to perform. While contractual obligations rarely contain the word *promise,* the language must communicate that the promisor has undertaken an obligation. Drafters often use words such as *shall, will,* or *agrees to.* The language of promise can be read as "has the duty to" if the promisor has manifested an intention to act, or "has the duty not to" if the promisor has manifested an intention to refrain from acting.

The promise creates in the promisor an obligation to so act or refrain from acting and creates in the promisee the right to expect the act. If the promisor does not act as promised, the promisor is in breach.

§ 10.3 Condition.

Legally enforceable promises create duties. However, a party is not in breach for not acting as promised unless that duty is immediately performable. Often some event must occur before a duty is immediately performable. Such an event is called a condition. Recall the definition of *condition* in Restatement (Second) of Contracts § 224:

> A condition is an event, not certain to occur, which must occur unless its non-occurrence is excused, before performance under a contract becomes due.

It is important to note that a condition is an *event,* as opposed to a promised performance. Lawyers often use the word in other senses; for example, to refer to the terms of a written agreement. It will be helpful to confine the meaning precisely to an event. In the Restatement definition, the event is "not certain to occur." This eliminates the mere passage of time as a condition. If, on September 1, *A* makes a legally enforceable promise to sell her horse to *B* on October 1, *A* is bound on September 1. Performance is due on October 1, but the occurrence of October 1 is not described as a condition of *A*'s performance.

Note particularly the relationship between the event and the performance. If we say *"A is a condition of B,"* then *we mean "if event A* happens, then performance *B* becomes due." If we say, "*A* is conditional on *B*," then we mean, "if event *B* happens, then performance *A* becomes due."

In scrutinizing an agreement, the drafter must determine whether one party has made only a promise or has also promised to bring about an event that must occur before performance by the other party is due. The latter is sometimes referred to as a *promissory condition*. Ask whether the party who controls the occurrence has a duty to make it occur. If so, there is a promissory condition. In the following provisions, a duty is subject to the occurrence of an event. Let us analyze the relationship of the promises and conditions. It is important to identify:

- the performance that is due
- the event that makes the performance conditional
- who has control over the occurrence of the event

---

1. The Owner shall pay the Contractor only if the Owner is satisfied with the Contractor's performance.

The Owner has a duty to pay the Contractor. This obligation is conditional on the occurrence of the Owner's satisfaction. Whether that event occurs is up to the obligor, the Owner. Although the Owner does not promise to be satisfied, the Owner is not free to exercise the satisfaction according to whim. A court will imply a promise on the Owner's part to exercise satisfaction according to a standard of good faith or reasonableness. Having recognized that the satisfaction clause contains a promise as well as a condition, the drafter may consider incorporating into the contract standards for exercising satisfaction. *See* § 2.9.

---

2. The Insurer shall pay for the loss on condition that the Insured furnishes proof of the loss within 60 days of the loss.

The Insurer has a duty to pay the Insured. This obligation is conditional on the occurrence of the Insured furnishing proof of loss. Whether that event occurs is up to the obligee, the Insured. The Insurer is indifferent as to whether the Insured performs or not, so the Insurer does not want the Insured to promise to bring about the event. It would not make sense to provide:

> The Insured shall furnish proof of loss. The Insurer shall pay for any loss within 30 days of receiving proof of loss from the Insured.

The Insurer's claim for damages for breach of the Insured's promise would not be meaningful. Therefore, the Insured's furnishing proof of loss should be stated not as a promise, but as a condition precedent to the Insurer's obligation to pay for the loss.

> 3. The Purchaser shall not be obligated to purchase the property if the purchase price exceeds the reasonable value of the property established by the Veteran's Administration.

The Purchaser has the duty to purchase the property. This obligation is conditional on the occurrence of the purchase price not exceeding the Veteran's Administration appraisal. Whether that event occurs is up to a third party, the VA. Because the VA is not a party to the contract, the parties cannot promise to bring about that event. A court would imply, however, that the Seller has an obligation to cooperate with the appraisal. The drafter could make that obligation explicit.

> 4. The Insurer shall pay the Insured for any loss by fire occurring on the premises.

The Insurer has the obligation to pay for fire loss. This obligation is conditional on the occurrence of a fire. Whether that event occurs is beyond anyone's control. Therefore, no additional promises are implied.

> 5. The sale of the automobile is conditional on Buyer finding a purchaser for her present automobile before September 1.

The Seller has a duty to sell the automobile and the Buyer has a duty to pay for it. These obligations are conditional on the occurrence of the Buyer finding a purchaser for her present automobile. Whether that event occurs is up to the Buyer. The parties probably intend that Buyer will make reasonable efforts to sell her present automobile. The parties may consider drafting this in the contract.

§ 10.4 Conditions precedent and conditions subsequent.

Restatement (Second) of Contracts does not distinguish between conditions precedent and conditions subsequent. The distinction can be shown through drafting. Where an event must occur before a party becomes liable, the condition is precedent. Where the party is already liable and will be relieved from liability on the happening of an event, the condition is subsequent. The duty is performable when a condition precedent occurs; a duty is discharged when a condition subsequent occurs. For example, an insurance policy may state:

> Insurer is not liable unless proof of death is submitted within 90 days of death.

or

> If proof of death is not submitted within 90 days of death, this policy is void and the company is released from all liability.

Here, the event — submitting proof of death — is first stated as a condition precedent and then as a condition subsequent. As another example:

> The insurer is released from liability if suit is not brought within one year from the date of death.

or

> It is a condition precedent to the liability of the company under this policy that suit is brought within one year of the insured's death.

Here, the event — bringing suit — is first stated as a condition subsequent and then as a condition precedent. Substantively, the different language does not produce a different result. However the condition is expressed, the event must occur for the insurer to be liable. The distinction is procedural, for the plaintiff has the burden of proving the performance of a condition precedent while the defendant has the burden of proving a condition subsequent.

§ 10.5 Drafting promises and conditions.

The law of promise and condition is a useful tool for a drafter to state contractual obligations. If *B* wants a certain performance by *A*, *B* can use three means to induce *A's performance:*

a. Have *A* undertake the duty and if *A* doesn't perform, claim damages. *A's* performance is a promise.

b. Make *B*'s performance conditional on *A*'s performance. *A*'s performance is a *condition,* an event that must occur before *B*'s performance is due.

c. Have *A* undertake the duty *and* make *B*'s performance conditional on *A*'s performance. *A*'s performance is both a promise and a condition; it is sometimes called a *promissory condition.*

For example, *B* hires *A* to perform construction services. It is essential to *B* that *A* begins work on or before October 1, 2004. *B* could draft the contract to provide:

> 1. *A* shall begin the construction on or before October 1, 2004.

or

> 2. *B* shall have no obligation under this agreement if *A* does not begin the construction on or before October 1, 2004.

or

> 3. *A* shall begin the construction on or before October 1, 2004. *B* shall have no obligation under this agreement if *A* does not begin the construction on or before October 1, 2004.

In Example 1, if *A* begins after October 1, *A* is liable for damages for breach of promise. In Example 2, if *A* begins after October 1, *A* is not liable for damages. The event (beginning on or before October 1) that had to occur before *B*'s performance became due did not occur. Therefore, *B* need not perform. But *A* did not promise to bring about that event, so *A* is not liable for breach. In Example 3, if *A* begins after October 1, *A* is liable for damages and *B* does not have to perform. Here, *A* promised to bring about the event that had to occur before *B*'s performance became due.

Lawyers often speak of "breach of condition." While this expression is useful, it is not exact. A condition is an *event,* and it is not possible to breach an event. The phrase "breach of condition" is shorthand for "breach of the promise to bring about the event that is a condition of performance by the other party." There can be no breach when a party has not promised to bring about the event, as in Example 2 above. Each case must be scrutinized to determine whether one party has made only a promise or has also promised to bring about an event that must occur before performance by the other party is due.

§ 10.6 Remedies.

The rules of promise and condition are closely tied to remedies for breach. If First Party's performance is conditional on the occurrence of an event, First Party will claim, "Because the event did not occur, I don't have to perform." And when the event is performance by Second Party, First Party will claim, "Because you didn't perform, I don't have to perform." Analysis of whether First Party's claim is justified requires an examination of at least three questions:

1. Who is supposed to go first?
2. If one party doesn't perform, must the other party perform anyway?
3. How much or what kind of nonperformance by one party excuses performance by the other party?

§ 10.6.1 Who is supposed to go first?

Stating in an agreement that a performance is conditional on an event is meaningful only if the event occurs before the performance is due. If *A* delivers goods before *B's* obligation to pay is performable, *A* cannot make delivery conditional on payment. It is therefore important to establish whose performance comes first. In the absence of an agreement between the parties, the law resolves this problem the same way children do. My brother and I often agreed to an exchange but did not trust each other's promise of future delivery. We each held on to the items being exchanged, then simultaneously released one while tugging the other. The law is equally practical. In the absence of an understanding to the contrary, the performances are due simultaneously. Restatement (Second) of Contracts § 234 states:

> (1) Where all or part of the performances to be exchanged under an exchange of promises can be rendered simultaneously, they are to that extent due simultaneously, unless the language or the circumstances indicate the contrary.

> (2) Except to the extent stated in Subsection (1), where the performance of only one party under such an exchange requires a period of time, his performance is due at an earlier time than that of the other party, unless the language or the circumstances indicate the contrary.

For example, *A* promises to sell her car to *B* for $5,000. *B*'s attorney must ask:

- What has each party promised to do?
- What has to happen before a party has to do what it promised?
- What happens if a party doesn't do what it promised to do?

One possibility is that *B* will pay the $5,000 and *A* will not tender the car. It would then be too late for *B* to withhold his performance. A party who performs first is limited in obtaining a remedy for the other's breach. *B* can sue *A* for breach of her promise, but that is an impractical and costly solution. One way to protect *B* is to make the performance simultaneous. If performance by one is a condition of performance by the other, then *B* need not perform if *A* does not perform.

An attorney can obtain important leverage for a client by structuring the order of performance in the contract. For example, contrast these provisions in a contract for the sale of goods:

---

1. Terms of payment: Net cash thirty (30) days.

---

2. Terms of payment: Cash on delivery.

In Example 1, the seller gives the buyer 30 days after delivery to pay. If the buyer does not timely pay, it is too late for the seller to withhold performance and the seller's only remedy is to seek damages. In Example 2, the seller demands cash at the time of delivery. If the buyer does not pay, the seller may withhold delivery of the goods.

It is not always possible to solve this problem by requiring simultaneous performance, for some exchanges cannot be simultaneous. Consider an agreement between attorney and client. The attorney cannot require simultaneous payment for the performance of services; one party will have to extend credit to the other. Under the rule stated in Restatement (Second) of Contracts § 234(2), it is the attorney, the one whose performance requires a period of time, who must go first and thereby extend credit to the client. To avoid this situation, the drafter must build other protection into the contract. For example, the agreement between attorney and client might state:

Client shall pay Attorney the sum of $100 per hour for Attorney's time spent in research, writing, consultation, conference with opposing parties, and other matters specifically related to the case.

Under this provision, the attorney will perform first and bill the client for the work done. If the client does not pay, it is too late for the attorney to withhold performance. The attorney's remedy is to seek damages. Alternatively, the attorney can structure the agreement to require the client to pay in advance. This arrangement is called a retainer agreement. It might look like this:[1]

---

[1] Ostberg, Using a Lawyer. Copyright © 1990 HALT, Inc. Reprinted with permission.

> Client shall pay Attorney a retainer of $_____ and Attorney shall give Client a signed receipt for this amount. Attorney shall deduct fees and all costs and expenses from the retainer. If the retainer exceeds the total cost of completing the case, Attorney shall return the remainder in full to Client. If the total cost exceeds the retainer, Client shall pay Attorney the additional amount within 30 days of receipt of an itemized statement.

When this provision is added, the client pays in advance and the attorney deducts payment for work done from the advance payment.

There are many other ways to structure an agreement so that one party is not extending credit to the other. In a contract between owner and contractor for the construction of a house, in the absence of an agreement between the parties, the owner's duty to pay would not be performable until the contractor completed the house. To protect the contractor, the drafter could provide for "progress payments," payments by the owner as the construction progresses. For example:[2]

PROGRESS PAYMENTS

Based upon Applications for Payment submitted to the Architect by the Contractor and Certificates for Payment issued by the Architect, the Owner shall make progress payments on account of the Contract Sum to the Contractor as provided in the Contract Documents for the period ending the _____ day of the month as follows:

Not later than _____ days following the end of the period covered by the Application for Payment _____ percent (_____%) of the portion of the Contract Sum properly allocable to labor, materials and equipment incorporated in the Work and _____ percent (_____%) of the portion of the Contract Sum properly allocable to materials and equipment suitably stored at the site or at some other location agreed upon in writing, for the period covered by the Application for Payment, less the aggregate of previous payments made by the Owner; and upon Substantial Completion of the entire Work, a sum sufficient to increase the total payments to _____ percent (_____%) of the Contract Sum, less such amounts as the Architect shall determine for all incomplete Work and unsettled claims as provided in the Contract Documents.

If a seller sells goods on the buyer's promise to pay the price later, the attorney could structure the agreement so that the seller takes a "security interest" in the goods. In other types of contracts, the attorney might help the client secure a lien to assist in enforcement of the promise.

---

[2] AIA Document A101. Copyright © 1987 the American Institute of Architects.

§ 10.6.2 If one party doesn't perform, must the other party perform anyway?

We have seen that some obligations are immediately performable while others are conditional on the occurrence of an event. The legal difference is of enormous consequence. The determination of whether an obligation is immediately performable (a promise) or conditional on the occurrence of an event (a condition) can be determined by:

- statute
- court decision
- agreement by the parties.

a. Statute. On rare occasions, statutes determine whether the performance of a contractual obligation is a promise or a condition. As part of the research into the substantive area of the contract, the drafter should note any applicable rules. For example, in a separation agreement incorporated in a decree of dissolution, the Husband promises the Wife child support of $100 per week and the Wife promises the Husband reasonable visitation rights. The Husband, who resides in a different state, fails to make a payment. The Wife says, "Since you didn't pay me, I'm not going to allow you to visit the child."

The Wife is claiming that the Husband's performance — payment of child support — is a condition of her allowing the visitation. She claims that his performance was not only promised but was a condition of her performance. Since he did not perform, she does not have to. Another way of saying this is that the promises are *dependent*. The Husband may claim that he is entitled to visitation even if he doesn't pay. He claims that his performance is a promise only; for the breach of it, the Wife may seek damages but is not relieved of her obligation to perform. Another way of saying this is that the promises are *independent*.

Are these promises dependent or independent? Uniform Reciprocal Enforcement of Support Act § 23 states in part, "The determination or enforcement of a duty of support owed to one obligee is unaffected by any interference by another obligee with rights of custody or visitation granted by a court." Many states have enacted this statute.

Under the facts, the Husband has breached his promise to pay support. Because the statute makes the promises *independent*, however, the fact that he failed to meet his obligation does not excuse the Wife's performance. She must still allow visitation. Her remedy is to seek damages for the Husband's failure to perform an immediately performable duty. Note that the result would be the same if the Wife did not permit visitation. Because the promises are independent, the Husband would have to continue to pay, but could seek a court order to enforce the Wife's promise.

b. Court decision. In the absence of a statute or the parties' expressed intent, courts will determine whether one party's performance is conditional on the other's performance. Since the 18th century, courts have generally held that each party's performance is a condition of the other's duty to perform. This principle is known as the rule of *constructive conditions* of exchange. As stated in Comment *a* to Restatement (Second) of Contracts § 237:

> Under the rule stated in this Section, a material failure of performance, including defective performance as well as an absence of performance, operates as the non-occurrence of a condition. . . . The occurrence of conditions of the type dealt with in this Section is required out of a sense of fairness rather than as a result of the agreement of the parties. Such conditions are therefore sometimes referred to as "constructive conditions of exchange."

For example, *A* promises to sell her car to *B* for $5,000 on August 1. Suppose on August 1, *B* tenders the $5,000. The following conversation ensues:

A: I don't have the car with me.

B: Then I'm not giving you the $5,000.

A: Then you are in breach of contract.

B: I admit I didn't perform. But I was justified in not performing because you didn't perform.

A: My performance has nothing to do with it. You promised me $5,000 and you didn't deliver. So you are a dirty contract breaker.

A's claim has a certain amount of logic going for it. *B* did promise to pay *A* $5,000 on August 1. *B* could perform and then sue *A* for damages for breach of contract. *B*'s contention commands our attention because it is more practical. *B* is saying, "It is true that I promised you $5,000. But it was a *condition* of my paying you the $5,000 that you tender the car. When that event failed to occur, I was relieved of my obligation."

B's claim indicates the practical importance of conditions. If a party merely promises a performance, then the only effect of nonperformance is that the other party has a claim for damages. But if that performance is a condition of the other party's performance, the other party may suspend its performance. After a period of time, which is either stated by the parties or is a reasonable time, the other party may treat its duty as discharged and the contract as terminated. If the first party promised to bring about the event that was a condition of the second party's performance, two consequences occur: the other party is not obligated to perform *and* is entitled to damages.

In the sale of the automobile, the parties stated no express conditions. Under the rule of constructive conditions, however, the law finds an implication that *A*'s performance is a condition of *B*'s performance and vice-versa. The contract can be broken down into the following promises and conditions:

Promise: *A* promises to tender a car.

Promise: *B* promises to tender $5,000.

Condition: *A*'s tendering the car is a condition of *B*'s tendering $5,000.

Condition: *B*'s tendering $5,000 is a condition of *A*'s tendering the car.

The obligations are both promises and conditions. We could also say that the promises are "dependent" or "promissory conditions."

c. Agreement by the parties. The rule of constructive conditions is premised on the idea that the parties expect an exchange of performances. The rule then fairly carries out the reasonable expectations of the parties. Because a court will infer a constructive condition in most circumstances, it is not always necessary for the parties to make the condition express. To express the contrary, the parties must be clear. Because the presumption of constructive conditions is so strong, it would be an unusual contract that would rebut it.

For example, in one case, an employee claimed that an employer breached an employment contract. The employer attempted to enforce against the employee a restrictive covenant. The contract stated:

> These [restrictive] covenants on the part of the employee shall be construed as an agreement independent of any other provision in this agreement, and the existence of any claim or cause of action of the employee against the company whether predicated on this agreement or otherwise, shall not constitute a defense to the enforcement by the Company of said covenants.

The court held that the intent of the parties was that the employee's promise contained in the restrictive covenant was to be performed even if the employer did not perform.

To say that the parties bargained in general for an exchange of performances is not to say whether a *particular provision* in a contract operates as a promise or a condition. For example, when *A* promised to sell her car to *B* for $5,000 on August 1, the rule of constructive conditions was invoked to provide that performance by one party was a condition of performance by the other. In a particular provision of that contract, the parties agreed that this exchange would take place on August 1. Suppose *B* tenders performance, but does so on August 2. *B* is in breach, but what is the consequence of that breach?

The consequence depends on whether that particular provision, payment on August 1, is a promise or a condition (note that since *B* promised to do it, if it is a condition, it is a promissory condition). If it is a promise, *B* is liable for damages because of his breach but *A*'s performance is not excused. If the event — payment on August 1 — is a condition of *A*'s performance and *B* promised to bring about the event, then *A*'s performance is excused when *B* did not cause the event to occur. The question of whether the provision is a promise or a condition has enormous practical significance for *A*. Suppose *A* treats the provision as a condition, excusing her performance. *B* may then claim that because the provision was merely a promise, *A* is in breach for failing to perform an immediately performable duty.

If the parties do not make clear the consequences of breach, a court has to interpret the provision. Recall that in interpreting an agreement, a court attempts to effectuate the intent of the parties. Whether a contractual provision is intended to be a promise or a condition is a question of the intent of the parties. A condition supplied by a court is called an *implied condition*. When the parties do not expressly provide that a duty is conditional on an event, a court may nevertheless find an implied condition. For example, an insurance policy states:

> The Insurer shall pay for any loss within 30 days of receiving proof of loss from the Insured.

The Insurer has the duty to pay for a loss. As worded, however, the Insurer's obligation is not expressly conditional on the occurrence of the Insured's furnishing proof of loss. A court would probably find an implied condition in these circumstances. The Insurer does not want the Insured's promise to furnish proof of loss. The Insurer is indifferent as to whether the Insured performs. The Insurer wants to place on the Insured the burden of doing its part if it wants the Insurer to perform.

The Insurer might redraft the agreement to make its obligation an express condition:

> The Insurer shall pay for any loss on condition that the Insured furnishes proof of loss. The Insurer shall pay for the loss within 30 days of receiving proof of loss from the Insured.

or

> The Insurer shall pay for any loss within 30 days of receiving proof of loss from the Insured. The Insurer is not liable for any loss for which the Insured does not submit proof of loss.

Sometimes the parties state a provision so ambiguously that it is difficult to determine whether they intended an event to be a condition. For example, an agreement between a Contractor and a Subcontractor provides:

> Contractor shall pay Subcontractor when Owner pays Contractor.

If the Owner does not pay the Contractor, must the Contractor pay the Subcontractor? If a condition is implied, the provision may be read as "Contractor shall pay Subcontractor *if* Owner pays Contractor." If payment is not conditional on that event, the provision may be read as "Contractor shall pay Subcontractor *not before* Owner pays Contractor, *but in any event within a reasonable time*." Because a Subcontractor would not normally assume the risk of nonpayment, a court would probably not find an implied condition. Contrast the above provision with this one from an agreement between the seller of a house and a real estate broker:

> Seller shall pay Broker on the passing of title.

What if the Broker finds a buyer but the deal falls through and title never passes? If a condition is implied, the provision may be read as "Seller shall pay Broker *if* the title passes." If payment is not conditional on that event, the provision may be read as "Seller shall pay Broker *not before* the passing of title, *but in any event within a reasonable time*." Because the risk of loss is part of the broker's business, a court would probably find an implied condition in the provision.

Perhaps the most famous illustration of this problem occurs in *Southern Surety Co. v. MacMillan Co.*[3] The surety agreement stated that "in the event of any default on the part of [the distributor], written notice thereof by registered letter, with a verified statement of the facts showing such default and the date thereof, shall within 60 days after such default be mailed to the Surety at its office in Des Moines, Iowa." MacMillan claimed that it was entitled to compensation by the Surety although MacMillan had not sent timely notice of default. In other words, MacMillan claimed the sending of notice was merely a *promise,* for the breach of which the Surety could recover damages, rather than a *condition,* an event that had to occur before the Surety became liable to it.

Courts often find that the *ambiguous* intention of the parties creates a promise. Restatement (Second) of Contracts § 227(1) states:

Standards of Preference with Regard to Conditions

1. In resolving doubts as to whether an event is made a condition of an obligor's duty, and as to the nature of such an event, an interpretation is preferred that will reduce the obligee's risk of forfeiture, unless the event is within the obligee's control or the circumstances indicate that he has assumed the risk.

---

[3] 58 F.2d 541 (10th Cir.), *cert. denied* 287 U.S. 617 (1932).

The parties to a contract may wish to remove themselves from the vagaries of judicial interpretation by expressly stating in their contract that particular provisions are promises or conditions. Contractual provisions containing conditions often include language such as *if, on condition that, in the event that,* or *subject to.* Because courts favor an interpretation that an event is not a condition, it is important that a drafter clearly state an express condition. For example, a homeowner's insurance policy states under the heading of "Agreement":

> We will provide the insurance described in this policy in return for the premium and compliance with all applicable provisions of this policy.

If the insured neglects to pay a premium, is the insurer relieved of its obligation to pay for losses? Or must it pay for the losses and make a claim against the insured for the unpaid premiums? To avoid any ambiguity, insurer desires to make its obligation expressly conditional on payment of the premium. It states under the heading of "Conditions":

> We may cancel this policy only for the reasons stated in this provision by notifying you in writing of the date cancellation takes effect. . . .
>
>   (1) When you have not paid the premium whether payable to us or to our agent or under any finance or credit plan, we may cancel at any time by notifying you at least 10 days before the date cancellation takes effect.

Only a material breach can operate as a condition. Therefore, when there is a breach, parties frequently argue about whether or not the breach was material. We have seen that they can take this issue out of the court's hands by making the term an express condition. Alternatively, they can define what is or is not material breach. For example:

> Service Level failures shall not constitute a material breach under the Agreement and Customer's sole remedy and Company's entire liability for any failure by Company to meet any Service Level shall be Customer's recovery of the Service Level Credits specified in the Statement of Work.

§ 10.6.3   How much or what kind of nonperformance by one party excuses performance by the other party?

Closely related to the question of promise and condition is the question of *materiality.* In the agreement between *A* and *B* for the sale of the car, the agreed performances, the exchange of the car for the $5,000, are material terms. It is not clear, however, whether the promise to conduct the transaction on a particular date, October 1, is a material term. When a court is determining whether a particular term is a promise or a condition, it looks to the materiality of the term. Breach of an immaterial term will not be treated as failure to bring about an event that is a condition of performance by the other party. *See* Restatement (Second) of Contracts § 241, Circumstances Significant in Determining Whether a Failure is Material.

In order to have a term enforced as a condition, therefore, the drafter must state it unambiguously. We have seen that if a court can find that a term is ambiguous, it may interpret it as a promise. Even if the term is clearly stated as a condition, however, a court may not always enforce the parties' characterization of the term. For example, suppose an agreement provided that exact performance of every obligation by *A* is a condition of payment by *B*. Such a provision could create a hardship for *A*, who may not be compensated because of an insignificant breach. If a court said that the provisions containing *A*'s obligations were promises and not conditions, *B* would still be required to perform but could recover damages for *A*'s breach.

It is often stated as black-letter law that express conditions are strictly enforced. Nevertheless, courts have developed a number of devices to lessen the harsh effects of the strict enforcement of conditions; for example, unconscionability, good faith and fair dealing, substantial performance, interpretation, waiver, estoppel, discharge, acceptance of performance, impossibility, and excuse to avoid forfeiture.

In the famous case of *Jacob & Youngs, Inc. v. Kent,*[4] the contract appeared to state that performance of the specifications was a condition of payment:

Art. IV. The Contractors shall provide sufficient, safe and proper facilities at all times for the inspection of the work by the Architect or his authorized representatives; shall, within twenty-four hours after receiving written notice from the Architect to that effect, proceed to remove from the grounds or buildings all materials condemned by him, whether worked or unworked, and to take down all portion of the work which the Architect shall by like written notice condemn as unsound or improper, or as in any way failing to conform to the drawings and specifications, and shall make good all work damaged or destroyed thereby.

Art. IX. . . . The final payment, or 15% of the total amount of this contract, shall be made within 30 days after the completion of the work

---

[4] 230 N.Y. 239, 129 N.E. 889 (1921).

> included in this contract, and all payments shall be due when certificates for the same are issued.

When the contractors failed to use the pipe called for in the specifications, the architect refused to issue the certificate. In other words, the owner treated the contractors' nonperformance as failure to bring about an event that had to occur before his performance became due (breach of condition). But the court held it was breach of promise, entitling the owner to damages only. On the motion for reargument, the court stated:

> The court did not overlook the specification which provides that defective work shall be replaced. The promise to replace, like the promise to install, is to be viewed, not as a condition, but as independent and collateral, when the defect is trivial and innocent. The law does not nullify the covenant, but restricts the remedy to damages.

§ 10.7 Drafting clear conditions.

Drafters who wish to have an express condition strictly enforced have their work cut out. Williston states that "[b]ecause the enforcement of conditions frequently leads to forfeitures and penalties, courts have always been indisposed to interpret contracts as containing conditional promises, unless the language is too clear to be mistaken."

How can the drafter indicate that a particular provision is material, so that a court will uphold its performance as a condition of performance by the other party? Courts often regard a promise to perform at a certain time as immaterial. The drafter may try to change this result by adding such language as "time is of the essence" in order to indicate that time is material and therefore should be treated as a condition. This technique may not work because a court may regard the language as boilerplate, not clearly indicating the intention of the parties.

To strengthen a term intended as a condition, drafters might consider the following:

- Be clear
- Be selective
- Use recitals
- Build the remedy into the contract
- Insert a non-waiver clause

a. Be clear. Clearly state the event that conditions performance. Clearly state the promise that is made conditional on the event. Make clear that the term is not merely stating a time for performance. Use clear language of condition. *See* § 17.6.3

b. Be selective. Drafting a blanket term indicating that all terms are material is probably less effective than enumerating a few well-chosen material terms. Select the term or terms which are most important and indicate that performance of that term is a condition. For example:

> Contractor shall use pipe of "Reading" manufacture. Owner has no obligation to make the final payment unless and until Contractor complies with this provision.

c. Use recitals. Instead of stating that "Time is of the essence of this agreement," state in recitals (the "premises" stated at the beginning of the contract), why time is material. For example:

> Buyer requires the goods at the time called for in the contract in order to re-ship them to its customers. Buyer has entered this agreement with Seller because Seller has represented that it will deliver the goods on time.

d. Build the remedy into the contract. For example:

> Seller shall deliver the goods on or before October 1, 2005. Timely delivery is a material term of this contract. Delivery of the goods on or before October 1, 2005 is a condition precedent to Buyer's obligation to perform its duties under this agreement.

e. Insert a non-waiver clause. Often an agreement states that an event is a condition, but when a party fails to bring about that event, the other party agrees to accept the performance. If the same thing happens again, a court may find that the non-breaching party has waived the right to treat the term as a condition. The non-breaching party might gain protection by including a non-waiver clause. For example:

> Waiver by either Seller or Buyer of a breach by the other of any provision of this agreement is not a waiver of future compliance with the provision, and the provision remains in full force and effect.

Because courts sometimes find that a party's behavior has waived the non-waiver clause, it is important for the attorney to advise the client that if there is a waiver, the client should not rely on the non-waiver clause but should send the other party clear and definite notice that strict compliance is expected in the future.

Even if the condition is clearly expressed, it is still subject to legal attack. Williston states that "[t]he courts have frequently disregarded plainly expressed conditions, because of their unwillingness to deprive a promisee of all rights on account of some trivial breach of condition." Nevertheless, express conditions will exhibit clearer thinking and will more forcefully express the parties' intentions. In the event of litigation, summary judgment is more likely when an agreement expressly states a condition; implied conditions raise issues of interpretation.

§ 10.8   Exercises.

1. Lease. In a residential lease agreement, the Tenant promises to pay for any damage to the premises. The Landlord requires a $200 security deposit to give the Landlord leverage in recovering for damage. After the Tenant has vacated the premises, the Landlord discovers $60 worth of damage. The Landlord sends the Tenant a check for $140. The Tenant demands return of the $60.

A statute provides that "Every landlord, within 30 days subsequent to the termination of a tenancy . . . shall provide the departing tenant with a written list of any damage and cleaning charges. . . . Delivery of such list shall be accompanied by payment of the difference, if any, between the security deposit and the permitted charges."

Did the Tenant have an immediately performable duty to pay for the damages?

2. Construction contract. A construction contract between Contractor and Subcontractor provides:

> All work shall be performed in a workmanlike manner, and in accordance with the best practices.
>
> Contractor shall make progress payments to Subcontractor each month during the performance of the work. Subcontractor must submit to Contractor, by the 25th of each month, a requisition for work performed during the preceding month. Contractor shall pay each requisition, less a retainer equal to ten percent (10%), by the 10th of the month following the month in which the Contractor receives the requisition.

On August 9, Subcontractor runs a bulldozer into a wall, causing damage of $3,400. On August 10, Contractor refuses to pay the requisition Subcontractor submitted in July. On September 10, Contractor refuses to pay the requisition Subcontractor submitted in August. On September 12, Subcontractor refuses to complete the job. The parties sue each other, making these claims:

The Subcontractor claims:

$ 1,484   for work performed
+ <u>1,340</u>   for lost profit (expectancy damages)
$ 2,824   total

The Contractor claims:

$ 3,400 bulldozer damage
+ 450 "cover" for hiring a replacement (expectancy
          damages)
$ 3,850 total

Analyze the contract and the claims in terms of promise and condition.

3. Sale of goods. Seller sold goods to Buyer under an installment sales agreement. The contract provides that Buyer may give Seller notice of latent defects. If Seller does not repair the defects, Buyer may have them repaired at Seller's expense. Buyer served notice of defects and Seller did not repair the goods. Buyer stopped making monthly payments. Seller sued for the monthly payments. Analyze the contract and the claims in terms of promise and condition.

4. Drafting Clear Conditions. If you were asked by your client to state the conditions in the following provisions (from unrelated contracts) more clearly, could you do so? Once you have stated the existing terms more clearly, what questions do you have for your client about the substance? Do you have any suggestions for changes in the substance?

a. Owner, by notice to Manager, may terminate this agreement, if Owner asserts a breach by Manager of the terms and conditions hereof, to the extent Manager is given a reasonable time to cure such breach.

b. Seller Installed Products. Seller will make reasonable accommodations if Buyer requests a delay in the originally scheduled In-Service Date, if Buyer gives Seller written notice prior to the CCD. If Buyer gives notice of a request for delay in the originally scheduled In-Service Date after the Change Control Date ("CCD"), requests more than one delay in the In-Service Date prior to the CCD, or causes a delay in the In-Service Date as a result of Buyer's failure to meet Buyer's obligations under this Agreement, Seller may: (i) deliver the Products and commence billing as of the originally scheduled In-Service Date for the Order, in which case installation will be scheduled at a mutually agreeable time and additional installation charges may apply; or (ii) cancel the order and bill Buyer for cancellation charges as set forth in Section XX.

c. Company grants Service Provider a non-exclusive, nontransferable right to purchase the Products for use in the Territory in creating and providing Network Services to End Users. Service Provider may resell Products to End Users who purchase Network Services, provided that the Products at the time of sale to the End User are intended to be used primarily in connection with access to Network Services, provided further that Service Provider shall indicate on its Purchase Order any Product units which are to be resold to third parties and shall report such sales as required in this Agreement.

5. Broker's listing agreement. In the following agreement[5] between Seller and Broker, what *promises* are made by each party? What performances are *conditional* on an event? What events must occur before the performances are due?

If the Broker did not use reasonable efforts to procure a buyer and after a few months the Seller found a buyer on his own, would the Seller have to pay the commission?

Which party must perform first? Could the drafter structure the agreement so that party does not extend credit to the other?

---

[5] Agreement for Exclusive Right to Sell. Copyright © 1984, 1987 Greater Boston Real Estate Board. This form has been made available through the courtesy of the Greater Boston Real Estate Board, and is protected by the copyright laws.

FROM THE OFFICE OF:

Agreement for Exclusive Right to Sell

DATE: _____ January 31, 2004 _____

This Agreement concerns the following property: _____ House and lot, 1107 Elm Avenue,

Springarden, Mass. _____

_____ PRICE $ __45,000.00__

In consideration of the mutual covenants and agreements herein contained, the undersigned Seller hereby gives to the undersigned Broker the sole and exclusive right to sell the said property for the price and on the terms and conditions herein set forth.

I. The Broker agrees:
   a. To use reasonable efforts to procure a ready, willing, and able Buyer of the property in accordance with the price, terms, and conditions of this Agreement.

II. The Broker is granted the sole authority to:
   a. Advertise the property;
   b. Post "For Sale" signs on the property; and
   c. Cooperate with other brokers.

III. The Seller agrees:
   a. To refer all inquiries and offers for the purchase of said property to the Broker;
   b. To cooperate with the Broker in every reasonable way;
   c. To pay the Broker a fee for professional services of ___six percent (6%)___ if:
     (1) A Buyer is procured ready, willing, and able to buy said property, or any part thereof, in accordance with the price, terms, and conditions of this Agreement, or such other price, terms, and conditions as shall be acceptable to the Seller, whether or not the transaction proceeds; or
     (2) The said property, or any part thereof, is sold through the efforts of anyone including the Seller; or
     (3) The said property, or any part thereof, is sold within _____ months after the term of this Agreement to anyone who was introduced to the said property through the efforts of the Broker or his agents prior to the expiration of said term. However, no fee will be payable under this clause if the said property is sold after said term with the participation of a licensed broker to whom the Seller is obligated to pay a fee under the terms of a subsequent written exclusive listing agreement.

Once an offer has been accepted in writing and a transaction is pending, the BROKER has no obligation to present further offers to the Seller.

IV. The Seller understands and agrees that the property will be marketed in compliance with all applicable fair housing laws.

V. The period of this Agreement shall be from _____ January 31 _____ , 20__04__ , to and including _____ June 30 _____ , 20__04__ . Time is of the essence hereof.

VI. Additional terms and conditions: _____

_____

IN WITNESS WHEREOF, the Seller and the Broker have hereunto set their hands and seals as of the ___31st___ day of _____ January _____ , 20__04__ .

_____ Leo Moore _____   Wanda Smith
BROKER   SELLER
BY _____   Karl Smith
                       SELLER
ITS _____
     duly authorized (title)

Chapter 11

MODIFICATION AND DISCHARGE

§ 11.1 Introduction.

The law is concerned with the stability of contracts. Changing circumstances, however, often lead parties to modify the agreement they have entered. The law must find ways to balance the need for stability with the need for flexibility. In doing so, it has imposed limitations on the ability of parties to modify their original agreement.

The principal doctrine by which the law imposes stability is known as the "pre-existing duty" rule. That doctrine rests on the premise that consideration is required for a promise to be enforceable. A contract binds a promisor to perform a certain duty. Under a modification of that contract, the promisor often promises to perform less than the full extent of that duty or demands an additional consideration for performing the duty. In that event, the promisor is only doing what he or she promised to do in the first place. Therefore, the modification is not enforceable. To induce the promisee to accept less or to pay an additional consideration, the promisor must supply a consideration. For example, A and B enter this agreement:

---

1. On October 1, A shall buy and B shall sell to A his 1985 Buick Skylark for $4,000.

The parties later modify this agreement to read:

---

2. On October 1, A shall buy and B shall sell to A his 1985 Buick Skylark for $3,500.

Under Agreement 1, A had a duty to pay B $4000. Under Agreement 2, A has a duty to pay B $3,500 to obtain the same consideration from B, the 1985 Buick. A is merely doing what A already had a duty to do, pay $3,500 as part of the $4,000. B has given up the right to receive $500 from A but has received no consideration from A for the promise to accept less than A was already bound to pay. According to the pre-existing duty rule, Agreement 2 is not enforceable.

A modification takes place before both parties have fully performed. Similar principles apply to the settlement of claims. Claims arise in contract when one party has completed performance and has a claim against the other, such as payment of a debt. Claims may also arise when one person

157

alleges that another has committed a tort. The pre-existing duty rule also requires consideration for the discharge of the debtor's or the tortfeasor's obligation. The law encourages settlement, but the parties must be careful to ensure that their settlement agreement complies with the pre-existing duty rule or with an exception to it.

For example, a debtor owes a creditor $1,000 and the creditor agrees to accept $800 in full payment. Consideration is required for the discharge of the debtor's obligation. The creditor has agreed to forgo $200 but has obtained nothing from the debtor in return. According to the pre-existing duty rule, the settlement agreement is not enforceable and the creditor has a right to collect the $200.

§ 11.2 Common law modification of executory agreements.

The common law found many ways around the pre-existing duty rule. The parties could rescind the original contract and enter a new one. For example, A gives up the right to receive the Buick and B gives up the right to receive the $4,000. Because each party to a mutual rescission surrenders a legal right, there is consideration for each party's promise. They can then make a new contract. The sequence of agreements looks like this:

---

1. On October 1, A shall buy and B shall sell to A his 1985 Buick Skylark for $4,000.

---

2. A and B release each other from the obligations contained in the above agreement.

---

3. On October 1, A shall buy and B shall sell to A his 1985 Buick Skylark for $3,500.

Alternatively, because the problem under the pre-existing duty rule is to find consideration for B's promise to forgo $500, A could promise to do something A had not previously promised to do. For example:

---

2. On September 30, A shall buy and B shall sell to A his 1985 Buick Skylark for $3,500.

---

or

2. On October 1, *A* shall buy and *B* shall sell to *A* his 1985 Buick Skylark for $3,500 and a ball-point pen.

Because the law does not generally inquire into the adequacy of consideration, it is up to the parties to determine whether payment at an earlier date or delivery of an additional item is worth $500.

§ 11.3 The modern rule.

Some states have abandoned the pre-existing duty rule in case law. The Uniform Commercial Code has also abandoned it with respect to contracts for the sale of goods. U.C.C. § 2-209(1) states:

> An agreement modifying a contract within this Article needs no consideration to be binding.

A thorough modification agreement could take this form:

Background. S. Co. (Seller) and B. Co. (Buyer), parties to a sales agreement dated October 1, 2005, agree that it is in their mutual interest to modify that agreement. Seller and Buyer agree that neither party exercised any duress or made any unreasonable demands in the negotiation of this modification, and each agrees that the other observed reasonable commercial standards of fair dealing in the trade during negotiations leading to the modification. This modification has become necessary because of an unanticipated national shortage of crucial materials used in producing the goods.

Therefore, Seller and Buyer agree as follows:

1. The price of the goods under their previous agreement will be increased by 10%.

2. The quantity of the goods under their previous agreement will be decreased by 20%.

3. All terms of the prior agreement between Seller and Buyer which are not specifically changed by this modification remain binding.

This modification agreement is to be governed by the Uniform Commercial Code as enacted and in force in the state of Nebraska on the date of this agreement.

Dated: February 1, 2006   S Co. by_____
                                  B Co. by_____

Abandonment of the pre-existing duty rule serves the goal of flexibility, but it may not serve the goal of stability. A modification may arise not when parties adjust to changing circumstances, but when one party coerces the other to pay more or to accept less than had been originally promised. These situations can be dealt with at common law by invoking the pre-existing duty rule and under the Code by invoking the statutory obligation of good faith. Consider the following problems, determining whether each modification should be enforced:

Contractor A agrees to put a new roof on X's garage for $750. A removes the old roof. He then tells X that heavy rain is predicted during the next few days and he can't possibly complete the job unless X pays him an additional $250. X promises to pay it.

Contractor B agrees to dig a well 20 feet deep for X for $750. B begins to work and hits solid rock 10 feet down that neither B nor X had anticipated. B tells X that she will need to get extra equipment and that the job is worth an extra $250 which she asks X to pay. X promises to pay it.

Supplier C agrees to deliver materials X needs for these projects on a certain day for $750. The day before delivery is due, C explains that the market has gone up and he plans to ship the goods to other customers unless X agrees to pay C $1,000 instead. X promises to pay it.

When the bills for $1,000 arrive, X sends A, B, and C each $750 with a note saying, "Ha Ha! Pre-existing duty rule! I don't have to pay you any more than our original agreement called for." If A, B, and C made a claim for the $250 from X, would they succeed?

The cases of A and B involve services rather than goods. Therefore the U.C.C. does not apply. Using common law principles as embodied in Restatement (Second) of Contracts § 89, the issue is whether A is taking advantage of the circumstances to coerce X into paying more or whether A is performing an additional service, such as working overtime to get the job done before the rains come. The case with B seems to be a fair and equitable modification in light of unanticipated circumstances. Case law would support enforcing the modification in spite of the pre-existing duty rule. Case C arises under the U.C.C. Although § 2-209 abrogates the rule, it appears that C is not acting in good faith as required by § 1-203. If C is not acting in good faith, the modification is not enforceable.

§ 11.4 Settlement of claims.

As when modifying an agreement, parties settling claims can get around the pre-existing duty rule if the obligee agrees to accept a different or additional performance from the obligor. (Recall that the *obligor* is the one who is obligated, such as a debtor or tortfeasor; the *obligee* is the one to whom he or she is obligated, such as a creditor or alleged victim.) For example, A owes B $1000 and A wishes to be released from the obligation. The parties may make one of these agreements:

> *B* agrees to release *A* from the obligation and *A* promises to deliver to *B* 5 shares of stock in XYZ Co.

or

> *B* agrees to release *A* from the obligation and *A* promises to pay *B* $800 and a ball-point pen.

If the parties do not agree to a different or additional performance, they may still enter into a binding settlement agreement. The new agreement must satisfy all the requirements of a contract, including offer, acceptance, and consideration. While the law favors settlement, any contract requires the free assent of the parties, with the offer clearly communicated and knowingly accepted.

To determine whether there is a consideration that will support the settlement, determine whether the obligation is:

- unliquidated or disputed; or
- liquidated and undisputed.

In general, there is consideration for the settlement of unliquidated or disputed obligations; there is no consideration for the settlement of liquidated and undisputed obligations. *Disputed* generally means that there is a good faith defense to payment. For example, a claim that services were inadequate or that goods were defective. *Liquidated* generally means fixed in amount by the parties or the court. In determining whether an obligation is liquidated, the concept of "account stated" may be helpful. Under this concept, when one party submits a computation to the other party, if the recipient does not question it during a reasonable period of time, the obligation will become liquidated in that amount.

§ 11.5   Unliquidated or disputed obligations.

If an obligation is unliquidated or disputed, the obligor's promise to pay a liquidated amount or to surrender a defense is consideration for the obligee's promise to settle for less than the amount claimed. For example:

1. Attorney *A* performed work for *B* with no discussion of the amount of the fee. *A* billed *B* $1,000. *B* claimed that the work was not worth that much. *B* offered to pay $800 and *A* accepted the offer.

2. *A* shipped goods to *B* in exchange for *B*'s promise to pay $1,000 to *A*. *B* claimed some of the goods were defective and offered to pay $800. *A* accepted the offer.

3. *A* shipped goods to *B* in exchange for *B*'s promise to pay $1,000 to *A*. *B* claimed that part of the shipment worth $800 was satisfactory but that

the other portion was worthless. *B* offered to pay $800 and *A* accepted the offer.

In Example 1, *A* and *B* did not agree on the amount of *B*'s obligation, making it unliquidated. *B*'s offer to pay $800 liquidates the debt in exchange for *A*'s agreement to discharge the obligation. The settlement agreement is supported by consideration. In Example 2, *B* has a good faith defense to his obligation, making it disputed. *B*'s offer to pay $800 surrenders his defense in exchange for *A*'s agreement to discharge the obligation. The settlement agreement is supported by consideration. Example 3 is tricky. *B* admits the $800 portion of the obligation but disputes the $200 portion. *A* could argue that the $800 portion is undisputed; by accepting $800 for an undisputed debt, *A* received no consideration for the discharge of the balance. Authority is split on whether this settlement agreement is supported by consideration. It might be prudent for *B* to offer *A* $801. The additional $1 would be consideration for *A*'s promise to discharge the disputed $200 obligation.

§ 11.6 Accord and satisfaction contrasted with substituted contract.

A fertile source of difficulty is the failure of the parties to a settlement agreement to distinguish between an *accord and satisfaction* and a *substituted contract*. In an accord and satisfaction, the obligee agrees to accept the *performance* of a promise in exchange for discharge of the obligation. The agreement is the accord. The performance is the satisfaction. The obligor's failure to perform is a breach of the accord. On breach, the obligee may sue on the accord or on the original obligation, which is revived by the breach.

In a substituted contract, the obligee agrees to accept the *promise* itself in exchange for discharge. Because the duty under the original agreement has been discharged, it may not be revived if the obligor does not perform as promised. The obligee's only recourse is to sue under the new, substituted contract. Whether the parties meant to have an accord and satisfaction or a substituted contract is a question of intent. For example:

1. *A* owes *B* $1,000 for goods sold and delivered. *A* offers, "I admit I owe you the money. Will you accept my promise to deliver 5 widgets on October 1 instead of my promise to pay the money?" *B* accepts. *A* does not deliver the widgets. *B* claims that she may revive the $1,000 debt but *A* claims that *B*'s only recourse is to sue for breach of the widget contract.

2. *A* owes *B* $1,000 for goods sold and delivered. *A* offers, "Some of those goods were defective. Will you accept the delivery of 5 widgets on October 1 in exchange for the discharge of the debt?" *B* accepts. *A* does not deliver the widgets. *B* claims that he may revive the $1,000 debt but *A* claims that *B*'s only recourse is to sue for breach of the widget contract.

3. *A* owes *B* $1,000 for goods sold and delivered. *A* offers, "Some of those goods were defective. I promise to deliver 5 widgets on October 1 in

exchange for the discharge of the debt." *B* accepts. *A* does not deliver the widgets. *B* claims that he may revive the $1,000 debt but *A* claims that *B*'s only recourse is to sue for breach of the widget contract.

Example 1 is probably a substituted contract. *B* has accepted one promise in place of another. Because *A*'s duty under the original contract has been discharged, *B*'s only recourse is to sue under the new contract. Example 2 is probably an accord. *B* has accepted an agreement in which a performance, delivery of the widgets, will discharge the debt. Because *A* has breached the accord, *B* may sue for damages either for breach of the original contract or for breach of the accord. Example 3 is more difficult. The language of the new agreement is "I promise to deliver." Because the circumstances indicate a dispute that performance of the new agreement was intended to resolve, the agreement is probably an accord.

§ 11.7 Liquidated and undisputed obligations.

It is more difficult for the parties to settle an obligation that is liquidated and undisputed. There is no consideration for the obligee's agreement to accept less than the full amount of the obligation; for example, creditor's agreement to accept $800 to discharge an admitted $1,000 debt. The parties may still use an additional or different performance to circumvent the pre-existing duty rule. However, they may not use liquidation of the amount or the surrender of a defense. A number of states permit discharge of a liquidated and undisputed obligation without consideration, either by case law or by statute. For example, California Civil Code § 1524 provides:

> Part performance of an obligation, either before or after a breach thereof, when expressly accepted by the creditor in writing, in satisfaction, or rendered in pursuance of an agreement in writing for that purpose, though without any new consideration, extinguishes the obligation.

This provision, like many other statutes, makes a writing an exception to consideration. *See* § 2.2. In complying with such a statute, it is important that the drafter keep in mind the common law requirement that an agreement must be knowingly made. That is, the statute dispenses with the consideration requirement. It does not dispense with the other aspects of contract formation, including offer and acceptance. For example, many jurisdictions have held that a notation on a check is not a sufficient offer, nor is the indorsement of a check a sufficient acceptance.

§ 11.8 Drafting a conditional check.

Debtors intending to enter into a settlement agreement often tender a "conditional check," stating that the creditor's acceptance of the check in full payment of the obligation is a condition of cashing it. For example, a debtor may write on the back of a check:

> Accepted in full settlement of my obligation.

As with any contract, principles of offer, acceptance, and consideration apply. An offer has to be clearly communicated. Most courts have held that the mere indorsement on the back of the check is not enough to constitute an offer without a separate communication. On the other hand, if the creditor, knowing of the offer to enter into an accord, strikes out the restriction and cashes the check, this act does not change the offer. The creditor may accept the offer or reject it, but may not change it and accept the changed offer. A creditor who puts the check in a drawer to think about the offer may accept it by inaction.

A creditor who knows of the offer will then accept it by indorsing the check under the debtor's statement:

> Accepted in full settlement of my obligation.
>   s/ John Creditor

Recall, however, that most jurisdictions require consideration to support a settlement. If the debt is unliquidated or disputed, there is consideration for the settlement. If the debt is liquidated and undisputed, there is no consideration. In those jurisdictions that accept the creditor's signed writing as a consideration substitute, cases have held that the indorsement alone does not satisfy the statutory requirement.

Sometimes a creditor will add a notation to the check, indicating that the creditor intends to reserve the right to seek the balance. For example, Debtor D owes Creditor C $1,000. D communicates a good faith dispute to C and sends C a check for $800. On the back of the check, D has written:

> Accepted in full settlement of my $1,000 obligation to you.

Creditor C adds:

> Accepted without prejudice.
>   s/ Creditor

Jurisdictions were divided as to whether a creditor's use of this language effectively prevented the discharge of an obligation by accord and satisfaction under U.C.C. § 1-207, which provided:

> A party who, with explicit reservation of rights, performs or promises performance or assents to performance in a manner demanded or offered by the other party does not thereby prejudice the rights reserved. Such words as "without prejudice," "under protest" or the like are sufficient.

The drafters of the U.C.C. put an end to this debate by placing the prior language in subsection (1) and adding a subsection (2) that provides:

Subsection (1) does not apply to an accord and satisfaction.

§ 11.9   Provisions barring modification and waiver.

Drafters seeking certainty and finality occasionally insert in the contract a provision stating that the agreement may not be modified except by a writing signed by the parties. Section 2-209(2) of the U.C.C. provides:

> A signed agreement which excludes modification or rescission except by a signed writing cannot be otherwise modified or rescinded, but except as between merchants such a requirement on a form supplied by the merchant must be separately signed by the other party.

A "no oral modification" clause might look like this:

All Modifications to be in Writing. This contract may be modified or rescinded only by a writing signed by both of the parties.

These provisions are sometimes enforced in contracts between merchants and in some jurisdictions are supplied by statute. Often, however, a court finds a way around the provision, largely through the use of the principle of waiver. For example, a contractor at a construction site orally agrees to changes in the specifications proposed by the owner. When the contractor seeks payment for the increased cost, the owner claims that because the modification was not in writing, the contract price governs. Waiver is the knowing surrender of a right. Here, the owner had the right to claim that the clause barred the modification, but a court could find a waiver when the owner allowed the contractor to act in reliance on the modification. This principle is codified in U.C.C. § 2-209(4), which provides:

> Although an attempt at modification or rescission does not satisfy the requirements of subsection (2) or (3) it can operate as a waiver.

The drafter may try to draft around the court's interference with a provision barring waiver. For example, an installment payment contract provides for payment on the first of the month. Debtor pays the first installment on the 8th of the month. Creditor takes no action. Debtor pays the second installment on the 8th of the month. Creditor claims breach. Debtor claims that Creditor waived its rights when it did not act on the first breach. Creditor would attempt to invoke the "non-waiver" clause in its defense. These are examples of a "non-waiver" clause:

> *Waiver.* No claim or right arising out of a breach of this agreement is discharged in whole or in part by a waiver or renunciation of the claim or right unless the waiver or renunciation is supported by consideration and is in writing signed by the aggrieved party.

or

> *Waiver.* Waiver by Seller of a breach by Buyer of any provision of this contract is not a waiver of future compliance, and that provision, as well as other provisions of this contract, remain in full force and effect.

As with the "no oral modification" clause, courts often hold that a "non-waiver" clause has itself been waived when the non-breaching party fails to insist upon performance of the contract as written. These provisions conflict with the autonomy of contracting parties. Parties to a present agreement cannot agree to surrender their power to make future agreements between themselves. Corbin's observation about statutes that prohibit oral modification may apply equally to contractual provisions:

> Like the statute of frauds, these statutes evidence the "yearning for certainty and repose", although as Holmes said "certainty is an illusion and repose is not the destiny of man." They operate against the innocent and the unwary as well as against those who might cheat and defraud; and they run counter increasingly to the practices of ordinary men in the making, modifying, and performing of their agreements. Men increasingly rely upon the spoken word, given in person or by telephone; and it is the function of the courts to do justice in such cases. It no longer serves for the court to throw a plaintiff out of court saying, "It was your folly not to get his signature."

The drafter using these provisions should be aware that they may not be enforceable.

§ 11.10 Exercises.

1. Research. Research the law in your jurisdiction. Does it permit parties to discharge a liquidated and undisputed obligation? Note carefully any drafting requirements. Does it permit a creditor to use § 1-207 to prevent formation of an accord and satisfaction?

2. The unpaid bill. A doctor treats a patient over a period of time with no mention of fees. On January 1, 2003, the doctor sends a bill for $1,000. At the bottom of the bill is this language: "Interest at the rate of 10% per year payable on all accounts paid more than 30 days late." Each month the doctor sends a copy of the bill to the patient. The patient does not respond. On February 1, 2004, the doctor turns the account over to you for collection. How much can you collect?

3. Settling a case. You represent P in a $5,000 personal injury claim against D. The day before trial, you settle the case for D's promise to pay $3,000, $1,500 payable in 10 days and $1,500 30 days after that. You draw up a stipulation and order of dismissal and file it with the court. Ten days later, D does not pay. What is your remedy?

Any difference if the suit were on a $5,000 debt?

How would you draft the stipulation to avoid this problem?

4. The disputed bill. You agree that I will handle your case at an hourly rate of $100. Two weeks later, I tell you the bill is now $1,000. You say you think the bill is too high. I ask you what you will pay, and you say $600. I send you a bill for $600 "for services rendered," and you don't pay it. What can I sue you for?

Any difference if we had originally agreed on a flat fee of $1,000?

How would you draft the bill to avoid this problem?

5. The conditional check. Megawatt Power Co. sends you a bill for $100. You send them a check for $60 with "accepted as payment in full" indorsed on the back. Megawatt Power cashes the check, then bills you for $40. Do you have to pay the $40?

What if you had first sent a letter explaining to Megawatt Power that you thought your electric meter was defective?

What if Megawatt Power crossed your indorsement off the check before cashing it?

What if Megawatt Power wrote "accepted without prejudice" under your indorsement?

Chapter 12

WARRANTIES

§ 12.1 Introduction.

The purpose of warranty law is "to determine what it is that the seller has in essence agreed to sell." Official Comment 4 to U.C.C. § 2-313. Recall that U.C.C. warranty law applies only to "transactions in goods." U.C.C. § 2-102. See § 2-105(1) for the definition of *goods*. While the U.C.C. applies to all transactions in goods, and not just those between merchants, on a few occasions the U.C.C. specifies that a provision is applicable only to merchants. This distinction between merchants and non-merchants arises in warranty law. See § 2-104(1) for the definition of *merchant*. The U.C.C. provides for a number of warranties. We are particularly concerned with three types:

1. Express warranty (U.C.C. § 2-313).

2. Implied warranty of merchantability (U.C.C. § 2-314).

3. Implied warranty of fitness for a particular purpose (U.C.C. § 2-315).

§ 12.2 Express warranty — § 2-313.

Express warranties are easy to make. They require no magic words and no intention on the part of the seller to make them. According to § 2-313(1)(a):

> Any affirmation of fact or promise made by the seller to the buyer which relates to the goods and becomes part of the basis of the bargain creates an express warranty that the goods shall conform to the affirmation or promise.

Express warranties may arise from:

a. Oral representations;

b. Written representations;

c. Description of goods;

d. Any sample or model shown;

e. Plans or blueprints;

f. Technical specifications;

g. Reference to a market or official standard;

h. Quality of goods sent to the buyer in the past; or

i. Brochures and advertisements.

Warranties are affirmations of fact or promises, not opinions. A great deal of litigation has ensued over whether the statements of a salesperson are statements of facts or merely "puffing." For example, Sally is selling her car to Barney. Sally makes the following statements:

---

1. This car is a real bargain.

---

2. This car gets great gas mileage.

---

3. This car gets at least 25 miles to the gallon around town.

---

4. LIMITED WARRANTY. Seller warrants these goods to be free from defects in material and workmanship for a period of one year from date of purchase provided that installation is performed as specified in instructions supplied by seller and included with this product.

Example 1 is probably sales "puffing," not an affirmation of fact. Example 2 is probably an opinion, not an affirmation of fact. Example 3 is probably an express warranty created by oral representation. The same unqualified statement contained in a window sticker or sales brochure, if part of the bargain, has the same effect. Example 4 is a more formal warranty statement.

Another issue that frequently arises is whether the express warranty is part of the "basis of the bargain." Representations that are made during negotiations but are not included in the written contract may be excluded because of the parol evidence rule. *See* Chapter 6, Parol Evidence. Other warranties may be excluded because they were not relied upon. Others may be excluded because they were not made at a time which is deemed to constitute the bargain. Most of these problems can be avoided by the careful drafter. Ask your client if promises or representations were made. Make sure those promises or representations are included in a document that represents the parties' final agreement.

§ 12.3 Implied warranty of merchantability — § 2-314.

Section 2-314(1) provides in part:

> Unless excluded or modified (Section 2-316), a warranty that the goods shall be merchantable is implied in a contract for their sale if the seller is a merchant with respect to goods of that kind.

Note that this warranty is implied by law only if the seller is a *merchant*. The warranty provides that the goods are "merchantable" as defined in § 2-314(2). The most common meaning of *merchantable* is found in § 2-314(2)(c): "Goods to be merchantable must be at least such as . . . are fit for the ordinary purposes for which such goods are used." For example:

1. Fred buys a can of "XYZ weed killer." In fact, the product does an excellent job of killing weeds but is also harmful to persons and animals coming in contact with it.

2. Charles purchases pork chops from Mario's Meat Market. Charles does not thoroughly cook the pork and contracts trichinosis.

3. Sally sells her used car to Barney. The car immediately fails to function.

In Example 1, XYZ impliedly warrants that the product is fit for killing weeds. The product is not merchantable due to its unreasonable propensity for harm. In Example 2, Mario impliedly warrants that the pork is fit for the ordinary purposes for which it is used. Mario did not breach the warranty, for pork is commonly sold in a condition that requires the consumer to cook it before eating. In Example 3, if she is not a merchant, Sally has not given an implied warranty of merchantability. If she is a merchant, Sally has warranted that the car is fit for the ordinary purposes for which a car is used. While courts generally find that the implied warranty applies to used goods, the seller's obligation varies with the condition of the goods. That is, it must be fit only for the purposes of a car with substantial mileage on it.

§ 12.4   Implied warranty of fitness for a particular purpose — § 2-315.

Section 2-315 provides:

> Where the seller at the time of contracting has reason to know any particular purpose for which the goods are required and that the buyer is relying on the seller's skill or judgment to select or furnish suitable goods, there is unless excluded or modified under the next section an implied warranty that the goods shall be fit for such purpose.

This warranty is implied by law only when the seller has reason to know any particular purpose for which the buyer requires the goods and the buyer relies upon the seller's skill or judgment in selecting the goods. It is given by sellers who are not merchants as well as by merchant sellers. For example:

1. A customer in a shoe store expresses a need for a good mountain climbing shoe. The salesperson recommends a particular shoe.

2. Brenda tells her friend Sarah that she needs word processing software that creates footnotes. Sarah says, "I just bought new software, so I'll sell you my old software."

In Example 1, in addition to the warranty of merchantability that the shoes will be fit for ordinary purposes, the seller has made a warranty that the shoes are fit for the particular purpose of mountain climbing. In Example 2, assuming the sale of software is a transaction in goods, Sarah has given an implied warranty that the software is fit for the particular purpose of creating footnotes. She gives this warranty even though she is not a merchant. If the software does an excellent job but does not have footnote capability, it is merchantable but it is not fit for the buyer's particular purpose.

§ 12.5 Disclaimer of warranties.

As an old saying goes, "The bold print giveth and the fine print taketh away." It could also be said that the law giveth and freedom of contract taketh away. For just as warranties are easily made and impliedly given by the Code, the Code also provides the means to disclaim or limit them.

Before turning to the means by which a drafter can accomplish this purpose under the Code, we should first consider other means of limiting liability. A warranty is essentially a promise. The drafter should include a merger clause in an agreement to make clear that there are no promises other than those contained in the writing. *See* § 6.4. The drafter should also include a "no oral modification" clause to make clear that the written agreement has not been modified. *See* § 11.9. To enhance limitations of liability that might seem contrary to public policy, the drafter might include recitals to state the purpose of the limitations. *See* § 15.4.4. Taking advantage of the freedom given by U.C.C. § 1-102(3), the drafter might make claims harder to assert by specifying notice requirements or by reducing the statute of limitations to the extent permitted. The drafter might also include an indemnity provision, making the other party liable for claims by third parties.

In examining the disclaimer of warranties under the Code, we will look at:

1. Disclaimer of express warranties — § 2-316(1).

2. Disclaimer of implied warranties — § 2-316(2) and (3).

3. The "conspicuousness" requirement — § 1-210(10).

§ 12.5.1 Disclaimer of express warranties — § 2-316(1).

Express warranties may be disclaimed orally with a statement such as "There are no express warranties" or with a written statement such as this:

> *Disclaimer of Express Warranties.* Seller warrants that the goods are as described in this agreement, but no other express warranty is made in respect to the goods. If any model or sample was shown Buyer, such model or sample was used merely to illustrate the general type and quality of the goods and not to represent that the goods would necessarily be of that type or nature.

Express warranties that are part of the basis of the bargain are hard to disclaim, however. According to U.C.C. § 2-316(1):

> Words or conduct relevant to the creation of an express warranty and words or conduct tending to negate or limit warranty shall be construed wherever reasonable as consistent with each other; but subject to the provisions of this Article on parol or extrinsic evidence (§ 2-202) negation or limitation is inoperative to the extent that such construction is unreasonable.

Under this provision, language creating a warranty and language disclaiming a warranty should be construed as consistent; if that is not possible, the warranty is made. For example, a seller says, "This car will get 25 miles per gallon around town. I disclaim all express warranties." The warranty has been both made and disclaimed. It is not possible to construe these statements as consistent with each other. Therefore, the warranty is given effect. This protects the buyer.

If, however, an express warranty is made during negotiations and the document embodying the final agreement of the parties disclaims all express warranties, then the disclaimer is probably effective because of the parol evidence rule, U.C.C. § 2-202. Most courts have interpreted the statutory language "basis of the bargain" in § 2-313(1)(a) in terms of time. If the statement was made during negotiations, but an integrated agreement did not contain the statement, it is not part of the bargain. This protects the seller against the buyer's fraudulent claims and against the statements of its own overzealous salespersons. For example:

1. The buyer of an automobile signs a contract which states:

> (a)   there are no express warranties;
>
> (b)   there are no terms other than those included in the contract; and
>
> (c)   there is a 30-day warranty on the clutch.

2. The buyer of an automobile signs a contract containing a merger clause which states that the writing constitutes the final expression of the parties. The agreement contains a disclaimer of "all warranties, express or implied." The buyer claims that the seller gave an oral warranty against latent mechanical defects.

3. The buyer of an automobile signs a contract that states:

> The seller's salesmen may have made oral statements about the merchandise described in this contract. Such statements do not constitute warranties, are not relied on by the buyer, and are not part of the contract for sale. The entire contract is embodied in this writing. This writing constitutes the final expression of the parties' agreement, and it is a complete and exclusive statement of the terms of that agreement.

The buyer claims that a salesman gave an oral warranty against latent mechanical defects.

In Example 1, the conflict between statements (a) and (c) is resolved by giving effect to the express warranty on the clutch. Despite the language of (b), parol evidence may be admitted to interpret the warranty. In Examples 2 and 3, the disclaimer is probably effective, with Example 3 providing protection for the seller in wider circumstances.

§ 12.5.2 Disclaimer of implied warranties.

Implied warranties can be disclaimed in a number of ways, including:

- Use of a specific disclaimer — § 2-316(2).
- Use of a general disclaimer — § 2-316(3)(a).
- When the seller requires the buyer to examine the product for defects, the seller effectively disclaims warranty for those defects which the buyer should have discovered — § 2-316(3)(b).
- By course of dealing, course of performance, or usage of trade — § 2-316(3)(c).

The disclaimers created under §§ 2-316(3)(b) and (c) do not raise drafting issues, except that the parties may by their agreement vary the provisions of the Code. *See* § 1-102(3). We will look more closely at the disclaimers that raise drafting issues. Note that there may be state variations on the Code provisions. A number of states prohibit the disclaimer of implied warranties in the sale of consumer goods. In that event, it might be a breach of a Consumer Protection Act to disclaim the warranties. Also, a number of states exclude implied warranties in the sale of livestock. In that event, the attorney for the buyer should draft an express warranty affirming that the livestock is free of disease.

a. Use of a specific disclaimer — § 2-316(2).

Section 2-316(2) provides:

> Subject to subsection (3), to exclude or modify the implied warranty of merchantability or any part of it the language must mention merchantability and in case of a writing must be conspicuous, and to exclude or modify any implied warranty of fitness the exclusion must be by a

writing and conspicuous. Language to exclude all implied warranties of fitness is sufficient if it states, for example, that "There are no warranties which extend beyond the description on the face hereof."

According to the statute, to effectively disclaim the implied warranty of merchantability, the disclaimer must mention merchantability by name and, if written, the disclaimer must be conspicuous. For example:

1. Seller orally states, "I am not giving you any warranty with this purchase."

2. Seller orally states, "I am not giving you a warranty of merchantability with this purchase."

3. Seller's form states:

WARRANTY. Seller warrants that the products sold by it will, when delivered, or when installed, if this contract provides for installation by Seller, be free of defects in workmanship or material. Should any failure to conform to this warranty become apparent during a period of one (1) year after date of installation, and not more than two (2) years after date of delivery, Seller shall, upon prompt, written notice and compliance by the customer with such instructions as it shall give with respect to the return of defective products or parts, correct such non-conformity by repair or replacement, F.O.B. factory, of the defective part or parts. Correction in the manner provided above shall constitute a fulfillment of all liabilities of Seller with respect to the quality of the products. The foregoing warranty is exclusive and in lieu of all other warranties of quality, whether written, oral or implied (including any warranty of merchantability).

---

4. Same as Example 3 except the last sentence states, "THE FOREGO-ING WARRANTY IS EXCLUSIVE AND IN LIEU OF ALL OTHER WARRANTIES OF QUALITY, WHETHER WRITTEN, ORAL OR IM-PLIED (INCLUDING ANY WARRANTY OF MERCHANTABILITY)."

In Example 1, the disclaimer is not effective because it does not mention merchantability by name. In Example 2, the disclaimer is effective. In Example 3, the disclaimer is not effective, because the disclaimer of the warranty is not conspicuous. This defect is cured in Example 4.

The statute provides that to effectively disclaim the implied warranty of fitness for a particular purpose, the disclaimer must be in writing and conspicuous. Note, however, that the term "fitness for a particular purpose" need not be used in the disclaimer. For example:

1. Same as Example 4 above.

2. Seller orally states, "I am not giving you a warranty of fitness for a particular purpose with this purchase."

In Example 1, the disclaimer is effective even though the warranty does not mention "fitness for a particular purpose" by name. In Example 2, the disclaimer is not effective because it is not in writing.

b. Use of a general disclaimer — § 2-316(3)(a).

Section 2-316(3)(a) provides:

Notwithstanding subsection (2):

(a) unless the circumstances indicate otherwise, all implied warranties are excluded by expressions like "as is", "with all faults" or other language which in common understanding calls the buyer's attention to the exclusion of warranties and makes plain that there is no implied warranty;

On the surface, use of this statutory provision makes it easy for a seller to disclaim implied warranties. The seller may use the phrases "as is," "with all faults," "as is, where is," or similar language. However, the general disclaimer is not effective if "the circumstances indicate otherwise." A court might find such circumstances in a consumer transaction in which the purchaser does not understand the meaning of the term or when the language is not conspicuous. Because of this danger, the drafter might wish to use the more complex disclaimer in § 2-316(2). For example:

1. A sales receipt states, "All goods sold as is."

2. The Federal Trade Commission Used Motor Vehicle Trade Regulation Rule requires a window sticker in which the seller of a used vehicle must inform the buyer whether the car is purchased with or without a warranty. Under the box marked AS IS-NO WARRANTY, the sticker states, "YOU WILL PAY ALL COSTS FOR ANY REPAIRS. The dealer assumes no responsibility for any repairs regardless of any oral statements about the vehicle."

The disclaimer in Example 1 is probably effective. Note, however, whether a consumer purchaser understood it and whether it was conspicuous. The FTC Rule in Example 2 is designed to prevent any dispute about whether the purchaser saw the disclaimer and understood its meaning.

§ 12.5.3 The "conspicuousness" requirement.

Extensive litigation has centered around the issue of conspicuousness. How is the § 2-316(2) requirement that a disclaimer of warranty be conspicuous satisfied? Should a requirement of conspicuousness be read into § 2-316(3)(a), the "as is" disclaimer? The intent of § 2-316 is "to protect a buyer from unexpected and unbargained language of disclaimer." Official Comment 1 to U.C.C. § 2-316. "Conspicuous" is defined in § 1-201(10) as follows:

"Conspicuous": A term or clause is conspicuous when it is so written that a reasonable person against whom it is to operate ought to have noticed it. A printed heading in capitals (as: NON-NEGOTIABLE BILL

OF LADING) is conspicuous. Language in the body of a form is "conspicuous" if it is in larger or other contrasting type or color. But in a telegram any stated term is "conspicuous". Whether a term or clause is "conspicuous" or not is for decision by the court.

For example:

---

1. EXCLUSIONS OF WARRANTIES: The parties agree that the implied warranties of MERCHANTABILITY and fitness for a particular purpose and all other warranties, express or implied, are EXCLUDED from this transaction and shall not apply to the goods sold.

---

2. IMPLIED WARRANTIES: The parties agree that the implied warranties of MERCHANTABILITY and fitness for a particular purpose and all other warranties, express or implied, are EXCLUDED from this transaction and shall not apply to the goods sold.

---

3. *The parties agree that the implied warranties of merchantability and fitness for a particular purpose and all other warranties, express or implied, are excluded from this transaction and shall not apply to the goods sold.*

The disclaimer in Example 1 satisfies the statutory definition that a printed heading in capitals is conspicuous. Perhaps the provision would be more conspicuous if capitalized, bold faced, and printed in a contrasting color. Interestingly, studies show that provisions written all in capitals are harder to read. In Example 2, the section caption, although conspicuous, may be misleading, for it seems to give warranties rather than exclude them. The conspicuousness test may not be met by an italicized disclaimer such as Example 3. One court stated, "it appears to be a classic case of attempting barely to comply with the letter of the law while circumventing its spirit. [The disclaimer] is not bolder, larger or different color type. It is not . . . indented, underscored or highlighted in any manner. It is not preceded by a distinctive legend or statement signifying the importance of that particular passage." The court's language suggests to the drafter ways to make a disclaimer conspicuous.

§ 12.6   Conflicts among warranties — § 2-317.

Conflicts when an express warranty is given and disclaimed are discussed in § 12.5.1. If express and implied warranties conflict, the intention of the parties governs. The statute establishes rules for determining that intention. One rule states that "express warranties displace inconsistent implied warranties." For example:

> A used car warranty states in full, "This vehicle is warranted to be free of defects for 2,000 miles or 2 months, whichever occurs first." A defect manifests itself at 2,500 miles.

The purchaser may claim that although the express warranty has expired, the seller did not effectively disclaim the implied warranty of merchantability. Most courts have held that the express warranty is not inconsistent with the implied warranty and therefore does not displace it. The result would be the same if the seller attempted a disclaimer but the disclaimer was not effective.

§ 12.7 Limitation of remedies — § 2-719.

Very often, a seller does not disclaim all warranties. Instead, the seller gives a warranty but limits the buyer's remedies under the warranty. In the absence of limitation, the remedies are those found in § 2-714(2) and (3):

> (2) The measure of damages for breach of warranty is the difference at the time and place of acceptance between the value of the goods accepted and the value they would have had if they had been as warranted, unless special circumstances show proximate damages of a different amount.
>
> (3) In a proper case any incidental and consequential damages under the next section may also be recovered.

Section 2-719 places a number of restrictions on the seller who limits remedies. The section provides:

> (1) Subject to the provisions of subsections (2) and (3) of this section and of the preceding section on liquidation and limitation of damages,
>
>> (a) the agreement may provide for remedies in addition to or in substitution for those provided in this Article and may limit or alter the measure of damages recoverable under this Article, as by limiting the buyer's remedies to return of the goods and repayment of the price or to repair and replacement of nonconforming goods or parts; and
>>
>> (b) resort to a remedy as provided is optional unless the remedy is expressly agreed to be exclusive, in which case it is the sole remedy.
>
> (2) Where circumstances cause an exclusive or limited remedy to fail of its essential purpose, remedy may be had as provided in this code.
>
> (3) Consequential damages may be limited or excluded unless the limitation or exclusion is unconscionable. Limitation of consequential damages for injury to the person in the case of consumer goods is prima facie unconscionable but limitation of damages where the loss is commercial is not.

The remedy is optional unless it is expressly agreed to be exclusive. If the remedy fails of its essential purpose, the buyer has available the other remedies provided in the U.C.C. Consequential damages may be limited or excluded unless unconscionable. In the case of consumer goods, limitation of consequential damages for personal injury is unconscionable. For example:

---

1. *Consequential Damages.* In the event of a breach or repudiation of this contract by Seller, Buyer shall not be entitled to any consequential damages in excess of $1,000. This limitation shall not apply, however, to damages for injury to the person if the goods are consumer goods.

---

2. Manufacturer agrees to repair or replace any defective part during the first 12 months after purchase.

The disclaimer in Example 1 is probably effective. A seller is free to limit consequential damages except in the case of consumer goods. Example 2 is a classic "repair or replace" warranty. The purchaser who is disappointed because of frequent unsuccessful repair attempts may claim under § 2-719(2) that the remedy fails of its essential purpose, which is to give the purchaser a defect-free product. The purchaser may then seek another remedy under the Code, such as revocation of acceptance. The failure of "repair or replace" automobile warranties to satisfy the purchasers of defective automobiles led many states to enact so-called "Lemon Laws."

§ 12.8   The Magnuson-Moss Warranty Act.

The Magnuson-Moss Warranty — Federal Trade Commission Improvement Act (Magnuson-Moss) was designed to protect consumers from deceptive warranty practices. It supplements U.C.C. warranty law. As stated in the report of a House committee:

> The paper with the filigree border bearing the bold caption "Warranty" or "Guarantee" was often of no greater worth than the paper it was printed on. Indeed, in many cases where a warranty or guarantee was ostensibly given the old saying applied: "The bold print giveth and the fine print taketh away." For the paper operated to take away from the consumer the implied warranties of merchantability and fitness arising by operation of law leaving little in its stead.

Magnuson-Moss gives consumers a federal cause of action for breach of warranty, including the possibility of recovering costs and attorneys' fees for breach of warranty. There are, however, a number of differences between U.C.C. warranty law and Magnuson-Moss. Magnuson-Moss applies only to warrantors of consumer products. Magnuson-Moss regulates only written warranties. "Written warranty" is a term of art under Magnuson-Moss, which does not employ the U.C.C. definition of warranty. Magnuson-Moss defines *written warranty* as:

(A) any written affirmation of fact or written promise made in connection with the sale of a consumer product by a supplier to a buyer which relates to the nature of the material or workmanship and affirms or promises that such material or workmanship is defect free or will meet a specified level of performance over a specified period of time, or

(B) any undertaking in writing in connection with the sale by a supplier of a consumer product to refund, repair, replace, or take other remedial action with respect to such product in the event that such product fails to meet the specifications set forth in the undertaking, which written affirmation, promise, or undertaking becomes part of the basis of the bargain between a supplier and a buyer for purposes other than resale of such product.

Because of the difference in definition, a warranty for purposes of the U.C.C. may not be a warranty for purposes of Magnuson-Moss. For example:

1. A sweater contains a label that states, "100% Cotton."

2. A used car dealer tells a consumer: "If anything goes wrong with the car in the next 30 days, we will fix it."

3. A used car dealer writes on a bill of sale to a consumer: "We will repair defects for 30 days on a 50-50 cost basis."

4. A supplier of a machine tool writes on a statement to a manufacturer: "We will repair any defects that show up in the next 30 days."

5. IBM buys a microwave oven that has a one-year warranty for the employee cafeteria.

Example 1 is a U.C.C. warranty but not a Magnuson-Moss warranty, for it does not pass the tests for a "written warranty" under the Act. Example 2 is a U.C.C. warranty but not a Magnuson-Moss warranty, for it is not written. Example 3 is a U.C.C. and a Magnuson-Moss warranty, for it promises that the car will meet a specified level of performance (no defects) over a specified period of time (30 days). Example 4 is a U.C.C. warranty but not a Magnuson-Moss warranty, for the transaction does not involve a consumer product. Example 5 is a Magnuson-Moss warranty; although IBM is not a consumer, the microwave is a consumer product.

Magnuson-Moss makes few substantive changes in warranty law. It does not require a seller to give any warranty, but a seller who does give a written warranty must make certain disclosures. The seller must designate the warranty as either "full" or "limited." A warrantor who gives a full warranty may not disclaim or limit the duration of implied warranties. A warrantor who gives a limited warranty may not disclaim the implied warranties, but may limit them to the duration of a written warranty of reasonable duration. For example:

1. A written statement to a consumer: "These goods are sold 'as is.' There are no warranties, express or implied."

2. A written statement to a consumer: "Limited Warranty. Seller expressly warrants that these goods will retain their color for 30 days. This warranty is in lieu of all other warranties, express or implied. THERE IS NO IMPLIED WARRANTY OF MERCHANTABILITY OR FITNESS FOR A PARTICULAR PURPOSE."

3. The following:

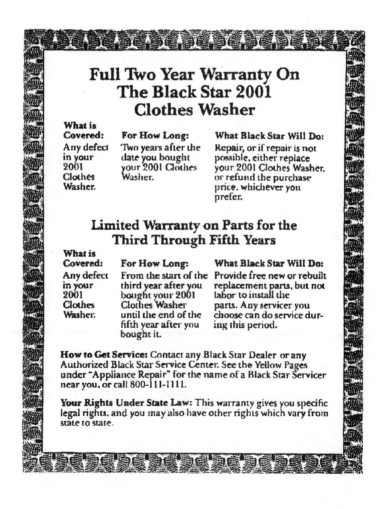

Full Two Year Warranty On The Black Star 2001 Clothes Washer

What is Covered:	For How Long:	What Black Star Will Do:
Any defect in your 2001 Clothes Washer.	Two years after the date you bought your 2001 Clothes Washer.	Repair, or if repair is not possible, either replace your 2001 Clothes Washer. or refund the purchase price. whichever you prefer.

Limited Warranty on Parts for the Third Through Fifth Years

What is Covered:	For How Long:	What Black Star Will Do:
Any defect in your 2001 Clothes Washer.	From the start of the third year after you bought your 2001 Clothes Washer until the end of the fifth year after you bought it.	Provide free new or rebuilt replacement parts, but not labor to install the parts. Any servicer you choose can do service during this period.

How to Get Service: Contact any Black Star Dealer or any Authorized Black Star Service Center. See the Yellow Pages under "Appliance Repair" for the name of a Black Star Servicer near you, or call 800-111-1111.

Your Rights Under State Law: This warranty gives you specific legal rights, and you may also have other rights which vary from state to state.

Example 1 is permissible under Magnuson-Moss, while Example 2 is not. The warrantor may limit the implied warranties but may not disclaim them. Example 3 demonstrates both a full and a limited warranty under Magnuson-Moss.

§ 12.9 Non-U.C.C. "warranties."

The U.C.C. governs only transactions in goods. In service transactions, attorneys often speak loosely of an implied warranty, defining the standard as one of "workmanlike conduct" or "workmanlike performance." These are actually negligence standards. Because warranty is a strict liability standard, a plaintiff making a U.C.C. warranty claim would merely have to show that there was a warranty and that the goods did not conform to that warranty. The plaintiff making a negligence claim would also have to show that the defendant failed to exercise due care. A case requiring a showing of negligence will doubtless be more difficult to prove than one requiring a showing of breach of warranty.

The drafter of a contract for services, therefore, should create the "warranties" by express promise. The particular specifications should be spelled out in detail so that the claim of defective performance can be brought as a breach of contract claim rather than as a negligence claim. A remedy for breach might also be included in the contract.

Many states have developed a common law "warranty of habitability" or "warranty of workmanlike skill and materials" in the sale of a new home. If this warranty is analogous to the U.C.C. warranty, then presumably it may be limited or disclaimed; if it derives from tort, presumably it may not be disclaimed. The drafter could attempt to limit or disclaim it, but should advise the client that if the applicable standard is tort, the contractual limitation will probably be ineffective.

§ 12.10 Exercises.

1. Research. Find out whether your jurisdiction has made changes in the uniform version of the warranties. What effect do these changes have on drafters?

2. Creation of warranties. In the following cases, what warranties did the seller give?

a. A drugstore employee told a customer that her own hair came out "very nice" and "very natural" following treatment with a hair dye, and that buyer would get very fine results from the product.

b. An auto dealer's sign stated "USED CARS 1 YEAR WARRANTY," but the sales contract contained no warranty terms.

c. The cover of an instruction booklet for a golf-training device contained the statement: "COMPLETELY SAFE BALL WILL NOT HIT PLAYER."

d. A sales brochure contained the following information regarding a printing press:

i. Paper sizes from 8″ × 10″ to 19″ × 25¼″;

ii. Thickness from 9 lb. onionskin to 6 ply card stock;

iii. Speeds to 8,500 impressions per hour;

iv. Superior inking system and precise inking controls.

e. A salesman stated that a trailer was supposed to be in perfect condition and would last a lifetime.

f. Buyer bought a boat from a dentist, who stated that the boat was free from dry rot and that seller would be responsible for any dry rot occurring in the first six months.

3. Disclaimers and limitations. Was the following language effective to disclaim or limit warranties?

a. On barrels of glue sold to a merchant, gummed labels on the end and on the side stated:

Important — Read Carefully Before Opening: We exclude all warranties, express or implied, with respect to these goods including warranties of fitness for a particular purpose and merchantability. This provision is the final agreement of the parties and can be modified only by one of our officers in writing. In any event, purchaser's damages shall not exceed the price of the goods. If purchaser does not want the goods subject to these terms, they should be returned unopened.

---

b. Seller stated: "This warranty is in lieu of all other warranties express or implied."

c. Seller stated on the back of the last page of a commercial agreement that consequential damages are excluded from buyer's remedies for breach of warranty. The exclusion was in a paragraph which did not have a heading, unusual capitalization, or contrasting type.

4. Magnuson-Moss. Which of the following written statements are warranties under U.C.C. § 2-313? Under Magnuson-Moss?

---

a. This coat is made of 100% nylon shell and 100% goose down filling. It may be dry cleaned or hand washed in a mild detergent solution.

---

b. Made of 100% nylon shell and 100% goose down filling. If for any reason you are dissatisfied with this product, you may return it for a refund of your money.

---

c. Satisfaction guaranteed. Full refund if you're not completely satisfied.

d. Satisfaction guaranteed. Full refund if you're not completely satisfied at any time within 30 days after purchase.

5. Purchase of a used car. On September 1, 2004, Terry Higgins went to Big Sky Motors to purchase a used car. The salesperson, Woody Ryman, showed him a 1984 Buick Skylark that Higgins was interested in. During a test drive, Terry commented that the standard transmission felt tight and that there was a whining noise under the car. Ryman replied that the car was in "Tip-top condition." He told Terry that every car was different and a person couldn't expect this one to feel or sound just like their last car.

Terry purchased the car for $4,995. He signed a purchase contract and received the Buyers Guide that was in the window and an Odometer Statement.

On September 5, after the car had been driven for 16.5 miles, Terry was driving into town. As he approached a red light, Terry heard a thud under the car. The car did not move when he tried to accelerate. He looked under the car and saw a large metal object on the road. It turned out to be the transmission.

Terry called AAA, which sent a tow truck to tow the car down the street to Marvin's Garage. After inspecting the car, Marvin told Terry that the transmission was completely shot and would have to be replaced. He estimated the repair cost at $1000. He said that the problem was a latent one that could not have been discovered without taking the car apart.

Terry called Big Sky to complain about the car. The service manager, Brooks Paxton, was very courteous but would do nothing for him. It was not unusual, he said, for a car with 30,000 miles on it to need transmission work. When Terry told him what the salesperson, Woody Ryman, had said, Paxton replied, "If he made a statement about the condition of the car, I'm sure it was just his opinion and we can't back that up. What we have to go by is the contract. You purchased the car 'as is,' which means that you are responsible for any repairs."

Terry wants to know if he has any legal claim against Big Sky Motors. These are the documents Terry obtained from Big Sky:

BIG SKY MOTORS
"YOUR VALUE HEADQUARTERS"

1750 Russell St.　　　　　　　　　　Sales:　555-2525
Missoula, MT　59802　　　　　　　　Service:　555-2526

Purchaser _TERRY HIGGINS_　　　Address _138 JACKSON ST._
City _MISSOULA_　　Postal Zone _59802_ State _MT._　Phone _555-1234_

I hereby agree to purchase from you, under the terms and conditions specified, the following:

STOCK No.	NEW	USED	YEAR	MAKE	MODEL	SERIAL NO.	COLOR
168		X	1984	BUICK	SKYLARK	1G1FP87F0FL502795	BLUE

USED VEHICLE TRADED IN AND/OR OTHER CREDITS		CASH DELIVERED PRICE OF VEHICLE	$ 4995
MAKE OF TRADE-IN			
YEAR MODEL BODY			
SERIES		ACCESSORIES	$ —
MVI NO.			
I CERTIFY THAT THE ODOMETER READING ON MY ABOVE TRADE READS___ MILES. THE ODOMETER HAS___ HAS NOT___ EXCEEDED 100,000 MILES. SIGNATURE X		THIS CAR IS SOLD "AS IS" NO WARRANTY	
BALANCE OWED TO			
DISCOUNT OVER ALLOWANCE	$		
CASH ACV ALLOWANCE			
BALANCE OWED ON TRADE-IN			
NET ALLOWANCE ON USED TRADE-IN	$		
DEPOSIT GOOD UNTIL			
CASH WITH ORDER	$ 5020		
TOTAL CREDIT (TRANSFER TO RIGHT COLUMN)	$ 5020		
		CASH PRICE OF VEHICLE & ACCESSORIES	$ 4995
		ADMINISTRATIVE EXPENSES	$ 25 00
		TOTAL PRICE OF UNIT	$ 5020
		TOTAL CREDIT TRANSFERED FROM LEFT COLUMN	$ 5020
		UNPAID CASH BALANCE DUE ON DELIVERY	0

Delivery of this purchase is to be made SEPTEMBER, 19 84, or as soon thereafter as possible. It is agreed, however, that neither the dealer nor the manufacturer will be liable for failure to effect delivery. Buyer assumes responsibility for any difference in payoff in excess of amount shown below, and will pay such difference in cash on demand. If not so paid, buyer authorizes dealer, at dealer's option, to increase the monthly payments and contract balance to cover the difference and finance charges thereon or repossess the car sold.

Delivery of this automobile is accepted by purchaser subject to credit approval by a financing institution, and in the event of a credit report unacceptable to the financing institution, the purchaser will return the automobile herein described immediately to the dealer.

Date _SEPTEMBER 1_, _2004_

THIS CAR IS SOLD AS IS AND
NOT GUARANTEED X _TH_
　　　　INITIAL

DISCLAIMER OF WARRANTIES

Any warranties on the products sold hereby, are the warranties of the manufacturer of those products. BIG SKY MOTORS hereby expressly disclaims all warranties, either express or implied, including any implied warranty of merchantability or fitness for a particular purpose, and the seller neither assumes nor authorizes any other person to assume for it any liability in connection with the sale of the vehicle. This disclaimer does not effect the manufacturer's warranty on this unit.

x _Terry Higgins_
　　Customer's Signature

Purchaser agrees that this Order cancels and supersedes any prior agreement and as of the date hereof comprises the complete and exclusive statement of the terms of the agreement relating to the subject matters covered hereby, and that THIS ORDER SHALL NOT BECOME BINDING UNTIL ACCEPTED BY DEALER OR HIS AUTHORIZED REPRESENTATIVE AND IN THE EVENT OF A TIME SALE, DEALER SHALL NOT BE OBLIGATED TO SELL UNTIL APPROVAL OF THE TERMS HEREOF IS GIVEN BY A BANK OR FINANCE COMPANY WILLING TO PURCHASE A RETAIL INSTALLMENT CONTRACT BETWEEN THE PARTIES HERETO BASED ON SUCH TERMS. Purchaser by his execution of this Order certifies that he is 18 years of age or older and acknowledges that he has read its terms and conditions and has received a true copy of this Order.
It is agreed that there are no other warranties, either express or implied, covering a new car sold hereunder. In the event the car sold hereunder is a used car, it is agreed that dealer assumes only such warranty obligations to Buyer as are set forth on the face of this order or in a separate written instrument, if any.

Buyer's Signature _Terry Higgins_
Referred By _____
Salesman's Name _Oakley Ryman_
Accepted _Brooks & Paxton_
　Must Be Accepted By An Authorized Representative of Dealer
Credit Approval _____

BUYERS GUIDE

IMPORTANT: Spoken promises are difficult to enforce. Ask the dealer to put all promises in writing. Keep this form.

BUICK _____ SKYLARK _____ 1984 _____ 1G1FP87F0FL502795 _____
VEHICLE MAKE   MODEL   YEAR   VIN NUMBER

_____ 168 _____
DEALER STOCK NUMBER (Optional)

WARRANTIES FOR THIS VEHICLE:

☒ AS IS-NO WARRANTY

YOU WILL PAY ALL COSTS FOR ANY REPAIRS. The dealer assumes no responsibility for any repairs regardless of any oral statements about the vehicle.

☐ WARRANTY

☐ FULL ☐ LIMITED WARRANTY. The dealer will pay _____% of the labor and _____% of the parts for the covered systems that fail during the warranty period. Ask the dealer for a copy of the warranty document for a full explanation of warranty coverage, exclusions, and the dealer's repair obligations. Under state law, "implied warranties" may give you even more rights.

SYSTEMS COVERED: **DURATION:**

_____   _____
_____   _____
_____   _____
_____   _____
_____   _____
_____   _____
_____   _____
_____   _____

☐ **SERVICE CONTRACT.** A service contract is available at an extra charge on this vehicle. Ask for details as to coverage, deductible, price, and exclusions. If you buy a service contract within 90 days of the time of sale, state law "implied warranties" may give you additional rights.

PRE PURCHASE INSPECTION: ASK THE DEALER IF YOU MAY HAVE THIS VEHICLE INSPECTED BY YOUR MECHANIC EITHER ON OR OFF THE LOT.

SEE THE BACK OF THIS FORM for important additional information, including a list of some major defects that may occur in used motor vehicles.

Form 803   Reynolds • Reynolds DAYTON OHIO LITHO IN U S A

Below is a list of some major defects that may occur in used motor vehicles.

Frame & Body
Frame—cracks, corrective welds, or rusted through
Dogtracks—bent or twisted frame

Engine
Oil leakage, excluding normal seepage
Cracked block or head
Belts missing or inoperable
Knocks or misses related to camshaft lifters and push rods
Abnormal exhaust discharge

Transmission & Drive Shaft
Improper fluid level or leakage, excluding normal seepage
Cracked or damaged case which is visible
Abnormal noise or vibration caused by faulty transmission or drive shaft
Improper shifting or functioning in any gear
Manual clutch slips or chatters

Differential
Improper fluid level or leakage excluding normal seepage
Cracked or damaged housing which is visible
Abnormal noise or vibration caused by faulty differential

Cooling System
Leakage including radiator
Improperly functioning water pump

Electrical System
Battery leakage
Improperly functioning alternator, generator, battery, or starter

Fuel System
Visible leakage

Inoperable Accessories
Gauges or warning devices
Air conditioner
Heater & Defroster

Brake System
Failure warning light broken
Pedal not firm under pressure (DOT specs.)
Not enough pedal reserve (DOT specs.)
Does not stop vehicle in straight line (Dot specs.)
Hoses damaged
Drum or rotor too thin (Mfgr. Specs)
Lining or pad thickness less than $1/32$ inch
Power unit not operating or leaking
Structural or mechanical parts damaged

Steering System
Too much free play at steering wheel (DOT specs.)
Free play in linkage more than $1/4$ inch
Steering gear binds or jams
Front wheels aligned improperly (DOT specs.)
Power unit belts cracked or slipping
Power unit fluid level improper

Suspension System
Ball joint seals damaged
Structural parts bent or damaged
Stabilizer bar disconnected
Spring broken
Shock absorber mounting loose
Rubber bushings damaged or missing
Radius rod damaged or missing
Shock absorber leaking or functioning improperly

Tires
Tread depth less than $2/32$ inch
Sizes mismatched
Visible damage

Wheels
Visible cracks, damage or repairs
Mounting bolts loose or missing

Exhaust System
Leakage

BIG SKY MOTORS
DEALER
1750 RUSSELL ST.
ADDRESS
MISSOULA MT. 59802
BROOKS T. PAXTON
SEE FOR COMPLAINTS

IMPORTANT: The information on this form is part of any contract to buy this vehicle. Removal of this label before consumer purchase (except for purpose of test-driving) is a violation of federal law (16 C.F.R. 455).

ODOMETER (MILEAGE) STATEMENT

(FEDERAL REGULATIONS REQUIRE YOU TO STATE THE ODOMETER MILEAGE UPON TRANSFER OF OWNERSHIP. AN INACCURATE OR UNTRUTHFUL STATEMENT MAY MAKE YOU LIABLE FOR DAMAGES TO YOUR TRANSFEREE, FOR ATTORNEY FEES, AND FOR CIVIL OR CRIMINAL PENALTIES, PURSUANT TO SECTIONS 409, 412, AND 413 OF THE MOTOR VEHICLE INFORMATION AND COST SAVINGS ACT OF 1972 (PUB. L. 92-513, AS AMENDED BY PUB. L. 94-364)) AND APPLICABLE STATE LAWS.

I, **BIG SKY MOTORS, INC.** , STATE THAT THE ODOMETER
TRANSFEROR'S NAME · SELLER · PRINT
MILEAGE ON THE VEHICLE

DESCRIBED BELOW NOW READS **30,000** MILES/KILOMETERS.
ODOMETER READING

CHECK ONE BOX ONLY:

[✓] (1) I HEREBY CERTIFY THAT TO THE BEST OF MY KNOWLEDGE THE ODOMETER READING AS STATED ABOVE REFLECTS THE ACTUAL MILEAGE OF THE VEHICLE DESCRIBED BELOW.

[ ] (2) I HEREBY CERTIFY THAT TO THE BEST OF MY KNOWLEDGE THE ODOMETER READING AS STATED ABOVE REFLECTS THE AMOUNT OF MILEAGE IN EXCESS OF DESIGNED MECHANICAL ODOMETER LIMIT OF 99,999 MILES/KILOMETERS OF THE VEHICLE DESCRIBED BELOW.

[ ] (3) I HEREBY CERTIFY THAT TO THE BEST OF MY KNOWLEDGE THE ODOMETER READING AS STATED ABOVE IS NOT THE ACTUAL MILEAGE OF VEHICLE DESCRIBED BELOW AND SHOULD NOT BE RELIED UPON.

MAKE	MODEL	BODY TYPE
Buick	SKYLARK	SEDAN

VEHICLE IDENTIFICATION NO.	YEAR	DEALER STOCK NO.
1G1FP87F0F502795	1984	168

CHECK ONE BOX ONLY:

[✓] (1) I HEREBY CERTIFY THAT THE ODOMETER OF SAID VEHICLE WAS NOT ALTERED, SET BACK OR DISCONNECTED WHILE IN MY POSSESSION, AND I HAVE NO KNOWLEDGE OF ANYONE ELSE DOING SO.

[ ] (2) I HEREBY CERTIFY THAT THE ODOMETER WAS ALTERED FOR REPAIR OR REPLACEMENT PURPOSES WHILE IN MY POSSESSION, AND THAT THE MILEAGE REGISTERED ON THE REPAIRED OR REPLACEMENT WAS IDENTICAL TO THAT BEFORE SUCH SERVICE.

[ ] (3) I HEREBY CERTIFY THAT THE REPAIRED OR REPLACEMENT ODOMETER WAS INCAPABLE OF REGISTERING THE SAME MILEAGE, THAT IT WAS RESET TO ZERO, AND THAT THE MILEAGE ON THE ORIGINAL

ODOMETER OR THE ODOMETER BEFORE REPAIR WAS_____ MILES/KILOMETERS.

TRANSFEROR'S STREET ADDRESS (SELLER)
1750 RUSSELL ST.

CITY	STATE	ZIP CODE
MISSOULA	MT.	59802

DATE OF STATEMENT	TRANSFEROR'S SIGNATURE (SELLER)
9/1/2004	x Brooks J. Paxton

TRANSFEREE'S NAME (BUYER)
TERRY HIGGINS

STREET ADDRESS
138 JACKSON ST.

CITY	STATE	ZIP CODE
MISSOULA	MT.	59802

I, x _Terry Higgins_ HEREBY CERTIFY THAT I HAVE
TRANSFEREE'S SIGNATURE · BUYER   RECEIVED A COPY OF THE ABOVE
                                      ODOMETER (MILEAGE) STATEMENT.
580.6 REV. 8/80

ORIGINAL — TRANSFEREE (BUYER)

6. Negotiation Exercise. Lynn Smith is a mechanic who repairs cars. On infrequent occasions, once or twice a year, a customer doesn't have enough money to pay for the repair, so Lynn buys the car from the customer, repairs it, and sells it.

Terry Palmer has agreed to buy one of these cars, a 1998 Ford Windstar, from Lynn. They have agreed on a price of $5000, which is the market price for this model, payable on delivery. Lynn worked on the transmission and is satisfied that the transmission is in good working condition, but Lynn has no knowledge about the condition of the other parts of the car. Lynn has made no statements or promises to Terry about the condition of the car. The car has 65,000 miles on it, and the manufacturer's warranty has expired.

Pair up and choose sides so that one of you is Lynn and the other is Terry. Negotiate and draft a warranty term in the contract between you. You are free to agree not to include a warranty term.

Chapter 13

DAMAGES

§ 13.1 Introduction.

In spite of the unrepresentative sample of cases you read in your Contracts casebook, the fact is that most contracts are performed as promised or with adjustments worked out by the parties during performance. Contracts are performed even though it might be economically profitable in the short run to breach them. If they are not performed, most injured parties don't sue because of the high transaction costs of bringing a claim.

Knowing that breach is always a possibility, particularly in one-shot transactions, lawyers must plan for it. The planner can build forms of protection into the contract that make a lawsuit unnecessary or that make the circumstances more favorable for a client should a lawsuit occur. For example, a creditor may be able to obtain advance payment, take a security interest in goods sold, obtain a lien in connection with the transaction, cut off services, or induce the debtor to pay in order to enhance the debtor's position in the community, for example, by improving its credit.

Parties to a contract generally contemplate performance, not breach. Lawyers, however, know that breach is always a possibility. The lawyer as planner must constantly ask, "What happens if one party doesn't perform as promised?" When breach occurs, the injured party may seek a remedy. That remedy is often money damages. If the contract is silent on damages, courts will apply the traditional rules descended from *Hadley v. Baxendale*.[1] The rules are not designed to compel the promisor to perform, but to compensate the promisee for the loss that occurs on account of breach.

These rules make it difficult for the injured party to receive full compensation for the breach. As Professor Arthur Leff observed, "Most people carry out their agreements because they carry out their agreements, not because awful things will happen to them if they don't." The rule of foreseeability limits damages to those losses the breaching party could reasonably have foreseen at the time of contracting. The rule of avoidable consequences denies the injured party recovery for losses that it could have prevented. The rule of certainty denies recovery for losses that cannot be established with reasonable certainty.

An injured party who succeeds in overcoming the hurdles imposed by these rules still has to pay the transaction costs of bringing an action. Statutory costs rarely cover all the expenses involved in bringing a lawsuit.

---

[1] 9 Exch. 341, 156 Eng. Rep. 145 (1854).

Most significant are attorneys' fees, which are often the greatest expense. Under the "American Rule," each side pays its own attorneys' fees, win or lose.

A lawsuit may also involve hidden costs, such as time and worry, that are hard to measure in economic terms. Win or lose, a party to a lawsuit suffers from uncertainty. The time spent in preparation can distract a person or a business from more productive endeavors. A great deal of time may pass between the breach and judgment. The injured party may recover statutory interest on a judgment, but that interest may be pegged below market rates. Because a judgment is not self-executing, additional costs may be expended in collection, which may be fruitless if the debtor is insolvent.

These limitations on recovery serve the goal of permitting "efficient breach." In theory, the breaching party may breach a disadvantageous contract, pay damages, and use the resources more productively. While preventing overcompensation of the injured party, the rules often favor the breaching party by making redress so costly. The lawyer as planner, thinking about what might happen if the contract is not performed, may build into the contract assistance to the non-breaching party. The parties can shift the risk of various losses, agree on a liquidated damages provision, allocate the award of attorneys' fees, or agree to have the dispute settled in a forum that requires less time and expense than the traditional legal system.

§ 13.2   Specific performance.

Specific performance of a contract is rarely awarded. There is little that drafters can do to compel a court to grant this relief. Because courts traditionally view the availability of equitable relief as a jurisdictional matter, it is doubtful that a court would allow the terms of the contract to invest the court with equity jurisdiction over the contract. However, the drafter might include in the contract language that would encourage the court to exercise its equity jurisdiction. For example, one of the criteria for specific enforcement is that damages, the remedy at law, must be inadequate. In contracts for personal services, which are usually unique, this criterion is often satisfied. A drafter might insert a provision reciting this fact. In baseball, the Uniform Player's Contract provides:[2]

---

2 Uniform Player's Contract. Reprinted with permission of Major League Baseball Players Association.

PLAYER REPRESENTATIONS

Ability

4.(a) The player represents and agrees that he has exceptional and unique skill and ability as a baseball player; that his services to be rendered hereunder are of a special, unusual and extraordinary character which gives them peculiar value which cannot be reasonably or adequately compensated for in damages at law, and that the Player's breach of this contract will cause the Club great and irreparable injury and damage. The Player agrees that, in addition to other remedies, the Club shall be entitled to injunctive and other equitable relief to prevent a breach of this contract by the Player, including, among others, the right to enjoin the Player from playing baseball for any other person or organization during the term of his contract.

Similarly, U.C.C. § 2-716(1) states: "Specific performance may be decreed where the goods are unique or in other proper circumstances." The parties could draft provisions indicating that these elements are present in the transaction. For example:

Uniqueness of Goods. Seller and Buyer affirm that the goods sold under this contract are unique and cannot be purchased on the open market or manufactured specially.

---

or

Special circumstances of sale. Seller and Buyer affirm that Buyer has foregone other opportunities to enter into a like contract for sale of similar goods; that Buyer cannot procure these goods from any other source without great difficulty and suffering irrevocable damage as a businessman; and that a repudiation or breach of this contract by Seller will prevent Buyer fulfilling his obligations under contracts with third parties.

---

§ 13.3   Money damages: Application of the *Hadley* rules.

A sends a package to *C* via the *B* Shipping Company. *B* charges $10 for the service and promises that the package "will absolutely, positively get there overnight." The package does not arrive on time. As a direct result, *A* loses a contract that would have earned her $10,000 in profits. What can *A* recover from *B*?

The answer, of course, is $10. Under the *Hadley* rules, *A* can recover damages for losses that are the natural result of breach and for losses that *B* should have reasonably known would occur as the probable result of a breach. A lost contract that would have earned a $10,000 profit does not fall under either of these rules.

A now realizes that the solution is to make *B* aware of the losses that may occur as a result of breach. The next time *A* sends a package, she gives *B* a paper stating:

> If this package does not arrive tomorrow, I will lose a contract that would have earned me $10,000. I will hold you responsible for this loss.

B is no fool. *B* says, "I'm sorry, I won't accept the package on those terms. I will accept the package only on my terms which are stated here:

> *Delay.* There is always a risk of late delivery or non-delivery. In the event of a late delivery, B Shipping Co. will refund all transportation charges paid. We will not be liable for any loss or damage resulting from delay, non-delivery or damage to a package except as noted above. This includes loss of sales, income, interest, profits, attorney fees and other costs, but is not limited to these items."

The law will honor these communications. The rules make business sense. *A,* foreseeing losses that she may suffer if *B* does not perform, may attempt to shift the risk of those losses to *B.* Under the *Hadley* rules, the breaching party is responsible for those losses which it knows or reasonably should have known at the time of contracting would result from breach. The promisee most clearly places the risk on the promisor by informing the promisor of the losses that may occur. Once *B* is aware of the possible losses, *B* may use the private law of contract to make a choice. *B* may offer to assume the risk, to shift the risk back to *A,* or to place a limit on the losses it will assume.

The U.C.C. provides many remedies for breach. One of the remedies, demonstrating an application of the *Hadley* rules, is that the buyer may recover damages when the seller repudiates and the buyer "covers" by purchasing the goods in the market. The U.C.C. specifies the buyer's remedies for "consequential damages" in § 2-715(2):

(2) Consequential damages resulting from the seller's breach include

   (a) any loss resulting from general or particular requirements and needs of which the seller at the time of contracting had reason to know and which could not reasonably be prevented by cover or otherwise; and

(b) injury to person or property proximately resulting from any breach of warranty.

To deal with consequential damages, the drafter might employ one of these provisions:

---

1. In the event of a breach or repudiation of this contract by Seller, Buyer shall not be entitled to any consequential damages as defined in § 2-715 of the Uniform Commercial Code except that if the goods sold are "consumer goods," personal injuries shall be recoverable.

---

2. In the event of a breach or repudiation of this contract by Seller, Buyer shall not be entitled to any consequential damages in excess of $_____. This limitation shall not apply, however, to damages for injury to the person if the goods are consumer goods.

---

3. In the event of a breach or repudiation of this contract by Seller, Buyer shall be entitled to recover as consequential damages, in addition to all other rights granted by the Uniform Commercial Code, any profit lost on a contract to resell the goods if Buyer is unable to cover.

In Example 1, the buyer gives up the right to recover consequential damages. Note, however, that in accordance with § 2-719(3), the provision excepts consequential damages for injury to the person in the sale of consumer goods. *See* § 12.7. In Example 2, the parties limit the consequential damages. In Example 3, the buyer informs the seller of lost profits on a contract to resell. This loss would probably not be foreseeable if seller did not have reason to know of it at the time of contracting.

§ 13.4   Liquidated damages.

It can be difficult to establish with certainty the losses that occur on breach, both at the time of contracting and at the time of breach. The drafter may be able to avoid this problem by incorporating a liquidated damages provision in the contract. By this provision, the parties agree at the time of contracting what the damages will be for breach. The principle that damages are assessed in order to compensate the injured party and not to deter the breaching party becomes important in drafting the provision, for the provision must not be a penalty that punishes a party for breach. Most courts will enforce a liquidated damages clause if the loss is difficult to ascertain and the liquidated amount is a reasonable forecast of the damages a court would award. U.C.C. § 2-718(1) states:

Damages for breach by either party may be liquidated in the agreement but only at an amount which is reasonable in the light of the anticipated or actual harm caused by the breach, the difficulties of proof of loss, and the inconvenience or nonfeasibility of otherwise obtaining an adequate remedy. A term fixing unreasonably large liquidated damages is void as a penalty.

The circumstances of each case must be examined. For example, consider the following situations:

1. Brown and Green agree to exchange tracts of land. Brown's lot is more valuable, so they also agree that Green will pay Brown $1000 a year after the exchange. To assure performance, they wish to provide that if one party does not perform, that party will pay a penalty of $500 to the other.

2. Smith agrees to deliver a large quantity of grain to Jones's ranch on or before September 1. To assure performance, Jones wishes to provide that if Smith does not perform by October 1, Jones will pay liquidated damages of $20,000.

3. Logger agrees with Owner that Logger will clear the timber on Owner's property, paying Owner for every merchantable tree cut. If Logger leaves merchantable trees uncut, Owner will not be able to sell them, for another logger would not take such a small job. Owner wishes to provide that Logger will pay $10 for every merchantable tree left uncut.

In Example 1, the contract concerns land. Often the remedy for breach is specific performance, which would not involve money damages. If the injured party sought damages, the damages could probably be readily ascertained as a function of the market value of the properties. Therefore, the liquidated damages provision appears to be a penalty and would not be enforceable. In Example 2, the contract concerns goods with an easily determinable market value. Furthermore, the penalty is the same irrespective of the length of the period of nonperformance beyond one month. The liquidated damages provision appears to be a penalty. In Example 3, it would be difficult to estimate the actual damages where there is no market for isolated logs. This factor and the fact that the amount of the liquidated damages would vary with the number of uncut trees would probably make this clause enforceable.

Construction contracts often contain liquidated damages clauses, for it is particularly difficult to estimate with certainty the damage caused by delay. For example:

> For each and every day work contemplated in this contract remains uncompleted beyond the time set for its completion, Contractor shall pay to Owner the sum of $_____, as liquidated damages and not as a penalty. This sum may be deducted from money due or to become due to Contractor as compensation under this contract.

§ 13.5 Arbitration.

When parties agree to arbitration, they will have the dispute resolved by a third party chosen by them rather than by a court.

Parties cannot be compelled to arbitrate disputes in the absence of a contractual provision providing for arbitration. Once the parties have agreed to arbitration, most states have enacted arbitration statutes that detail how the arbitration is to be conducted. A few states have statutes that restrict arbitration, but these statutes have generally been pre-empted by the Federal Arbitration Act, 9 U.S.C. § 1 *et seq.*, which allows for arbitration in disputes involving interstate commerce. Even if the parties do not have a pre-dispute agreement to arbitrate, they can agree to arbitrate an existing dispute.

In their contract, the parties may determine what disputes are within the scope of arbitration and what remedies are available. An arbitrator does not have the power to award punitive damages unless the agreement expressly permits the award. The American Arbitration Association recommends this clause for insertion in commercial contracts:

> Any controversy or claim arising out of or relating to this contract, or the breach thereof, shall be settled by arbitration in accordance with the Commercial Arbitration Rules of the American Arbitration Association, and judgment upon the award rendered by the arbitrator(s) may be entered in any court having jurisdiction thereof.

As with any provision, the drafter should not incorporate an arbitration clause without being sure it meets the need of the parties to a particular contract. For example, the parties might want a particular person or organization to arbitrate the dispute. If they are located in different cities, the parties might want to indicate the site of the arbitration. The vast body of cases interpreting arbitration agreements indicates the importance of careful drafting. The parties might desire a narrowly drafted clause, with only certain issues being referred to arbitration. For example:

> All work under this specification shall be subject to inspection by the owner or his representative. All parts of the work shall be accessible to the inspector. The contractor shall correct such work as is found defective under the specifications. If the contractor does not agree with the inspector, the arbitration or settlement procedure established in the contract shall be followed.

§ 13.6 Attorneys' fees.

The common law rule in the United States is that each side to a lawsuit pays its own legal fees regardless of the outcome. This rule has been changed by many statutes, particularly in the area of consumer law. For example, while attorneys' fees are not recoverable under the U.C.C. for breach of warranty, the transaction may also give rise to a claim under Magnuson-Moss, which authorizes an award of attorneys' fees. *See* § 12.8.

The parties may also provide in their contract for the payment of attorneys' fees in the event of litigation. For example:

> 1. In the event of default in payment, Buyer shall pay Seller's reasonable attorneys' fees incurred to enforce payment.

> 2. If you have to sue me, I also agree to pay your attorneys' fees equal to 15% of the amount due, and court costs. But if I defend and the court decides I am right, I understand that you will pay my reasonable attorneys' fees and the court costs.

> 3. The prevailing party in any lawsuit arising under this Agreement or as a result of its cancellation may recover reasonable attorneys' fees from the loser.

In Example 1, attorneys' fees are payable for only one event, default in payment, and only to the Seller. In Example 2, the fees are payable in the event of any lawsuit and to either party. In Example 3, fees are payable to the prevailing party. Note that this example uses the discretionary *may;* this probably means that a court is not obligated to award fees but may exercise its discretion.

§ 13.7 Punitive damages.

Punitive damages are not available for breach of contract. The traditional doctrine of "efficient breach" allows a party to a contract to breach and pay only compensatory damages. However, punitive damages are available in a tort action and when permitted by statute. Sometimes breach of contract may give rise to an independent tort. One independent tort is "breach of the implied covenant of good faith and fair dealing," which is often referred to as "bad faith."

Courts have generally determined that a tort remedy is available only where there is a "special relationship" between the parties. The classic case is the relationship of insurer and insured. One element of the special relationship is that one party has inherently superior bargaining power. In that event, a clause repudiating the tort remedy would probably be unenforceable. Therefore, parties outside the special relationship should plan their remedies within the predictable confines of the *Hadley* rules. Within the special relationship, the party with superior bargaining power must not rely on drafting but must monitor its conduct to avoid bad faith.

Punitive damages may also be available when a contract claim is brought under a statute, such as a state Consumer Protection Act that prohibits "unfair or deceptive acts or practices." The drafter of a consumer contract must scrutinize the contract to be sure that provisions violative of the Act are not included. *See* § 4.7.

§ 13.8   Exercises.

1. Research. Research the law in your jurisdiction to determine any rules regarding attorneys' fees provisions, arbitration clauses, and torts that may be invoked in a contract action. How do those rules affect the drafter of a contract?

2. Creditor's remedies. A debtor has the following bills to pay. She is short of funds. As you look over the list, consider what will happen if she doesn't perform her obligation to pay. Which creditors have probably built remedies into the agreement?

$400/month house payment to a bank secured by a conventional mortgage

$1,000 from a contractor who replaced part of the roof

$500 county tax bill

$75/month bill from the Power Company for electricity and gas

$40/month TV bought from a large retail store on credit

$200 credit card bill for miscellaneous purchases

$220 bills from local merchants who sold on credit

$250/month car payment to a finance company

$100 lawyer's bill

3. The lost deal. On Saturday you go to a used car lot and find the car you have been looking for. You buy the car for $1,200, which is the suggested retail price listed in the "Blue Book," but because you are short of cash, you and the seller agree that payment and delivery will take place on Monday. You enter into a written agreement reflecting these terms. On Monday, when you go to pick up the car, the seller says, "Ha Ha! I got a better offer Saturday afternoon, so I sold it to someone else." What claim do you have? *See* U.C.C. §§ 2-712 and 2-713.

4. The missed game. A group of Red Sox fans in Maine charter a bus from Yankee Coach Lines to see a big game in Boston. The normal charge for the charter is $500. Fred Rice, the organizer of the fans, reads the proposed contract and finds that Yankee's liability in the event of breach is limited to the charge for the service. He offers an additional $250 consideration in return for Coach Lines' promise to pay liquidated damages of $10,000 to the fans in the event of breach. Bucky Nettles, President of Coach Lines, agrees and they draft the provision in the contract.

On the day of the big game, the bus never shows up. Nettles explains that at the last minute he got a better offer from a Yankee fan club and "money talks." Nettles had consulted a lawyer and was advised that the liquidated damages provision was unenforceable as a penalty and that emotional distress — even the distress of missing a Red Sox game — was not compensable. Nettles was advised that Yankee Coach Lines could return the Red Sox fans' money, pay any compensatory damages, and still come out ahead, so he followed the lawyer's advice.

Is the provision enforceable?

5. Over-lawyering — or sound preventive law? Consider the following advice, given by Mark H. McCormack in his book, THE TERRIBLE TRUTH ABOUT LAWYERS:[3]

BEWARE OF BEING OVER-LAWYERED

One of the truly terrible things about many Western legal systems is that *the lawyers themselves are given such broad discretion in determining the pace and complexity — i.e., the cost — of most procedures by which they make their living.*

Built into the systems are all sorts of incentives for lawyers to be slow, obscurantist, contentious, long-winded. Law schools might deny it, but there is the most obvious temptation for lawyers to do more lawyering than really needs doing.

For a slightly comical example of over-lawyering at its worst, consider these two versions of so-called grant clauses typically included in licensing contracts:

Licensor hereby grants to Company the right to use Licensor's trademarks on and in connection with the advertisement, distribution and sale of athletic shoes and athletic shoes only.

The above wording is perfectly clear and legally watertight. Now here is what an overly zealous lawyer might add to it (and in fact *has* added to it, this example being from our files!):

Use by Company of the Licensor trademark on products other than athletic shoes shall result in immediate termination of this agreement and the forfeiture by Company of its rights hereunder, including the right to dispose of any inventory bearing Licensor's trademarks. Company agrees that Licensor shall have the right to enforce this obligation by injunctive relief and Company hereby indemnifies Licensor for any and all costs, expenses, damages, claims and expenses, including attorneys' fees, for any breach by Company of the foregoing obligations.

---

[3] MARK MCCORMACK, THE TERRIBLE TRUTH ABOUT LAWYERS (1987). Copyright © 1987 Mark McCormack Enterprises, Inc. Reprinted with permission of William Morrow and Co., Inc.

Just what in the name of heaven is the second version all about? It adds virtually nothing of substance to the first simple clause.

One party to a contract can *always* seek relief if the other party violates the contract's provisions; that's why they call it a contract!

Damages can *always* be sought—again, by definition.

So the second version does nothing except keep the billing meter running while the lawyer belabors basic points of law that are implied in any contract anyway.

Do you agree with McCormack that the second version adds "virtually nothing of substance" to the first version? Recall Chapter 10, Promise and Condition.

6. The Shipment Contract. ABC Company pays Delivery Company $15 to deliver a parcel overnight to one of its plants. The parcel contains a computer chip worth $1,000. If the chip is not delivered on time, ABC will suffer down time costing $10,000 per day. The back of the form that ABC filled out contains the following Terms and Conditions:

Limitations On Our Liability and Liabilities Not Assumed

- Our liability in connection with this shipment is limited to the lesser of your actual damages or $100, unless you declare a higher value, pay an additional charge, and document your actual loss in a timely manner. You may pay an additional charge for each additional $100 of declared value. The declared value does not constitute, nor do we provide, cargo liability insurance.

- In any event, we will not be liable for any damage, whether direct, incidental, special, or consequential in excess of the declared value of shipment, whether or not Delivery Company had knowledge that such damages might be incurred including but not limited to loss of income or profits.

Money-Back Guarantee In the event of untimely delivery, Delivery Company will, at your request and with some limitations, refund or credit all transportation charges.

ABC's parcel does not get there overnight and ABC suffers losses of $20,000 before it can replace the chip. Did the drafter effectively limit liability for damages? Would it have mattered if ABC had told Delivery Company what losses it would suffer? What could ABC have done?

7. Ethics. You are the lawyer for ABC Corporation. The President of ABC has unwisely ordered 1,000 widgets from X Co. The President wants to know if ABC can breach the contract with X Co. There is nothing wrong with the widgets and the loss of the contract will cause a hardship for X Co. Can you advise your client to break a contract? If you are familiar with the tort of tortious interference with contract, is the President or the lawyer committing that tort if they advise ABC to break the contract with X Co.?

Chapter 14

THIRD PARTIES

§ 14.1 Introduction.

A contract often affects parties other than those who entered it. Third parties may acquire an interest as a beneficiary of the contract. Or the parties to the contract may assign their rights or delegate their duties under the contract. In this respect, contract rights are similar to interests in property. If *A* has the right to receive 100 widgets on October 1, *A* has something that can be bought and sold. On the other hand, a party who considers the contract rights to be personal may wish to prohibit their transfer. The lawyer as planner can build these various rights and prohibitions into the contract. As always, the planner must consider the needs of the particular client and cannot solve a problem by using boilerplate forms.

In this area of the law, it is hard to keep track of the players without a scorecard. In planning transactions involving third parties, it is helpful to diagram the transaction. When drafting the transaction, it is important to use vocabulary that properly expresses the parties' meaning. Think of a contract as containing rights and duties. For example, *A* and *B* agree that *A* will sell a pen to *B* for $10:

PEN

$$A \rightleftarrows B$$

$10

This contract may be seen as containing these rights and duties:

Rights	Duties
B to a pen	*A* to tender a pen
A to $10	*B* to tender $10

It is also helpful to think in terms of the parties' obligations:

A party who has the obligation to perform a duty is an *obligor*;

A party who has the right to receive a performance is an *obligee*.

In an *assignment,* rights are *assigned:*

The obligee who assigns is the *assignor;*

The third party to whom the assignment is made is the *assignee.*

In a *delegation,* duties are *delegated:*

The obligor who delegates is the *delegating party* (or *delegator*);

The third party to whom the delegation is made is the *delegate* (or *delegatee*).

In a *transfer,* rights are assigned *and* duties are delegated:

The party who assigns and delegates is the *transferor*;

The third party to whom the assignment and delegation are made is the *transferee.*

In the previous example, if A assigns to C the right to receive a performance from B (the payment of $10), and B delegates to D the obligation to perform a duty owed to A (the payment of $10), the transaction may be illustrated:

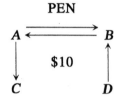

A is the *assignor.* C is the *assignee.*

B is the *delegating party.* D is the *delegate.*

If we follow the arrows, we see that the $10 is now coming from D and going to C. In the actual transaction, D will pay C directly instead of going through B and A.

In a more common transaction, A assigns to E the right to receive the $10 and A also delegates to E the duty to tender the pen. This transaction may be illustrated:

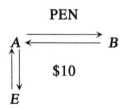

This transaction is a *transfer.* A is the *transferor.* E is the *transferee.*

In the actual transaction, E and B will perform directly, bypassing A. A does not drop out of the picture, however. Recall that in a delegation, the delegating party (the original obligor) remains liable to the obligee for performance and breach if the delegate does not perform. The obligee may not hold the delegate liable for performance and breach unless the delegate has *assumed* the obligation by promising to perform. If the delegate promises to perform, as it usually does, the obligee is a third party beneficiary of that promise.

If the obligee agrees to look to the delegate for performance and agrees to discharge the original obligor, there is a *novation*. In the last example, if *B* and *E* entered into a novation, *B* could look only to *E* for performance, as *A*'s obligation would be discharged. The transaction may be illustrated:

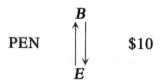

PEN $10

§ 14.2 Third party beneficiaries.

A third party acquires a right to enforce a contract only if that party is an "intended" beneficiary of a promise. An obvious example is the naming of a beneficiary in a life insurance contract. For example:

> The ABC Mutual Life Insurance Company of Milwaukee, Wisconsin agrees to pay at its Home Office immediately upon receipt of due proof of the death of
>
> **THE INSURED**_____
>
> **THE FACE AMOUNT**_____ **DOLLARS** to
>
> **THE DIRECT BENEFICIARY** _____
>
> with reservation to the Insured of the right of revocation and change of Direct Beneficiary.

In other cases it may not be as clear whether someone is a third party beneficiary of the parties' agreement. Ascertaining intent is always difficult, but can be made clearer through drafting. When a third party may enforce the contract, the scope of the promisor's duty is greater than if the promise was enforceable only by the promisee. It would be helpful to have some indication that the promisee bargained for this greater undertaking. As a drafting matter, the parties to the contract can clearly express their intent in the agreement. For example:

Example 1.

1. A claimant is defined as one having a direct contract with the Principal or with a Subcontractor of the Principal for labor, material, or both, used or reasonably required for use in the performance of the Contract, . . .

2. The above named Principal and Surety hereby jointly and severally agree with the Owner that every claimant as herein defined, who has not been paid in full before the expiration of a period of ninety (90) days after the date on which the last of such claimant's work or labor was done or performed, or materials were furnished by such claimant, may sue on this bond for the use of such claimant, prosecute the suit to final judgment for such sum or sums as may be justly due claimant, and have execution thereon. The Owner shall not be liable for the payment of any costs or expenses of any such suit.

Example 2.

NO THIRD PARTY BENEFICIARY. It is specifically agreed between the parties executing this contract that it is not intended by any of the provisions of any part of the contract to create the public or any member thereof a third party beneficiary hereunder, or to authorize anyone not a party to this contract to maintain a suit for personal injuries or property damage pursuant to the terms or provisions of this contract. The duties, obligations, and responsibilities of the parties to this contract with respect to third parties shall remain as imposed by law.

Example 1 is from a payment bond. The contract is between a contractor ("Principal") and a bonding company ("Surety") for the benefit of an Owner. Often the contractor does not pay a subcontractor, who looks to the bonding company for payment. A number of courts have held that subcontractors and suppliers could not recover on payment bonds because only the Owner appeared to be a beneficiary. The example makes clear that subcontractors and suppliers can recover. In Example 2, the parties to a construction contract have made clear that they do not intend any third party to be a beneficiary of their agreement.

§ 14.3 Assignment of rights.

Often contracts do not mention assignment. In that case, a court may have to determine whether assignment is permissible. There is a strong public policy in favor of assignment. Sometimes a contract will not directly mention assignment but will provide:

> This agreement is binding on the heirs, representatives and assigns of the parties.

By providing that the agreement is binding on "assigns" (by which the drafter means "assignees"), the drafter has created an implication that rights may be assigned. The drafter may wish to state clearly that assignment is permitted. For example:

> Either Seller or Buyer may assign its rights under this agreement in whole or in part.

In an effective assignment, the right to the obligor's performance is taken from the assignor and given to the assignee. To be enforceable, the assignment agreement should make clear the assignor's intention to make a present transfer and should recite a consideration. For example, assume that Landlord A has the right to receive money from tenants under rental agreements.

1. For a consideration, Landlord A agrees to pay over to B any money she receives.

2. Landlord A gives to Charity C the right to receive the money.

3. Landlord A sells the building to Landlord D. The contract provides that as of the closing date, D has the right to receive the tenants' payments under the present leases.

Example 1 is not an assignment. A has a contractual obligation to pay B the money she receives. B can enforce this right against A. But because A has not made a present transfer of her rights, B has no claim against the tenants. Example 2 is an assignment, but it is not effective. If the tenants pay C, their obligation to A is extinguished. But because it is a gift assignment, A may terminate it. Because A has no contractual obligation to C, she has not given up the right to enforce the tenants' obligations. Example 3 is an effective assignment. The contract should also provide for the parties to notify the tenants to pay D rather than A.

In a contract involving the sale of goods, the assignment agreement might look like this:

> ABC Co., Seller, assigns to DEF Co. all money due from XYZ Co., Buyer, under an agreement between Seller and Buyer dated August 1, 2003 for the sale of 1,000 widgets for $5,000. Dated: September 1, 2003.

DEF then might send a notice like this to XYZ:

> You are hereby notified that on September 1, 2003, ABC Co. as Assignor, assigned to me as Assignee, the right of Assignor to receive payments due under an agreement between you and ABC Co. dated August 1, 2003 for the sale of 1,000 widgets for $5,000.
>
> I am enclosing a copy of the assignment. Please send all payments due under the agreement to me at the above address. Dated: September 2, 2003.

§ 14.4 Delegation of duties.

As with assignment of rights, contracts often do not mention delegation of duties. While policy favors delegation, duties involving personal choice may not be delegated. The issue of whether a particular duty may be delegated is often a close question. The drafter can make clear that the parties contemplate delegation. For example:

> Either Seller or Buyer may delegate its duties under this contract in whole or in part. If any delegation is made, the delegating party must give notice to the non-delegating party at least 5 days prior to the delegation. The delegating party remains fully liable for performance of the delegated duties.

A delegation occurs when the obligor confers upon the delegate the power to perform. Recall, however, that the delegating party remains liable for performance. If the delegate does not perform, the obligee may hold the delegating party liable. The obligee may not enforce the agreement against the delegate unless the delegate promised to perform. In that case, the obligee may be a third party beneficiary of the delegate's promise. For example:

1. The *A* Construction Co. contracts to erect a building for Owner. *A* invites *B*, a new company looking for experience, to pour the foundation.

2. *A* Construction Co. contracts with *C* to pour the foundation for $1,000.

The first issue is whether the delegation is effective. In general, a party may delegate duties unless the obligee has a substantial interest in performance by the party it contracted with. Because of the policy favoring delegation, if the parties intend to prohibit delegation, they should state the prohibition in the agreement. Here, both delegations are effective. In both examples, *A* has conferred on the delegate the power to perform. In Example 1, *B* has made no promise to perform. If the foundation is not poured, Owner has a claim against only *A*. In Example 2, *C* has promised to perform. If the foundation is not poured, Owner has a claim against either *A* or *C*. When the delegate promises to perform, the delegate is said to have *assumed* the obligation. The drafter should make clear that the delegate has assumed the obligation. For example, when a purchaser of real property agrees to assume the seller's mortgage obligation, the purchaser signs a mortgage assumption agreement, which states in part:

Purchaser hereby assumes and agrees to pay the obligation secured by the above-described mortgage according to the terms of the mortgage and those of the note accompanying it.

---

§ 14.5   Is an assignment a transfer?

Drafters often use language permitting the "assignment of the contract." This phrase is ambiguous. A contract consists of rights and duties. Rights are *assigned* but duties are *delegated*. It is not clear in an "assignment of the contract" whether the parties intended to permit only assignment of rights or also delegation of duties. Public policy favors assignment and delegation. Therefore this phrase is interpreted broadly as a *transfer*, which is both an assignment of rights and a delegation of duties. A drafter who intends something less than a transfer should make this intention clear. For example:

No right or interest in this contract shall be assigned by either Buyer or Seller without the written permission of the other party and any attempted assignment shall be wholly void and totally ineffective for all purposes. This clause is meant to prohibit assignment of rights but not delegation of duties and the parties specifically intend to negate the provision of Section 2-210(3) of the Uniform Commercial Code.

---

§ 14.6   Contractual prohibitions.

Often parties do not want rights assigned or duties delegated. A party may not want a right assigned because the assignment might have an adverse effect on the obligor's duty. For example, if A assigns to C the right to receive goods from B, B may be concerned that A will have less incentive to tender payment, for A will have to pay without receiving performance. B may wish to prohibit the assignment.

Similarly, a party may want performance by the party it bargained with and may not want the obligation delegated to a stranger. For example, A may have contracted with B because B has a reputation for prompt, courteous service. If B delegates to C the obligation to perform, A may be concerned about the quality of performance. A may wish to prohibit the delegation. Of course, B remains liable for performance and breach, but A wants performance and not a legal claim.

Nevertheless, because of the strong policy favoring the free transfer of rights and duties, assignment and delegation are generally permitted in the absence of an understanding to the contrary. The drafter should expressly state in the contract that there is a restriction on assignment or delegation. Some assignments, such as the assignment of the right to receive money, are so important to the market economy, that a prohibition of assignment is unenforceable. *See* U.C.C. § 9-406.

Drafters often use language prohibiting the "assignment of the contract." Again the phrase is ambiguous, for it is not clear whether the parties intended to prohibit only assignment of rights or also delegation of duties. Public policy favors assignment and delegation. Therefore this phrase is interpreted narrowly as a prohibition only of delegation. A drafter who intends something more than a prohibition of delegation must make this intention clear. For example:

---

1. This contract may not be assigned.

---

2. No right or interest in this contract shall be assigned by either Buyer or Seller without the written permission of the other party, and no delegation of any obligation owed by either Buyer or Seller shall be made without the written permission of the other party. Any attempted assignment or delegation shall be wholly void and totally ineffective for all purposes.

In Example 1, the prohibition of "assignment" will be interpreted as a prohibition of delegation of duties and not a prohibition of assignment of rights. Example 2 makes clear that both delegation of duties and assignment of rights are prohibited.

When drafting a promise, the drafter must always ask, "What happens if a party doesn't do what it promised to do?" What are the consequences of breach of a provision prohibiting assignment or delegation? Because of the public policy favoring free transfer, courts often regard breach of the provision as a breach of promise, the remedy for which is damages, and not as an event that voids the assignment or delegation. Parties intending that breach voids the assignment or delegation should make this intention clear. For example:

1. The power of either Buyer or Seller to assign rights and delegate duties acquired or imposed under this contract is not limited. However, if either party makes an assignment or delegation without the written permission of the other party, the assignor or delegating party shall be liable for any damages caused the other party by the assignment or delegation.

2. Neither Buyer nor Seller shall assign any right or interest in this contract without the written permission of the other party, and neither Buyer nor Seller shall delegate any duty owed without the written permission of the other party. Any attempted assignment or delegation shall be wholly void and totally ineffective for all purposes.

Recall that a breach may give rise only to damages or it may relieve the other party of its obligation to perform. Example 1 makes clear that the assignment or delegation is effective; the consequence of breach is that the breaching party must pay damages. Example 2 makes clear that the attempted assignment or delegation is ineffective. Example 2 does not make clear whether the non-breaching party may also regard the breach as an event that terminates its obligations under the agreement. *See* Chapter 10, Promise and Condition.

§ 14.7　Novation.

A delegating party often informs the obligee of the delegation. Unless the duty is personal or the contract prohibits delegation, the obligee usually has no choice but to accept performance by the delegate. The fact that the obligee accepts or consents to the delegation is not legally meaningful. Acknowledgment does not discharge the obligation of the original obligor.

A novation is a contract in which the obligee agrees to discharge the original obligor in consideration of the delegate's promise to perform. For example, Wife owes $500 to Doctor A. In a separation agreement, Husband and Wife agree that Husband assumes this obligation. As between themselves, Husband and Wife have delegated to Husband the duty to pay Doctor A. But Doctor A may enforce the agreement against either party, for the delegation does not discharge Wife, the original obligor. To discharge the obligation of Wife requires a novation, a contract between Doctor A and Husband.

The drafter of a novation should make clear that the obligee intends to accept the performance of the delegate in lieu of performance of the original obligor. For example:

Doctor *A* acknowledges, that in consideration of Husband having assumed the liability of Wife to pay $500 for services performed on October 1, 2003, Doctor *A* releases all the claims which he had against Wife under the original contract. In lieu of those claims, Doctor *A* accepts the liability of Husband for the obligation of Wife under the original contract.

§ 14.8   Exercises.

1. Language of assignment and delegation. The following provision appears in a contract for the sale of goods. Revise the agreement for greater clarity:

I, ABC Co., assignor, hereby delegate to DEF Co., assignee, the performance of all undertakings to be performed by assignor as specified in Sections 5 and 6 of an agreement dated October 1, 2004, between myself and XYZ Co. for the sale of 1,000 widgets for $5,000.

In consideration of the performance of the undertakings by assignee, I shall pay assignee the amount of $4,800 payable 30 days after delivery.

Dated September 1, 2004.

2. Sale of a business. *A* operates a small business. *A* has a long term contract to buy parts from *B* and a long term contract to sell finished goods to *C*. *D* wants to buy the business from *A*. *D* asks you to draft the contract between *A* and *D*. What provisions in the contracts between *A* and *B*, and between *A* and *C*, would you look for? What provisions would you put in the contract between *A* and *D*?

3. Resale of a business. Immediately after *D* buys the business from *A*, *D* has an opportunity to sell it to *E*. *D* asks *A* if *A* would agree to discharge *D*'s obligations under the agreement and substitute *E*. *A* agrees. What provisions would you put in a contract between the parties?

Part II

How the Principles of Drafting Are Exemplified in Contracts

Chapter 15

THE FRAMEWORK OF A CONTRACT

§ 15.1 Introduction.

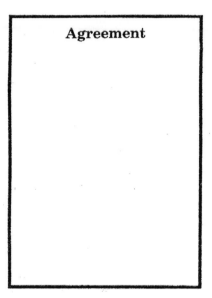

How do lawyers begin drafting a contract? They usually do not begin with a blank page (or, in the modern office, a blank screen). They begin with a model — a contract that the office has used previously, or a form from a formbook. In a law office, the following scenario is all too common. A partner calls an associate and says, "Draft an agreement for Newman. We did this kind of agreement in the Olsen case. Pull the Olsen file and use that agreement as a model." In many offices, the form will be indexed and filed on computer, bypassing the problem of erratic memory.

All the form tells you is that for one particular client in one particular situation at one particular time, the transaction looked like this. The form does not tell you how Newman's problem differs from Olsen's, whether the Olsen agreement was properly drafted in the first place, and whether the law has changed since the Olsen agreement was drafted.

While the form may be found, much of the institutional wisdom that went into it may not have been preserved. *See* Chapter 19, Drafting with a

Computer. The drafter who relies on an office form may lack the advantage of a discussion of the substantive purposes of the provisions. Why were some included and others omitted? Was it because of a legal requirement? A drafter's eccentricity? An unusual fact situation? A negotiated concession? A mistake (heaven forbid!)? Often all the WHY is lost and all that remains is the WHAT.

Early in my practice I asked the lawyer with whom I was negotiating an agreement the meaning of a provision in his draft. "I don't know what it means," he replied, "but it is always found in this type of agreement." I must confess that at the time I accepted this response. Now I realize that drafting is a process of legal analysis. Ideally, an attorney should research the substance of the transaction and the history of the agreement to understand the role of each provision. Although a practitioner cannot always take the time for the research, it is important to take the first step and to determine the meaning of the provision. If you don't know what it means, how do you expect it to be meaningful to your client or to a court?

Whether taken from a previous agreement or from a formbook, the model is only a guide. As a drafter, you must consider whether the language serves the purposes of the agreement you are drafting. Based on your discussions with the client, your substantive research into the area in which you are drafting, and your knowledge of contract law, you may find that the existing provisions must be altered or supplemented with additional provisions. To integrate the provisions into a working document, you must understand the purpose served by each provision in the agreement and how the provisions interrelate. Should a client ask about the meaning of a particular provision, you don't want to respond, "I don't know," or "That is language from another agreement that is not appropriate for your agreement."

§ 15.2 The use of forms.

A form which served the needs of other parties may not serve the present parties and must be examined anew. At the same time, precedent cautions us to stick with what has gone before, and efficiency persuades us to rely on assembly-line products rather than tailor-make each new item. These are legitimate concerns that must be balanced. Sidney F. Parham states:[1]

> No one can ever hope to be even passably competent in this field [drafting], unless and until he recognizes that each legal document involves to a greater or lesser extent an effort in original composition.

Most importantly, do not be in awe of forms. A practitioner who, as a law student, never saw a form may tend to clutch it as a drowning person grabs whatever flotsam comes within reach. The form may represent the "answer" that has been hidden by a devious instructor. A form is neither a taboo object, never to be touched, nor an object of veneration, to be respectfully copied. It is a guide, perhaps a checklist. The most useful formbooks

---

[1] SIDNEY F. PARHAM, JR., THE FUNDAMENTALS OF LEGAL WRITING 11–12 (1967).

key the presentation of the provisions to a discussion of their substance. The form must be subjected to the same critical thinking involved in all legal analysis.

Rare is the form that cannot be improved. Most antiquated forms and models, and many modern ones, would benefit from an analysis of both their substance and their style. Many formbooks claim to be "litigation-tested." It seems hardly a recommendation for a form that it was the subject of litigation! Having seen the problems caused by the form, the drafter should feel free to improve upon the original. In order to work with a model, whether from a formbook or from an office file, you must always:

- Compare the facts of each situation
- Understand the substance of the transaction
- Update the law
- Update the language

After you have completed these tasks, you are ready to build the document. Drafters speak of the "architecture" of an agreement. The term "architecture" is a good one, for it suggests that the assembly of a document is an art. Just as a building must be assembled according to a plan, so must an agreement. A document is composed of individual provisions, but those provisions must be assembled in a clear and coherent manner. It is unproductive to generalize about the correct architecture for agreements, for as with a building, form follows function. Each agreement requires the structure that is logical and systematic for that particular transaction.

A living agreement should not be filed away and forgotten. It should be accessible to the parties. The user should be able to locate and understand a particular provision and other provisions affecting that provision. Sometimes the law *requires* you to draft certain agreements in plain language. Many plain language laws require that a contract be "appropriately divided and captioned by its various sections." When the agreement is divided and captioned, the reader can find provisions more easily. Aesthetics are important to agreements. A well-drafted instrument gains force not only from its contents but also from its appearance.

The use of a decimal system for numbering paragraphs can be useful. The decimal system makes it easier to add or delete paragraphs and to subordinate one provision to another. It is also easier to find a particular paragraph. The decimal system is illustrated by the Shareholders' Agreement in § 17.12 and by the Standard Form Listing Contract in § 18.6.

§ 15.3 Zero-base drafting.

A drafter may find that no model serves the needs of a particular transaction. In this case, you must think about the legal principles in question and how they find expression. In "zero-base" drafting, the agreement is built from the principles rather than from a model. If you understand the principles and how language can be used to express them, you will be able to make drafting decisions with greater confidence.

To begin zero-base drafting, start with an original form that can serve as an outline and with the appropriate legal authority, usually case law and legislation. Then follow these four steps:

Step 1: Outline the document based on the contents of the original.

Step 2: Evaluate the rights and responsibilities of both parties as stated in the legal authorities.

Step 3: Assess the issues involving business risk, based on provisions from the original document and an evaluation of business records. This assessment may show the need for new provisions or even whole new categories of information.

Step 4: Draft the document using plain language techniques.

For example, a residential lease might be constructed based on the statutes and case law that govern the transaction. A model could then be used as a checklist to determine whether any appropriate provisions were omitted. The landlord should be consulted to determine which provisions have a business justification and whether any additional concerns might be addressed. Because most clients don't know the meaning of the boilerplate in the agreements they commonly use, this discussion should contribute to the education of the client as well as the attorney. The final document should more accurately reflect the state of the law than many landlord-oriented forms that unnecessarily overreach.

§ 15.4   The structure of a contract.

Whether adapted from a form or written using zero-base techniques, most agreements can be built on the following framework:

1.   Description of the instrument

2.   Caption

3.   Transition (language of agreement)

4.   Recitals

5.   Definitions

6.   Operative language and boilerplate terms

7.   Closing

§ 15.4.1   Description of the instrument.

At the top of the page, you might want to indicate the type of agreement you are creating. This heading has no substantive significance, but can be useful to readily identify the document. A heading such as "AGREEMENT" serves little purpose. You might want to specify "CONTRACT FOR DEED" or "BILL OF SALE" or "LAST WILL AND TESTAMENT OF MILDRED PIERCE."

§ 15.4.2   Caption.

The main function of the caption (sometimes formally called the *exordium*) is to identify in a nutshell the *names* of the parties and the *legal action* they are taking. For example:

John Doe as landlord and Richard Roe as tenant agree to a residential lease on the following terms.

This example has identified the names of the parties (John Doe and Richard Roe) and the legal action they are taking (entering a lease agreement).

In addition, the caption may provide a shorthand way to identify the parties and may specify a date. We will examine these aspects of the caption and then edit a caption.

a. Identifying the parties. You will assist the reader of the document if you provide a shorthand way of identifying the parties throughout the agreement. Once you have identified each party, make sure you use the same identification throughout the agreement. Also, make sure the shorthand is appropriate under the circumstances. For example, in a mortgage agreement between First Bank of Tiny City and Mary Smith, you could use any of the following shorthand references:

---

1. Mortgage agreement dated October 1, 2003, between First Bank of Tiny City ("Bank") and Mary Smith ("Smith").

---

2. Mortgage agreement dated October 1, 2003, between First Bank of Tiny City ("Mortgagee") and Mary Smith ("Mortgagor").

---

3. Mortgage agreement dated October 1, 2003, between First Bank of Tiny City ("Lender") and Mary Smith ("Borrower").

---

4. Mortgage agreement dated October 1, 2003, between First Bank of Tiny City ("you," "your," or "yours") and Mary Smith ("I," "me," "mine," or "my").

Example 1 works well to identify the parties to a one-shot agreement. However, it would not be practical for a party such as a bank, which frequently uses a standardized agreement, to enter the customer's name

("Smith") throughout the document. Example 2 is more practical. Each time the bank enters an agreement with a new customer it will have to write a new caption, but the shorthand "Mortgagor" and "Mortgagee" will remain the same throughout the agreement. However, this shorthand could be confusing to a lay person, who may be unable to keep straight who is "Mortgagor" and who is "Mortgagee." Example 3 solves that problem by referring to the parties by their readily identifiable roles as "Lender" and "Borrower."

Example 4 employs an informality that will be used throughout the agreement to make the agreement more personal (e.g., "If I fail to timely pay any amount due under this agreement, you may. . . ."). The parties should have no difficulty understanding the text as long as they recall who is "you" and who is "I." In some jurisdictions, a plain language law may require that a consumer contract refer to the parties either by personal pronouns or by their actual or shortened names.

b. Date. What is the point of a date in an agreement? Obviously it is a useful reference, particularly to distinguish one agreement among many. Often it may have legal consequences, such as tax ramifications, that are dependent on a date. Too often, however, the agreement contains a number of dates and they are not synchronized. There may be a *formal* date, the date in the caption. There may be a *signature* date, the date the document is executed. There may be a *performance* date, the date performance of the agreement begins, which may occur before or after the signature date.

The performance dates will often be drafted into the agreement and are less subject to change than the formal date or the signature date. Because of the legal consequences attached, the signature date should be an exact date and might well be left blank to be filled in when the signatures are added. The formal date can either be omitted or, if included, could be stated "as of" a certain date, generally the date of performance. The "as of" term will prevent needless explanations of why a document dated October 1 was in fact signed on October 5. ("What else in this agreement was my client told to disregard, counselor?")

There is no reason to write out the date in words, as in "this First day of October, 2003." "October 1, 2003" will do the job. For example:

---

1. September 20, 2003

   John Doe as landlord and Richard Roe as tenant agree to a residential lease on the following terms.

---

2. Residential lease agreement dated as of October 1, 2003, between John Doe as landlord and Richard Roe as tenant.

3. John Doe as landlord and Richard Roe as tenant agree to a residential lease on the following terms.

. . . .

Dated: September 20, 2003

c. Editing a caption. To decide whether you should add language to a caption you have drafted or whether you should delete language from a form caption, ask what purpose the language serves. If it serves no purpose, it can be discarded. If it serves a substantive purpose, it belongs in the body of the agreement. For example:

Agreement made and entered this 1st day of October, 2003, by and between ABC Corp., 200 West 16th St., New York, N.Y., a Delaware corporation (hereinafter referred to as "Buyer") and XYZ Corp., 100 East 54th St., New York, N.Y., a New York corporation (hereinafter referred to as "Seller").

While none of this language is fatal, most of it is surplusage. You can edit the following overblown expressions:

Before	*After*
made and entered	made
this 1st day of October, 2003	October 1, 2003
by and between	between
hereinafter referred to as "Buyer"	"Buyer"

What purpose is served by including the business addresses? If they serve a substantive purpose, for example, to indicate the address to which notices must be sent, they belong with that substantive provision. If they serve no purpose other than convenience, they clutter the caption and might better be placed at the end of the document.

What purpose is served by including the states of incorporation? If they serve a substantive purpose, for example, to represent that the business is in fact incorporated or to indicate the law governing the agreement, they belong with that substantive provision. If they serve no substantive purpose, they may be deleted.

Your edited draft of this caption might look like this:

Agreement made as of October 1, 2003, between ABC Corp. ("Buyer") and XYZ Corp. ("Seller").

§ 15.4.3 Transition (language of agreement).

Your agreement should contain language signifying that the parties have entered an agreement. Words of agreement could be added in a number of ways:

Example 1.

APARTMENT RENTAL AGREEMENT
Dated: October 1, 2003

Susan Potter ("Tenant") and ABC Corporation ("Owner") agree as follows:

1. PREMISES

   Apartment No. 5, Valley View Apartments, Lubbock, Texas.

2. RENT

   Tenant shall pay each month in advance. . . .

Example 2.

APARTMENT RENTAL AGREEMENT

Agreement made October 1, 2003

1. BETWEEN

   Tenant: Susan Potter

2. AND

   Owner: ABC Corporation

3. ON

   Apartment No. 5, Valley View Apartments, Lubbock, Texas.

   THE PARTIES AGREE AS FOLLOWS:

4. RENT

   Tenant shall pay each month in advance. . . .

Example 3.

APARTMENT RENTAL AGREEMENT
Dated: October 1, 2003

1. BETWEEN

   Tenant: Susan Potter

2. AND

   Owner: ABC Corporation

3. ON

   Apartment No. 5, Valley View Apartments, Lubbock, Texas.

4. RENT

   Tenant shall pay each month in advance. . . .

Example 1 uses the simple form "*A* and *B* agree as follows." Example 2 sets out the parties' names and then states "The parties agree as follows." In Example 3, the agreement is well-edited to be clear and logically organized. The words of agreement, however, are found in the description of the instrument. Instead of pressing the description into substantive service the drafter should incorporate other words of agreement between the parties.

Traditionally, agreements contain words of transition between the caption and the body of the agreement. These expressions are often archaic and should be avoided. For example:

WITNESSETH:

KNOW ALL MEN BY THESE PRESENTS:

NOW, therefore, in consideration of the premises and the mutual promises herein contained, the parties hereby agree as follows:

Transitional words are usually included because drafters have always done it that way. They are surplus, but harmless surplus. If the caption does not contain words of agreement, however, the transitional words may supply them. In Example 2 above, the transitional words "The parties agree as follows" between provisions 3 and 4 serve this useful purpose. These expressions are modern and direct:

THE PARTIES AGREE AS FOLLOWS:

IT IS AGREED:

§ 15.4.4   Recitals.

Drafters often begin instruments with a statement of background. They may do this to clarify the parties' intentions or to resolve problems of interpretation. Although the practice may be helpful, it is often overdone. More importantly, the drafter must be careful not to cast in the form of recitals provisions that are in fact representations or agreements. For example:

Whereas, Buyer and Seller entered into a contract dated March 15, 2003 in which Seller promised to deliver 100 widgets to Buyer for $1,000;

Whereas, 40 of the widgets were defective; and

Whereas, Buyer and Seller desire to enter into an accord to resolve the dispute between them;

The parties agree as follows:

Because this agreement resolves problems that arose under a previous agreement, the recitals are useful to provide background. What does the recital mean, however, when it states that the parties "entered into a contract"? Does this mean that they agree that the previous transaction was an enforceable contract, precluding them from later litigating that issue? What does the recital mean when it states that "40 of the widgets were defective"? Under the substantive law of accord and satisfaction, a dispute must be raised in good faith. Does this mean that the parties agree that 40 widgets were defective, precluding Seller from later claiming that Buyer did not raise the dispute in good faith?

The recitals could be rewritten as follows:

Whereas, on March 15, 2003, Seller promised to deliver 100 widgets to Buyer;

Whereas, Buyer alleges that 40 of the widgets were defective;

Finally, the use of *whereas* to introduce each recital has only tradition going for it. A modern drafter might enumerate the recitals after introducing them with a word such as *Background* or *Premises*. For example:

Background:

1. On March 15, 2003, Seller promised to deliver 100 widgets to Buyer.

2. Buyer alleges that 40 of the widgets were defective.

3. Buyer and Seller desire to enter into an accord to resolve the dispute between them.

The parties agree as follows:

Recitals may also be used to secure a remedy by informing the court of the substantive importance of a term. For example, one of the eternal

questions of contract law is: How close to the stated obligation must performance be? *See* § 10.6.3. The parties may specify in the contract the
consequences of inexact performance. Alternatively, the parties could tell
the court in recitals how exact performance must be. For example:

Premises:

 Buyer is in the business of building high-technology components. In
this business, exact tolerances are crucial to proper performance. The
slightest deviation will result in a substandard product. Therefore, it
is the intention of the parties that the specifications agreed to by Seller
must be met exactly.

 Similarly, in the event of ambiguity, the guiding principle of interpretation is "the intent of the parties." The parties can express that intent in
recitals. If the recitals themselves are ambiguous, one court suggested this
commonsense solution:

> If the recitals are clear and the operative part is ambiguous, the recitals
> govern the construction. If the recitals are ambiguous, and the operative
> part is clear, the operative part must prevail. If both the recitals and
> the operative part are clear, but they are inconsistent with each other,
> the operative part is to be preferred.

 Parties sometimes erroneously state representations as recitals. For
example:

Whereas, Debtor is a duly qualified corporation with full licensing authority to engage in the business of. . . .

---

or

Whereas, Seller owns full title to the premises, free and clear of any
and all liens and encumbrances. . . .

 If it turns out that a representation made by one party is not true, does
the other party have any remedy? To make clear that these representations
are not agreements of the parties, the drafter should move them from the
recitals to the body of the agreement. They may be removed as recitals and
rewritten as substantive provisions:

> Debtor represents that it is a duly qualified corporation with full licensing authority to engage in the business of. . . .

or

> Seller represents that it owns full title to the premises, free and clear of any and all liens and encumbrances. . . .

The statement of the representation in this form should trigger the drafter to ask, "What if the representation is not true?" The drafter can then provide a remedy for that contingency. *See* Chapter 16, Operative Language and Boilerplate Terms.

§ 15.4.5 Definitions.

The parties may begin the agreement with a series of definitions in order to achieve clarity without repetition. For example:

> In this agreement, the word *structure* shall mean an office building of no less than 20 stories.

Definitions should be written in the present tense. This definition can be rewritten as:

> In this agreement, the word *structure* means an office building of no less than 20 stories.

When you have created a definition, make sure you use it and that you use it consistently. Richard Robinson gives this example of a definition that is not used:

> Humpty Dumpty stipulates a new meaning and uses it once only. He is like a man who, wishing to say that the sky is overcast, says instead: "By 'soda' I shall mean that the sky is overcast. Soda." He uses eleven words to say what four would say better, and these four are included in his eleven.

A good way to test whether you have used a definition consistently is to use your word processor's "find and replace" function to replace each use of the defined term with the definition. You can then determine whether the definition has been properly used. For example, a contract defines "Acceptance Period" as follows:

> Acceptance occurs when the System performs without Major Failure over a period of thirty (30) days after delivery ("Acceptance Period").

A later paragraph uses the defined term:

> If at any time during the Acceptance Period the System has experienced Major Failures, Buyer shall notify Seller in writing in a timely manner, at which time the current Acceptance Period shall terminate and Seller shall cure any pending outage or failure. Seller shall thereafter notify Buyer that a new Acceptance Period has commenced. In no event, however, shall the Acceptance process extend beyond the forty-fifth (45th) day after delivery.

Replacing the defined term [Acceptance Period] with the definition [period of thirty (30) days after delivery] each time the defined term occurs, we get the following:

> If at any time during the [period of thirty (30) days after delivery] the System has experienced Major Failures, Buyer shall notify Seller in writing in a timely manner, at which time the current [period of thirty (30) days after delivery] shall terminate and Seller shall cure any pending outage or failure. Seller shall thereafter notify Buyer that a new [period of thirty (30) days after delivery] has commenced. In no event, however, shall the Acceptance process extend beyond the forty-fifth (45th) day after delivery.

It is readily apparent that the definition does not work.

Another problem with definitions is the "elegant variation." When learning composition, most of us were instructed to consult a thesaurus so that we would use a variety of words. In drafting, this can be disastrous, for the Golden Rule of Drafting is:

> Never change your language unless you wish to change your meaning, and always change your language if you wish to change your meaning.

For example, an agreement states that "the parties shall use *reasonable efforts* to timely perform this contract." A later provision states that "the seller shall use *best efforts.*" This change in language may suggest that the parties intended the meaning of *best efforts* to be something other than *reasonable efforts,* perhaps requiring more heroic efforts.

§ 15.4.6   Operative language and boilerplate terms.

Operative language and boilerplate terms are discussed in detail in Chapter 16, Operative Language and Boilerplate Terms.

§ 15.4.7   Closing.

Substantively, the closing of an agreement (sometimes formally called the *testimonium*) should demonstrate that the parties assent to it. They do this by affixing their signatures. For example:

> Buyer   Seller

It is important that the parties who sign the agreement are the same parties recited in the caption. For example, if Buyer and Seller are corporations, the corporation must sign the agreement. Of course, a corporation can do this only through an authorized person:

> ABC Corporation   XYZ Corporation
> by _____   by _____

Traditionally, other language of closing is used, but it is usually of no substantive effect. For example:

> IN WITNESS WHEREOF, the parties have hereunto set their hands and seals this 15th day of October, 2003:

This language provides a visual break between the text and the signatures but it is archaic. *Whereof* and *hereunto* should be avoided. *Seals* have no effect in most jurisdictions. If the date has been stated earlier, repeating it is at best redundant and at worst contradictory. If it has not been previously stated, the date is substantively important, but can be stated in a simplified manner:

> Signed October 15, 2003.

If not stated elsewhere in the agreement, the parties' addresses might also be added. For example:

> October 15, 2003.
>
> Buyer   Seller
> Buyer's address: Seller's address:
> 260 West 21st St.   60 East 42nd St.
> New York, NY 10011   New York, NY 10017

§ 15.5 Exercises.

1. Revising a form. John Zilch, owner and operator of Zilch's Good Stuff Gift Shoppe in your town, wants to buy pottery produced locally by Sheila

Smith. If the pottery sells well, Zilch and Smith want to continue the arrangement.

John asks you to draft a contract to use for this agreement and perhaps for similar deals in the future. After Zilch leaves your office, you find the following form in a form book:

MEMORANDUM OF AGREEMENT

This memorandum of agreement, made this _____ day of _____, 20____, by and between _____, of the city of _____, county of _____, state of _____, hereinafter sometimes referred to as the party of the first part and _____ of the city of _____, county of _____, state of _____, hereinafter sometimes referred to as the party of the second part, witnesseth the agreement of the aforesaid parties hereto, as follows, to wit:

1. The party of the first part agrees to purchase and the party of the second part agrees to sell _____ for a total price of _____ dollars ($_____).

2. The party of the second part agrees to deliver the goods as described in paragraph 1 hereinabove to the party of the first part at _____, on the _____ day of _____, _____.

3. The party of the first part agrees to pay the party of the second part the total price set forth in paragraph 1 hereinabove at the time of delivery as set forth in paragraph 2 hereinabove.

4. In witness whereof, the parties have set their hands and seals to this Agreement as of the date first above written.

_____(s)   _____(s)
Party of the first part   Party of the second part
Address _____   Address _____

_____   _____

---

a. Revise this form for style. One consideration is to be sure the parties understand their agreement.

b. In addition to making the agreement clear, you will want to analyze whether it serves your client's purposes. What questions should you ask Zilch before you reduce the agreement to writing? What provisions would you consider adding to the form?

2. Zero-base drafting. The following provision regarding security deposits is found in a lease used in Tennessee:

SECURITY DEPOSIT

LESSEE agrees to pay LESSOR the sum of $_____ as a security deposit upon the execution of this lease, the receipt of which is hereby acknowledged. If LESSEE shall promptly pay the rent as provided herein, and if he shall comply with each and all of the terms and conditions of this written lease which are to be performed be LESSEE during LESSEE'S entire tenancy, then upon the termination of this tenancy, and after the surrender of the possession of the leased premises according to the terms of this lease, in good and clean condition, reasonable wear and tear excepted, LESSOR will refund to LESSEE the said sum within two (2) weeks following 30 day written notice. It is understood and agreed that this Security Deposit is forfeited if for any reason the Applicant does not occupy these quarters also. If this lease is signed by more than one person as LESSEE, the LESSOR may make return of the Security Deposit or any part thereof to any one or more of the persons constituting the LESSEE without further liability therefor to any other person or LESSEE who may have contributed all or part of said deposit. LESSEE understands and agrees that only that portion of the Security Deposit above the fair and reasonable cost necessary to repair the walls, floors, cabinets, carpet, drapes, windows, plumbing fixtures, range, refrigerator and furniture or premises, will be refunded.

ESCROW All monies paid as deposits shall be held in _____ in escrow account number _____.

Revise this provision twice, once using the traditional techniques of drafting, and then using zero-base drafting. To accomplish the latter task, you may use your traditional draft as an outline, but the content should be based on the substantive law. Because this provision is from a Tennessee lease, we must examine the Tennessee statute, which is based on the Uniform Residential Landlord and Tenant Act. The relevant section provides:

§ 66-28-301. Security deposits

(a) All landlords of residential property requiring security deposits prior to occupancy shall be required to deposit all tenants' security deposits in an account used only for that purpose, in any bank or other lending institution subject to regulation by the state of Tennessee or any agency of the United States government. Prospective tenants shall be informed of the location of the separate account and the account number.

(b) At the termination of occupancy, the landlord shall inspect the premises and compile a comprehensive listing of any damage to the unit which is the basis for any charge against the security deposit and the estimated dollar cost of repairing such damage. The tenant shall then have the right to inspect the premises to ascertain the accuracy of such listing. The landlord and the tenant shall sign such listing, which signatures shall be conclusive evidence of the accuracy of such listing. If the tenant shall refuse to sign such listing, he shall state specifically in writing the items on the list to which he dissents, and shall sign such statement of dissent. If the tenant has moved or is otherwise inaccessible to the landlord, the landlord shall mail a copy of the listing of damages and estimated cost of repairs to the tenant at his last known mailing address.

(c) No landlord shall be entitled to retain any portion of a security deposit if the security deposit was not deposited in a separate account as required by subsection (a) and if the final damage listing required by subsection (b) is not provided.

(d) A tenant who disputes the accuracy of the final damage listing given pursuant to subsection (b) may bring an action in a circuit or general sessions court of competent jurisdiction of this state. Tenant's claim shall be limited to those items from which the tenant specifically dissented in accordance with the listing or specifically dissented in accordance with subsection (b) of this section; otherwise the tenant shall not be entitled to recover any damages under this section.

(e) Should a tenant vacate the premises with unpaid rent due and owing, and without making a demand for return of deposit, the landlord may, after thirty (30) days, remove the deposit from the account and apply the moneys to the unpaid debt.

(f) In the event the tenant leaves not owing rent and having any refund due, the landlord shall send notification to the last known or reasonable determinable address, of the amount of any refund due the tenant. In the event the landlord shall not have received a response from the tenant within sixty (60) days from the sending of such notification, the landlord may remove the deposit from the account and retain it free from any claim of the tenant or any person claiming in his behalf.

(g) This section does not preclude the landlord or tenant from recovering other damages to which they may be entitled under this chapter.

3. Organization of an Agreement. The following is the Table of Contents of a contract that has been organized in a logical manner. How would you rearrange the order of the provisions? What organizing principle did you use in rearranging?

Table of Contents

1. Appropriations Refinancing Act Incorporated by Reference
2. Assignment
3. Billing and Payment

4. Commencement Date

5. Contract Revisions and Waivers

6. Definitions

7. Delivery

8. Effective Date and Term

9. Entire Agreement

10. Governing Law and Dispute Resolution

11. Notices and Information Exchange

12. Obligations Upon Expiration or Termination

13. Recitals

14. Sale Charges

15. Sale of Other Products or Services

16. Sale Quantities

17. Sale Scheduling Provisions

18. Signatures

19. Termination of Prior Agreement on Commencement Date

20. Uncontrollable Forces

4. Organization of a Term. Here is a contractual provision that is organized in a logical way. What is the organizing principle? Are there any problems with this plan? Is there a better way to organize the term?

---

15. ENERGY EFFICIENCY SERVICES

(1) **Duties of BPA**

(a) BPA shall provide an Energy Efficiency Task Order in response to Customer's request for service.

(b) BPA shall commence implementation of the Task Order when it receives and accepts the Task Order from Customer. BPA may accomplish the work, at the discretion of BPA, by using BPA employees or through the use of partners.

(c) BPA or its partners shall perform agreed-upon services as specified in the Energy Efficiency Task Order approved by Customer.

(d) BPA may elect to accept, counter propose, or reject a Customer Task Order.

(2) **Duties of Customer**

(a) Customer shall request BPA services under this Agreement.

(b) Customer shall provide BPA with a signed Energy Efficiency Task Order within 45 days indicating its acceptance or rejection of BPA's offer to provide the services requested.

(c) Customer shall provide BPA with access to necessary information and facilities as agreed to by the Parties necessary to provide the energy efficiency products and services.

(d) Securing necessary environmental permits or waivers are the responsibility of Customer, unless other arrangements are made by the Parties.

5. The Personal Management Contract. The first page of a contract that you found in a formbook looks like the below. How might you revise it?

EXCLUSIVE PERSONAL MANAGEMENT AGREEMENT

This Agreement, made this _____ day of _____, 20_____, by and between _____, hereinafter called "MANAGER" and _____, also known as _____, hereinafter called "Artist."

WHEREAS, THE Artist is engaged in the field of entertainment and is desirous of utilizing the services of a manager to aid Artist in furthering Artist's career,

1. APPOINTMENT

WHEREAS, the Personal Manager desires to manage the Artist and assist Artist in the furtherance of Artist's professional career as an entertainer in the Entertainment Industry, and Manager hereby accepts such appointment. "Entertainment Industry" and "Entertainment" as used in this Agreement means the fields of music, recording, motion picture, television, video, audio visual devices, radio, theater, live performance, literature, advertising and endorsements, and the licensing of Artist's name and likeness here now known or hereafter invented.

2. TERM

Manager is hereby engaged as Artist's exclusive personal manager, representative, the advisor, director of all Artist's personal business and affairs in all branches of the entertainment industry, throughout the universe. The Agreement will continue for _____ (_____) years (hereinafter the "initial term") from the date hereof, and will be renewed for _____ (_____) year(s) periods (hereinafter "renewal period(s)") automatically unless either party gives written notice of termination to the other not later than thirty (30) days prior to the expiration of the initial term or the then current renewal period, as applicable, subject to the terms and conditions hereof.

3. SERVICES

Manager's duties hereunder are to use reasonable efforts to further Artist's professional career and business interests, and to guide and advise the Artist with respect to Artist's career and to act as Artist's advisor and Personal Manager in all matters concerning their professional interest, whenever Manager may be reasonably called upon to do so.

NOW, THEREFORE, be it resolved that in consideration of the covenants contained herein, the Artist and the Manager agree as follows:

6. The Golden Rule of Drafting. Can you find a violation of the Golden Rule in these provisions?

a. Buyer is responsible for removal of any hazardous material (e.g., asbestos) or correction of any hazardous condition that affects Seller's performance of services. Services will be delayed until Buyer corrects the hazardous condition; Seller shall not be liable to Buyer as a result of such delays.

b. The MOU and Order(s) placed hereunder shall be subject to Company's standard Telecommunications Service Provider Purchase and License Agreement, a copy of which has been previously provided to Customer and is incorporated herein by this reference, until Customer signs the Company Telecommunications Service Provider and License Agreement.

Subject to the terms and conditions contained herein, Company agrees to apply a total discount of XX% to the list price of all Company products ordered by Customer upon execution of the Telco and Service Provider Agreement.

c. Export. The Receiving Party shall not transmit, directly or indirectly, the Confidential Information or any technical data received from Company, nor the direct product thereof outside the United States without Company's prior written consent and in accordance with all export laws and regulations of the United States. The Receiving Party agrees that it does not intend nor will it directly or indirectly, export or re-export any Confidential Information to any end-user who it knows or has reason to know will utilize the Confidential Information in the design, development or production of nuclear, chemical or biological weapons or to any end-user who has been prohibited from participating in U.S. export transactions by any federal agency of the U.S. Government.

Chapter 16

OPERATIVE LANGUAGE AND BOILERPLATE TERMS

§ 16.1 Introduction.

The term "operative language" refers to the language that affects legal relationships. The drafter must choose language with care. In giving guidance to the drafter, however, it is not possible to say, do it a certain way and you will obtain a certain result. Contracts are for the parties to make and the first rule of interpretation is to carry out the parties' intentions. *See* § 7.1. Words are not magical incantations like "abracadabra." You must consider what it is you want to say and how you can best say it.

The word "boilerplate" is often used to describe the all-purpose language that is found in every contract. Usually boilerplate provisions appear at the end of the contract, often under a heading such as "Miscellaneous." The frequency with which these terms appear may cause the drafter to pass over them, saying in effect, "that is just boilerplate." But particularly because word processing makes it so easy to change the wording of a term, you should not assume that you know what the term means without reading it, and you should never underestimate its importance. As you saw in Part I, a term can be worded in different ways to serve different purposes. That is also true for boilerplate terms.

Determining what to call the separate sections of a contract is itself a difficult task. Often drafters refer to the "terms and conditions" of the agreement. This expression may have once been a term of art, distinguishing between those provisions that operated as promises and those that operated as conditions. Today the phrase is not used precisely. *See* § 10.3. To avoid any misunderstanding, the modern drafter may wish to employ a single word, such as *terms, provisions, clauses,* or *paragraphs* to describe the various sections of the agreement and use it consistently.

The futility of attempting to impose exact meaning on a word is illustrated in a passage from Corbin's treatise. Corbin had strong opinions on the appropriate legal meaning of the word *condition*. Yet he sensibly realized that when the word is found in a contract, it should not always be interpreted according to the meaning he reserved for it:

> Now, however beautiful and exact may be the usage and terminology of this book, comparatively few people will read it; and it is impossible to compel millions of contractors to conform to it. It will not even be possible to induce lawyers, and other supposedly skilled draftsmen of contracts and statutes and constitutions, to conform to it. The courts, and the

lawyers and law writers, must take the raw material that is prepared for them by contractors and draftsmen and determine its meaning and operation. The problem is one of interpretation and construction and the problem now before this writer is to give aid in this process of interpretation and construction. Most assuredly, it is not to force meanings upon contractors that they did not intend, or to penalize them for not choosing their words according to a system that is more beautiful and exact.

While unfailing precision cannot be attained, drafters pay a heavy price for sloppy language. It is good preventive lawyering to take the time to improve the language during the drafting stage rather than to litigate the meaning later. Often language is not clear because the thinking that preceded it is not clear. First be sure of what you want to say, then find the language to express it clearly.

§ 16.2   Stating obligations.

By definition, a contract is a set of promises. Recall the definition of *promise* in Restatement (Second) of Contracts § 2(1):

> A promise is a manifestation of intention to act or refrain from acting in a specified way, so made as to justify a promisee in understanding that a commitment has been made.

An agreement does not usually contain the word *promise*. But the agreement must communicate that the promisor has undertaken some obligation that the promisee has a right to expect. Language of promise is best communicated by the word *shall*. If *shall* is used to express promises, then it must not be used to express the future. The problem of expressing future action is solved by drafting obligations in the present tense; on rare occasions when the future is needed, use *will*.

For example, the "Fair Clause" found in § 9.5 states in part:

> If either party hereto shall believe that a new situation described in § 15.2 shall have arisen, then, at the request of either party hereto, the parties shall promptly consult with a view toward reaching a mutually acceptable agreement dealing with such situation.

The first *shall* does not communicate an obligation. Delete it and use the present tense: If either party hereto *believes*. Similarly, the second *shall* may be deleted and the past tense substituted: that a new situation described in § 15.2 *has arisen*. The third *shall* properly states promises: the parties *shall* promptly consult. With these changes and the archaic *hereto* and the misused *such* removed, the provision looks like this:

> If either party believes that a new situation described in § 15.2 has arisen, then, at the request of either party, the parties shall promptly consult with a view toward reaching a mutually acceptable agreement dealing with the situation.

There is no single correct way to state an obligation. While I prefer *shall*, other language of promise includes *will*, *covenants*, and *agrees to*. Whichever term you use, state the obligation consistently and clearly. Make sure that the language of promise can be read as "has the duty to" if the promisor has manifested an intention to act, or "has the duty not to" if the promisor has manifested an intention to refrain from acting.

For example, an agreement discussed in § 10.1 provides:

> *A* shall deliver her horse "Black Beauty" to *B*. The horse shall be in good health.

By stating "*A* shall deliver her horse," the drafter provides that *A* has a duty to act in a certain way, to deliver a particular horse. The statement "The horse shall be in good health" is more difficult to characterize. Part of the problem is created by making *horse* the subject of the sentence. Certainly the horse is not the actor and did not undertake an obligation. If *A* is obligated to do something, that duty could be more clearly stated by making *A* the subject of the sentence:

> *A* shall deliver the horse in good health.

This phrasing is better, for it indicates that *A* has promised something. What, exactly, has *A* promised? The phrase "good health" is vague. It covers a wide spectrum of the horse's condition. *See* § 7.6. Part of that spectrum includes *de minimis* breaches, for which the law would not grant a remedy. Part of it includes immaterial breaches that could be atoned for with damages. And part includes material breaches that would justify *B* in considering his performance excused.

The parties may intend that *A* promises to pay damages to *B* if the horse is not in good health. Or the parties may intend that the horse's health is a representation of fact; if the fact is not true, *B* may avoid the contract. Or they may intend that the horse's good health is a condition, an event that must occur before *B*'s performance becomes due.

This example indicates the kinds of problems that arise when a drafter employs promises without stating the consequences of breach. Every time you state an obligation you must ask, what happens if the party does not perform? After you phrase this obligation in the active voice so that it is clearly an obligation of *A*, you can then provide for what happens if *A* does not do as promised. If you want a particular remedy, you must provide for it; otherwise, a court will interpret the language depending on the facts and circumstances. The use of a particular word will not necessarily guarantee a result, for the words are often used sloppily.

For example, the drafter might state:

> Conditions: 1. *A* shall deliver the horse in good health.

B might argue that this statement is an express condition, with the result that *A*'s nonperformance excuses *B*'s performance. As Corbin indicated, however, the word *condition* does not have this exclusive meaning. It may simply refer to a term of the agreement. The drafter could spell out the condition:

> *A* shall deliver the horse in good health. If the horse is not in good health, *B*'s performance under this agreement is discharged.

This draft still does not solve the problem of defining "good health," in order to determine whether *A* is in breach. One alternative is for the parties to define the term:

> In this agreement, "good health" means suitable for quarter horse racing.

Another alternative is to leave it to the determination of one of the parties:

> *A* shall deliver the horse in good health. If the horse is not in good health, as determined by *B* in his absolute discretion, *B*'s performance under this agreement is discharged.

Another alternative is to leave the meaning to the determination of a third party:

> *A* shall deliver the horse in good health. If the horse is not in good health, as determined by a veterinarian licensed by the American Quarter Horse Racing Association, *B*'s performance under this agreement is discharged.

Of course, the drafter could go crazy preparing every provision with this thoroughness. That thoroughness may be unnecessary where custom and usage of trade supplies the meaning of obligations, or where a problem is unlikely to occur. In this area the client, who usually knows the business better than the attorney, can provide guidance to the attorney. Which provisions are the most important to the client? Which are the most likely to go wrong and jeopardize the deal? Those are the terms on which the drafter's energies should be concentrated.

§ 16.3 Representations and warranties.

A promise creates an obligation of *future* performance. Often, however, parties to a contract make statements about the present. For example, "This business has a net worth of $1,000,000," or "This automobile is in good operating condition." These statements are intended as representations of existing fact. Representations appear in at least two contexts in contract law: misrepresentation and warranties. Actions alleging actual fraud (intentional misrepresentation) or constructive fraud (innocent misrepresentation) are based on representations made to *induce* the contract. These claims allege that no contract was formed. *See* § 5.3. Therefore, if the injured party proves all the elements of the claim, the contract is avoided.

A warranty is defined in U.C.C. § 2-313(1)(a) as "[a]ny affirmation of fact or promise . . . which becomes *part of the basis of the bargain . . . .*" A warranty can be either a representation or a promise; the warrantor may be saying that something is presently in a certain condition or that it will be in that condition in the future. Actions alleging breach of warranty are based on representations expressly or impliedly made. *See* § 12.1. These claims allege that a contract was formed and breached. Therefore, an injured party who proves all the elements of the claim recovers damages.

The careful drafter will include all representations in the contract to avoid the problems that arise under the parol evidence rule. *See* Chapter 6, Parol Evidence. But what does the drafter intend to happen if the representation is false? The intention may be that the party to whom it was made may rescind. For example, if a seller represents that a business has a net worth of $1,000,000 and it does not, the buyer may wish to escape from the contract. The intention may be, however, that the party who made the representation promises to make it true or promises to pay damages for its falsity. For example, if a seller promises that an automobile is in good operating condition and it is not, the seller may promise to put it in good condition or to indemnify the buyer for the loss.

The drafter should not rely on a particular word such as *representation* or *warranty* to convey a precise meaning, but should identify the legal consequences that attach to each operative part of a contract. When drafters sloppily employ legal terms, courts interpreting agreements look to the intentions of the parties. The meaning of terms varies with the context. For example, in an insurance contract, the term "representation" often refers to a statement that is not found in the document. And the term "warranty" often means that the fact warranted is a *condition* of the insurer's obligation to pay rather than a *promise* for breach of which the insurer is entitled to damages.

To muddy the waters even more, drafters often use the phrase "warrants and represents." Do they intend to give the injured party a right to elect either the remedy of rescission or damages, or are they simply following the lawyer's custom of using two words where one will do? The drafter who wants a specific remedy to follow a breach, or alternative remedies to be available, or a specific remedy to be exclusive, should spell out the remedy in the agreement. Otherwise a court will interpret the language according to the facts and circumstances.

The drafter can make the language more precise by asking questions about the intended meaning. When an agreement recites a promise, a representation, or a warranty, the drafter must ask:

- What if the promise is not kept?
- What if the fact is not as represented?
- What remedies are contemplated?

The drafter may then determine whether to provide for the consequences in the agreement. *See* Chapter 13, Damages.

§ 16.4   Example: Providing for the consequences of breach.

We will take the following steps to use legally operative words in a way that more clearly expresses the intended meaning:

- Step 1. Underline all the legally operative words.
- Step 2. Analyze the intended legal consequences by asking what happens if a party does not perform as promised or if a representation is not true.
- Step 3. Provide for the legal consequences with precise language.
- Step 4. Write the provision in plain language.

Let us examine the following provisions in a contract for the sale of a business:

---

1. Conditions Precedent to Buyer's Obligations

Buyer's obligation to perform and complete the transactions provided for herein shall be subject to the Sellers performing, on or before the closing date, all acts required of them, and shall be further subject to

---

the material accuracy and correctness of the representations and warranties of Sellers contained herein, and to the further conditions that:

(a) On or before the closing date, Sellers shall have caused the resignation of the officers and directors of company.

(b) Sellers shall deliver to Buyer, on the closing date, a certificate of Sellers to the effect that the representations and warranties of Sellers contained herein are substantially true as of the closing date.

2. Sellers' warranty as to absence of litigation

Sellers hereby represent and warrant that there is no pending administrative, civil, or criminal litigation involving the business sold, nor any demands or claims that would materially and adversely affect the same or Sellers' financial condition.

In the event of breach of this warranty, Buyer may rescind this agreement and any consideration paid by it to Sellers will be returned.

Let us look first at Provision 1. Step 1. Here is the provision with operative words emphasized:

1. _Conditions Precedent_ to Buyer's _Obligations_

Buyer's _obligation_ to perform and complete the transactions provided for herein _shall be subject to_ the Sellers performing, on or before the closing date, all acts required of them, and _shall be further subject to_ the material accuracy and correctness of the _representations and warranties_ of Sellers contained herein, and to the further _conditions_ that:

(a) On or before the closing date, Sellers _shall have caused_ the resignation of the officers and directors of company.

(b) Sellers _shall deliver_ to Buyer, on the closing date, a certificate of Sellers to the effect that the _representations and warranties_ of Sellers contained herein are substantially true as of the closing date.

Step 2. Analysis of the intended consequences. The caption is confusing. The conditions are not precedent to Buyer's obligations, but to Buyer's _performance_ of its obligations. Recall that legal rules can be thought of as "If . . . then" propositions, with the result following from the satisfaction of the enumerated conditions. Here, the result — Buyer's obligation to perform — follows from the satisfaction of four enumerated events, i.e., conditions. What is Buyer's obligation to perform? Presumably to pay money, which will occur at closing. We must therefore specify what Sellers must do before closing and what Buyer may do if Sellers do not bring about those events.

Step 3. Use of precise language. Language other than "subject to" might make the condition clearer. Similarly, even the words "further conditions" may not make clear that the performance is conditional, for *condition* sometimes means term or provision. These conditions — the events that must occur before Buyer needs to perform — may be expressed in the present tense and with parallel construction in this way:

---

1. Conditions Precedent to Buyer's Performance

Buyer's obligation to perform and to complete the transaction is conditional upon:

(a) Sellers' performance, on or before the closing date, of all acts required of them;

(b) the material accuracy and correctness of Sellers' representations and warranties;

(c) the resignation of the officers and directors of the company on or before the closing date; and

(d) Sellers' delivery to Buyer, on the closing date, of a certificate stating that Sellers' representations and warranties are substantially true as of that date.

Now that drafting has made the conditions clearer, we can examine their substance to determine whether they make sense. For example, how will Buyer determine whether Sellers have complied with item (b)? Do they comply with (b) by complying with (d), in which case (b) is superfluous? Or does (b) intend to state a remedy, that Buyer may rescind if the representations are false? Because that fact will probably not be known at closing, the event is not really a condition precedent, but a remedy that Buyer may exercise later. How does Buyer determine whether Sellers have complied with item (c)? Must Sellers take some affirmative step, such as submitting an affidavit, corporate minutes, or written resignations? Or is this event also not a condition precedent but a remedy that Buyer may exercise later? We must resolve these questions before we can express the intended consequences.

Let us examine Provision 2. Step 1. Here is the provision with the operative language underlined:

---

2. Sellers' <u>warranty</u> as to absence of litigation

Sellers hereby <u>represent and warrant</u> that there is no pending administrative, civil, or criminal litigation involving the business sold, nor any demands or claims that would materially and adversely affect the same or Sellers' financial condition.

> In the event of <u>breach of this warranty</u>, Buyer may <u>rescind</u> this agreement and any consideration paid by it to Sellers will be returned.

Step 2. Analysis of the intended consequences. The heading and second paragraph state that this provision is a warranty, but the first paragraph uses two words where one will do. Because this is a statement of existing fact, *represents* expresses it clearly. If we decide to use the word *representations,* then in the second paragraph we should no longer refer to *breach.* In providing for the consequences if a representation is not true, this provision uses a passive construction, "will be returned." State the actor who is to do something.

Step 3. Use of precise language. We might rewrite the provision as follows:

> ## 2. Sellers' representation as to absence of litigation
>
> Sellers represent that there is no pending administrative, civil, or criminal litigation involving the business sold, nor any demands or claims that would materially and adversely affect the business or Sellers' financial condition.
>
> If any of these representations is not true, Buyer may rescind this agreement and Sellers shall return any consideration paid by Buyer.

Step 4. Plain language. It is unclear whether the clause beginning "that would materially affect the business" modifies only demands or claims or also litigation. In other words, if Sellers failed to disclose a minor matter that was being litigated, would the representation be false? For additional clarity, we could tabulate the representations:

> Sellers represent that:
>
> a. there is no pending administrative, civil, or criminal litigation involving the business sold; and
>
> b. there are no demands or claims that would materially and adversely affect the business or Sellers' financial condition.

§ 16.5 Boilerplate

Boilerplate terms are usually declarations in which parties state the private law that will govern their contract. The art of drafting involves prediction. The drafter must constantly ask, "What if . . . ?" In the declarations, the parties provide answers to these questions. In earlier chapters, we have considered the drafting of boilerplate provisions such as

Severability (§ 4.6), Merger (§ 6.4), Force Majeure (§§ 9.4 and 9.5), Modification and Waiver (§ 11.9), Remedies (Chapter 13), and Assignment and Delegation (§ 14.6). Other declarations may include provisions regarding:

- Headings
- Choice of law
- Choice of forum
- Waiver of jury trial
- Notice

§ 16.5.1 Headings.

A declaration used by overly-careful drafters provides that headings in a contract have no substantive significance. For example:

> The headings and subheadings of clauses contained in this agreement are used for convenience and ease of reference and do not limit the scope or intent of the clause.

This declaration may have little substantive effect. For example, in a case in which the plaintiff sued in tort for defective construction of a building, the defendant raised in its defense the following provision from the contract:

> ONE YEAR LIMITED WARRANTY — Contractor warrants all work and materials furnished under this contract to be free from defects in materials and faulty workmanship under normal use which appear within one (1) year . . . THIS WARRANTY IS EXPRESSLY IN LIEU OF ANY OTHER WARRANTY, EXPRESSED OR IMPLIED, INCLUDING ANY IMPLIED WARRANTY OF MERCHANTABILITY OR FITNESS FOR A PARTICULAR PURPOSE AND OF ANY OTHER OBLIGATION OR LIABILITY ON THE PART OF THE CONTRACTOR.

The court held that although the provision excluded "any other obligation or liability," it did not bar a claim in tort. Part of the reasoning was that the provision was captioned "ONE YEAR LIMITED WARRANTY," apparently limiting its scope to contract liability. It is unlikely that a declaration limiting the scope of captions would change that result, particularly where the provision failed to communicate adequately that a party was giving up significant rights. *See* Chapter 4, Enforceability.

§ 16.5.2 Choice of law.

When we refer to choice of law, we don't mean the jurisdiction in which the case is heard. Rather, we mean once jurisdiction is established, it is the law that the judge will apply to the case. There are many reasons parties establish choice of law in their contract. For one, in the absence of the parties' agreement, the default rule may be uncertain. Many parties would rather know what law applies. In addition, a party may feel that a certain jurisdiction's law gives them an advantage, or they may just want law that is familiar. U.C.C. § 1-105 and Restatement (Second) of Conflict of Laws § 187 permit parties to choose law that bears a "reasonable relation" to the transaction, although the Uniform Computer Information Transactions Act and U.C.C. Revised Article 1 have eliminated this requirement.

Before automatically choosing the law of a particular state, the drafter should be sure that it is a desirable choice and that the provision will produce the desired result. For example, suppose a drafter for a California business included this choice of law provision in a contract for the sale of goods between her company and a Canadian company:

> The validity, interpretation, and performance of this Agreement shall be controlled by and construed under the laws of the State of California.

What law will govern? The answer, of course, is the United Nations Convention on Contracts for the International Sale of Goods. California is part of the United States, and conventions entered into by the United States are part of the law of California. If the drafter wanted the agreement to be governed by California state law, she would have to add something like this:

> The validity, interpretation, and performance of this Agreement shall be controlled by and construed under the laws of the State of California, as if performed wholly within the state and without giving effect to the principles of conflict of law. The parties specifically disclaim the UN Convention on Contracts for the International Sale of Goods.

§ 16.5.3 Choice of forum.

This provision does refer to the jurisdiction in which a claim must be brought. For example:

> Any legal suit, action or proceeding arising out of or relating to this Agreement shall be commenced in a federal court in the Commonwealth of Virginia, and each party hereto irrevocably submits to the non-exclusive jurisdiction and venue of any such court in any such suit, action or proceeding.

§ 16.5.4 Waiver of jury trial.

Some courts are becoming increasingly hostile to contracts in which parties surrender fundamental rights that may be given to them by a state constitution, such as the right of access to the court system or the right to a jury trial. In such an environment, the drafter might wish to draft the waiver so that it is conspicuous, in case the court gives more weight to a knowing waiver.

§ 16.5.5 Notice.

A contract often requires that one party notify or send notice to another party. Often giving the notice is a condition, an event that must occur before some result occurs, such as asserting a warranty claim, terminating a lease, or recovering on an insurance policy. For example:

U.C.C. § 2-607(3)(a) provides:

> the buyer must within a reasonable time after he discovers or should have discovered any breach notify the seller of breach or be barred from any remedy.

A lease provides:

> Lessor or Lessee may cancel this agreement at any time during the original term thereof upon giving the other party written notice at least thirty (30) days in advance of the next due date for payment of rent.

An insurance contract provides:

> In the event of any occurrence, written notice shall be given by or for the insured to the company as soon as practicable.

It is important that the notice be given correctly, for the result does not occur if it is not. Furthermore, a court may carefully scrutinize whether the party gave proper notice, for the issue of whether notice was given often determines whether the other party suffers a substantial loss.

We will use a number of drafting techniques to make sure that we have an appropriate notice provision. These techniques include:

- "What-iffing" the term
- Ascertaining the default rules
- Contracting around the default rules
- Updating the form book and drafting for clarity

1. "What-iffing the" term. The reader or drafter of the notice provisions should "what-if" the term, looking ahead to conjure up various scenarios. One issue is whether there is any particular medium in which the notice must be given. Can the notice be oral? Is personal delivery required? Is an e-mail effective? Another issue is whether receipt is required. It is easy to imagine a scenario in which one party sends notice but the other party never receives it. A related issue is whether notice sent to an address that the other party no longer uses is effective.

2. Ascertaining the default rules. In determining how to draft the provision, it will be helpful to know what the default rules are. If the default rule is clear and helpful to our client, we will worry less about crafting this provision. The U.C.C. rule may be an easier place to start than the common law rule. Section 1-201(26) provides:

> (26) A person "notifies" or "gives" a notice or notification to another by taking such steps as may be reasonably required to inform the other in ordinary course whether or not such other actually comes to know of it.

Under this rule, the means by which notice is given are flexible, in the usual U.C.C. fashion, depending on reasonableness and the ordinary course. On the other hand, it is clear that notice given in this manner does not need to be received to be effective. Finding the common law rules may be more problematic, particularly when the notice required may vary with the circumstances.

3. Contracting around the default rules. Parties may wish to establish their own rules because the default rules are not clear, as with the common law, or are uncertain in their application, as with the U.C.C. rules. In the absence of regulation, the parties are free, within the bounds of reasonableness, to establish their own rules on notice. For example, the U.C.C. rule does not require written notice, but as a practical matter, parties may want to require written notice.

4. Updating the form book. The parties may not be well served by language from a form book. The drafter must ask whether the language is appropriate for these parties in this transaction at this time. A form book notice, for example, might refer to means of communication that are obsolete and might not refer to other means that are widely available. For example, a notice provision states:

> All notices shall be in writing (including telecopier, telegraphic or telex communication) and mailed, telecopied, telegraphed, telexed or delivered to the relevant party at its address on Schedule 1. Notices shall, when mailed, telecopied, telegraphed or telexed, be effective when deposited in the mails, telecopied, delivered to the telegraph company or confirmed by telex answerback, respectively.

Does your client use these forms of communication? The drafter has provided that notice is effective when dispatched. But if mail or delivery is used, how will the sender evidence that there has been notice? What happens when, as is too often the case, Schedule 1 is not attached to the agreement? After thinking through these questions, in consultation with the client, the drafter may wish to update the form, using the techniques you have learned in this book.

§ 16.6 Example.

Let us examine the obligations, representations or warranties, and declarations found in the kind of informal agreement neighbors might make when selling a car:

WHEREAS, *A* has good title to a red 1985 Buick Skylark ("the car"):

1. *A* shall transfer and deliver the car to *B* on August 1.

2. *B* shall pay *A* the sum of $5000 cash at the time of delivery.

3. *B* shall not assign his rights or delegate his duties under this agreement to any third party.

> 4. This agreement is governed by the Uniform Commercial Code as enacted and in force in the State of Texas on the date of this agreement.

The recital (the clause beginning with "Whereas") is poorly drafted. A recital should contain background information rather than substantive provisions. *See* § 15.4.4. Do the parties mean that *A* promises she has good title? Do they mean they have agreed that *A* has good title? What if it is not true? This provision should probably be redrafted as a representation or warranty:

> 1. *A* represents that she has good title to a red 1985 Buick Skylark ("the car").

or

> 1. *A* warrants that she has good title to a red 1985 Buick Skylark ("the car").

As redrafted, *A* represents that she has good title as an existing fact. If the representation turns out to be false, *B* may have a claim for misrepresentation or for breach of warranty.

Paragraphs 1 and 2 contain obligations. In these paragraphs, *A* promises to deliver the car and *B* promises to pay for it. These statements manifest the parties' intentions to act in specified ways. They have undertaken the duty to do the thing promised.

In Paragraph 3, *B* promises *not* to assign his rights and duties. This is a promise to refrain from acting, or a duty not to do something. This provision can also be seen as a declaration, stating the law that governs *B*'s rights.

Paragraph 4 does not contain obligations. It contains a declaration known as a "choice of law" provision. The parties agree that the governing law is the U.C.C. as enacted in Texas.

§ 16.7 Exercises.

1. The coal contract. The following provision is from a long term contract for the sale of coal. Use the techniques discussed in § 16.4 to redraft this provision. You will find it helpful first to determine what the drafter meant to say, then to use concepts of legal analysis and drafting to state that meaning, and finally to state it with clarity.

5. **Failure of Seller to Deliver Coal of Prescribed Quality.** It being essential that the coal covered by this contract shall meet the requirements of the Gas Company in the production of coke and gas of substantially the same structure and strength as that heretofore produced from coal furnished by the Coal Company to the Gas Company and that said coal shall contain on an average of thirty per cent (30%) of volatile matter, it is understood that if the coal delivered hereunder, as sampled and analyzed dry basis, after being crushed ready to go to the ovens of the Gas Company, fails for thirty (30) consecutive days to maintain an average for said thirty (30) days sufficient to produce coke of such structure as that heretofore produced from coal furnished by said Coal Company, and it is practicable for the Gas Company to remedy such deficiency in quality by the mixture of not exceeding thirty per cent (30%) of other coal with the coal furnished by the Coal Company, the Gas Company may to the extent necessary for the purpose of such mixture purchase other coal; and to the extent that other coal may be thus purchased, the amount which it shall be required to take of the Coal Company shall be reduced; but in the event it is impossible to remedy such deficiency by such mixture of not exceeding thirty per cent (30%) of other coal, the Gas Company shall be entitled to cancel this contract; but the Coal Company shall not be responsible for any damages which the Gas Company may suffer from any such deficiency or from the cancellation of such contract; except as provided in Sections 8 and 9.

2. Redrafting a form provision. In a form book, you find the following notice provision. How might you update it and revise it for clarity?

Notices. All notices required or permitted under this Agreement will be in writing and will be deemed given: (a) when delivered personally; (b) when sent by confirmed telex or facsimile (followed by the actual document in air mail/air courier); (c) three (3) days after having been sent by registered or certified mail, return receipt requested, postage prepaid (or six (6) days for international mail); or (d) one (1) day after deposit with a commercial express courier specifying next day delivery (or two (2) days for international courier packages specifying 2-day delivery), with written verification of receipt. All communications will be sent to the addresses set forth on the cover sheet of this Agreement or such other address as may be designated by a party by giving written notice to the other party pursuant to this paragraph.

Chapter 17

THE LANGUAGE OF DRAFTING

§ 17.1 Introduction.

The three P's of drafting are PREDICT, PROVIDE, and PROTECT:

- PREDICT what may happen;
- PROVIDE for that contingency; and
- PROTECT your client with a remedy.

Whether you are adapting a model or form to fit your needs or using zero-base drafting techniques, the language you use reflects your command of the three P's. Drafting is not a passive process, a matter of filling in the blanks or responding to prompts on the computer screen. You must constantly talk back to the draft, asking whether the language clearly, directly, and completely states the agreement.

The suggestions that follow should help guide you to that end:

- Draft in the present tense.
- Draft in the active voice. Ask who is obligated to do something or to refrain from doing something.
- Use gender-neutral language.
- Delete unnecessary language of agreement.
- State obligations with the word *shall*. When you have used *shall*, ask if you can substitute "has the duty to."
- State authorization with the word *may*. When you have used *may*, ask if you can substitute "is authorized to."
- State conditions precedent with the word *must*. When you have used *must*, ask if you can substitute "has to do X before Y will happen."
- Consider whether you have used a term that requires greater specificity. *Predict* whether the term may cause problems in the future.
- Constantly ask "What if . . . ?" *Provide* for the significant contingencies.
- When you have stated an obligation, ask, "What happens if the obligor doesn't do it?" *Protect* the obligee by stating a remedy in the contract.
- Cross-check the agreement for internal references. Make sure the references are consistent.

§ 17.2 Use the present tense.

Contracts describe events that will take place in the future. Yet because the parties see a contract as continuously speaking, the drafter should write the contract in the present tense. For example:

> If any party to this agreement shall die, then. . . .

can be rewritten to provide:

> If any party to this agreement dies, then. . . .

This technique also preserves *shall* to indicate language of obligation rather than the future tense. When the future is required, use *will*. See the discussion in § 16.2.

§ 17.3 Use the active voice.

Contractual obligations require that a person do something or refrain from doing something. Who is that person? When drafters use the active voice, the name of the actor is clear. For example, consider this lease provision:

> The premises shall be kept in good repair.

It is not clear whether this is an obligation of the tenant or the landlord. When rewritten in the active voice, the provision clearly indicates the person who is obligated:

> The tenant shall keep the premises in good repair.

or

> The landlord shall keep the premises in good repair.

An agreement can bind only the parties to it, not third parties. When the drafter writes the agreement in the active voice, the persons who are obligated stand out. For example:

> The apartment shall be occupied by no person other than the tenant, his spouse, children, and temporary guests, without the written consent of the landlord.

It makes no sense to impose an obligation on the apartment. This use of *shall* creates a "false imperative," for it commands a result rather than an action. This provision can be rewritten in the active voice as:

> No person other than the tenant, his spouse, children, and temporary guests shall occupy the apartment without the written consent of the landlord.

After the provision is written in the active voice, it is clear that the actor is *no person*. It does not make sense for a contract to impose obligations on *no person*; the contract should impose obligations on the *parties*. This provision can be rewritten as follows:

> The tenant shall not permit a person other than the tenant, or the spouse, child, or temporary guest of the tenant, to occupy the apartment without the written consent of the landlord.

§ 17.4 Draft in gender-neutral language.

There are a number of reasons why drafters should use gender-neutral language. Use of gender-specific language, such as the words "he" or "his" to refer to attorneys or clients, is not only inaccurate, but may also be offensive.

Additionally, documents employing gender-neutral language make better models. You will use most of your documents as forms or primary documents for transactions that will sometimes refer to a man, sometimes to a woman, sometimes to both, and sometimes to a neuter such as a corporation. When assembling a new document based on a model, you have a number of choices:

- Replace the gender-specific pronouns every time to suit the particular transaction.
- Use a sophisticated program that will guide you to choose the appropriate gender.
- Use a boilerplate clause that deems inappropriate language to be appropriate. For example, U.C.C. § 1-102(5)(b) provides:

words of the masculine gender include the feminine and the neuter, and when the sense so indicates words of the neuter gender may refer to any gender.

- Replace the pronouns *once* with gender-neutral language that will be appropriate for all transactions.

The fourth choice — replacing the pronouns once — will prove most effective and efficient. For example, consider this sentence:

When drafting, a lawyer should be sensitive to the needs of his client.

There are a number of techniques you may employ to rewrite the sentence in a gender-neutral style:[1]

1. Write the statement in the plural, since *they, them,* and *theirs* are gender-neutral pronouns:

When drafting, lawyers should be sensitive to the needs of their clients.

2. Use the second person, since *you* is also gender-neutral:

When drafting, you should be sensitive to the needs of your clients.

3. Use an article instead of a pronoun:

When drafting, a lawyer should be sensitive to the needs of the client.

4. Use the name of the actor throughout the sentence:

When drafting, a lawyer should be sensitive to the needs of the lawyer's clients.

5. Change the subject of the sentence or use the passive voice:

In the drafting process, sensitivity to the needs of the client is important.

---

[1] I hope the reader has not noticed that this entire book has been written using these techniques.

6. Use both the masculine and feminine pronoun:

> When drafting, a lawyer should be sensitive to the needs of his or her client.

7. Employ the masculine and feminine in alternating sentences:

> When drafting, a lawyer should be sensitive to the needs of his client. She must interview her client to ascertain those needs.

When redrafting a document, follow these three steps to eliminate gender-specific language:

- Step 1. Identify the language that needs to be changed.
- Step 2. Think about whether the language, when made gender-neutral, will cover all contingencies.
- Step 3. Consider an appropriate revision.

Let us redraft the following provision from an attorney retainer agreement by following the steps:

> Client agrees to keep the Law Firm advised of his whereabouts at all times and to cooperate in the preparation and trial of his case, to appear on reasonable notice for depositions and court appearances, and to comply with all reasonable requests made of him in connection with the preparation and presentation of his case.

Step 1. Identify the language that needs to be changed. This task is easily accomplished with a word processing macro that will search for and highlight gender-specific words such as *he, she, it, his, him, her, hers, its*:

> Client agrees to keep the Law Firm advised of *his* whereabouts at all times and to cooperate in the preparation and trial of *his* case, to appear on reasonable notice for depositions and court appearances, and to comply with all reasonable requests made of *him* in connection with the preparation and presentation of *his* case.

Step 2. Think about whether the language, when made gender-neutral, will cover all contingencies. This is a *substantive* question, a question that requires examining the meaning of the language.

For example, is it possible that the client will be a corporation? If so, gender-neutral language will take the place of the neuter, but does the provision make any sense in the context of a corporate client? Consider the provision that the client will keep the law firm advised of its whereabouts. In the context of a corporation, perhaps the provision should be addressed to the *actors* on behalf of the corporation, the officers. For example:

> *The officers of the corporation* agree to keep the Law Firm advised of *their* whereabouts at all times and to cooperate in the preparation and trial of *the* case, to appear on reasonable notice for depositions and court appearances, and to comply with all reasonable requests made of *them* in connection with the preparation and presentation of *the* case.

Step 3. Consider an appropriate revision. For this particular paragraph, plurals would not be appropriate where the client may be an individual. It might be effective to write the entire agreement in plain language. *See* Chapter 18, Plain Language. Using these techniques, the drafter might refer to the Law Firm as *we, us, our,* or *ours,* and the Client as *you, your,* or *yours*:

> *You* agree to keep *us* advised of *your* whereabouts at all times and to cooperate in the preparation and trial of *your* case, to appear on reasonable notice for depositions and court appearances, and to comply with all reasonable requests made of *you* in connection with the preparation and presentation of *your* case.

In this case, it would not be appropriate to use the passive voice and it may be awkward to use the names of the actors throughout the sentence. Using both the masculine and the feminine can be awkward if repeated too often, but this technique might be used in conjunction with use of an article:

> Client agrees to keep the Law Firm advised of *his or her* whereabouts at all times and to cooperate in the preparation and trial of *the* case, to appear on reasonable notice for depositions and court appearances, and to comply with all reasonable requests made of *him or her* in connection with the preparation and presentation of *the* case.

§ 17.5 Language of agreement.

Once the caption or transitional words have incorporated language of agreement, the text does not need to restate the fact that the parties have made an agreement. *See* § 2.5. Consideration is found in the mutual promises contained in the agreement. The fact of agreement does not have to be repeated throughout. For example:

> Landlord and tenant agree that tenant shall pay each month in advance. . . .

> It is mutually agreed by and between the parties to this agreement that tenant shall pay each month in advance. . . .

> In consideration of the mutual promises herein contained, tenant agrees to pay each month in advance. . . .

These provisions can be rewritten as:

> Tenant shall pay each month in advance. . . .

§ 17.6   Language of obligation, authorization, and condition.

Useful rules on the use of *shall, may,* and *must* in legislative drafting are stated by Reed Dickerson:[2]

The problems of "shall," "may," and "must" are best seen against the broad spectrum of creating or negating rights, legal authority, duties, or conditions precedent. For these basic legal contingencies the following conventions seem to be lexicographically sound:

(1)   To create a right, say "is entitled to."

(2)   To create discretionary authority, say "may."

(3)   To create a duty, say "shall."

(4)   To create a mere condition precedent, say "must" (e.g., "To be eligible to occupy the office of mayor, a person must . . .")

(5)   To negate a right, say "is not entitled to."

(6)   To negate discretionary authority, say "may not."

(7)   To negate a duty or a mere condition precedent, say "is not required to."

(8)   To create a duty not to act (i.e., a prohibition), say "shall not."

---

[2] REED DICKERSON, THE FUNDAMENTALS OF LEGAL DRAFTING (2nd ed. 1986). Copyright 1986 © F. Reed Dickerson. Reprinted with permission of Aspan Publishers.

We will look more closely at the usages found most commonly in contracts:

1. Language of obligation.

2. Language of authorization.

3. Language of condition.

§ 17.6.1 Language of obligation.

When a party undertakes an obligation, the drafter should use the word *shall* to state the duty. *See* § 16.2. Note that if the drafter writes in the present tense, there will be no confusion between *shall* indicating the future and *shall* indicating obligation. In thinking whether *shall* is used in the sense of obligation, try substituting the phrase "has the duty to." If the substitution works, *shall* is used correctly. For example:

> Seller shall deliver 30 widgets, each of which shall not exceed 20 pounds in weight.

The first *shall* is correct; seller "has the duty to" deliver 30 widgets. The second *shall* is incorrect; it makes no sense to state that each widget "has the duty to" not exceed 20 pounds. This obligation can be rewritten as:

> Seller shall deliver 30 widgets, each not exceeding 20 pounds in weight.

§ 17.6.2 Language of authorization.

When a party does not undertake an obligation, but exercises a right or privilege, the drafter should use the word *may*. In thinking whether *may* is used in the sense of authorization, try substituting the phrase "is authorized to." For example:

> If Buyer fails to make any payment on time, Seller *shall* send a Notice of Default.

There is no obligation on the part of Seller to send a notice. If there were an obligation on the part of Seller, then Buyer would have a claim for Seller's breach. But it is absurd to think of Buyer suing Seller for failure to send the notice! Because the action is discretionary on the part of Seller, the provision may be rewritten as:

> If Buyer fails to make any payment on time, Seller *may* send a Notice of Default.

§ 17.6.3 Language of condition.

The drafter may wish to make clear that a party is required to do something before taking some further action. For example, Seller is required to send a Notice of Default before seeking a remedy against Buyer. In this case, the Seller is not required to send the notice because of an obligation to the Buyer. Rather, the action — sending the notice — is a condition, an event that must occur before Seller may seek a remedy. To indicate that the action is required to bring about the consequences, some drafters use the word *must*. For example:

> If Buyer fails to make any payment on time, Seller *must* send a Notice of Default before seeking any remedy.

Seller has no obligation to send a notice, but if Seller does not send it, then Seller may not seek any remedy. In thinking whether *must* is used in the sense of a condition, try asking whether the party "has to do X before Y will happen." For example:

> Seller shall deliver on the first day of each month. If Buyer is dissatisfied with Seller's performance in any particular month, Buyer *shall* notify Seller on or before the 10th day of that month.

Although *shall* was used, the drafter did not intend that Buyer has a duty to notify Seller. Rather, Buyer has to give timely notice before Seller will do anything about unsatisfactory performance. The notice is not an obligation but a condition. The provision can be rewritten as:

> Seller shall deliver on the first day of each month. If Buyer is dissatisfied with Seller's performance in any particular month, Buyer *must* notify Seller on or before the 10th day of that month.

To state conditions, drafters often use terms such as *if, in the event that, provided that*, or *on condition that*. When drafting conditions, it is more important to use language that clearly shows the relationship between the two events than to use any particular words. In fact, although it may have a defined meaning in legislative drafting, the use of the word *must* may be problematic in contract drafting. For example, an insurance contract states:

> Insurer shall pay for covered losses. Insured must provide Insurer with written proof of loss within 90 days of the loss.

If Insured provides Insurer with written proof of loss 100 days after the loss, does Insurer have to pay for the loss? Insurer will claim that its intention was for the word *must* to create a condition, with its performance (paying for the loss) conditioned on occurrence of the event (Insured submitting proof within 90 days). A court might find, however, that *must* is just a way of stating an obligation — that it means *shall*. If the language creates an obligation on Insured's part rather than a condition, Insurer is entitled to damages for Insured's breach but Insurer must still perform its obligations.

To accomplish its goal, Insurer would be safer using language that clearly spells out the relationship between the events. For example:

> Insurer shall pay for covered losses. Insured must provide Insurer with written proof of loss within 90 days of the loss. If Insured does not provide written proof of loss within 90 days of the loss, Insurer has no obligation to pay for the loss.

Now there is no doubt about the relationship between the two events, a relationship that is signaled with the word *if*. It might be argued that we have now made the provision twice as long. While brevity is a goal, clarity is a higher goal to which brevity must sometimes give way.

§ 17.7 Fleshing out the agreement for completeness.

The art of drafting often involves deciding when to be general and when to be specific. When drafters use the passive voice, the details of what the actor must do are often obscured. For example, a lease provides:

> The premises shall be kept in good repair.

Because this provision does not obligate a person to do something, the reader does not think about what that person is obligated to do. In the active voice, the actor is identified:

> The tenant shall keep the premises in good repair.

Now the lack of detail stands out — exactly what is the tenant's obligation? The drafter must constantly ask, "What does that mean?" The drafter may choose not to define a term for fear of breaking a deal. This is a judgment call. The strengths and weaknesses of using indefinite language can be discussed profitably with the client.

Drafters may also prefer to leave a term indefinite rather than flesh it out and in the process leave something out. Courts often invoke the maxim *expressio unius est exclusio alterius* (the expression of one thing is the exclusion of another) to narrow the meaning to the items enumerated. If the drafter believes this is a case in which the provision should be made more specific, consider a definitional provision. To make clear that the list is not intended to be exclusive, use language such as "including but not limited to." For example:

> In this agreement, *good repair* includes but is not limited to . . . .

§ 17.8   Declarations.

Declarations provide answers to the question, "What if?" Because they do not state obligations of the parties, drafters should not use *shall* when stating declarations. For example:

> If weather, fire or an act of God shall render the premises uninhabitable, this lease shall terminate.

The drafter intends that *shall* indicate the future. If the drafter reserves *shall* for obligations, it does not make sense that weather and fire are under an obligation. This declaration should be rewritten in the present tense. The drafter's habitual use of *shall* could lead to the argument that "shall terminate" means termination at a later time. Presumably, immediate termination is contemplated. This provision may be written as:

> If weather, fire or an act of God renders the premises uninhabitable, this lease terminates.

Sometimes drafters use the word *deemed* as a convention to indicate a declaration. For example:

> Notice shall be deemed effective if delivered in writing to either party at the address set forth below.

If *shall* means "has the duty to," this provision makes no sense. The word *deemed* may be deleted and the declarative verb *is* substituted:

> Notice *is* effective if delivered in writing to either party at the address set forth below.

Note that this provision is written in the passive. This is an acceptable use of the passive, for the actor is not known; it may be either of the parties. The provision could be rewritten in the active voice as:

> A party gives effective notice by delivering the notice in writing to the other party at the address set forth below.

§ 17.9 Remedies.

Every time the agreement states an obligation, the drafter should ask, "What happens if the party doesn't do it?" The answer to this question may indicate the need to state further obligations or to impose a sanction for breach. For example:

> Tenant shall pay the rent on the first day of the month at the office of the manager.

This provision states three obligations of the tenant:

1. to pay rent;

2. to pay it on the first day of the month; and

3. to pay it at the office of the manager.

The drafter should consider the effect of breach of each of these obligations. What happens if:

1. the tenant does not pay at all;

2. the tenant pays, but after the first day of the month; or

3. the tenant pays, but at a place other than the office of the manager.

The agreement may have a sweeping default provision, such as:

> **EVICTION** It is agreed in the event the TENANT is delinquent in the payment of any rental installment, then this lease shall automatically terminate and the TENANT specifically waives the right to receive a notice to quit.

Does the landlord really intend such a drastic remedy to occur automatically, even for a minor breach? The drafter might consider a series of graduated remedies, such as money damages when the payment is received late and eviction only if the failure to pay continues for a substantial period.

§ 17.10 Cross-references.

Always check the final agreement for both internal consistency and consistency with external documents. This practice is particularly important when generating documents on a computer, when a variable written for one transaction may accidentally be incorporated into the documents for another. Dates should be checked for completeness and accuracy. When using a phrase such as *set forth below*, the drafter should make sure the information is in fact stated in another provision. Rather than relying on a mental note, the drafter might indicate a specific paragraph, leaving the space blank until the agreement is completed. For example:

> Notice is effective if delivered in writing to either party at the address set forth in paragraph _____.

In the final proofing, the blank space will be a reminder to cross-check the agreement to be sure the provision referred to has been added.

Alternatively, use the word processor to perform your searches or to mark your cross-references. To use the search method, as you draft, insert a letter combination that rarely occurs, such as *xx*, where each variable will occur. For example:

> Notice is effective if delivered in writing to either party at the address set forth in paragraph xx.

Then have your word processor search for *xx* and replace the *xx* with the appropriate entry. You can also use the word processor to mark the cross-references as you draft. When you type the reference, e.g., "set forth in paragraph 7," mark the text and also mark the target, e.g., "¶ 7." When the drafting is complete, generate a table of cross-references. You can then check them for accuracy and update any that need to be changed or eliminated. You might also mark references to external documents, such as schedules. The cross-reference will then be a reminder to add the list. There is nothing so embarrassing as having a client search in vain for "Schedule A attached"!

When stating that another document is "incorporated by reference," check whether you literally intend the entire document to be incorporated. The other document may contain provisions that are not appropriate or that increase your client's obligations or liability. The incorporation can be more narrowly drawn by reference to particular provisions. Here, too, you can use a computer to mark the provision to prompt you to review the incorporated material.

§ 17.11 Example of the language of drafting.

We will rewrite a portion from a contract for the sale of goods, paying particular attention to the language of drafting. In this provision a number of legally operative words are used improperly. We will use the following steps from § 16.4 to rewrite the provision:

- Step 1. Underline all the legally operative words.
- Step 2. Analyze the intended legal consequences by asking what happens if a party does not perform as promised or if a representation is not true.
- Step 3. Provide for the legal consequences with precise language.
- Step 4. Write the provision in plain language.

The provision states:

It is mutually agreed that on delivery, the Seller shall be paid the reasonable value of the goods. The Buyer shall be notified within 10 days if the amount of payment is not satisfactory. If the parties cannot agree on the payment amount, the amount shall be determined by a third party to be chosen by the parties.

Consider the following language:

- *It is mutually agreed that.* This is language of agreement that can be deleted from each provision.
- *[T]he Seller shall be paid.* Who is the actor? If it is the Buyer, this obligation can be rewritten in the active voice as: *The Buyer shall pay the Seller.*
- *The Buyer shall be notified.* Who is the actor? If it is the Seller, this obligation can be rewritten in the active voice as: *The Seller shall notify the Buyer.* What is the Seller obligated to do? In fact, it makes little sense to think of giving notice as an obligation, for the Buyer will be happy if the Seller doesn't do it. This obligation can be rewritten as a condition precedent, for the Seller indicates that the payment is unsatisfactory by giving notice: *The Seller must notify the Buyer.* Once it is clear that the Seller is the actor, the drafter may give some thought to fleshing out the notice requirement.
- *[T]he amount shall be determined by a third party to be chosen by the parties.* Who is the actor? Note that it is not the third party, who assumes no obligations under a contract to which he or she is not a party. That the third party has no obligation becomes clear when we rewrite the passage in the active voice: *A third party to be chosen by the parties shall determine the amount.* The obligations of the *parties* must be put in the active voice, for they are the actors who are bound by the agreement: *The parties shall choose a third party who shall determine the amount.* Because the third party has no obligation under this agreement, the second *shall* in this sentence reflects the future. To avoid confusion, *will* should be used for the future: *The parties shall choose a third party who will determine the amount.*

Once the drafter has made clear that the parties have the obligation to choose a third party, he or she might give some thought to fleshing out this obligation. For example, the drafter should consider how the parties will choose the third party and what happens if they don't agree on a third party.

A rewrite might look like this:

On delivery, the Buyer shall pay the Seller the reasonable value of the goods. The Seller must notify the Buyer within 10 days if the amount of payment is not satisfactory. If the parties cannot agree on the payment amount, the parties shall choose a third party who will determine the amount.

---

§ 17.12   Exercises.

1. Editing. Rewrite the following provisions where appropriate:

a. Acceptance shall be deemed to have occurred when the Multiservice System performs without Major Failure over a period of thirty (30) days after delivery ("Acceptance Period"). Major Failure(s) shall be defined as follows.

b. All shipping, rigging, and other destination charges shall be paid by Buyer.

c. Seller shall pay Broker a commission of 6% if a buyer is procured.

d. Service Provider shall indicate on its Purchase Order any Product units which are to be resold to third parties and shall report such sales as required in this Agreement.

e. Service Provider will not distribute the Products to third parties, including resellers, other than for use in conjunction with Network Services.

f. Service Provider is free to determine its resale prices unilaterally.

g. Company represents that all Hardware delivered to Service Provider shall be free of liens and encumbrances.

h. During the term of this Agreement, Company may make the Products which are to be supplied outside the United States available for order in and delivery from an alternate central location and/or a Company affiliate, if it chooses. In the event that Company does so, Service Provider will order the Products according to the procedures set forth at the time such delivery becomes available. At such time, orders in conformance with Company's policies will be shipped according to the availability and expedited leadtimes described in the procedures. Company shall have the right to change delivery terms and include additional charges, if any, at the time such alternate order and delivery process is implemented by Company.

i. Purchaser agrees to the following:

(1) UM Productions will receive signed copies of all Artist contracts negotiated by Purchaser in connection with the engagement not later than 21 days prior to performance.

(2) Artist contract riders associated with this performance will be sent to UM Productions immediately upon return of this signed contract. Requirements contained in the Artist contract rider are subject to approval by UM Productions.

2. The coal contract. Using the techniques discussed in this chapter, revise the following quality term from a long term contract for the sale of coal. The term provides:

---

2. **Quality.** The coal to be delivered shall, in all respects, closely approximate in character and quality the coal heretofore delivered to the Gas Company by the Coal Company from its said mines and shall analyze on a dry basis approximately as follows:

Volatile Matter	30.00 per cent
Fixed Carbon	63.25 per cent
Ash	6.75 per cent
Sulphur in Ash	.65 per cent

The Coal Company guarantees that said coal, upon fair tests, dry basis, in carload lots, will not show less than twenty-eight and one-half per cent (28½%) volatile matter, will not show more than eight per cent (8%) ash, and will not show more than eight-tenths of one per cent (.8 of 1%) sulphur in ash.

The Gas Company may test each carload of coal upon receipt at its plant, and if it shall not meet the requirements specified herein, the Gas Company shall at once notify the Coal Company of the fact and set said car aside as subject to the order of the Coal Company. If the Coal Company shall question the correctness of such test, it shall have the right to have such carload of coal tested by a competent chemist of its own selection. If the chemists of the parties disagree in the results of their respective tests, then the parties shall select a third chemist competent and disinterested in every way, who shall test said car of coal and whose determination shall be final and binding on both parties. Provided, however, that the failure of the Gas Company at any time to make such tests and to make complaint shall not estop it from thereafter making such tests and complaint of the quality of the coal, although there may be no apparent change in such quality.

---

3. Restrictions on transfer from a shareholders' agreement. Revise the following excerpt from a shareholders' agreement, employing the following drafting considerations:

1. The caption.
2. The recitals.
3. Definitions.
4. The active voice.
5. The present tense.
6. Language of obligation, authorization, and condition precedent.
7. Number.
8. Gender-neutral language.
9. Words to avoid.
10. Architecture.

The provision states:

SHAREHOLDERS' AGREEMENT

This is an Agreement entered into on _____, 20_____, between _____ ("Corporation"), and _____ (collectively referred to as the "Shareholders" and individually as the "Shareholder").

PREMISES

WHEREAS, the Shareholders own all shares of the common Stock ("shares") of the Corporation; and

WHEREAS, the Shareholders and the Corporation desire to restrict the transferability of shares in order that the Corporation remain closely held and in order to avoid incompatible owners; and

WHEREAS, the Shareholders desire to create a market for the shares owned by deceased Shareholders.

THEREFORE, the parties agree as follows:

AGREEMENT

1. *Restrictions on Transfer.*

1.1 *Offer of Sale.* Except to the extent expressly permitted by this Agreement, Shareholders may not sell, transfer, assign, pledge, encumber or otherwise dispose of or convey (by operation of law or otherwise) any or all of the shares of the Corporation unless such shares are first offered to the Corporation and remaining Shareholders in accordance with Section 1 of this Agreement.

1.2 *Time and Form of Offer.* At least 90 days prior to the date the Shareholder desires to sell, transfer, assign, pledge, encumber or otherwise dispose of or convey any of the shares of the Corporation,

---

the Shareholder must offer to sell such shares to the Corporation and remaining Shareholders in accordance with the terms of this Agreement. The offer to the Corporation and remaining Shareholders must (i) be written; (ii) be executed by the Shareholder; (iii) be subject to the terms of this Agreement; and (iv) be transmitted to the Secretary of the Corporation. At the same time such offer is transmitted the Shareholder shall transmit a written statement concerning the proposed sale, transfer, assignment, pledge, encumbrance, disposition or conveyance, which states (i) how the Shareholder proposes to sell, transfer, assign, pledge, encumber or otherwise dispose of or convey any or all of his shares; (ii) the number of shares to be transferred; (iii) the proposed transfer date; (iv) the name, business and residence address of the proposed transferee; (v) the price for which the shares are to be transferred, including the value of any property to be received for the shares (or the amount of the proposed pledge or encumbrance); and (vi) the terms of the proposed transfer (including time of payment of purchase price, interest rate on deferred payments, type of collateral offered to secure purchase price and value of collateral offered to secure purchase price). The Secretary of the Corporation shall, upon receipt of any such offer and statement, transmit a copy of the offer and statement to the remaining Shareholders.

1.3 *Corporation's Option to Purchase.* The Corporation shall have the option to purchase all of the shares proposed to be sold, transferred, assigned, pledged, encumbered, disposed of or otherwise conveyed (the "Subject Shares") for the purchase price per share set forth in Section 3.2 and upon the other terms provided in this Agreement. The Corporation must send a notice of its election to exercise such option to the Shareholder intending to transfer the Subject Shares within 60 days of the Corporation's receipt of the offer described in Section 1.2. If the Corporation does not send such notice of its election within such 60 day period, the Corporation's option to purchase the Subject Shares will be considered to have expired. At the end of such 60 day period, the Secretary of the Corporation shall notify all shareholders whether or not the Corporation elected to exercise the option described herein.

1.4 *Shareholder's Option to Purchase.* If the Corporation does not elect to exercise its option described in Section 1.3, any or all of the remaining Shareholders may elect to purchase all of the Subject Shares for the purchase price per share set forth in Section 3.2 and upon the other terms provided in this Agreement. All Shareholders wishing to purchase all of the Subject Shares must send written notice to the Corporation within 75 days of the date they received the offer described in Section 1.2. If more than one Shareholder proposes to purchase all the Subject Shares, then those Shareholders will be entitled to purchase the shares of Transferring Shareholder on the basis of their pro rata ownership of the shares. The Secretary of the Corporation shall forthwith send to all Shareholders a notice of which Shareholders, if any, elect to purchase the shares, together with a statement as to the number of shares which each of the Shareholders shall purchase.

1.5 *Intervening Death.* If a Shareholder proposes to transfer shares and dies prior to the closing of the sale and purchase contemplated by this Section 1, the Subject Shares shall be the subject of sale and purchase under Section 2.

1.6 *Effect of Non-Exercise of Options.* If the Corporation and Shareholders do not exercise their purchase options, then the Subject Shares may be transferred at any time within 90 days after the expiration of the Shareholders' option to the transferee named in the offer required by Section 1.1, and upon the terms therein stated. In such case the Subject Shares shall be free forever of the terms of this Agreement.

1.7 *Exceptions.* Nothing herein shall prevent the inter vivos transfer by gift, sale or any other means of the stock of this Corporation to those person(s) or trust(s) listed on Exhibit A hereto or any descendants of these individuals listed on Exhibit A, but only if such individual(s) or trust(s), prior to transfer of the stock, agree to be bound by the terms of this Agreement with respect to such stock.

Chapter 18

PLAIN LANGUAGE

§ 18.1 Introduction.

The present interest in plain language, or plain English, as it is sometimes called, represents the confluence of two concerns: interest in language and the consumer movement. These concerns are expressed in a proposed plain language law in Maine:

> The purpose of this chapter is to enable the average consumer, who makes a reasonable effort under the circumstances, to read and understand the terms of so-called form contracts and the like without having to obtain the assistance of a professional.

The idea of plain language, that contracts should be written with clarity, should not be associated solely with statutory requirements. Clarity is a goal for all contracts. Nevertheless, much of the impetus for plain language has come from government. After World War II, the federal government found itself ensnared in the "gobbledygook" of its own regulations. In a fireside chat in 1977, President Carter promised that government regulations would be written in plain English and followed up with a 1978 Executive Order. The Securities and Exchange Commission requires that a securities prospectus be written in plain language. In a number of states, statutes in the areas of insurance and consumer protection were enacted to regulate the typography and wording of private contracts.

In 1977, New York State enacted the first broad plain language law. New York's efforts seem to have been inspired by the fact that its largest bank, Citibank, developed readable consumer credit forms, which were a success with the public. Other businesses followed suit, demonstrating that the regulation would not be perceived as "anti-business." A number of states have now enacted plain language laws. These statutes are generally of two types. One contains general, subjective criteria for plain language. The other contains specific, objective tests.

§ 18.2 Subjective standards of plain language.

The New York statute is an example of a subjective plain language law. Under that statute, a covered agreement must be:

1. Written in a clear and coherent manner using words with common and every day meanings.

2. Appropriately divided and captioned by its various sections.

271

These intentionally vague standards seem appropriate to address the evils of form contracts without causing undue hardship to those who draft them. Plain language drafting can present a hardship at two extremes. It is not cost effective to burden the drafter of a one-shot contract with detailed regulations. Nor should the large interstate business have to adapt its forms to comply with differing regulations in each state. Drafters in both of these situations can comply with subjective standards by drafting for clarity without worrying about nit-picking details.

§ 18.3   Objective standards of plain language.

The Model Life and Health Insurance Policy Language Simplification Act, which has been enacted in many jurisdictions, illustrates objective plain language requirements.[1] Part of it provides:

(A) . . . [N]o policy forms . . . shall be delivered or issued for delivery in this state on or after the dates such form must be approved . . . unless:

(1) the text achieves a minimum score of 40 on the Flesch reading ease test . . . ;

(2) it is printed, except for the specification pages, schedules, and tables, in not less than 10-point type, 1-point leaded;

(3) the style, arrangement, and overall appearance of the policy give no undue prominence to any portion of the text of the policy or to any endorsements or riders; and

(4) it contains a table of contents or an index of the principal sections of the policy, if the policy has more than 3,000 words printed on 3 or fewer pages of text, or if the policy has more than 3 pages regardless of the number of words.

(B) For the purposes of this Section, a Flesch reading ease test score shall be measured by the following method:

(1) For policy forms containing 10,000 words or less of text, the entire form shall be analyzed. For policy forms containing more than 10,000 words, the readability of two 200 word samples per page may be analyzed instead of the entire form. The samples shall be separated by at least 20 printed lines.

(2) The number of words and sentences in the text shall be counted and the total number of words divided by the total number of sentences. The figure obtained shall be multiplied by a factor of 1.015.

(3) The total number of syllables shall be counted and divided by the total number of words. The figure obtained shall be multiplied by a factor of 84.6.

---

[1] Model Life and Health Insurance Policy Language Simplification Act. Copyright 1984 © the National Association of Insurance Commissioners. Reprinted with permission.

(4) The sum of the figures computed under (2) and (3) subtracted from 206.835 equals the Flesch reading ease score for the policy form.

(5) For the purposes of paragraphs (B)(2),(3), and (4), the following procedures shall be used:

(a) A contraction, hyphenated word, or numbers and letters, when separated by spaces, shall be counted as one word;

(b) A unit of words ending with a period, semicolon, or colon, but excluding headings and captions, shall be counted as a sentence; and

(c) A syllable means a unit of spoken language consisting of one or more letters of a word as divided by an accepted dictionary. If the dictionary shows two or more equally acceptable pronunciations of a word, the pronunciation containing fewer syllables may be used.

The objective test uses the Flesch test of reading ease. The Flesch test measures two factors: number of syllables in a word and number of words in a sentence. The premise is that reading ease is a function of short words and short sentences. While this premise may be true, always remember that the overall purpose is clarity, not a mechanical result. For example, compare these two provisions:

---

1. Agreement dated October 1, 2003 between Sam and Ben. Sam is known as the party of the first part. Ben is known as the party of the second part. The party of the first part shall sell his pen to the party of the second part. The party of the second part shall pay $10 to the party of the first part.

---

2. Agreement dated October 1, 2003 between Sam ("Seller") and Ben ("Buyer"). Seller shall sell his pen to Buyer and Buyer shall pay Seller $10.

Measured by the objective test, both versions qualify as plain language (minimum score of 40). Example 1 receives a better score than Example 2 (89 to 68), however, because the formula gives much greater weight to word length than to sentence length. Both Examples 1 and 2 have about 12 words per sentence. But Example 1 achieves a better score by using a greater proportion of smaller words. The score is achieved at the expense of clarity, however. The reader can more easily keep track of who is to perform an obligation when a party is called "Seller" rather than "party of the first part."

Note that for purposes of the objective standard, a sentence may end with a colon or semicolon. One way to achieve a high objective score — and probably also high readability — is to use tabulation, for each enumerated item in the list is counted as a sentence. *See* § 7.5.2. For example:

---

1. Plain language laws often do not apply to consumer contracts in excess of $50,000, purchase of securities or commodities, life and disability insurance, government agencies, public utilities providing services under tariffs approved by the PSC, the transfer of real estate, language required or authorized by court decisions, statutes, or governmental agencies, or legal description of real property.

---

2. Plain language laws often do not apply to:

   a. consumer contracts in excess of $50,000;

   b. purchase of securities or commodities;

   c. life and disability insurance;

   d. government agencies;

   e. public utilities providing services under tariffs approved by the PSC;

   f. the transfer of real estate;

   g. language required or authorized by court decisions, statutes, or governmental agencies; or

   h. legal description of real property.

Example 1 is difficult to read because of the sentence length. The listing in the sentence may also create ambiguities. For example, it is hard to tell whether "legal description of real property" is a separate phrase or is part of the clause that begins "language required or authorized by." Because it is written in tabulated form, Example 2 is easier to read and avoids the ambiguity in items *g* and *h*. Under the objective test of plain language, Example 1 counts as one sentence of 57 words; Example 2 counts as 9 sentences with an average length of 6.33 words.

§ 18.4 Plain language and substance.

Plain language is often thought of as a matter of style. However, one of the most significant, and probably unanticipated, effects of drafting in plain language is its effect on the substance of the contract. The process of rewriting a document in plain language is not merely a matter of translation. The process requires the drafter to examine the content of the language to determine its meaning and to determine whether that content should be perpetuated.

One commentator who analyzed consumer loan agreements found that many clauses are "misinformational." The clauses are legally unenforceable, but give the impression that the creditor has more rights or the debtor less rights than the law gives them. In comparing forms used in New York prior to and subsequent to passage of the plain language law, he found that the types of clauses most often deleted were the misinformational ones. Examples of deleted clauses included those stating that the debtor waived the statute of limitations, that the creditor's opinion as to default was conclusive, and that the creditor had the right to modify the terms of any contract assigned as collateral.

As an example of the effect of plain language on both style and substance, consider the reform of the Citibank loan agreement. The "old" and "new" agreements provide graphic evidence of the typographic and stylistic advantages of plain language.[2]

---

[2] Old and New Citibank Consumer Loan Notes. Reprinted with permission of Citibank, N.A.

"Old" Agreement

SHERMAN BUSINESS FORMS, INC. 33-40 57TH ST. WOODSIDE, NEW YORK 11377

PBR 668 REV 9-74

FIRST NATIONAL CITY BANK
PERSONAL FINANCE DEPARTMENT - NEW YORK
APPLICATION
NUMBER _____
**ANNUAL PER-
CENTAGE RATE** _____ %
$ _____
            TOTAL OF PAYMENTS (4) + (7)

PROCEEDS TO BORROWER .... (1) $ _____
PROPERTY INS. PREMIUM .... (2) $ _____
FILING FEE .... (3) $ _____
AMOUNT FINANCED (1) + (2) + (3) ..... (4) $ _____
PREPAID FINANCE CHARGE .... (5) $ _____
GROUP CREDIT LIFE INS. PREMIUM ...... (6) $ _____
FINANCE CHARGE (5) + (6) .... (7) $ _____

FOR VALUE RECEIVED, the undersigned (jointly and severally) hereby promise(s) to pay to FIRST NATIONAL CITY BANK (the "Bank") at its office at 399 Park Avenue, New York, New York 10022 (i) THE SUM OF

_____ ($ _____) (TOTAL OF PAYMENTS)
( ) IN _____ EQUAL CONSECUTIVE MONTHLY INSTALMENTS OF $ _____ EACH ON THE SAME DAY OF EACH MONTH, COM-
MENCING _____ DAYS FROM THE DATE THE LOAN IS MADE; OR ( ) IN _____ EQUAL CONSECUTIVE WEEKLY INSTALMENTS
OF $ _____ EACH ON THE SAME DAY OF EACH WEEK, COMMENCING NOT EARLIER THAN 5 DAYS NOR LATER THAN 45 DAYS FROM
THE DATE THE LOAN IS MADE; OR ( ) IN _____ EQUAL CONSECUTIVE BI-WEEKLY INSTALMENTS OF $ _____ EACH, COM-
MENCING NOT EARLIER THAN 10 DAYS NOR LATER THAN 45 DAYS FROM THE DATE THE LOAN IS MADE, AND ON THE SAME DAY
OF EACH SECOND WEEK THEREAFTER; OR ( ) IN _____ EQUAL CONSECUTIVE SEMI-MONTHLY INSTALMENTS OF $ _____
EACH, COMMENCING NOT EARLIER THAN 10 DAYS NOR LATER THAN 45 DAYS FROM THE DATE THE LOAN IS MADE, AND ON THE
SAME DAY OF EACH SEMI-MONTHLY PERIOD THEREAFTER, (ii) A FINE COMPUTED AT THE RATE OF 5¢ PER $1 ON ANY INSTALMENT
WHICH HAS BECOME DUE AND REMAINED UNPAID FOR A PERIOD IN EXCESS OF 10 DAYS, PROVIDED (A) IF THE PROCEEDS TO THE
BORROWER ARE $10,000 OR LESS, NO SUCH FINE SHALL EXCEED $5 AND THE AGGREGATE OF ALL SUCH FINES SHALL NOT EXCEED
THE LESSER OF 2% OF THE AMOUNT OF THIS NOTE OR $25, OR (B) IF THE ANNUAL PERCENTAGE RATE STATED ABOVE IS 7.50% OR
LESS, THE LIMITATIONS PROVIDED IN (A) SHALL NOT APPLY AND NO SUCH FINE SHALL EXCEED $25 AND THE AGGREGATE OF ALL
SUCH FINES SHALL NOT EXCEED 2% OF THE AMOUNT OF THIS NOTE, AND SUCH FINE(S) SHALL BE DEEMED LIQUIDATED DAM-
AGES OCCASIONED BY THE LATE PAYMENT(S); (iii) IN THE EVENT OF THIS NOTE MATURING, SUBJECT TO AN ALLOWANCE FOR
UNEARNED INTEREST ATTRIBUTABLE TO THE MATURED AMOUNT, INTEREST AT A RATE EQUAL TO 1% PER MONTH AND (iv) IF
THIS NOTE IS REFERRED TO AN ATTORNEY FOR COLLECTION, A SUM EQUAL TO ALL COSTS AND EXPENSES THEREOF, INCLUDING AN
ATTORNEY'S FEE EQUAL TO 15% OF THE AMOUNT OWING ON THIS NOTE AT THE TIME OF SUCH REFERENCE, FOR NECESSARY COURT COSTS.
THE ACCEPTANCE BY THE BANK OF ANY PAYMENT(S) EVEN IF MARKED PAYMENT IN FULL OR SIMILAR WORDING, OR IF MADE AFTER ANY
DEFAULT HEREUNDER, SHALL NOT OPERATE TO EXTEND THE TIME OF PAYMENT OF OR TO WAIVE ANY AMOUNT(S) THEN REMAINING
UNPAID OR CONSTITUTE A WAIVER OF ANY RIGHTS OF THE BANK HEREUNDER.

IN THE EVENT THIS NOTE IS PREPAID IN FULL OR REFINANCED, THE BORROWER SHALL RECEIVE A REFUND OF THE UNEARNED
PORTION OF THE PREPAID FINANCE CHARGE COMPUTED IN ACCORDANCE WITH THE RULE OF 78 (THE "SUM OF THE DIGITS" METHOD),
PROVIDED THAT THE BANK MAY RETAIN A MINIMUM FINANCE CHARGE OF $10, WHETHER OR NOT EARNED, AND, EXCEPT IN THE CASE OF A
REFINANCING, NO REFUND SHALL BE MADE IF IT AMOUNTS TO LESS THAN $1. IN ADDITION, UPON ANY SUCH PREPAYMENT OR REFINANCING,
THE BORROWER SHALL RECEIVE A REFUND OF THE CHARGE, IF ANY, FOR GROUP CREDIT LIFE INSURANCE INCLUDED IN THE LOAN EQUAL
TO THE UNEARNED PORTION OF THE PREMIUM PAID OR PAYABLE BY THE HOLDER OF THE OBLIGATION (COMPUTED IN ACCORDANCE WITH
THE RULE OF 78), PROVIDED THAT NO REFUND SHALL BE MADE OF AMOUNTS LESS THAN $1.

AS COLLATERAL SECURITY FOR THE PAYMENT OF THE INDEBTEDNESS OF THE UNDERSIGNED HEREUNDER AND ALL OTHER
INDEBTEDNESS OR LIABILITIES OF THE UNDERSIGNED TO THE BANK, WHETHER JOINT, SEVERAL, ABSOLUTE, CONTINGENT, SECURED,
UNSECURED, MATURED OR UNMATURED, UNDER ANY PRESENT OR FUTURE NOTE OR CONTRACT OR AGREEMENT WITH THE BANK (ALL
SUCH INDEBTEDNESS AND LIABILITIES BEING HEREINAFTER COLLECTIVELY CALLED THE "OBLIGATIONS"), THE BANK SHALL HAVE, AND IS
HEREBY GRANTED, A SECURITY INTEREST AND/OR RIGHT OF SET-OFF IN AND TO (a) ALL MONIES, SECURITIES AND OTHER PROPERTY OF
THE UNDERSIGNED NOW OR HEREAFTER ON DEPOSIT WITH OR OTHERWISE HELD BY OR COMING TO THE POSSESSION OR UNDER THE
CONTROL OF THE BANK, WHETHER HELD FOR SAFEKEEPING, COLLECTION, TRANSMISSION OR OTHERWISE OR AS CUSTODIAN, INCLUDING
THE PROCEEDS THEREOF, AND ANY AND ALL CLAIMS OF THE UNDERSIGNED AGAINST THE BANK, WHETHER NOW OR HEREAFTER EXISTING,
AND (b) THE FOLLOWING DESCRIBED PERSONAL PROPERTY (ALL SUCH MONIES, SECURITIES, PROPERTY, PROCEEDS, CLAIMS AND PERSONAL
PROPERTY BEING HEREINAFTER COLLECTIVELY CALLED THE "COLLATERAL": ( ) Motor Vehicle ( ) Boat ( ) Stocks, ( ) Bonds, ( ) Savings.
and/or
SEE CUSTOMER'S COPY OF SECURITY AGREEMENT(S) OR COLLATERAL RECEIPT(S) RELATIVE TO THIS LOAN FOR FULL DESCRIPTION.
IF THIS NOTE IS SECURED BY A MOTOR VEHICLE, BOAT OR AIRCRAFT, PROPERTY INSURANCE ON THE COLLATERAL IS REQUIRED
AND THE BORROWER MAY OBTAIN THE SAME THROUGH A PERSON OF HIS OWN CHOICE.
IF THIS NOTE IS NOT FULLY SECURED BY THE COLLATERAL SPECIFIED ABOVE, AS FURTHER SECURITY FOR THE PAYMENT OF THIS
NOTE, THE BANK HAS TAKEN AN ASSIGNMENT OF 10% OF THE UNDERSIGNED BORROWER'S WAGES IN ACCORDANCE WITH THE WAGE
ASSIGNMENT ATTACHED TO THIS NOTE.

In the event of default in the payment of this or any other Obligation or the performance or observance of any term or covenant contained herein or in any
note or other contract or agreement evidencing or relating to any Obligation or any Collateral on the Borrower's part to be performed or observed; or the
undersigned Borrower shall die; or any of the undersigned become insolvent or make an assignment for the benefit of creditors; or a petition shall be filed by or
against any of the undersigned under any provision of the Bankruptcy Act; or any money, securities or property of the undersigned now or hereafter on deposit with
or in the possession or under the control of the Bank shall be attached or become subject to distraint proceedings or any order or process of any court; or the Bank
shall deem itself to be insecure, then and in any such event, the Bank shall have the right (at its option), without demand or notice of any kind, to declare all or any
part of the Obligations to be immediately due and payable, whereupon such Obligations shall become and be immediately due and payable, and the Bank shall have
the right to exercise all the rights and remedies available to a secured party upon default under the Uniform Commercial Code (the "Code") in effect in New York
at the time, and such other rights and remedies as may otherwise be provided by law. Each of the undersigned agrees (for purposes of the "Code") that written notice
of any proposed sale of, or of the Bank's election to retain, Collateral mailed to the undersigned Borrower (who is hereby appointed agent of each of the undersigned
for such purpose) by first class mail, postage prepaid, at the address of the undersigned Borrower indicated below three business days prior to such sale or election
shall be deemed reasonable notification thereof. The remedies of the Bank hereunder are cumulative and may be exercised concurrently or separately. If any provision
of this paragraph shall conflict with any remedial provision contained in any security agreement or collateral receipt covering any Collateral, the provisions of such
security agreement or collateral receipt shall control.
Acceptance by the Bank of payments in arrears shall not constitute a waiver of or otherwise affect any acceleration of payment hereunder or other right of
remedy exercisable hereunder. No failure or delay on the part of the Bank in exercising, and no failure to file or otherwise perfect or enforce the Bank's security
interest in or with respect to any Collateral, shall operate as a waiver of any right or remedy hereunder or release any of the undersigned, and the Obligations of the
undersigned may be extended or waived by the Bank, any contract or other agreement evidencing or relating to any Obligation or any Collateral may be amended
and any Collateral exchanged, surrendered or otherwise dealt with in accordance with any agreement relative thereto, all without affecting the liability of any of the
undersigned. In any litigation (whether or not arising out of or relating to any Obligation or Collateral or other matter connected herewith) in which the Bank and
any of the undersigned may be adverse parties, the Bank and each such undersigned hereby waives their respective right to demand trial by jury and, additionally,
each such undersigned waives his right to interpose in any such litigation any counterclaim of any nature or description which he may have against the Bank. In
addition, the Bank shall not be deemed to have obtained knowledge of any fact or notice with respect to any matter relating to this note or any Collateral unless
contained in a written notice mailed, postage prepaid, or personally delivered to the Personal Finance Department of the Bank at its address set forth above. Each of
the undersigned, by his signature hereto, hereby waives presentation for payment, demand, notice of non-payment, protest and notice of protest with respect to the
indebtedness evidenced by this note, and each such undersigned hereby agrees that this note shall be deemed to have been made under and shall be construed in
accordance with the laws of the State of New York.
Each of the undersigned hereby authorizes the Bank to date this note as of the day the loan evidenced hereby is made, to correct patent errors herein and
at its option, to cause the signatures of one or more co-makers to be added without notice to any prior obligor.

"New" Agreement

First National City Bank

Consumer Loan Note   Date_____ ;9____

(In this note, the words I, me, mine and my mean each and all of those who signed it. The words you, your and yours mean First National City Bank.)

Terms of Repayment   To repay my loan, I promise to pay you _____ Dollars ($_____). I'll pay this sum at one of your branches in _____ uninterrupted _____ installments of $_____ each. Payments will be due _____, starting from the date the loan is made.

Here's the breakdown of my payments:

1. Amount of the Loan $_____
2. Property Insurance Premium $_____
3. Filing Fee for Security Interest $_____
4. Amount Financed (1+2+3) $_____
5. Finance Charge $_____
6. Total of Payments (4+5) $_____

Annual Percentage Rate_____ %

Prepayment of Whole Note   Even though I needn't pay more than the fixed installments, I have the right to prepay the whole outstanding amount of this note at any time. If I do, or if this loan is refinanced—that is, replaced by a new note— you will refund the unearned finance charge, figured by the rule of 78—a commonly used formula for figuring rebates on installment loans. However, you can charge a minimum finance charge of $10.

Late Charge   If I fall more than 10 days behind in paying an installment, I promise to pay a late charge of 5% of the overdue installment, but no more than $5. However, the sum total of late charges on all installments can't be more than 2% of the total of payments or $25, whichever is less.

Security   To protect you if I default on this or any other debt to you, I give you what is known as a security interest in my O Motor Vehicle and or _____ (see the Security Agreement I have given you for a full description of this property), O Stocks, O Bonds, O Savings Account (more fully described in the receipt you gave me today) and any account or other property of mine coming into your possession.

Insurance   I understand I must maintain property insurance on the property covered by the Security Agreement for its full insurable value, but I can buy this insurance through a person of my own choosing.

Default   I'll be in default:
1. If I don't pay an installment on time; or
2. If any other creditor tries by legal process to take any money of mine in your possession.

You can then demand immediate payment of the balance of this note, minus the part of the finance charge which hasn't been earned figured by the rule of 78. You will also have other legal rights, for instance, the right to repossess, sell and apply security to the payments under this note and any other debts I may then owe you.

Irregular Payments   You can accept late payments or partial payments, even though marked "payment in full", without losing any of your rights under this note.

Delay in Enforcement   You can delay enforcing any of your rights under this note without losing them.

Collection Costs   If I'm in default under this note and you demand full payment, I agree to pay you interest on the unpaid balance at the rate of 1% per month, after an allowance for the unearned finance charge. If you have to sue me, I also agree to pay your attorney's fees equal to 15% of the amount due, and court costs. But if I defend and the court decides I am right, I understand that you will pay my reasonable attorney's fees and the court costs.

Comakers   If I'm signing this note as a comaker, I agree to be equally responsible with the borrower. You don't have to notify me that this note hasn't been paid. You can change the terms of payment and release any security without notifying or releasing me from responsibility on this note.

Copy Received   The borrower acknowledges receipt of a completely filled-in copy of this note.

       Signatures   Addresses

Borrower: _____   _____

Comaker: _____   _____

Comaker: _____   _____

Comaker: _____   _____

Hot Line   If something should happen and you can't pay on time, please call us immediately at (212) 559-3061.

Personal Finance Department
First National City Bank

Buried in the old agreement is this provision for default:

> In the event of default in the payment of this or any other Obligation or the performance or observance of any term or covenant contained herein or in any note or other contract or agreement evidencing or relating to any Obligation or any Collateral on the Borrower's part to be performed or observed, or the undersigned Borrower shall die; or any of the undersigned become insolvent or make an assignment for the benefit of creditors; or a petition shall be filed by or against any of the undersigned under any provision of the Bankruptcy Act; or any money, securities or property of the undersigned now or hereafter on deposit with or in the possession or under the control of the Bank shall be attached or become subject to distraint proceedings or any order or process of any court, or the Bank shall deem itself to be insecure, then. . . .

In the new agreement, the provision reads:

> **Default** I'll be in default:
>
> 1. If I don't pay an installment on time; or
> 2. If any other creditor tries by legal process to take any money of mine in your possession.

It is readily apparent that the style has been changed. The provision has a heading ("Default"). A long sentence has been broken down into a tabulation. The informal "I" and "you" replace "Borrower" and "Bank." Notice that not only the form but also the substance of the agreement has been altered. At least eight events of default have been reduced to two. A thorough lawyer generally tries to foresee all possible problems and to provide for them. Here, the drafters realized that most of the foreseeable events would quickly manifest themselves in failure to pay on time. Furthermore, the Bank would not be concerned about the event if timely payment nevertheless continued. The drafters could therefore reduce those many possible events to one significant event. They developed a rule of thumb: "For commercial agreements, if a problem can be foreseen, draft for it. For consumer agreements, unless a problem seems likely, consider dropping it."

§ 18.5 The process of plain language drafting.

Drafting often begins with the revision of a form or model. An alternative approach is "zero-base" drafting, in which the drafter begins with the issues and the law, using the model only as a checklist. *See* § 15.3. Zero-base drafting can be helpful when an agreement has drifted too far from its origins. For example, attorneys for landlords often use agreements that do not embody the statutes that govern them. It might be wise to draft such an agreement using the statutes rather than a later-generation form as a model.

The following steps will help you draft or revise any agreement in plain language. Computer programs are also available to evaluate your draft and to help you write it in plain language. *See* § 19.2.2.

- Step 1. Read for style.
- Step 2. Identify the problem.
- Step 3. Read for precision.
- Step 4. Outline a solution.
- Step 5. Know the law.
- Step 6. Organize for clarity and accessibility.
- Step 7. Make it look good.

We will look more closely at these seven steps and then apply them to the revision of a document. The steps are not always followed in the same order, but can be followed flexibly as the demands of the document dictate.

Step 1. Read for style. When confronting a draft that is stylistically poor, the drafter is probably wise to start by improving the style. This suggestion is made not just for aesthetic purposes, although aesthetics are important. Eliminating the stylistic problems will help clarify the substance. Problems of style can also lead to misinterpretation of the document.

Lawyers sometimes fear that clients will not think they are getting their money's worth unless the agreement contains a sprinkling of legalese. This concern is expressed in the following cartoon:

The Wizard of Id. Copyright 1991 North American Syndicate, Inc. Reprinted by permission of Johnny Hart and Creators Syndicate, Inc.

This concern makes no sense. Much of lawyering is communicating in one form or another. Drafting is communicating to the parties, sometimes to third parties, occasionally to a court. If your style is not appropriate for that audience, you are not doing your job.

Some of the stylistic steps to improve a draft include the following:

- Avoid archaic words.

- Use gender-neutral language.

- Shorten overlong sentences. Recall that readability is largely a function of sentence length. Tabulation can be a helpful tool.

- Use words appropriate to your audience. Recall that one factor in readability is word length. While the drafter can presume that law school graduates are familiar with many unusual words, many documents are drafted for the general public.

- Use proper punctuation.

Step 2. Identify the problem. What is it you are trying to accomplish through this transaction? Have you covered all aspects of the situation? A sample contract or formbook can be useful as a checklist, to remind you of all sides of the problem, but feel free to modify it.

Step 3. Read for precision. What language is vague or ambiguous and may come back to haunt you later? One of your jobs as a lawyer is to predict what may go wrong and take steps to provide for those situations at the outset. This is good preventive lawyering.

Step 4. Outline a solution. Your outline is a table of contents for the draft, providing for all the relevant provisions and organizing them in a clear and logical manner.

Step 5. Know the law. You cannot draft without knowing the substantive law of the area you are concerned with. It may also be important to check the statutes for required language, prohibitions, and the like. Research whether the law has changed since you last worked in the area.

Step 6. Organize for clarity and accessibility. At this point you should have either drafted an original document or analyzed a draft submitted to you. In either event, pull it apart now to make sure it is thorough and well-organized. If you want parties to honor a document, it should be accessible to them. Can the parties find enumerated points easily? Arrange topics in a logical order, gathering all material relevant to each topic. Use headings to break up text and to orient the reader.

Step 7. Make it look good. As with style, appearance is not merely a matter of aesthetics. It is a matter of communication. To communicate clearly, use readable typefaces and readable print. Use white space to break up text. Highlight important provisions. Don't use all capital letters.

§ 18.6   Example of plain language drafting.

The following passage is from a Standard Form Listing Contract between a broker and the owner of real property. With reference to the steps to follow for plain language drafting, we will revise the provision that addresses payment of the broker's commission:

---

1 I agree to pay you _____ percent (_____%) of the selling
2 price as and for your compensation hereunder in the event
3 that you or any broker cooperating with you shall find a
4 buyer ready and willing to enter into a contract for said
5 price and terms, or at such other price and terms as I
6 accept, for the sale or exchange of said real property by
7 you or any other, including myself, while this contract is
8 in force. I agree to pay you such compensation should a
9 sale or exchange be made or an agreement to sell or
10 exchange be entered into, or in the event I lease, rent or
11 lend such property and such arrangement is ultimately
12 consummated in a sale, by me within one hundred twenty
13 (120) days after the termination of this authorization, to
14 or with parties with whom you negotiated during the term

15 hereof, or to or with parties who became interested in
16 said property, directly or indirectly, as a result of any
17 of the activities or efforts of you or your agents,
18 including, but not limited to, the placing of a "For Sale"
19 sign, advertising or personal referrals or contracts;
20 unless such sale or exchange is made or agreement or
21 exchange entered into during the term of a valid,
22 exclusive authorization to sell given by me to a licensed
23 real estate broker other than you after the termination of
24 this agreement. I agree to pay you said percent of the
25 listing price if I withdraw said property from sale or
26 exchange or otherwise prevent performance hereunder by
27 you.

First, let us determine whether this provision is presently written in plain language. How does the passage rate on a subjective test of plain language? Recall the New York requirements:

- Is it clear and coherent?

- Does it use words with common, every day meanings?

- Is it divided and captioned by sections?

The answer to the first and third questions is clearly *no.* Our consideration of these questions suggests steps to take in revision. The provision contains three sentences, one of which is extremely long. The provision does not clearly convey to the reader any particular substance. In fact, without divisions and captions, it is hard to discover exactly what the provision is about. Interestingly, the drafter has called the parties "you" and "I." While this technique is used by many drafters to promote reading ease, this provision makes painfully clear that the technique is not sufficient to achieve the goal of clarity. Put yourself in the shoes of the seller of real property who signs it. Does that seller know what he or she is agreeing to? In particular, would the seller know when he or she must pay the broker a commission?

How does the passage fare on an objective test? Refer to the provisions of the Model Life and Health Insurance Policy Language Simplification Act, which contains the calculations we must make to answer this question.

In this provision, there are 4 sentences, 261 words, and 404 syllables:

words/sentences x 1.015	=	66.22
syllables/words x 84.6	=	130.28
total	=	196.50
206.835 − 196.50	=	10.33

This agreement does not pass the objective test, for the required minimum score for plain language is 40.

Step 1. Read for style. In general, the drafter will read for style when the draft is complete. There are some words and phrases, however, that can be eliminated early on as they tend to gum up the draft as you work on it. In this passage we find the following:

	Before	After
twofers:		
	as and for (line 2)	define and use commission
	lease, rent or lend (lines 10–11)	rent
	activities or efforts (line 17)	efforts
	to or with (lines 13–14, 15)	to
words to avoid:		
	hereunder (lines 2, 26)	delete
	said (lines 4, 6, 16, 24, 25)	the
	such (lines 8, 20)	the
	hereof (line 15)	delete
simplify:		
	in the event that (lines 2–3, 10)	if

There is also an error. In line 19, the word should be *contacts*, not *contracts*.

Steps 2 and 3. Identify the problem and read for precision. Now we will read through the draft raising questions of substance. The drafter must read actively, talking to the draft, carrying on a conversation with it.

First sentence:

". . . a buyer ready and willing to enter into a contract" (lines 3–4). Does this mean the broker gets paid even if the buyer doesn't actually enter the contract, or if the buyer enters the contract but breaches it? The substantive meaning must be clarified to specify what the broker has to do to earn the commission.

"sale or exchange" (line 6). Does this mean the broker can perform by getting the seller a property in exchange for his or her property? Would the seller have wanted this? Clarify what kind of a transaction the seller will agree to.

What does "by you" (lines 6–7) modify? It should modify "find" (line 3), not "sale or exchange" (line 6). Clarify who can obtain the buyer that will get the broker the commission. This same question may help to clarify "you or any broker cooperating with you" (line 3). Isn't that phrase redundant, given "any other" (line 7)?

Second sentence:

What does "within 120 days after the termination of this authorization" (lines 12–13) modify? The text identifies three events: 1) sale or exchange, 2) agreement to sell or exchange, 3) lease that ultimately (when?) results in a sale. Note the variation in language — events 1 and 2 refer to sale or exchange, but event 3 refers only to sale. Does 120 days relate to just the first of these three events? Before answering this, what does "by me" (line 12) modify? Note the use of the passive voice — "by me" means I do something. What is that something?

The purpose of this section seems to be to identify events that will result in the broker earning a commission even after the agreement has terminated. Otherwise, the two sentences would be redundant. Clarify the circumstances in which the commission is payable after termination of the contract.

What do lines 13–19 mean, beginning with "to or with"? The purpose is to say that sale after 120 days doesn't always result in payment of a commission. Clarify the exceptions.

Following the semicolon (line 19):

This is another exception to when the commission is not payable during that 120 days. Clarify it. Note the lack of parallel construction. "Such" (line 20) refers to the first two events in the preceding sentence, but not the third. Was this intentional?

Last sentence:

What is the "listing price" (line 25)? Note the term used in lines 1–2 was "selling price." Is this an oversight or is there a reason for using different language?

This sentence enumerates additional circumstances in which the commission is payable. What are they? How can seller prevent performance by broker? How else can seller prevent full performance? Clarify this.

Steps 4 and 5. Outline a solution and know the law. We are now in a position to make an outline. We are only drafting one section of the agreement. If there are phrases that are frequently used in the agreement, we should define them at the beginning. Once we have defined them, we can use them throughout the agreement. In drafting this section, let us assume we have previously defined these terms:

- I = seller
- you = broker
- the property = this particular property
- the price and terms = sales terms established by the seller
- the termination date = date this contract is terminated

We can organize our outline of the agreement around the issues we have raised from questioning the model, the existing text. However, we should also check whether our model has covered all of the issues. We raised some substantive questions that we will want to check with our client. For example: Is the commission payable if the sale does not go through? Is the commission payable for an exchange?

We can also check the model against checklists, form contracts, and other models to see if there are additional issues we should consider. Finally, we should check the statutes and case law in our jurisdiction to see if the substance or the language in our agreement has been subjected to legislative or judicial scrutiny.

Let us assume we have done that. Our client states that the commission is payable when a buyer "ready and willing to purchase is found," and our research indicates that the case law supports this interpretation. Our client acknowledges that most sellers contemplate a sale, so exchange should be omitted. The outline raises these issues:

1. What does the broker have to do to earn the commission?

2. Who can obtain the buyer that earns the broker the commission?

3. Under what circumstances is the commission payable after the contract has been terminated?

   a. What the seller must do

   b. What the broker must do

   c. Exception: if there is another broker's contract

4. Under what circumstances is the commission payable if there is no sale?

   a. What are the events?

   b. How is the commission computed?

Step 6. Organize for clarity and accessibility. We can now organize our draft by stating clearly provisions that answer the questions we have raised:

I agree to pay you a percent of the selling price

   I pay it if you find a buyer ready and willing to enter a contract for the sale [or exchange?] of my property

   I also agree to pay if any broker cooperating with you finds a buyer

      I pay if the contract is for the above price and terms or other price and terms I accept

      I pay if the buyer is found by you or any other, including me

I agree to pay you

   if a sale or exchange is made

   if an agreement to sell or exchange is entered into

   if I lease, rent, or lend the property and the arrangement ultimately results in a sale by me

But I only have to pay you

   if these events occur within 120 days after termination *and*

   if the sale, agreement, or lease is made

---

to parties with whom you negotiated during the term *or*

to parties who became interested in the property as a result of your efforts

"efforts" includes placing a "For Sale" sign, advertising, personal referrals, contacts

I do not have to pay you if the sale is made during the term of an exclusive authorization to sell I give to another licensed real estate broker after termination

I agree to pay you based on the listing price

if I withdraw the property from sale; or

if I prevent performance by you

Step 7. Make it look good. We can now state the points raised in the outline in a precise and orderly fashion, arranging them meaningfully on the page:

1. Broker's commission.

1.1. I agree to pay you _____ percent of the selling price (your "commission") if, during the term of this contract, you find a buyer ready and willing to purchase or to enter a contract to purchase the property for the above price and terms.

1.2. I will pay you the commission if, during the term of this contract:

1.21. I agree to a sale at any other price or terms; or

1.22. any other person, including myself, finds a buyer.

1.3. I will pay you the commission if, within 120 days from the date this contract expires, I have:

1.31. sold or exchanged the property; or

1.32. entered into a contract to sell or exchange the property; or

1.33. rented the property and the rental results in a sale before or after 120 days from the date this contract expires;

and

1.34. the property came to the knowledge of the buyer, directly or indirectly, as a result of your efforts. "Efforts" includes, but is not limited to, listing, negotiation, the placing of a "For Sale" sign, advertising, personal referrals, and contacts.

1.4. Paragraph 1.3 does not apply if any of the events itemized as 1.31, 1.32, or 1.33 occurs during the term of a valid, exclusive contract between me and a licensed real estate broker.

1.5. I will pay you a commission based on the price in the sales terms if:

1.51. I withdraw the property from sale; or

1.52. I prevent your performance; or

1.53. I prevent performance by a ready and willing buyer.

Let us examine some of the changes we have made:

- We have added a caption, "Broker's commission," describing what this part of the agreement is about. We could break the provision down further and make captions for each of the subsections.

- In 1.1, we have defined a term, "commission," and used it throughout the agreement. We have dropped "exchange" from "sale or exchange." We have used a phrase "price and terms," that we earlier defined.

- In 1.2, we have eliminated the redundancies. We have kept the phrase "including myself," however, to make absolutely clear to the seller the fact that the seller must pay the commission even if the seller makes the sale. Because this concept leads to frequent misunderstandings, we might look for additional ways to make it conspicuous.

- In 1.3, we have included "exchanged" in "sold or exchanged." Here we have changed the language because we have changed the meaning. 1.1 dealt with when the broker receives a commission for his or her acts; we did not want the broker to arrange an exchange. 1.3 deals with when the broker receives a commission on account of the acts of the seller; the broker is paid if the seller transfers the property by any means, including exchange. 1.33 clarifies that the broker receives a commission for a sale that occurs any time after the 120 days has expired. 1.34 defines "efforts," using the helpful phrase "including but not limited to." Note how the enumerations are connected by an *and*, indicating that two events must occur before the commission is payable.

- 1.4 refers to specific paragraphs for clarity.

- 1.5 deals with the payment of a commission if no sale occurs. Therefore, it cannot be based on the sales price, but must be based on the price at which the property was listed. The variation in language was intentional. We have added a provision, 1.53, that was not in the original but was suggested by another form.

Finally, we can check this draft under the objective test for plain language. In this revision, there are 15 sentences, 228 words, and 341 syllables.

words/sentences x 1.015	=	15.42
syllables/words x 84.6	=	126.05
total	=	141.47
206.835 − 141.47	=	65.36

Recall that a minimum passing score is 40, so this draft easily qualifies.

§ 18.7 Is plain language drafting worth the trouble?

As we saw when revising the provision from the Listing Contract, drafting in plain language requires considerable effort. We revised just part of the agreement, payment of the broker's commission. Is the expense incurred by spending the time to draft in plain language justified?

This is a standard form contract. It will be used by many brokers and sellers. The time spent by the drafter in putting it together will benefit many transactions. It might be harder to justify economically drafting an agreement that is used only once. This is one of the reasons plain language statutes apply only to consumer contracts, form contracts that will be used on a number of occasions. Even an agreement drafted for a particular transaction, however, is often used in an office as a model for other agreements, particularly when the office uses its forms in computerized document assembly.

Furthermore, there has been a great deal of litigation over the particular problem of when a broker's commission is payable. The amount of litigation indicates that this is an area where the agreement should clearly express the agreement so that both parties understand it. Understanding is particularly important when the parties probably enter the agreement without the assistance of an attorney to explain it. The time spent in drafting the agreement in plain language may be economical in the practice of preventive law. It may be expensive to take the time carefully to draft the agreement, but a lawsuit may be even more expensive.

Some drafters are concerned that in the process of "translating" a form into plain language, they will inadvertently change the substantive meaning. Perhaps a horror story circulates to support this concern. "If it ain't broke," the opponent might conclude, "let's not fix it." I must say I question the premise: if it is not written with clarity, it *is* "broke." The drafter examining the language is practicing sound preventive law. In analyzing the text, the drafter will probably find a number of ambiguities, unenforceable and possibly unconscionable provisions, and unstated remedies. Each of these represents a sleeping dog that may later awaken to haunt the drafter. Of course, any attempt to fix a potential problem can make it worse. The drafter must use caution, always returning to the client to check the intended substantive meaning of a provision.

There is some backlash against plain language. The complaint is twofold: that commercial lawyers understand the text even if a lay person does not, and that lawyers should be able to rely on established language. As to the first complaint, we write for an audience. Plain language is essentially a consumer movement, and lawyers who understand exactly what they are saying can communicate without short sentences and short words. Take the first sentence of a legal opinion:

> Appellant (plaintiff below) sought to recover $670 as liquidated damages under a contract for improvements on appellees' home. Appellees' defense was that the contract never came into existence because of an unfulfilled condition precedent. This appeal raises the sole question of whether the parol evidence rule required exclusion of all testimony regarding the alleged condition.[3]

Pat yourself on the back. Before you began law school, those sentences would have meant little to you. Now they are quite clear. The clarity was attained, not by lowering the reading level, but by raising your level of education. Further clarity for that audience is not needed.

As for the second complaint, forms have value in leveraging up experience. Over the course of time, the language becomes more refined as it addresses more and more contingencies. In the course of that development, it may become convoluted. Nevertheless, if the language is used in a sophisticated transaction, used by specialized practitioners, or is drafted to comply with a statute, there may be good reason to stick with form language that works. Clarity is the goal, but efficiency is a competing consideration. Lawyers need not spend much time assessing familiar language, but would have to carefully parse and analyze any changes. On the other hand, if the language could lead to ambiguity and litigation even among an audience that "knows what it means," then it is time to look at it again. Most importantly, it is always necessary to ask whether the form language is appropriate for this client, in this transaction, at this time.

§ 18.8 Computer assistance.

Computers can be very helpful in plain language drafting. Word processing programs can search for words in a document that you may wish to replace. Grammar checking programs will indicate when your sentences are too long or when you have used difficult words. You can also modify most of the programs to search for specific terms, such as the archaic terms and legalese that clutter up legal documents. The program will give you a Flesch score or other readability score. *See* § 19.2.2.

You may wish to obtain a score before and after you have made your revisions. In some jurisdictions where plain language drafting is required, a good faith effort to draft in plain language is a defense to an alleged violation. Running the document through the grammar program,

---

[3] *Luther Williams, Jr., Inc. v. Johnson*, 229 A.2d 163 (D.C. Ct. App. 1967).

incorporating suggested changes, and demonstrating an improved readability score would probably satisfy the good faith requirement.

§ 18.9 Summary: The elements of plain language.[4]

a. In General

1. As the starting point and at every point, design and write the document in a way that best serves the reader. Your main goal is to convey your ideas with the greatest possible clarity.

b. Design (for consumer documents especially)

1. Use at least 8-to 10-point type for text, and a readable typeface.

2. Try to use between 50 and 70 characters a line.

3. Use ample white space in margins, between sections, and around headings and other special items.

4. Use highlighting techniques such as boldface, underlining, and bullet dots. But don't overuse them, and be consistent throughout the document.

5. Avoid using all capital letters, except possibly for main headings.

6. Use diagrams, tables, and charts as needed to help explain the text.

c. Organization

1. Divide the document into sections, and into smaller parts as needed.

2. Put related material together.

3. Order the parts in a logical sequence. Usually, put the more important before the less important, the general before the specific, and the ordinary before the extraordinary.

4. Omit unnecessary detail. Try to boil down the information to what your reader needs to know.

5. Use informative headings for the main divisions and subdivisions.

d. Sentences

1. Prefer short and medium-length sentences. As a guideline, keep the average length under 25 words.

2. In most sentences, put the subject near the beginning; keep it short and concrete; make it something the reader already knows about; and make it the agent of the action in the verb.

3. Put the main action in strong verbs, not in abstract nouns. ("If the seller delivers the goods late, the buyer may cancel the contract." Not: "Late delivery of the goods may result in cancellation of the contract.")

4. Keep the subject near the verb, and the verb near the object (or complement). Avoid intrusive phrases.

---

4 Joseph Kimble, *Plain English: A Charter for Clear Writing,* 9 Thomas M. Cooley L. Rev. 1, 11–14 (1992). Copyright 1992 © Thomas M. Cooley Law Review. Reprinted with permission.

5. Put your strongest point, your most important information, at the end.

6. Prefer the active voice. Use the passive voice if the agent is unknown or unimportant. Or use it if, for continuity, you want to focus attention on the object of the action instead of the agent. ("No more legalese. It has been ridiculed long enough.")

7. Connect modifying words to what they modify.

8. Use parallel structure for parallel ideas. Consider using a list or tabulation if the items are at all complicated, as when you have multiple conditions or rules.

e. Words

1. Prefer familiar words — usually the shorter ones.

2. Avoid legal jargon: stuffy old formalisms, *here-*, *there-*, and *where-* words, unnecessary Latin, and all the rest.

3. Avoid doublets and triplets.

4. In consumer documents, explain technical terms that you cannot avoid using.

5. Omit unnecessary words.

6. Replace wordy phrases.

7. In consumer documents, consider making the consumer "you."

8. Avoid multiple negatives.

9. Be consistent; use the same term for the same thing, without guilt.

§ 18.10   Exercises.

1. Contract for deed. The following provision is from the default clause of a contract for deed, an agreement for seller financing of real property. Revise it in plain language. Note any substantive questions that arise in the process.

---

1   9. DEFAULT—In case of the failure of the said
2 Purchasers to make any of the payments of principal or
3 interest, or to perform any of the covenants on their part
4 hereby made and entered into, then the whole of said
5 payments and interest shall, at the election of said
6 Seller, become immediately due and payable, except as
7 hereinafter provided, and this Contract shall, at the
8 option of Seller, be forfeited and determined by giving to
9 the Purchasers sixty (60) days' notice, in writing, of the
10 intention of the Seller to cancel and determine this
11 Contract and any covenants and payments which the Pur-
12 chasers have failed to perform and make, if any; and the

13 time when and the place where payment can be made;
14 should the said Purchasers make good such default within
15 said 60-day period, then their rights under this Contract
16 shall be fully reinstated, and said acceleration of said
17 payments shall fail; however, should said Purchasers fail
18 to make good any such default within said 60-day period,
19 said acceleration shall be good and this Contract may
20 be terminated by the Sellers as aforesaid.
21 It is mutually understood and agreed by and between
22 the parties to this Contract that 60 days is a reasonable
23 and sufficient notice to be given said Purchasers in case
24 of their failure to perform any of the covenants on their
25 part hereby made and entered into and shall be sufficient
26 to cancel all obligations hereunto on the part of the said
27 Sellers and fully invest them with all right, title and
28 interest agreed to be conveyed, and the said Purchasers
29 shall forfeit all payments made by them on this Contract,
30 and all right, title and interest in all buildings, or
31 other improvements shall be retained by the said Sellers,
32 in full satisfaction and as a reasonable rental for the
33 property above described and in liquidation of all damages
34 by them sustained, and they shall have the right to take
35 possession of the land and premises aforesaid.

2. Lease. The following provision is from a lease. Revise it in plain language. Note whether all the subjects addressed in the provision belong under its heading.

DAMAGE TO PREMISES. The LESSEE further covenants and agrees to take good care of the premises hereby leased, and the fixtures of same, and commit and suffer no waste of any kind therein; that LESSEE shall pay for all repairs required to be made to the floors, walls, ceilings, paint, plastering, plumbing work, pipes, fixtures or any other part of leased premises, whenever damage or injury to same shall have resulted from any misuse or neglect on the part of Lessee or members of family, guests, or employees of LESSEE; that Leased premises shall be used only as a family dwelling. LESSEE shall not perform any maintenance, adjustment, or repair on heating or air conditioning, and plumbing, stoves, refrigerators or other appliances or equipment of LESSOR but said maintenance, adjustment or repair shall be done only by LESSOR'S employees, contractors or agents, and LESSEE agrees to notify LESSOR accurately and promptly of any problem arising from such equipment, its location and cause, if possible; Lessee agrees to allow repairmen to enter leased premises to remedy said problems; and LESSOR shall not be liable for damages due to the temporary breakdown or discontinuance of same. Locks may not be changed, nor any additional locks put on any doors without written permission of the LESSOR. LESSOR is not responsible to provide access to the premises in the event LESSEE accidently or otherwise locks himself/herself out of the premises. LESSEE is responsible for the cost of lost keys or the replacement of locks. Nails, tacks, brads, screws, stick-on picture hangers or tape shall not be used on the woodwork, walls, floors or ceilings of said premises. It is permissible to use small nails that are specifically designed for hanging pictures on the walls. The use of gasoline and/or similar combustibles for cleaning or for other purposes is strictly prohibited. LESSEE shall so use the premises so as not to cause any increase in the insurance rates. LESSOR shall not be responsible or liable to the LESSEE, or any other person claiming by or through LESSEE, for any injury or damage resulting from bursting, stoppage or leaking of plumbing, gas, water, sewer, or other pipes; nor for any damage or injury arising from the acts or neglect of co-tenants, their families or guests or any owners or occupants of adjacent or contiguous property; nor for any damage or injury caused by fire, water damage, snow, ice, wind or any other natural calamity. No outside or attic aerials or antennas will be permitted on the building or premises. LESSOR and/or his representatives may enter the leased premises at any reasonable time to make such repairs and alterations as may be deemed necessary by LESSOR for the safety and preservation of the premises, or exhibiting the leased premises for sale, lease or mortgage financing.

3. The Owner Operator Lease Agreement. The provisions that follow are from a contract between a trucking company and its drivers. Do you think this contract passes either the objective or subjective test for plain language? Using the techniques from this chapter, revise it to make it more readable.

OWNER OPERATOR LEASE AGREEMENT

THIS AGREEMENT, made and entered into this _____ day of _____, 20____, by and between _____ Trucking (a Corporation) hereinafter referred to as the "CARRIER" and

_____

(Name) (Address) (City) (State) (Zip)

hereinafter referred to as the "CONTRACTOR".

PREMISES

A. CARRIER is a for-hire motor carrier engaged in the transportation of commodities in the United States and Canada, and holds operating authority from the Interstate Commerce Commission and from one or more state and Canadian provincial agencies responsible for the regulation of motor carrier operations.

B. CONTRACTOR is the owner of certain motor carrier equipment, more particularly described in Appendix A attached to and hereby made a part of this Agreement, and, as an independent contractor, operates or employs drivers to operate said motor carrier equipment.

C. It is the desire of the parties to this Agreement that the CONTRACTOR lease to the CARRIER the aforesaid equipment, furnished with driver, under terms and conditions hereinafter set forth.

NOW THEREFORE, in consideration of the premises and of the mutual covenants and promises set forth herein, the parties hereto agree as follows:

1. CONTRACTOR hereby leases to CARRIER the equipment described in Appendix A, for the period _____ to _____. CONTRACTOR represents to CARRIER that it holds full legal title or that it has the legal right to exercise full control over the equipment covered by this Agreement, and agrees to furnish CARRIER all necessary information and documents of title or registration to enable CARRIER to properly identify said equipment.

2. Possession and use of the equipment involved is, for the period of the Agreement, entirely vested in CARRIER, in such a way as to be good against all the world, including CONTRACTOR.

3. CONTRACTOR warrants that the equipment covered by this Agreement is complete with all required accessories, and is in good, safe, and efficient operating condition and appearance, and shall be so maintained at no expense to CARRIER throughout the duration of this Agreement. The choice of location and persons to perform any necessary repairs of maintenance is exclusively vested in CONTRACTOR.

4. CONTRACTOR agrees to submit the said equipment for CARRIER's inspection at the time CARRIER takes possession and periodically thereafter as required by the Department of Transportation rules and regulations. Before taking possession of the equipment, CARRIER, or a person duly authorized by CARRIER, shall inspect the said equipment to make certain that equipment complies in every respect with the rules, regulations, and laws of the Interstate Commerce Commission and the Department of Transportation, and of various state and local governments relative to the condition of such equipment. If the original inspection provided for herein reveals that the equipment does not comply with any aspect of the said rules, regulations, and laws, the equipment must be placed into such operating condition by CONTRACTOR in order to fully comply with such rules, regulations, and laws or this Agreement shall immediately terminate.

5. CONTRACTOR agrees to exercise this Agreement in the manner of an independent contractor. The parties hereto understand that CARRIER is subject to rules and regulations of the Interstate Commerce Commission (Commission) under the provisions of the Interstate Commerce Act; that the Commission has adopted certain rules and regulations relating to the

leasing of equipment by carriers by motor vehicle; that it is the intent of the parties that CARRIER shall fully comply with all such rules and regulations but that CARRIER does not have the right to and will not control the manner or prescribe the method of doing that portion of the operations which are contracted for in this Agreement, except such control as can reasonably be construed to be required by said rules and regulations.

6. For and in consideration of the lease of said motor vehicle equipment furnished with driver(s), and for and in consideration of full and proper performance of each trip made by the CONTRACTOR pursuant to this Agreement, CARRIER agrees to pay the CONTRACTOR for each such trip in accordance with the Schedule of Compensation attached hereto as Appendix B. In the event the parties desire to modify Appendix B, said modifications may be effected either (a) by notation thereon initialed by both parties, or (b) by substituting therefor and appending hereto duly signed and dated replacement Appendix B.

7. Settlements for completed use of the said equipment shall be paid to CONTRACTOR within fifteen (15) days (or at such more frequent intervals as CARRIER desires) of the return to CARRIER of the properly prepared executed paperwork, including signed delivery tickets, bills of lading, drivers' logs, and other trip documents as required to enable CARRIER to secure payment from shippers. CONTRACTOR agrees to furnish CARRIER such additional trip documents as CARRIER may require, but understands that the furnishing of such additional documents is not required as a condition precedent to CONTRACTOR receiving payment.

8. CARRIER shall at the time of settlement make available to CONTRACTOR for inspection, a copy of the rated freight bill, subject to the right of CARRIER to delete the names of shippers and consignees, in those cases where settlements are based on a percentage of gross freight revenue for a shipment. In any event, CONTRACTOR shall have the right to examine copies of CARRIER's applicable tariff.

9. CARRIER shall not be liable to CONTRACTOR for any loss of or damage to the vehicles and equipment furnished by CONTRACTOR hereunder unless caused by the intentional or negligent act of CARRIER's employees while acting within the scope of their employment, and in such latter event, CARRIER will be liable only to the extent CONTRACTOR is not compensated for such loss or damage by insurance or otherwise.

10. CONTRACTOR assumes the risk of any injury or death to any person resulting from performance of this Agreement, whether caused by CONTRACTOR's own equipment or equipment furnished to it by CARRIER, or by the employees of CONTRACTOR or CARRIER, unless caused by the intentional or negligent acts of CARRIER's employees while acting within the scope of their employment.

11. In the event CARRIER incurs any liability, expense, cost or attorneys' fees resulting from performance or nonperformance of the Agreement, CONTRACTOR agrees to indemnify and save harmless CARRIER from such liability, expense, cost, or attorneys' fees.

12. In the event CARRIER supplies the trailer equipment for use by CONTRACTOR, CARRIER will maintain, or cause to be maintained, the trailer and accessorial equipment furnished by CARRIER, including the cost of the fuel for the operation of such accessorial equipment. CONTRACTOR shall be responsible and liable for all loss of or damage to any said trailer and accessorial equipment occurring while in the possession or custody of CONTRACTOR, excepting such loss or damage as CARRIER is compensated for under any applicable insurance or otherwise, and CONTRACTOR will indemnify CARRIER against any loss on account thereof. In the event CONTRACTOR supplies the trailer equipment under this Agreement, then CONTRACTOR shall be responsible as provided heretofore for the maintenance of the trailer and accessorial equipment furnished by CONTRACTOR and shall also be responsible for the cost of the fuel for the operation of the accessorial equipment; and shall also be responsible for insurance on the trailer equipment in accordance with Paragraph 15.

4. Notice to Guests. I found this notice hanging on the back of the door in a motel room in (eat your heart out) Butte, Montana. How might you revise it?

NOTICE TO GUESTS

How exempted from liability. Whenever the proprietors of any hotel or inn shall provide a safe or other secure place of deposit therein for the safe-keeping of any money, jewels, ornaments, or other articles of value, belonging to any guest or guests of such hotel or inn, and shall cause to be posted and maintained printed notices thereof in the office or public room, and within every guest's room of such inn or hotel, the proprietor or proprietors thereof shall not be liable to any such guest or guests who shall neglect to deliver their money, jewels, ornaments, or other articles of value to the proprietor or other person in charge of such safe or place of deposit for deposit and safe-keeping therein, for any loss of such money or other articles which may be sustained by such guest by theft or otherwise. — Montana State Code section 7674.

5. Computer exercise: Plain language. The computer can be used to check a document for grammar and readability. There are a number of programs available for this purpose. Look to see if you have one in your word processing program under Tools. The information gained from the program can be extremely valuable to you in revising the draft. For example, the program will pick up long sentences, archaic language, the passive voice, and difficult words. The program will also give you a readability score, such as the Flesch Test of readability or the Flesch-Kincaid grade level test.

Run the texts of the Exercises through a grammar checking program and use the suggestions in your revision. After you are satisfied with your revision, run it again for more suggestions. Compare your readability scores before and after the redraft to measure your progress.

Chapter 19

DRAFTING WITH A COMPUTER

§ 19.1 Introduction.

"Computers will never replace attorneys, but attorneys who use computers may replace attorneys who don't." More and more attorneys are beginning, perhaps begrudgingly, to agree with that sentiment. Some think the proper place for a computer is in front of the secretary, not in front of them. After all, they say, "I am not a typist." Even when working with quill pens, attorneys as drafters have always feared being regarded as a "mere scrivener." That is exactly the point — you are not a mere scrivener. Used effectively, computers will remove much of the repetitiveness and tedium from legal work, leaving attorneys with more time to employ the analytical talents that are their stock in trade.

Should you have a computer in front of you? Yes, without a doubt. Many attorneys draft documents on traditional legal pads, or dictate, or both. The chief advantages of word processing over these methods are flexibility and higher standards of excellence. The computer facilitates legal thinking. Most lawyers do not proceed linearly from one step to the next, but engage in a conversation with a draft, circling back and forth over the work in progress. When changes are easily made, you will find yourself less often saying, "It's good enough." Your standards will be higher because it is easier to attain higher standards. You say you don't know how to type? Get a computer program to teach you how!

In addition to your own ability to manipulate text, you will find many other uses for the computer. You should have instant access not only to traditional sources of legal research, but also to your own and your firm's institutional knowledge and experience. You will have greater access to the world, through electronic mail and other communication technologies. At present, we revise documents largely by exchanging drafts or by holding face-to-face meetings. Interactive computers will let us revise the draft on screen as we discuss it with a client or with counsel for the other party. With a computer in front of you, the drafting process can be completed more quickly and with better results.

§ 19.2 Word processing.

Drafting with a computer begins with word processing, although, as we shall see, it does not end there. It is obvious why word processing is so helpful to attorneys. Most legal written products:

- combine past experience with original thought

297

- are hard to read
- are repetitious

Word processing increases your efficiency and productivity because it:

1. guides you through original thought
2. improves your written expression
3. quickly repeats past experience

§ 19.2.1 Word processing guides you through original thought.

Just as you rarely start drafting with a blank page, so you do not need to start with a blank screen. If you lack a model, computer programs can help you problem-solve by prompting your thinking or by guiding you through checklists to tailor a document for you. An idea processor or outliner can help turn that blank screen or those random thoughts into a coherent document. Even if you do not use document assembly, which will be discussed later in this chapter, your word processor can store a drafting database to help you with the first draft of contracts. You can call up a checklist to remind you of the usual contents or issues and clauses to address each issue.

§ 19.2.2 Word processing improves your written expression.

The features of the word processor can save you from mistakes and can also make your good writing better. You can conduct searches, for example, for legalese or for gender-specific language that may offend some readers. *See* § 17.4. Gender-neutral language will also give you a model that can be used for future transactions without change. You can also search for words that are potentially ambiguous, such as *and* and *or,* in order to examine them closely. *See* § 7.4.2. When you use a definition, you can search for each use to be sure the term is used consistently. *See* § 7.5.1. If you leave blanks or cross-references in an agreement, you can mark them for a final search to check them for accuracy. Many of these searches can be conducted with macros, making the task simpler. *See* § 17.10.

Many word processing programs improve your written expression by offering such functions as spell-checking, thesaurus, outlining, and by generating cross-references, a Table of Authorities, Table of Contents, or Index. More sophisticated programs will check your citations for proper form. Other programs will help you draft in plain language. Others will check your writing for grammatical and structural problems. You can instruct these programs to look for particular problems or words.

We will examine how computer software can assist the drafter with:

- Grammar checking
- Readability

- Aesthetics

a. Grammar checking. As an example of the help you can get from grammar checking programs, consider this passage from a brief:

Buyer was damaged by Seller's delay in shipment. To then obtain the goods, Buyer had to make a number of telephone calls, which caused some disruption of his business, inconvenienced him, and exacerbated the situation because it caused him to lose a sale by the time he was able to find them somewhere else.

These are comments on the passage from Grammatik:

Check: was damaged

Rule Class: Passive voice

Advice: Passive voice: was damaged. Consider revising using active voice. See Help for more information.

* * *

Check: To then obtain

Rule Class: Split infinitive

Advice: Avoid splitting the infinitive "to obtain." Try changing the position of the intervening modifier(s).

* * *

Check: a number of

Rule Class: Long-winded or wordy

Advice: Simplify.

* * *

Check: his/him/he

Rule Class: Gender specific

Advice: It is possible to revise and avoid using "his," "him," or "he." Use of "their," "them," or "they" is now considered acceptable.

* * *

Check: by the time

Rule Class: Long-winded or wordy

Advice: Simplify.

* * *

Check: able to

Rule Class: Long-winded or wordy

Advice: Simplify. Try form of "can."

* * *

Check: To then obtain the goods, Buyer had to make a number of telephone calls, which caused some disruption of his business, inconvenienced him, and exacerbated the situation because it caused him to lose a sale by the time he was able to find them somewhere else.

Rule Class: Long sentence

Advice: Long sentences can be difficult to read and understand. Consider revising so that no more than one complete thought is expressed in each sentence.

It is no surprise that this passage, like most legal writing, includes the passive voice, long-winded or wordy expressions, gender specific language, and long sentences. The drafter can use this advice to redraft the passage:

> Seller's delay in shipment damaged Buyer. To obtain the goods elsewhere, Buyer had to make a number of telephone calls. This disrupted his business and caused him inconvenience. Furthermore, by the time he was able to find another source, he lost a sale.

The redrafted passage is stronger because it does not use the passive voice. The long sentence has been cut down, improving reading ease. Wordy phrases are eliminated. The gender specific language has been retained, for here the drafter is referring to a specific Buyer.

These are the comments on the revised passage, omitting the comments on gender specific language:

Check: a number of

Rule Class: Long-winded or wordy

Advice: Simplify.

* * *

Check: Furthermore

Rule Class: Overstated or pretentious

Advice: Simplify.

* * *

Check: by the time

Rule Class: Long-winded or wordy

Advice: Simplify.

* * *

Check: able to

Rule Class: Long-winded or wordy

Advice: Simplify. Try form of "can."

b. Readability. Many of these grammar checking programs can check your draft for readability. This function could be very important in complying with a plain language law. *See* Chapter 18, Plain Language. If the law has objective standards of plain language, the program will assure compliance. If the law has subjective standards, your good faith attempt to comply by using the computer to check for readability would probably constitute a defense to a claim against you. For example, these are some of the Readability Statistics generated on the above example:

Flesch Reading Ease: 46

Gunning's Fog Index: 17

Flesch-Kincaid Grade Level: 14

These are the statistics on the revised passage:

Flesch Reading Ease: 61

Gunning's Fog Index: 13

Flesch-Kincaid Grade Level: 8

c. Aesthetics. Documents prepared with word processing look good. You can experiment with such features as type size, white space, underline, bold, italics, and graphics to get a good look. Appearance can be important for complying with statutes as well. For example, disclaimers of warranties are often subject to attack as inconspicuous. *See* § 12.5.3. You can use various techniques to make a provision conspicuous. Consider these ways of presenting the same substantive provision, an exclusion of warranties:

1. The foregoing warranty is exclusive and in lieu of all other warranties of quality, whether written, oral or implied (including any warranty of merchantability or fitness for purpose).

2. WARRANTY. THE FOREGOING WARRANTY IS EXCLUSIVE AND IN LIEU OF ALL OTHER WARRANTIES OF QUALITY, WHETHER WRITTEN, ORAL OR IMPLIED (INCLUDING ANY WARRANTY OF MERCHANTABILITY OR FITNESS FOR PURPOSE).

3.   <u>EXCLUSION OF WARRANTY</u>. The foregoing warranty is exclusive and in lieu of all other warranties of quality, whether written, oral or implied (including any warranty of merchantability or fitness for purpose).

4.   The equipment covered hereby is sold subject only to the applicable manufacturer's standard printed warranty, if any, in effect at the date hereof, receipt of which is hereby acknowledged, and no other warranties, express or implied, including without limitation, the implied warranties of *merchantability and fitness for a particular purpose shall apply.*

Example 1 states the exclusion in standard text. Nothing calls it to the attention of the Buyer. Example 2 adds the caption "WARRANTY." This caption is misleading, as in fact the provision is an exclusion of warranty. The drafter has used all capital letters, making the text harder to read than the standard text. When everything stands out, nothing stands out. Example 3 is accurately captioned "Exclusion of Warranty." To make the provision conspicuous, only the caption is underlined and capitalized. The entire provision has a box around it to make it stand out. Example 4 lacks a heading or other devices to call it to the attention of the buyer. It does use italics to emphasize part of the exclusion. The problem is, however, that the emphasized part states that the warranties *shall apply.* A court found the disclaimer ineffective because the emphasis created the appearance of a warranty.

§ 19.2.3   Word processing quickly repeats past experience.

New documents are often assembled by the old-fashioned scissors and paste method. Computerized document assembly has made this technique obsolete. The building block of document assembly is word processing. When the document is in word processing format, it can be edited without the necessity of re-typing it every time. The document can be:

- Originally created on a word processor;
- Transcribed by a typist onto a word processor; or
- Mechanically scanned by an optical scanner.

Once you have made the decision to computerize your office, you will create new documents on the word processor and can then use either of the other methods — one labor intensive and the other capital intensive — to convert other documents.

Word processing quickly repeats past experience because of its capacity for storage. Your computer is the "institutional memory" of your office. When properly catalogued, any important document can be retrieved for future use. Virtually all drafters adapt past experience, often captured in a form or model, to the needs of the present transaction. Document assembly is premised on the idea that legal drafting involves largely the use of forms or models, with original composition to tailor the form or the model to the needs of a particular client.

Using the document as a form or model, you have the efficiency of mass production for the terms that *do not* change. Your basic correspondence, wills, pleadings, contracts, and so forth become templates for future documents. Using alternative provisions, you can tailor the draft for the terms that *do* change. We will call the form or model the *primary document* and the variable provisions the *secondary document*.

Simple document assembly can use any of the following techniques:

- The typeover method
- The place marker method
- The semi-automatic merge
- The automatic merge

a. The typeover method. The typeover method uses the power of word processing in a very unsophisticated way. You simply take the primary document and edit out the changes you wish to make, substituting the new variables. A letter to Jones becomes a letter to Smith. There are a number of problems with this approach. The drafter may not detect all the variables, leading to an embarrassing situation. We have probably all received the letter saying something like "Say hello to Thelma and the kids" that was appropriate for the previous recipient, but not for us.

More importantly, when changes are made, the reasons for the changes become lost. If a paragraph is deleted or a thought changed when the Jones letter becomes the Smith letter, that paragraph and thought are not available to the next drafter when the Smith letter becomes the Brown letter. Contracts may pile up in the form files to be used as models, but the legal analysis behind them is not documented. It may remain in the mind of the drafter, but that knowledge is not directly available to others. An opportunity for efficient education of future lawyers is lost.

b. The place marker method. The place marker method is not much of an improvement. Each variable in the primary document is marked with a symbol such as *xxx*. The drafter then searches for the variable, decides upon the appropriate entry at that point in the document, and goes on to the next variable. The primary document is then retained intact for the next user. This method will prevent many of the mistakes made with the typeover method, but it does not facilitate the sharing of the institutional memory.

c. The semi-automatic merge. The semi-automatic merge uses the power of the word processor to join the primary document with the variables. The variables are extracted from the document and each place where a variable appears is coded F1, F2, F3, etc. In a semi-automatic merge the processor stops at each code to await your entry.

d. The automatic merge. In an automatic merge the word processor replaces each code with appropriate information from a secondary document.

§ 19.3 Preparing a document for document assembly.

Use the following steps to prepare the primary document and the secondary document for document assembly.

- Step 1. Identify the *variables* in the primary document. A variable is language that may change with each use of the form. Imagine, for example, that the form was first filled in for John Brown as a client and was later used for Mary Smith. Or, it was used for one of John Brown's transactions and was later used for another. What language had to be changed or might have been changed?

- Step 2. Bracket each variable in the primary document.

- Step 3. Create the *secondary document* by listing the variables in the primary document. Make up a short name that clearly identifies each variable. Following the identifying name, explain briefly what information is needed to complete that part of the form.

   Imagine you are handing the secondary document to a secretary or paralegal who will obtain the needed information from a client. Make sure that 1) the list includes every variable in the primary document, and 2) the list clearly identifies what information is needed for that variable.

- Step 4. Test your secondary document with some actual facts. Does it provide for every variable? Does it clearly identify the needed information? Is any additional information required? What is the source of that information? A contract, for example, always contains the agreement of at least two parties. Note which information is to be gathered from each party.

Let us apply these steps to prepare the following attorney's retainer agreement for document assembly:

ATTORNEY'S RETAINER AGREEMENT

Retainer. I, _____, of _____, County of _____, State of _____, retain Able, Baker, and Charles, Attorneys at Law, to represent me in my claim against _____, of _____. I suffered damages arising from personal injuries I sustained through the negligence of _____, as the result of an accident occurring on or about the _____ day of _____, 20____.

Payment. I agree to pay you, for services you render pursuant to this retainer the following amount of all sums recovered on my claim or which I receive in settlement:

one-third (1/3) without suit or up to actual trial; and forty percent (40%) if the action is tried or trial is commenced.

Settlement. I agree to pay you this amount whether the settlement is made by me, through my attorneys or by any other person. I also agree to pay, from my share of the recovery, all reasonable and necessary expenses, if any, paid or incurred by you for me in connection with your handling of the claim.

Investigation. The attorneys accept this claim on the condition that they will first investigate it. If it appears to be recoverable, they will handle it on the terms set forth above.

Dated:

_____

Claimant
Able, Baker & Charles
By _____
Attorneys for Claimant

Steps 1 and 2. Identify and bracket the variables. The blanks in the agreement are a helpful start. The percentages retained by the attorneys might also be a variable. Entire provisions might also be variables. For example, some cases might be accepted without the reservation for investigation. We might mark and bracket the variables as follows:

ATTORNEY'S RETAINER AGREEMENT

Retainer. I, [name], of [name of city], County of [name of county], State of [name of state], retain Able, Baker, and Charles, Attorneys at Law, to represent me in my claim against [defendant], of [defendant's city]. I suffered damages arising from personal injuries I sustained through the negligence of [defendant], as the result of an accident occurring on or about [date of accident].

Payment. I agree to pay you, for services you render pursuant to this retainer the following amount of all sums recovered on my claim or which I receive in settlement:

[one-third (⅓)] without suit or up to actual trial; and [forty percent (40%)] if the action is tried or trial is commenced.

Settlement. I agree to pay you this amount whether the settlement is made by me, through my attorneys or by any other person. I also agree to pay, from my share of the recovery, all reasonable and necessary expenses, if any, paid or incurred by you for me in connection with your handling of the claim.

[Investigation. The attorneys accept this claim on the condition that they will first investigate it. If it appears to be recoverable, they will handle it on the terms set forth above.]

Dated: [date of agreement]

[name]
Claimant
Able, Baker & Charles
By _____
Attorneys for Claimant

Step 3. Create the secondary document. We can now create a secondary document listing the variables:

name of client:

client's city of residence:

client's county of residence:

client's state of residence:

name of defendant:

defendant's city of residence:

date of accident:

percentage up to trial:

percentage after trial is commenced:

investigation provision? [Note: if yes, we are not committed to take the case without investigation. If no, we are committed to take the case on signing. If in doubt, choose yes]:

date of agreement:

Step 4. Test the document. If we asked the client the questions necessary to satisfy the secondary document, we would probably be able to complete the retainer agreement. It is evident, however, that there is other information we will need from this client. We can satisfy both of our purposes by using a more extensive checklist while interviewing the client. We can then extract from that checklist the information needed for the retainer agreement, enter it at the appropriate place in the secondary document, and instantly generate the document.

§ 19.4   Document assembly.

Document assembly is the process of combining the primary document with the information in a completed secondary document. There need not even be a primary document. The drafter could compile a checklist of all provisions used in a transaction and then check the ones to be combined into a particular document. The secondary document could then contain the information to tailor this document for a particular transaction. Just as document assembly puts together all the constituent parts of a document, so can "project assembly" put together all the documents required for a transaction. Project assembly can be an invaluable checklist to make sure that all the pieces are present and are consistent with each other.

Simple document assembly can be accomplished with the use of word processing macros. Document assembly programs are also available that work over word processing. More sophisticated document assembly programs are specifically tailored for the legal profession. Some of these programs will generate documents for you. Lawyers who used to be in the habit of reaching for formbooks will now reach for computer disks. Document assembly is not a cookbook, however. It cannot substitute for legal analysis of the *content* of the document. In fact, the ease with which the document can be reshaped should lead to deeper thought about the content of the document.

Sophisticated document assembly is often described as "rule based." The compiler must first reduce legal rules to "If . . . then" propositions. A complex document is reduced to a decision tree containing a series of choices. Sometimes the law school experience seems like a battle between the professor's view that nothing is certain and the student's desire for certainty, for black-letter rules. While rule-based document assembly may suggest that the student's view has won, a system would be defective if it did not take account of areas of uncertainty. The best of these programs contain text discussing each decision point or allow you to enter your own notes. More sophisticated expert systems, by modeling the thought process of an attorney, take account of these gray areas.

§ 19.5 Expert systems.

Expert systems are similar to document assembly systems. Expert systems attempt to capture the thought process a lawyer would use in analyzing a problem. They then guide the user through the process. For example, a document assembly system might ask if you represent buyer or seller. If you respond, *buyer,* its logic system may be directed to choose a provision that is more favorable to buyer. If that is as far as the system goes, the attorney is back to being a mere scrivener. The provision was originally drafted by an expert in the transaction. The expert knows what the provision means, how it relates to the rest of the transaction, what authority supports it, why particular wording was chosen, what alternatives are available in the event of negotiation, and so forth. A good expert system makes all of this information available to the user. In this way, the user does not simply use the material passively. Instead, the knowledge of the expert is "leveraged down" so that the user can eventually become an expert. The expertise of that attorney is not lost if the attorney leaves the firm. Furthermore, the knowledge can also be "leveraged up." As users employ the system, they can add their own experience to the knowledge base, so it grows in a systematic way.

Often the concept of "hypertext" is used in expert systems. Hypertext is language found "behind" the text in a computer display. A hypertext data base is not linear, but allows the user to browse through documents, statutes, cases, alternative language, comments, and so forth, in a systematic way. For example, a document assembly system on the topic of residential contract for deed might contain these provisions:

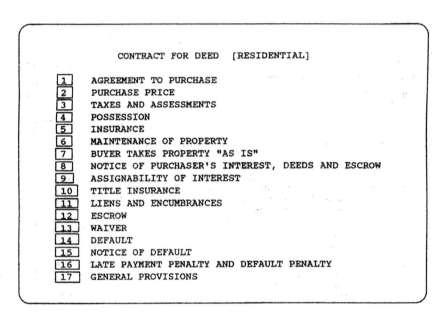

```
                CONTRACT FOR DEED   [RESIDENTIAL]

      1    AGREEMENT TO PURCHASE
      2    PURCHASE PRICE
      3    TAXES AND ASSESSMENTS
      4    POSSESSION
      5    INSURANCE
      6    MAINTENANCE OF PROPERTY
      7    BUYER TAKES PROPERTY "AS IS"
      8    NOTICE OF PURCHASER'S INTEREST, DEEDS AND ESCROW
      9    ASSIGNABILITY OF INTEREST
     10    TITLE INSURANCE
     11    LIENS AND ENCUMBRANCES
     12    ESCROW
     13    WAIVER
     14    DEFAULT
     15    NOTICE OF DEFAULT
     16    LATE PAYMENT PENALTY AND DEFAULT PENALTY
     17    GENERAL PROVISIONS
```

In a document assembly environment, the drafter could be asked to make a choice of clauses. This could be accomplished in a number of ways. The drafter could be asked:

```
   Do you represent:

       1   Buyer

       2   Seller
```

and the system would automatically insert the clause that would be most advantageous for the choice selected. This method requires no analysis by the drafter. Alternatively, the drafter could be asked:

```
Which "Assignability of Interest" clause do you choose:

    [1] Non-assignment
    [2] Assignment with consent
    [3] Freely assignable
```

With this method, the drafter would have to be familiar with the meaning of the choice. Hypertext in the program could describe the advantages and disadvantages of each choice for the drafter who wants additional information. For example, if we choose Number 9, asking for more information about ¶ 9, ASSIGNABILITY OF INTEREST, we might see this:

```
9.  Assignability of Interest: [Choose either 1, 2, or 3]

        [1] [Non-Assignment]

        Buyer may not assign this contract.  If Buyer
    assigns the contract, the assignment is not valid and
    Buyer has committed an act of default under this
    agreement.

        [2] [Assignment with Consent]

        Buyer may not assign this contract without the
    written consent of Seller, which consent may not be
    unreasonably withheld.

        [3] [Freely assignable]

        Buyer may assign its rights under this contract
    in whole or in part.
```

At another level, hypertext could explain the consequences of each choice. For example, if we chose to see more about provisions 1, 2, or 3, we might see these screens:

> 1. This provision is the strongest for Seller, prohib-
> iting Buyer from assigning. Do not use if our client is
> the Buyer.

> 2. This provision is a compromise. While it purports
> not to permit assignment, in most circumstances the contract
> will in fact be assignable, for consent may not be unreason-
> ably withheld.

> 3. This provision is the most desirable for Buyer, per-
> mitting Buyer to assign. Do not use if our client is the
> Seller.

On another level, the system could contain authority containing information about the choice made. For example, if we chose to go another level behind number 2 from the above choices, we might find this explanation:

> 2. Withholding of consent.   In *Erban v. Monforton*,
> 227 Mont. 531, 740 P.2d 677 (1987), the contract for deed
> contained this clause:
>
>> Assignment. This agreement shall not be assigned, nor
>> shall the real property which is the subject of this
>> Agreement be encumbered by the second party without
>> receiving written consent from the first party, said
>> written consent not to be unreasonably withheld by the
>> first party.
>
> Buyer sought consent from Seller, who responded through
> his attorney, "consent was not extended by Joe." The Su-
> preme Court upheld the District Court's determination that
> Seller breached the contract when he did not explain the
> reasons for withholding consent. The Court cited with
> approval the District Court's finding that "reasons of
> sound business judgment, or where the justification for
> refusing consent is clearly explained, would suffice."

Beyond hypertext is the capacity for hypermedia. Pictures and video images can be digitized and accessed along with text. We think of drafting in terms of words, not pictures, so there may be few instances in which hypermedia would be used in drafting. Still, drafters should be alert to the possibilities. Representations of conditions or descriptions of property, for example, could be backed up with visual images of the property.

§ 19.6　Other uses for computers in drafting.

§ 19.6.1　Comparison by computer.

Redlining is the process of comparing successive drafts in order to detect changes. Redlining is a laborious and often error-prone process. Computers have made redlining easier. Computer programs can quickly scan drafts and indicate changes and additions.

Computers have, however, also created a greater need for redlining. Unlike changes made in printed forms or typewritten drafts, changes made in drafts printed from word processors can be extremely difficult to detect. "Boilerplate" provisions in forms, for example, may not remain the same in perpetuity but may be changed as easily as other provisions.

For example, *Hand v. Dayton-Hudson* [1] indicates the ease with which an unscrupulous party can sneak unexpected language into a contract. Dayton-Hudson discharged Hand, an employee who also happened to be an attorney, offering him $38,000 if he agreed to sign a release given to him by Dayton-Hudson. Hand later agreed to the terms and Dayton-Hudson signed the release Hand brought with him.

After receiving the money, Hand sued Dayton-Hudson. Dayton-Hudson raised the affirmative defense of release. Hand pointed to the language of the agreement. Following Hand's agreement to release all claims he had against Dayton-Hudson was the phrase "except as to claims of age discrimination and breach of contract." Hand had copied the document in the same type style so that the change was not readily apparent. When Dayton-Hudson cried foul, Hand reminded Dayton-Hudson of the first rule of contract law: you are responsible for what you sign, so *read the contract.* Although the court properly found that Hand had committed fraud, preventive law practices counsel the drafter to be more careful.

The problems created by technology can sometimes be solved by technology. If all the documents are on disk, then the final version can be compared to an earlier draft or to the standard form. The Compare feature of a word processing program will indicate phrases that have been altered. More sophisticated redlining software will home in on the specific words that have been changed.

§ 19.6.2　Virtual drafting.

It is technologically possible for two attorneys to negotiate and draft a contract on a computer from distant locations in real time. The clients could

---

[1] 775 F.2d 757 (6th Cir. 1985).

then electronically sign the document, producing what the U.C.C. calls an authenticated record. I don't recommend this practice except for the most routinized fill-in-the-blanks transactions. As discussed in Part III, How to Read and Analyze a Contract, contract drafting is a nonlinear, iterative process. On the computer screen, it is hard to follow how a provision you altered may affect something later in the contract. Paper has its uses, and laying contracts out so they can be read is one of them. Before your client signs, print the contract, read through it, and make sure it is acceptable.

§ 19.7 Exercises.

1. Document assembly. The following provisions are from an agreement between employer and employee. Using the techniques described in § 19.3, use this agreement to prepare a primary document and a secondary document for document assembly.

EMPLOYMENT AGREEMENT

AGREEMENT made February 1, 2003, between Washington Corporation, a corporation duly organized and existing under the laws of the State of Montana ("Company"), and Trevor Burnham ("Employee").

Company and Employee agree as follows:

ARTICLE I
Term

The term of this Agreement shall commence as of the date set forth above and shall continue for three years.

ARTICLE II
Duties

Company shall employ Employee as Corporate Counsel of Company with the following responsibilities:

all legal matters relating to intellectual property, including patents, trademarks, and copyrights.

Employee shall report to Company's President and shall be under the supervision and control of Company's President. Employee shall be available to perform such duties on a full-time basis.

ARTICLE III
Compensation

3.1 *Base Salary.* Company shall pay Employee a salary of $50,000 per annum ("Base Salary") payable in equal monthly installments. The

Base Salary is subject to periodic review (with the first review being on August 1, 2003) and may be adjusted from time to time by mutual agreement of Employee and Company's Board of Directors ("the Board").

3.2 *Other Benefits.* In addition to the Base Salary, Company shall provide Employee, in the discretion of the Board, such other benefits as management employees in similar positions in Company receive, except that Employee will be subject to any qualification requirements contained in Company's insurance or benefit plans.

3.3 *Auto.* Company shall, at its discretion, provide Employee with either a Company Automobile or a $200 per month auto allowance.

---

2. Redlining. Below are successive drafts of a provision from a mortgage assumption agreement.

a. Compare the drafts by hand, noting the changes you detect.

b. Compare the drafts using the Compare feature of your word processing software.

c. Optional. Compare the drafts using a sophisticated document comparison program.

The drafts:

---

2. <u>Assumption of Indebtedness</u>. Buyer hereby covenants, promises and agrees (a) to assume the payment for $450,000.00 of the Note and to pay at the times, in the manner and in all respects as therein provided, (b) to perform each and all of the covenants, agreements, and obligations in the Mortgage and in the other security instruments securing the Note to be performed by Mortgagor therein, at the time, in the manner and in all respects as therein provided, and (c) to be bound by each and all of the terms and provisions of the Note and the Mortgage as though such documents had originally been made, executed and delivered by Buyer.

2. <u>Assumption of Indebtedness</u>. Buyer hereby covenants, promises and agrees (a) to assume the payment for $400,000.00 of the Note and to pay at the times, in the manner and in all respects as therein provided, (b) to perform each and all of the covenants, agreements, and obligations in the Mortgage and in the other security instruments securing the Note to be performed by Mortgagor therein, at the time, in the manner and in all respects as therein provided, and (c) to be bound by each and all of the terms and provisions of the Note and the Mortgage as though such documents had originally been made, executed and delivered by Smith and Buyer.

Part III

HOW TO READ AND ANALYZE A CONTRACT·

* This material first appeared in 45 Arizona Law Review 133 (2003).

HOW TO READ AND ANALYZE A CONTRACT

Introduction

People are reluctant to read contracts — and for good reason. A contract often appears to be a formidable foe. The aspiring reader contemplates the ranks of terms and conditions lined up in neat rows, considers an assault, and quickly decides to retreat. Whether the document is found on the computer screen or the printed page, the reader would prefer to click or sign, taking a chance on the terms of surrender, rather than read it. Familiarity with the terrain seems to make little difference. Even attorneys and sophisticated business persons are reluctant to attempt to scale these walls.

This phenomenon should not surprise us, for most people do not know how to read a contract. They know how to read as such, but research into the process of reading informs us that there is reading and there is *reading*. That is, the protocols — the procedures and skills — the reader employs to read a novel are not the same as those employed to read a poem, a statute, or a contract. Although we must know the protocols in order to read each kind of text, we are rarely taught them expressly. We are simply told, for example, to "read the contract" and left to our own devices. Because those who do know how to read contracts are generally unconscious of the protocols they employ, their value as teachers is limited. They can do it, but they cannot tell you how they do it. I try here to make explicit the implicit protocols employed by an experienced reader of contracts and attempt to convey those protocols to the novice.

Contract law tells us that a contract is formed by "objective manifestation of assent." Once you have manifested assent to a contract, whether by signing, clicking, or some other means, you are bound by its terms whether or not you have read them or understood them. The audience for a primer on contract reading must therefore be the general reader of contracts, whether attorney or not, for everyone is expected to read and understand contracts. The pronoun "you" will be used throughout to stand for the contract reader, whatever his or her background.

You read contracts under many different circumstances but the protocols remain essentially the same in all circumstances. You may, for example, read contracts at different times in the life of a transaction. Sometimes you read a contract after the fact, that is, after you have agreed to its terms. For example, an insured might pull out the insurance contract to find out whether he or she has a claim after a loss has occurred, or a client might point out certain contract language to an attorney to find out whether the other party is in breach of the agreed-upon terms. At other times, you read the contract before the fact. For example, an attorney may read it in order to advise a client on what terms might be negotiated; the client might read it to decide whether to sign it. When reading after the fact, you are likely to start with the particular term in issue and work back to put that specific term in the general context of the agreement. When reading before the fact, you are likely to do the opposite, starting with the general theme of the contract in order to put the particular terms in context.

You may also have different goals to achieve through contract reading at different times. For example, if you are reading an on-line contract, you have no opportunity to negotiate its terms. Your goal may be to determine your rights and duties under the proposed contract in order to decide whether you should enter into the transaction, or, if you have decided to enter the transaction in any event, to at least understand what you have gotten into. If you are an attorney reading a contract proposed to a client, your goal may be to negotiate terms that protect your client's interests. But no matter when you are reading it or what your goals are, the protocols require you to take both the narrow view and the long view: the narrow view to examine the particular language in careful detail, and the long view to see that detail in the context of the transaction and the law of contracts.

Contract reading is:
- Nonlinear — Do not begin at the beginning and end at the end.
- Imaginative — Consider what the future might bring and how the text might provide for it.
- Nonliteral — Supply text that does not appear on the page.
- Transformative — Look for opportunities to change the text.
- Iterative — Explore the text many times for different purposes.

These different contract-reading scenarios indicate some of the important differences between reading contracts and reading many other texts. Contract reading is nonlinear, imaginative, nonliteral, transformative, and iterative. Contract reading is *nonlinear* because you do not begin at the beginning and end at the end. You must move around from place to place as you gather information and perceive relationships between the parts of the contract. It is an *imaginative* process because, even though contracts are written in the present, they govern the future. You must use your imagination to consider what that future might bring in order to determine whether the contract provides for it. Contract reading is *nonliteral* because you must supply text that does not appear on the page. The rules of contract law, applicable regulations, and custom and usage all provide additional text that you must consider. Contract reading is *transformative* because the text is not always static. You may have the opportunity to change the text through redrafting or negotiation.

Most importantly, contract reading is *iterative*. Because a contract is such a complex text, you will not be able to grasp the significance of every term in one reading. Whether you are reading the contract before or after the fact and no matter what your goal, reading the contract involves exploring the text many times for different purposes. I have divided contract-reading into five different explorations of the text. I call each of the explorations a "pass," in the sense of a sweep over a target. The name of each of the five passes describes the principal purpose of that pass. The boundaries between passes are, of course, somewhat artificial, and there is considerable overlap between them. For example, during your first four passes you will be gathering information that you will evaluate during the fifth pass. Nevertheless, if you are a novice reader, you will find it helpful to work through each pass before moving on to the next. As you gain expertise, you will find that you are able to compress the process and will achieve more of your goals in fewer passes. The following is a brief description of what you are expected to accomplish with each pass.

1. First Pass: Orientation

In the Orientation pass, you will discover the general theme of the contract and the legal relationship of the parties. You will also begin to see the structure around which the contract is built. You will then pause to consider the goals of the parties and how those goals might be reflected in the contract.

2. Second Pass: Explication

In the Explication pass, you will identify the boilerplate declarations and focus on the rights and duties of each party. You will also detect when those rights and duties are expressly conditional on the happening of some event.

3. Third Pass: Implication

In the Implication pass, you will read into the contract terms and conditions that are not expressly stated in the contract. You will continue to explore the relationships between the contract terms, particularly those relationships that are not expressly stated.

4. Fourth Pass: Remediation

In the Remediation pass, you will ascertain the consequences of nonperformance of the parties' duties. Some of these consequences are expressly found in the agreement, but others must be implied.

5. Fifth Pass: Evaluation

In the Evaluation pass, you will make normative judgments about the terms of the agreement. You might find weaknesses in language, terms that are too harsh, terms that are missing, or terms that may be negotiated.

Outline of the Passes

The following Outline contains the various steps that comprise each of the five passes. I then describe the steps in detail, demonstrating how they can be applied to read a contract. As you make your passes over a contract, you should take notes about what you find. To take notes, use both the contract itself and the Outline.

The contract itself. Get in the habit of "talking back" to the text of the contract. Ask what a term means and put a big question mark next to it if you do not understand it. Underline terms that strike you as important. Draw lines between related terms. Question whether language might be changed to make it clearer or simpler. You will learn to see the contract not as a completed text, but as a work in progress that is open to change.

The Outline. The Outline of the five passes is more than a table of contents. You can use it to organize the information you gather and your thoughts about the contract as you work through the passes. For example, if terms you envisioned are not included in the contract, note them on the Outline and later determine whether you wish to include them. Note any inquiry you may wish to make about the default rules of contract law or applicable regulation.

1. First Pass: Orientation

In the Orientation pass, you will discover the general theme of the contract and the legal relationship of the parties. You will also begin to see the structure around which the contract is built. You will then pause to consider the goals of the parties and how those goals might be reflected in the contract.

§ 1.1.   Ascertain the general theme of the contract. Look to:

§ 1.1.1.   The description of the instrument

§ 1.1.2.   The caption

§ 1.1.3.   Recitals

§ 1.1.4.   The primary exchange of promises

§ 1.2.   Detect the structure of the contract:

§ 1.2.1.   Foundation or cathedral?

§ 1.2.2.   Stepping stone or final agreement?

§ 1.2.3.   What are the parts of the contract?

- Description of the instrument
- Caption
- Language of transition
- Recitals
- Definitions
- Operative language
- Boilerplate terms
- Closing

§ 1.3.   See the transaction against a larger background.

§ 1.3.1.   What are the goals of the parties?

§ 1.3.2.   What are the applicable rules of contract law?

§ 1.3.3.   Is there applicable regulation?

2. Second Pass: Explication

In the Explication pass, you will identify the boilerplate declarations and focus on the rights and duties of each party. You will also detect when those rights and duties are expressly conditional on the happening of some event.

§ 2.1. Identify the boilerplate terms. Boilerplate provisions frequently include:

§ 2.1.1. Merger

§ 2.1.2. Modification

§ 2.1.3. Assignment and delegation

§ 2.1.4. Force majeure

§ 2.1.5. Severability

§ 2.1.6. Headings

§ 2.1.7. Dispute resolution. Dispute resolution terms frequently include:

§ 2.1.7.1. Arbitration

§ 2.1.7.2. Choice of law

§ 2.1.7.3. Choice of forum

§ 2.1.7.4. Attorneys' fees

§ 2.2. Ascertain the rights and duties of each party:

§ 2.2.1. Identify promises

§ 2.2.2. Watch for promises that are beyond customary norms

§ 2.2.3. Determine the duration of the contract

§ 2.2.4. Identify conditions. Who controls the happening of the event?

§ 2.2.4.1. Neither party

§ 2.2.4.2. The party whose performance is conditional on the event

§ 2.2.4.3. The other party

§ 2.3. Consider creating a graphic

3. Third Pass: Implication

In the Implication pass, you will read into the contract terms and conditions that are not expressly stated in the contract. You will continue to explore the relationships between the contract terms, particularly those relationships that are not expressly stated.

§ 3.1. Read in the default rules

§ 3.2. Read in the implied conditions

§ 3.2.1. Is one party's entire performance a condition of the entire performance of the other party?

§ 3.2.2. Who performs first?

§ 3.2.3.   Did the party who performed first protect itself?

§ 3.3.   Read in trade usage, course of dealing, and course of performance

4. Fourth Pass: Remediation

In the Remediation pass, you will ascertain the consequences of nonperformance of the parties' duties. Some of these consequences are expressly found in the agreement, but others must be implied.

§ 4.1.   Is a party's nonperformance breach? Nonperformance might be excused by:

§ 4.1.1.   Changed circumstances

§ 4.1.2.   Modification or waiver

§ 4.1.3.   Nonoccurrence of a condition

§ 4.1.4.   Trade usage

§ 4.2.   If nonperformance is not excused, what happens?

§ 4.2.1.   The nonbreaching party may recover damages. To determine damages:

§ 4.2.1.1.   Ask what the nonbreaching party would have had if the contract had been performed

§ 4.2.1.2.   Look for express terms relating to damages

§ 4.2.2.   The nonbreaching party's counterperformance may not be due. Whether counterperformance is due may depend on whether:

§ 4.2.2.1.   The entire performance was not given

§ 4.2.2.2.   A part of the performance was given

§ 4.2.2.3.   The performance was not timely given

§ 4.2.3.   Create a visual representation

§ 4.3.   Look for terms that address remedies. These may include:

§ 4.3.1.   Specific performance

§ 4.3.2.   Liquidated damages

§ 4.3.3.   Limitation of remedies

§ 4.3.4.   Dispute resolution

5. Fifth Pass: Evaluation

In the Evaluation pass, you will make normative judgments about the terms of the agreement. You might find weaknesses in language, terms that are too harsh, terms that are missing, or terms that may be negotiated.

§ 5.1.   Assemble your concerns:

§ 5.1.1.   Should you expressly state omitted terms?

§ 5.1.2.   Do you understand and agree with all the stated terms?

First Pass: Orientation

In the Orientation pass, you will discover the general theme of the contract and the legal relationship of the parties. You will also begin to see the structure around which the contract is built. You will then pause to consider the goals of the parties and how those goals might be reflected in the contract.

In this pass you will:

- Ascertain the general theme of the contract
- Detect the structure of the contract
- See the transaction against a larger background

§ 1.1. Ascertain the general theme.

The general theme of the contract is the nature of the transaction and the legal relationship of the parties. For example, it may be an agreement between a landlord and tenant for the rental of an apartment, or an agreement for the sale of goods between a commercial seller and a consumer buyer. Most of us do not read contracts for pleasure, so you probably have an interest in the transaction. Note which party is you or your client. Useful questions to ask to ascertain the general theme include:

- What is this transaction about?
- Who are the parties? Which one am I?
- What is the relationship between the parties?

To answer these questions, look to the following sources:

- The description of the instrument
- The caption
- Recitals

- The primary exchange of promises

§ 1.1.1. The description of the instrument.

The description of the instrument is the shorthand heading that frequently appears in bold letters at the top of the contract. Like the title of a book, it might give you some idea of the contents of the document. If it says *Residential Lease, Contract for the Sale of Goods,* or *Consumer Loan,* it has given you some help in discovering the general theme. If it says *Agreement*, it is not particularly helpful.

§ 1.1.2. The caption.

The caption, usually found directly below the description of the instrument, contains the names of the parties, sometimes contains shorthand terms by which the parties are described in the agreement (usually in a parenthetical following each name), and sometimes describes the legal relationship between the parties. The names may tell you what kinds of legal entities are involved in the transaction. For example, the caption may tell you whether the agreement is between two corporations, between a corporation and an individual, or between two individuals. The shorthand terms may also tell you something about the nature of the transaction and the legal relationship between the parties.

For example, the caption:

> Agreement dated January 1, 2001 between First Bank of New York ("Lender") and John C. Smith ("Borrower")

provides you with much information. The names (First Bank of New York and John C. Smith) tell you that the parties are a bank and an individual. The shorthand terms ("Lender" and "Borrower") tell you the nature of the transaction and the legal relationship between the parties: this is a loan agreement in which the Bank is lending money to Smith.

This caption:

> John Doe, hereinafter described as Landlord, and Richard Roe, hereafter described as Tenant, agree to a residential lease on the following terms

tells you that the parties are both individuals, that the nature of the transaction is a residential lease, and that the legal relationship between the parties is that Doe is leasing the property to Roe.

On the other hand, a caption that states:

> Agreement entered into this 1st day of January, 2001 between Owens Chemical, Inc. ("Company") and John Bartos ("Contractor")

provides virtually no clues to the general theme of the contract, so you will have to look elsewhere.

In the previous examples there are only two parties to the agreement, which makes it easier for you to keep the relationships straight. If there are more than two parties, then you need to ascertain the legal relationships among all the parties. For example, this caption:

> Agreement dated January 1, 2001 between First Bank of New York ("Secured Party"), Jones Corp. ("Debtor"), and Mary Jones ("Guarantor")

indicates that the nature of the transaction is a security agreement. The Bank is the secured party, Jones Corp., a corporation, is the debtor, and Mary Jones, individually, is a guarantor. As you continue your passes, you will have to determine what the legal relationships between the various parties are and which of these legal relationships is affected by each term of the agreement.

§ 1.1.3. Recitals.

Recitals are statements of background, often containing "whereas" clauses, that sometimes appear at the beginning of a contract. If the agreement contains recitals, your job has been made easier, for the purpose of recitals is to provide the reader with the background necessary to see the agreement in context. If the drafter has done the job well, then the nature of the transaction should be clear to you from the recitals. For example, if the recitals state:

> Background: On March 15, 2003, Seller promised to deliver 100 widgets to Buyer. Buyer alleges that 40 of the widgets were defective. Buyer and Seller desire to enter into an accord to resolve the dispute between them.

then you have been handed the general theme of the contract on a platter. You will not always be so lucky.

§ 1.1.4. The primary exchange of promises.

The substantive provisions of the agreement provide the remainder of the clues to help you discover the general theme. Because a contract is an exchange of promises, you will always find promises made by each party.

Among them, usually toward the beginning of the contract, there is often a primary exchange of promises that contains the essence of the transaction. Because the parties do not typically use the word *promise*, look for language of commitment such as *shall, will, must,* or *agrees to.*

Consider the following example:

---

1. Description of Work. Contractor shall devote full time and use best efforts to make sales of chemical products to Company's customers.

. . .

3. Commission. Company shall pay to Contractor a commission of six percent (6%) of gross sales. Payment shall be made on the 15th of each month for sales made during the previous month.

In this contract, Contractor has agreed to sell Company's products and Company has promised to pay Contractor a commission.

§ 1.2. Detect the structure of the contract.

In order to explore the contract, you will find it helpful to study its architecture. One reason contracts are intimidating is that they appear monolithic — a giant wall that does not allow easy entrance. But when you get to know the document, you may see that it has a structure, a pattern that allows you to make distinctions. The ability to recognize a contract's structure is a trait that separates the novice contract reader from the expert contract reader. The expert, perceiving the pattern, unconsciously places the terms of the contract into various categories. When you begin to perceive these patterns, you are on your way to becoming an expert who can penetrate any contract. There are a couple of patterns that you can identify early on in the contract-reading process:

- Whether the contract is a foundation or a cathedral
- Whether the contract is a stepping stone or a final agreement

In addition, identifying the parts of the contract will help you discern its structure.

§ 1.2.1. Foundation or cathedral?

Experts know that documents are structured differently for different purposes, perhaps following the adage that "form follows function." For example, a contract may provide just the foundation for the agreement, the primary exchange of promises. This is frequently the European and Japanese model. As contingencies occur, the parties must add the details that were not constructed in advance. Alternatively, the contract may have the intricacy of a Gothic cathedral if it attempts to predict and provide for every contingency. Many American drafters strive for this construction. Having recognized these different structures, you must be prepared to work out the details in the first structure and find them in the second.

§ 1.2.2. Stepping stone or final agreement?

Sometimes the agreement is a stepping stone to a later agreement. Parties negotiating a complex agreement may build their agreement in stages, like a structure that is initially built small but with the capacity for later growth. The parties may, for example, call their initial agreement a "Memorandum of Understanding" or "Letter of Intent," often specifically providing that they do not consider themselves bound by the agreement unless and until they reach a later stage of agreement. In real estate transactions, parties may sign a "buy-sell agreement" or "escrow agreement" that does bind them, but contemplates a later contract that contains additional terms. Alternatively, the parties may make clear that their initial agreement, however skeletal, is the final agreement.

§ 1.2.3. What are the parts of the contract?[1]

Within these different structures, you will often see a pattern that allows you to break the contract down into smaller pieces. A common structure frequently includes the following parts, in this order:

- Description of the instrument
- Caption
- Language of transition
- Recitals
- Definitions
- Operative language
- Boilerplate terms
- Closing

During this pass, when you ascertained the general theme, you saw that the structure usually includes a *description of the instrument*, a *caption*, and a *closing* that contains signature lines (or the on-line equivalent, such as a button that says "I agree"). *Language of transition* often appears after the caption or before the closing, providing a transition from the caption to other text or from other text to the closing. For example:

---

[1] *See* § 15.4.

In consideration of the mutual covenants set forth below, the parties hereby agree as follows:

In witness whereof, the parties have executed this agreement on the day and year first above written.

This transition language generally serves no purpose and can be disregarded.

Some contracts may contain *recitals* or *definitions*. The recitals provide background information that enables you to put the transaction in a context. If the contract contains recitals, you look at them in order to determine the general theme. When you encounter definitions, you should set them aside, reading them only when an operative term uses the defined term. We will return to definitions in that context.

The remaining portion of the contract is the *boilerplate terms* and the *operative language*. The boilerplate terms do not contain rights and duties of the parties but declare the ground rules the parties have agreed to follow in certain circumstances. They are the housekeeping details that appear in virtually every contract. The boilerplate may be set off with a heading such as "Miscellaneous" (but never "Boilerplate") at the end of the document. More likely, these terms are mingled with the other terms, usually toward the end of the document. For now, just identify the boilerplate terms and set them aside; you will scrutinize the boilerplate in the next pass. The operative language is the heart of the contract, containing the promised performances of the parties and the events that must occur before those performances are due. Sometimes the operative language is broken down into sections that reveal the structure of the contract. For example, a homeowner's insurance policy may be organized around sections called "What we will cover" and "What we will not cover," while a residential lease may be broken down into "Landlord's Obligations" and "Tenant's Obligations."

More frequently, however, the document itself does not expressly reveal its detailed structure. Nevertheless, as you read it, you will see patterns, terms that may be grouped together around a common theme. A sales contract, for example, may contain Delivery Terms (Seller's obligations to deliver), Payment Terms (Buyer's obligations to pay), and Warranty Terms (Seller's obligations after delivery). Look for those organizing principles as you continue your passes.

§ 1.3. See the transaction against a larger background.

After you have ascertained the general theme and the structure of the contract, you will find it helpful to pause in your reading. Take a few moments to reflect on the transaction. You should see the transaction against the background of:

- The goals of the parties
- The rules of contract law
- Regulation

§ 1.3.1.   What are the goals of the parties?

Ask what each party wants to get out of the transaction, that is, what their goals are. The answers to this question are not always found in the contract, but your imaginative search will pay dividends. You can better understand the transaction when you see that certain provisions are inserted to further the goals of the parties in that particular transaction.

I call this use of the imagination "what-iffing" the contract. It is what makes contracts such interesting reading, for every contract is an adventure in time travel! Even though the contract is written in the present, it describes events that are going to arise in the future. But the future is unpredictable. Because the events may not occur, the parties are taking risks. A prudent party may try to predict those future risks and seek protection from them in the contract. The "Three P's" of contract drafting are *Predict, Provide* and *Protect*:

- Predict what may happen in the future,
- Provide for that contingency in the contract, and
- Protect the party with a remedy.

Because much of the law of the contract involves risk-shifting, your imagination and your close reading will lead you to observe provisions where one party shifted a risk to the other party or where there is an opportunity for risk-shifting.

For example, in a transaction involving the sale of goods, what are the goals of the seller and the buyer? One goal of the seller is to avoid claims by the buyer. In predicting the future, the seller may foresee a claim by the buyer that the goods are defective. The seller may therefore provide terms that shift the risk that the goods are defective to the buyer. Because the buyer's goals include getting defect-free goods, the buyer can be expected to shift this risk to the seller.

§ 1.3.2.   What are the applicable rules of contract law?

The technique of identifying goals will also alert you to terms that the parties did *not* include in the contract. You will need a knowledge of contract law to determine the consequences if an issue arises that is not addressed in the contract. The rules supplied by contract law are often called the "default rules." Just like the default settings on your word processor, they are the rules that apply unless you change them — which you are generally free to do. But if the contract is silent on a rule, contract law will generally read in the rule that reasonable parties would have written if they had thought about the omission.

For example, another goal of the seller of goods is to get paid. The contract may state, "Seller shall deliver the goods on July 1 and Buyer shall pay Seller $1000 on August 1." The reader must "what-if" the contract by time traveling ahead to August 1 and asking, "What happens if Buyer does not pay?" If the contract does not provide for this contingency, the reader must use contract law to determine the consequences. The default rule where the seller has delivered the goods is that the seller's remedy is to recover the money from the buyer, ultimately through a lawsuit. Knowing this rule after the fact, the seller can determine his or her options. Knowing the rule before the fact, he or she may negotiate for cash on delivery or negotiate for terms that protect her when extending credit, such as a down payment or a security interest.

§ 1.3.3. Is there applicable regulation?

An important exception to the parties' freedom of contract arises when state or federal law regulates the transaction. The parties' freedom of contract may be limited in that they may not include certain terms or they must include certain terms. In some jurisdictions, the form of the contract may be regulated. Often the contract makes no reference to this body of law that provides additional rules. You must research the law and detect whether the contract terms are in violation of those rules. For example, residential leases are regulated in most jurisdictions. The regulations may provide how a landlord must proceed when evicting a tenant. Because these are not default rules but regulations, they must be followed despite what the contract may say.

To find the terms that are expressly stated in the contract, we turn to the Second Pass: Explication.

Second Pass: Explication

In the Explication pass, you will identify the boilerplate declarations and focus on the rights and duties of each party. You will also detect when those rights and duties are expressly conditional on the happening of some event.

In the previous pass, you examined the structure of the contract and separated out everything but the boilerplate terms and the rights and duties of the parties. In this pass, you will:

- Identify the boilerplate terms
- Ascertain the rights and duties of each party

§ 2.1. Identify the boilerplate terms.[2]

Before we turn to the terms that govern the legal relationship between the parties in a particular transaction, it will be helpful to first weed out the boilerplate provisions. The boilerplate terms do not contain rights and

---

[2] *See* § 16.5.

duties of the parties but declare the ground rules the parties have agreed to follow in certain circumstances. They are the housekeeping details that appear in virtually every contract.

If you are familiar with contract law, you will carefully ascertain the function of each boilerplate term as you set it aside. The boilerplate terms cannot be disregarded just because they appear in every contract. Take a second look to determine whether the boilerplate provision is in fact the same term found in most contracts or whether it has been altered or tailored to fit this transaction. For example, a *force majeure* clause answers the question, "What if performance becomes impracticable because of an event beyond the control of the party who promised it?" The provision usually reflects the default rule that unanticipated events that are beyond the control of the parties excuse nonperformance. However, it might enumerate specific events that could occur in this transaction. On occasion, it might change the default rule to provide that no event excuses nonperformance. Because they do not always state standard terms, you cannot gloss over these boilerplate provisions, no matter how dull they appear.

Boilerplate provisions frequently include the following:

- Merger
- Modification
- Assignment and delegation
- Force majeure
- Severability
- Headings
- Dispute resolution

§ 2.1.1.　Merger.[3]

This declaration answers the question, "Where is our agreement found and will provisions not included in the written agreement be enforceable?" It generally states that promises not found in the writing are not part of the agreement. For example:

> This agreement signed by both parties constitutes a final written expression of all the terms of this agreement and is a complete and exclusive statement of those terms.

This innocent-sounding provision can cause a lot of problems when a party later claims that an oral promise was made. For example, you are buying a used car and during the sales pitch, the seller says that he or she will fix anything that goes wrong with the car in the next two weeks. The

---

[3] *See* Chapter 6.

written contract states that the purchase is "AS IS," which means the seller has no obligation to fix the car. If the contract has a merger clause, the writing will probably govern over the spoken statement. The lesson here is clear — if anyone made promises or representations to you that are not found in the written contract, ask for them to be included in the contract before you sign.

§ 2.1.2. Modification.[4]

This declaration answers the question, "If we later decide to change our agreement, is the original agreement or the modified agreement effective?" For example:

> *All Modifications to be in Writing.* This contract may be modified or rescinded only by a writing signed by both of the parties.

This provision can cause hardship because, in spite of the boilerplate agreement, people frequently make changes to their contracts after they have been signed and do not write them down. For example, you have an auto loan that is payable on the first of the month and the bank can repossess your car if you do not pay on time. You call the bank and ask if you can pay on the tenth this month. The bank tells you that will not be a problem. On the seventh, they repossess your car. When you point out that the agreement was modified to allow payment on the tenth this month, the bank will say that the oral modification does not count because of the boilerplate that requires all modifications to be in writing! While you may ultimately prevail, you can save yourself a lot of hassle by doing what the boilerplate says and getting the modification in writing.

§ 2.1.3. Assignment and delegation.[5]

This declaration answers the question, "Can the rights and duties under this agreement be delegated or assigned?" For example:

> Either Seller or Buyer may delegate its duties under this contract in whole or in part. If any delegation is made, the delegating party must give notice to the non-delegating party at least 5 days prior to the delegation. The delegating party remains fully liable for performance of the delegated duties.

The operation of this provision can also take you by surprise, because it allows the parties to have someone else perform the work they promised

---

[4] *See* Chapter 11.

[5] *See* Chapter 14.

to do. For example, you shop around and learn that ABC Pools, Inc. has a good reputation for constructing swimming pools, so you hire them to install your pool. You look out the window and there is Sleazy Pool Co. building your pool. You call ABC and they say, "The boilerplate provision in our contract says we can freely delegate our duties. That is what we did." If you want performance by the party you contracted with, you had better put in the contract that duties are *not* delegable.

§ 2.1.4.　Force majeure.[6]

This declaration answers the question, "What if performance becomes impracticable because of an event beyond the control of the party who promised it?" For example:

> *Force majeure.* Neither party shall be held responsible if the fulfillment of any terms or provisions of this contract are delayed or prevented by revolutions or other disorders, wars, acts of enemies, fires, floods, acts of God, or without limiting the foregoing, by any other cause not within the control of the party whose performance is interfered with, and which by the exercise of reasonable diligence, the party is unable to prevent, whether of the class of causes hereinbefore enumerated or not.

§ 2.1.5.　Severability.[7]

This declaration answers the question, "If a court refuses to enforce part of our agreement, will it give effect to the remainder?" The provision may not be meaningful when a drafter is concerned that a term in the agreement may be unconscionable, for a court will generally determine whether the offensive provision goes to the essence of the agreement. The language might look like this:

> The invalidity, in whole or in part, of any term of this agreement does not affect the validity of the remainder of the agreement.

§ 2.1.6.　Headings.[8]

A declaration used by overly-careful drafters provides that headings in a contract have no substantive significance. For example:

---

[6] *See* Chapter 9.

[7] *See* Chapter 4.

[8] *See* § 16.5.1.

> The headings and subheadings of clauses contained in this agreement are used for convenience and ease of reference and do not limit the scope or intent of the clause.

§ 2.1.7. Dispute resolution.[9]

Terms relating to dispute resolution are important boilerplate terms. Dispute resolution terms might include:

- Arbitration
- Choice of law
- Choice of forum
- Attorneys' fees

§ 2.1.7.1. Arbitration.

The default rule is that parties have the right to take their dispute to court. Therefore, if the parties want to require a party to take a future dispute to arbitration, they must include an arbitration clause in the agreement. An arbitration clause might look like this:

> Any controversy or claim arising out of or relating to this contract, or the breach thereof, shall be settled by arbitration in accordance with the Commercial Arbitration Rules of the American Arbitration Association, and judgment upon the award rendered by the arbitrator(s) may be entered in any court having jurisdiction thereof.

§ 2.1.7.2. Choice of law.

This declaration answers the question, "If we have a dispute, what law will apply?" The choice of law clause provides for the body of law that will be applied to resolution of the dispute, but does not limit the place where the trial will be held. The parties are generally free to specify the applicable law, subject to relevance and to the public policy of the jurisdiction asked to apply it. For example:

> This agreement is governed by the law of the State of Kansas.

---

[9] *See* Chapter 13; § 16.5.

§ 2.1.7.3.　Choice of forum.

While a choice of law clause identifies the applicable law, it does not identify the location where the parties must bring their dispute. A choice of forum clause does that by specifying the jurisdiction in which the plaintiff must bring the claim. For example:

Any claim arising from this transaction must be filed in Dade County, Florida.

---

§ 2.1.7.4.　Attorneys' fees.

The default rule on attorneys' fees is that each side pays its own attorneys' fees, win or lose. The parties are free to change that rule by providing that the loser must pay the winner's attorneys' fees. A provision such as this changes the default rule:

The prevailing party in any lawsuit arising under this Agreement or as a result of its cancellation may recover reasonable attorneys' fees from the loser.

---

§ 2.2.　Ascertain the rights and duties of each party.[10]

You should now ascertain the rights and duties of each party and the relationships between one party's rights and duties and the other party's rights and duties. To accomplish this task:

- Identify promises
- Watch for promises that are beyond customary norms
- Determine the duration of the contract
- Identify conditions

§ 2.2.1.　Identify promises.

The contract's expression of the parties' promises may take various forms. The contract language rarely uses the word *promise*, but conveys a commitment or obligation to do or not to do something. Look for language such as *shall, will, must,* or *agrees to.* Your goal is to determine for each party:

- What do we have a duty to do or not to do?
- When do we have to do it?

---

[10] *See* Chapters 10, 16.

- What do we have a right to receive?
- When do we receive it?

For example, a residential lease may provide:

- Lessee agrees to pay Lessor $1,000 per month on the first of each month.
- Lessee shall take good care of the premises and the fixtures, and commit and suffer no waste of any kind.
- Lessee must use the premises only as a family dwelling.
- Lessee will neither change locks nor install additional locks on any doors.
- Lessee's use of nails, tacks, brads, screws, stick-on picture hangers or tape on the woodwork, floors or ceilings of the premises is strictly prohibited.

These provisions all contain duties of the tenant. The Lessee has the duty to pay rent on the first and to care for the premises in the specified ways during the term of the tenancy. The terms might all be found in one part of the contract called something like "Duties of Tenant," but if they are not, you can nevertheless detect this relationship among the promises. Note that every duty creates a corresponding right in the other party. In our example, Lessor has the right to receive rent on the first of the month and has the right to expect Lessee to care for the premises. Notice the duties may be stated as negative duty — a party may have a duty *not* to do certain things.

Sometimes you have to use inferences — reading between the words — to determine what the promises are. For example, a franchise agreement provides:

Franchisee shall have the exclusive right to distribute Franchisor's products in Musselshell County.

What are the promises here? First, you may need to refresh your memory of who the parties are. Going back to the caption, you determine that Franchisor is the corporation that owns the franchise name and that Franchisee is the person who is buying the rights to this particular franchise, probably you. The contract states that you have the "right" to distribute the products. You know that every right has a corresponding duty, so this also means that you have the duty to distribute the products. How much of a duty do you owe? If the contract does not say, the default rule is that you promise to make "reasonable efforts" to distribute the products. You have detected two promises by you: a promise to distribute the products in Musselshell County and a promise to make reasonable efforts to do so. You would also infer a promise not to distribute the products anywhere else.

What did Franchisor promise? Franchisor is granting you a right, but most importantly it is an *exclusive* right. That is, there is a negative duty by Franchisor not to give the same right to anyone else. If Franchisor did not give you the exclusive right, it would not be a breach of Franchisor's promise if Franchisor granted the same right to others.

Sometimes operative language appears as declarations rather than as promises. In that case, ask why the parties would make such a declaration. This process may help you determine what the rights and duties are. For example, a contract drafted by a company that engages a sales person declares:

---

4. *Relationship of Parties.* The parties intend that an independent contractor relationship will be created by this contract. The Company is interested only in the results to be achieved and the conduct and control of the work will lie solely with the Contractor.

What was the company's purpose in making this declaration? The term states that the sales person's status is that of independent contractor, presumably to distinguish his or her status from that of an employee. There are advantages to the company in having the sales person be an independent contractor rather than an employee. For example, if the sales person is an independent contractor, the company is not liable for the sales person's negligence and the sales person is not entitled to certain statutory employment benefits. Therefore, you may read the declaration as a promise by the sales person not to assert employee status even though it may be in his or her interest to do so.

§ 2.2.2. Watch for promises that are beyond customary norms.

A term that is illegal is not enforceable. Some terms, while not illegal, are so oppressive or "unconscionable" that they may shock the conscience of the court, and the court may decline to enforce them. Knowing the substantive area of law can help you identify promises that push the envelope of customary practices. Identifying these provisions can be useful for negotiation. If they cannot be altered, as in an Internet transaction, identifying them can at least help you decide whether to enter into the transaction. For example, an employment contract provides:

> In the event either party terminates this contract, Employee agrees not to work in a similar field of employment in this state or any adjacent state for a period of three years.

You may have identified this term as a restrictive covenant. Note that it applies even if the employee is fired and that its scope is broad. The employee may wish to determine whether it is enforceable and whether it is customarily found in all such contracts in the industry. This information will aid in negotiating the final contract. For example, if case law in your state indicates that the provision is enforceable and every employer in your field includes it, you may have little power to change it.

One reason we do not generally read form contracts, such as car rental contracts or insurance contracts, is that we have an expectation of what we will find in them and we do not expect surprises. The drafters of these form contracts know that if they slip an unusual term into such a contract, a court may refuse to enforce the term because it is beyond your reasonable expectations. The drafters also know that their chances of having these unusual provisions enforced are better if they make the term conspicuous. If you see bold print, a term that must be separately clicked on or signed, or some other device calling your attention to the provision, you should be alerted that the provision may be onerous. Make sure you understand its significance.

For example, the Federal Trade Commission (FTC) became concerned that used car dealers were misleading buyers by not clearly disclosing when the buyer was not getting any warranty. Now, the FTC requires that the used car dealer place a sticker on the window informing the buyer whether the seller is providing a warranty or not. If the seller has checked the box next to the bold print statement **"AS IS — NO WARRANTY,"** the buyer has been alerted that the risk of defects in the car has been shifted to the buyer. Instead of warranting that the car is merchantable, the dealer is promising nothing about its condition. The buyer is assuming the risk of all defects in the automobile.

As another example, before you order goods online, the seller asks you to agree to the terms and conditions. At the top of the terms and conditions, you see this notice:

> **THIS AGREEMENT CONTAINS A DISPUTE RESOLUTION CLAUSE. PLEASE SEE SECTION 8 BELOW.**

The fact that this language appears in capital letters and bold print alerts you to its importance. You scroll down to Section 8, which also contains bold print:

---

8. Dispute Resolution

. . .

You understand that, in the absence of this provision, You would have had a right to litigate disputes through a court, including the right to litigate claims on a classwide or class-action basis, and that You have expressly and knowingly waived those rights and agreed to resolve any Disputes through binding arbitration in accordance with the provisions of this paragraph.

If you later attempt to take the seller to court to resolve a dispute, the seller will claim that a reasonable person should have been aware that this contract contained an arbitration clause. You may well be stuck.

§ 2.2.3. Determine the duration of the contract.

Once you have identified the duties of the parties, determine when in time they must be performed. Often a contract has a date in the caption or in the signature lines, but those dates are not always meaningful. For example, on February 7, the parties sign a one-year lease that begins on March 1. The significant dates to identify are the start date, here March 1, and the end date, here one year from March 1. The February 7 date is not significant. If another term provides that rent is due on the first day of each month, that is a significant date as well, because it identifies when a performance is due. If the contract term is renewable, note when the notice of renewal must be given. For example, if an agreement states:

This lease is automatically renewed for an additional term of one year unless either party gives notice to the other at least 30 days before the renewal date

---

then note the date thirty days before the end of the first year as the date by which notice must be given. Enter the significant dates on a time line or tickler file.

Sometimes a contract contains no date for the performance of a duty. For example, a contract for the sale of goods may provide that "Seller shall sell a type X widget to Buyer for $100,000." The default rule for time of performance in the absence of a time stated by the parties is a reasonable time. Seller has a reasonable time to tender the widget to Buyer. Sometimes a performance is not due on a particular date, but after another performance is given. This observation brings us to conditions.

§ 2.2.4. Identify conditions.[11]

A party's duties are not always immediately performable. Often some event must occur before a party has to perform a duty. Such an event is called a condition. Confusingly, drafters frequently call the provisions of a contract the "terms and conditions" without intending the designation "condition" to have any legal effect. They usually just mean *terms*. You will have to identify those provisions that really have the legal effect of conditions. Ask if some event has to occur before a party has a duty to perform. If the answer is yes, that event is a condition.

Conditions can be either express or implied. We will first look at express conditions. To find express conditions, look for language such as *if, in the event that, provided*, or *subject to*. For example:

The Purchaser shall not be obligated to purchase the property if the purchase price exceeds the reasonable value of the property established by the Veteran's Administration.

In the event this note is prepaid in full or refinanced, the Borrower shall receive a refund of the unearned portion of the prepaid finance charge.

After you have identified the condition, the event that must occur before a performance is due, it is helpful to ask two questions:

- Who controls the happening of the event?
- Did a party promise to bring it about?

The answer to the first question, "Who controls the happening of the event?" may be that the event is within the control of:

- Neither party
- The party whose performance is conditional on the event
- The other party

§ 2.2.4.1. The event is within the control of neither party.

Some conditions are pure conditions, that is, they are not within the control of either party to bring about. For example, assume Buyer and Seller agree:

---

[11] *See* Chapter 10.

> If the U.S. government lifts export restrictions to China, Seller agrees to sell Buyer 1,000 Type Y widgets for $100,000.

You identify the promises — Seller has a duty to sell the widgets and Buyer has a duty to pay for them. But you also note that those promises are not immediately performable. They are conditional on the occurrence of an event — the U.S. government lifting export restrictions to China. If this event does not occur, the parties have no duties. If the event does occur, the duties are immediately performable. When you ask, "Who controls the happening of the event?" The answer is neither party. When you ask, "Did a party promise to bring it about?" The answer is no. Because neither party promised to bring it about, neither party is in breach if it does not occur.

§ 2.2.4.2.   The event is within the control of the party whose performance is conditional on the event.

It may not seem logical to allow a party to control whether or not it performs. Nevertheless, there are circumstances in which a party can condition its own performance. For example, a contract for the sale of real estate frequently provides that the buyer's duty to purchase is "subject to the buyer obtaining mortgage financing." This condition is an event that is within the control of the buyer. Now you ask if the buyer has a duty to obtain financing. The answer is *not exactly*. It would not make sense to require the buyer to *obtain* financing, since the reason for the condition is to protect the buyer in case the buyer cannot obtain financing, but it does make sense to require the buyer to *look* for financing. Even though the term is stated as a condition, you would read in a promise by the buyer to make good faith efforts to bring about the event.

Sometimes the party's control seems to provide the party with a way to avoid the party's contractual duties. "Satisfaction" clauses are a notorious example. In a satisfaction clause, the promisor conditions his or her performance on his or her satisfaction with something. For example, a contract commissioning a work of art might provide:

> Owner shall pay Artist the sum of $5,000 if Owner is satisfied with the work.

Performance of Owner's promise to pay for the work is conditional on the occurrence of the event — satisfaction with the work. It would appear that Owner has an easy out from the duty to pay — Owner can say "I'm not satisfied," and then not pay. Not surprisingly, it is not quite that easy. Now you ask if the party has a duty to bring about the event. The answer is that Owner has no duty to bring about his or her satisfaction, but he or she does have a duty to act honestly or reasonably. When the satisfaction is based on subjective factors, such as artistic judgment, courts have found an implied promise by the party to exercise his or her satisfaction in good faith. When the satisfaction is based on objective factors, such as operative fitness, courts have found an implied promise by the party to act like a reasonable person in exercising his or her satisfaction.

§ 2.2.4.3.   The event is within the control of the other party.

Often one party has to do something before the other party has to perform its duty. For example, a life insurance contract provides:

> If insured does not submit proof of death within 90 days of death, this policy is void and the company is released from all liability.

This condition provides that the insurance company does not have to perform its promise to pay the death benefit unless a certain event occurs, submission of proof of death. This event is within the control of the insured. Did the insured promise to bring it about? No. In fact, the insurance company would be happy if the insured did not do it! So this is a condition without a promise.

More often, a party has promised some performance and that performance is the event that has to occur before performance by the other party is due. In that case, the promise is also a condition. Sometimes the event that conditions performance is stated in the contract. If so, it is called an express condition. For example:

> Seller shall deliver the horse Dirty Contract Breaker in good health to Buyer at Buyer's place of business by June 1. If the horse is delivered as promised, Seller shall pay Buyer $100,000.

Here, Buyer's duty to pay is expressly made conditional on performance of Seller's promises. More frequently, however, the condition is not expressed but must be implied. For example, if the buyer's duty in a contract for the sale of goods is to "pay net 30 days from delivery," you must read in that the buyer's duty to pay is not performable until the goods have been delivered, and even then the buyer has thirty days to pay.

§ 2.3.   Consider creating a graphic.

Because the terms of the contract are related, a graphic can help you visualize those relationships. Sometimes a time line or a flow chart will help you visualize who has to do what, when they have to do it, and what events condition the performances. For example, a contract between the Seller of real property and a Broker provides in part:

The Seller agrees:

a. To refer all inquiries and offers for the purchase of said property to the Broker;

b. To cooperate with the Broker in every reasonable way;

c. To pay the Broker a fee for professional services of _____ percent (_____%) if:

(1) A Buyer is procured ready, willing, and able to buy said property, or any part thereof, in accordance with the price, terms, and conditions of this Agreement, or such other price, terms, and conditions as shall be acceptable to the Seller, whether or not the transaction proceeds; or

(2) The said property, or any part thereof, is sold through the efforts of anyone including the Seller; or

(3) The said property, or any part thereof, is sold within _____ months after the term of this Agreement to anyone who was introduced to the said property through the efforts of the Broker or the Broker's agents prior to the expiration of said term. However, no fee will be payable under this clause if the said property is sold after said term with the participation of a licensed broker to whom the Seller is obligated to pay a fee under the terms of a subsequent written exclusive listing agreement.

The conditions in subsection (c) can be recast as IF-THEN statements to make clear the events that must occur before payment is due:

IF

- A buyer is procured who is ready willing, and able to buy the property; or
- The property is sold by anyone including the Seller; or
- The property is sold within X months after the term of the agreement to anyone introduced to the property by the Broker during the term of the agreement, unless the Seller must pay a fee to another licensed broker

THEN

- The Seller shall pay the Broker a fee of x %

We will read in implied conditions along with other implied terms in the Third Pass: Implication.

Third Pass: Implication

In the Implication pass, you will read into the contract terms and conditions that are not expressly stated in the contract. You will continue to explore the relationships between the contract terms, particularly those relationships that are not expressly stated.

The process of ascertaining the parties' duties is more easily accomplished when the terms are expressly stated in the contract, but one of the difficulties of reading contracts is that the terms do not always appear in the contract! Why do parties leave terms out of written contracts? They might have been hasty or careless. More likely, they did not want to take the trouble to hammer out all the details or they may not have foreseen all the possibilities. Sometimes, they may have foreseen them but they did not wish to raise them for fear of jeopardizing the deal.

It is not reasonable or desirable to plan for everything that may happen. As you continue to reflect on the goals of the parties and "what-if" the contract, you may determine that certain terms should have been included. In this pass, you will read in three kinds of terms that do not appear in the contract:

- Default rules
- Implied conditions
- Trade usage

§ 3.1. Read in the default rules.[12]

When the parties omit a term, contract law will generally supply the "default" rule. The process of determining the default rules is easier if you are familiar with the substantive area of law. If you are not familiar with the transaction, you may have to do some research to determine what the default rules are. You can then more easily determine whether the contract term:

- Is omitted, so the default rule must be read in;
- States the default rule; or
- Changes the default rule.

For example, a contract between a widget dealer and a buyer states:

> Seller shall deliver 100 widgets to Buyer on June 1.

The contract does not state what quality of widgets Seller must deliver. The default rule, found in U.C.C. § 2-314, is that a merchant seller gives the buyer an implied warranty of merchantability. This warranty is a

---

[12] *See* Chapters 3, 12.

promise that the widgets are fit for the ordinary purposes for which widgets are used. Even though it is omitted from the contract, you must read in the default rule that the seller is promising that the widgets are merchantable.

Alternatively, the contract might state:

> Seller shall deliver 100 widgets to Buyer on June 1. Seller promises that the widgets are merchantable.

Thanks for nothing, you might say, because that provision merely states the default rule. As we saw above, you would read the rule in even if it was not stated in the agreement. On the other hand, if the contract provides:

> Seller shall deliver 100 widgets to Buyer on June 1. All goods are sold AS IS.

then you may conclude that Seller has shifted the risk that the widgets are defective to Buyer, for the phrase "AS IS" effectively disclaims the implied warranties. The parties have used their freedom of contract to change the default rule. As the buyer, you might note this change as a negotiating point.

§ 3.2. Read in the implied conditions.[13]

In the last pass, you identified the promises. In this step, you must determine whether the relationship between the promises is a condition. Recall that a condition is an event that must occur before some performance is due. In the last pass, you identified the express conditions. You will now identify implied conditions. You will ask:

- Is one party's entire performance a condition of the entire performance of the other party?
- Who performs first?
- Did the party who performed first protect itself?

§ 3.2.1. Is one party's entire performance a condition of the entire performance of the other party?

One goal of a party is to get the other party to perform. One way to achieve that goal is for the party to make its promised performance conditional on performance by the other party. For example, the contract

---

[13] *See* Chapter 10.

states that the seller promises to deliver a widget to the buyer, and the buyer promises to pay $10,000 for it on delivery. No express conditions are stated. You now time travel and ask what happens if, at the time of delivery, the buyer refuses to pay for the widget. Does the seller have to deliver it? The answer is no, because the default rules will supply an implied condition — in the absence of an agreement to the contrary, the performance of one party's promise is a condition of the performance of the other party's promise. The buyer invoked that rule to give the seller an incentive to perform and to protect the buyer when the seller did not perform.

§ 3.2.2.   Who performs first?

The technique of making your performance conditional on the other party's performance only works if the performances are simultaneous. If one party performs first, that party has lost the ability to condition its performance on performance by the other party. In that situation, the party who performed first has become a creditor and may use other devices to reduce the risk that the other party will not perform. For example, if the contract states that the seller promises to deliver a widget to the buyer, and the buyer promises to pay $10,000 for it *30 days later*, then the buyer's performance is not an event that had to occur before the seller had to perform. By extending credit, the seller has made its duty to deliver independent of the buyer's duty to pay. As another example, if the builder promises to build a house for the owner for $300,000, the default rule is that the builder must go first because the builder's performance will take time. The builder must take the risk that the owner will not pay on completion.

§ 3.2.3.   Did the party who performed first protect itself?

You must first determine whether a party has made its performance conditional on performance by the other party, either expressly or impliedly. If a party has not, look for provisions that protect the party who has performed. In our example, where the seller has promised to deliver before receiving payment, the seller takes a risk of not receiving the buyer's performance — payment. The seller has become a creditor, for the seller is unable to make her performance conditional on receiving payment. In this situation, look for other steps the seller has taken to protect herself. The seller might, for example, have required the buyer to grant the seller a security interest, giving the seller the right to repossess the goods if the buyer does not pay for them. Or the seller might have insisted that a third party guarantor promises to pay for the goods if the buyer does not. In the Builder-Owner contract, the builder will insist that the owner perform first. But the owner will complain that his or her completion of performance will give the builder no incentive to perform. The result will be a compromise — the owner will agree to make "progress payments" when the builder's performance has reached certain stages.

§ 3.3. Read in trade usage, course of dealing, and course of performance.[14]

Parties frequently omit terms, sometimes intentionally and sometimes unconsciously, because they are so familiar with the usages in their business that they assume those practices are part of the contract. Often trade practices come from the parties' trade or business, but they can also be established by the parties' course of dealing over a series of transactions or their course of performance over a single contract. These assumptions can be dangerous when a party is not familiar with the practices or when the parties wish to change the practice.

As an example of trade practice, assume the seller is selling the buyer 100,000 bushels of wheat. Parties in the wheat business know that because of the inexactness of measurement and the moisture content, they cannot expect exactly the quantity specified, but only a quantity plus or minus a certain percentage. To avoid disputes, particularly with someone who is not familiar with the practice, it might be best to state expressly in the contract that the quantity promised is "100,000 bushels plus or minus 5%."

As an example of course of performance, assume that a contract for the sale of an automobile states that the price includes the seller's duty to change the oil "at reasonable intervals" for the next two years at the seller's expense. During the first year, the seller changes the oil every 5,000 miles. Now the buyer demands that the seller change it every 3,000 miles. The parties' course of performance over the first year has probably established that the meaning of "reasonable intervals" is 5,000 miles. If the buyer wanted more frequent oil changes, the buyer could have expressly stated it in the contract or not acquiesced in the course of performance.

In the Fourth Pass: Remediation, we will look for the consequences of a party's nonperformance of its duties.

Fourth Pass: Remediation

In the Remediation pass, you will ascertain the consequences of nonperformance of the parties' duties. Some of these consequences are expressly found in the agreement, but others must be implied.

In the First Pass: Orientation, you saw the importance of "what-iffing" the contract in order to predict the future. This process is particularly important in the area of remediation, because you must always ask what happens if a party does not do what it promised to do. In this pass, you will see that sometimes nonperformance is not breach. But if it is breach, remedies supplied by the rules of contract law and by the terms of the contract will come into play.

---

[14] *See* Chapter 3.

§ 4.1. Is a party's nonperformance breach?

Breach of contract generally occurs when a party does not do what it promised to do. However, nonperformance is not always breach of contract because the nonperformance might be excused. Nonperformance might be excused by:

- Changed circumstances
- Modification or waiver
- Nonoccurrence of a condition
- Trade usage

§ 4.1.1. Changed circumstances.[15]

An unexpected event, such as an Act of God, might excuse nonperformance. Check the boilerplate *force majeure* clause or the default rule for the events that excuse nonperformance.

§ 4.1.2. Modification or waiver.[16]

The parties might have modified the terms of the contract so that there was nonperformance under the original terms but not under the terms as modified, or vice-versa. Resolution of the issue will often turn on whether the modification was effective. Waiver may arise when the parties have not made a formal modification, but one party's conduct has lulled the other into a reasonable belief that nonperformance is not breach. For example, a loan agreement provides that the borrower will pay on the first of the month, that time is of the essence, and that the lender may repossess the borrower's car if the borrower does not timely pay. The borrower establishes a course of conduct of paying late and the lender takes no action. The lender has probably waived its right to treat nonperformance of borrower's promise to pay on the first of the month as a breach that would entitle lender to repossess the car.

§ 4.1.3. Nonoccurrence of a condition.[17]

Nonperformance is not breach if performance was conditional on an event and that event did not occur. Sometimes the condition is an express condition, such as a time for performance that has not arisen. At other times it may be an implied condition. For example, if Party A's performance was impliedly conditional on Party B's performance and Party B has materially breached, then Party A's nonperformance is excused because the event that had to occur before A's performance was due has not occurred.

---

[15] *See* Chapter 9.

[16] *See* Chapter 11.

[17] *See* Chapter 10.

§ 4.1.4. Trade usage.[18]

As you have seen, trade usage may excuse nonperformance. For example, if a seller promises 2,000 Grade A sheets of plywood and 100 of them are not up to the Grade A standard, the seller has not done what the seller promised to do. However, the seller may not be in breach if a 5% deviation from the specified grade is acceptable in the trade.

§ 4.2. If nonperformance is not excused, what happens?[19]

If the nonperformance has not been excused, then the nonperformance is probably breach of contract. If the nonperformance is breach, what are the remedies? The promises and conditions in the contract are inextricably bound up with the remedies available to a party for nonperformance by the other party. After you have identified the promise that has not been performed, ask, "What happens if a party does not do what it promised to do?" The answer may be:

- Damages; or
- Counterperformance is not due.

Creating a visual representation may help you figure out what happens in the event of breach.

§ 4.2.1. The nonbreaching party may recover damages.

In general, the nonbreaching party can recover money damages for the breach of promise. To determine damages:

- Ask what the nonbreaching party would have had if the contract had been performed
- Look for express terms relating to damages

§ 4.2.1.1. Ask what the nonbreaching party would have had if the contract had been performed.

The default rule is that the injured party may recover the expectancy — the amount which will put him or her where he or she would have been if the contract had been performed on both sides. For example, a contractor enters a contract with an owner to build a house for $200,000, of which $180,000 represents the cost of labor and materials and $20,000 represents profit. The owner immediately breaches. The contractor is entitled to the $20,000 profit that the contractor would have received if the contract had been performed. If the owner breaches after the contractor has spent $30,000 on labor and materials, then $50,000 represents the contractor's expectancy. Alternatively, assume that after the contractor has spent $30,000 on labor and materials for which the owner has paid the contractor,

---

[18] *See* Chapter 3.

[19] *See* Chapters 10, 13.

the contractor breaches by walking off the job. The owner has the house finished by another contractor at a cost of $190,000. The owner's damages are $20,000, for if the owner pays Contractor 1 $10,000 and Contractor 2 $190,000, the owner will have what he or she expected — the promised house for $200,000.

§ 4.2.1.2. Look for express terms relating to damages.

You may find provisions relating to damages expressly stated in the contract. For example, in a lease, the tenant promises to pay rent on the first of the month. What if he or she does not do what he or she promised to do? The contract may provide that he or she promises to pay a $10 late fee for rent paid after the fifth of the month. What if he or she does not do that? Another provision may provide that the landlord may evict the tenant for nonpayment. The landlord will probably not be permitted to evict the tenant when he or she first breaches his or her promise. The contract will contain a number of promises and conditions related to this remedy, including, for example, any required notices. You must find all of these provisions, which may be scattered throughout the contract, and must figure out the relationships between them. Sometimes in a regulated area such as residential landlord and tenant law, the procedure is found not only in the contract but in statutes.

§ 4.2.2. The nonbreaching party's counterperformance may not be due.

You saw in Pass Three: Implication that one party's performance of its promise can be an implied condition, an event that has to occur before the other party's performance is due. In addition to recovering damages, often when one party does not perform, the other party does not have to perform. This consequence is usually not expressly stated but must be implied. However, whether the counterperformance is excused may depend on whether:

- The entire performance was not given;
- A part of the performance was given; or
- The performance was not timely given.

§ 4.2.2.1. The entire performance was not given.

Generally, when the performances are due simultaneously but one party does not perform entirely, the other party's performance is excused. For example, assume the contract states:

> Seller shall deliver 100 widgets to Buyer by July 17. Buyer shall pay Seller $100,000 on delivery.

Assume Seller delivers no widgets. Because Seller did not give its entire performance, Buyer does not have to perform by paying. That term is not stated in the contract, but Seller's entire performance is an implied condition, an event that has to occur before Buyer has to perform.

§ 4.2.2.2.　A part of the performance was given.

It is hard to determine when less than the entire performance by one party relieves the other party of its duty to perform. Assume Seller delivers 75 of 100 widgets on July 17. Seller has clearly breached its promise, so Buyer is entitled to damages. But since Seller gave partial performance, is Buyer entitled to reject the widgets and consider its contract duties discharged? This is one of the abiding problems of contract law. The courts usually resolve the problem by determining whether a breach is "material." If the breach is material, Buyer may consider its duties discharged, but if the breach is immaterial, its remedy is limited to damages. The reader should know that the courts do not favor a conclusion that a breach is material. Look for a provision that would change this default rule. For example, the parties are free to state that failure to deliver any quantity less than 100 is a material breach.

As another example, assume you are having a contractor build a swimming pool to a depth of nine feet. What happens if the contractor does not build it to that depth? If the breach is held to be immaterial, you may be entitled to damages, but you will not have the pool you wanted. If the term is important to you, spell it out in the contract. You might want to provide that this term is material and that you have no obligation to pay in the event of nonperformance. Put this provision in bold letters to emphasize its importance or use some other means to call it to the attention of the contractor.

§ 4.2.2.3.　The performance was not timely given.

Performances that are not timely given pose a problem similar to that posed by partial performance. Assume Seller delivers all 100 widgets, but delivers them on July 20. Seller has breached a promise, so Buyer is entitled to damages. But is Buyer entitled to reject the widgets and consider its contract duties discharged? The default rule is that a breach with respect to time is generally immaterial. Therefore, Buyer still has to perform and its remedy is limited to deducting damages. Suppose, however, the contract states:

> Seller shall deliver 100 widgets to Buyer by July 17. Buyer shall pay Seller $100,000 on delivery. Time is of the essence of this agreement.

By adding the provision, "time is of the essence of this agreement," the parties intend to make a breach with respect to time material. If Seller delivers on July 20, Buyer may be justified in saying, "I do not have to accept or pay for the goods." In other words, the language attempts to make Seller's performance a condition, an event that has to occur before Buyer has to perform. However, courts do not always give weight to boilerplate language like "time is of the essence." If the contract expressly stated, "If Seller delivers after July 17, Buyer does not have to accept the goods," the courts would be more likely to enforce the remedy.

§ 4.2.3. Create a visual representation.

Making a diagram or flow-chart of the consequences of nonperformance can help you visualize them. For example, in a loan agreement, a debtor promises to pay a debt of $3,000 at a rate of $300 per month and grants the creditor a security interest in his or her automobile to secure payment. In the event of debtor's nonpayment, the remedies may look something like this:

> IF the debtor does not timely pay
>
> THEN the creditor may:
> - Sue for the missed payment, plus late fees and attorney fees; or
> - Accelerate the debt, and
>   - Sue for the entire amount plus attorney fees, or
>   - Repossess the car and sue for any deficiency after sale.

§ 4.3. Look for terms that address remedies.[20]

Provisions in the contract that address remedies may include:
- Specific performance
- Liquidated damages
- Limitation of remedies
- Dispute resolution

[20] *See* Chapter 13.

§ 4.3.1. Specific performance.

Often a party does not want the money damages for nonperformance but wants the actual performance. Such a demand is called specific performance. The general rule, which the parties cannot contract around, is that specific performance can generally not be obtained for personal services and can only be obtained when the breaching party did not deliver something that is unique. For example, because real estate is considered unique, the purchaser or the seller can generally request specific performance. The contract may provide:

The Purchaser agrees that this contract does authorize the Seller to enforce the remedy of specific performance. The Seller agrees that this contract does authorize the Purchaser to enforce the remedy of specific performance.

---

§ 4.3.2. Liquidated damages.

Because the amount of damages can be difficult to ascertain, contracts sometimes contain a liquidated damages clause in which the parties agree on the damages in advance. For example:

For each and every day work contemplated in this contract remains uncompleted beyond the time set for its completion, Contractor shall pay to the Owner the sum of $500, as liquidated damages and not as a penalty. This sum may be deducted from money due or to become due to Contractor as compensation under this contract.

Courts look carefully at liquidated damages provisions. An ironclad rule is that the goal of contract damages is to compensate the nonbreaching party, not to punish the breaching party. Therefore, a court will scrutinize a liquidated damages provision to make sure it is not punitive.

§ 4.3.3. Limitation of remedies.

While they may not provide for damages that overcompensate, parties are nevertheless generally free to limit the remedies for breach. For example, you saw earlier that a warranty is a promise relating to the quality of the goods. The default rule is that a merchant seller gives an implied warranty that the goods are merchantable. If the seller breaches that warranty, the default rule is that the buyer recovers all resulting damages. You have seen that the seller may change the default rule by shifting the risk of defects to the buyer by giving no warranty. More frequently, however, the seller gives the buyer a warranty in one term of the contract and in another limits the remedy for breach of that warranty. For example, a seller promises:

> Seller warrants these goods to be free from defects in material and workmanship for a period of one year from date of purchase

and also provides:

> *Consequential Damages.* In the event of a breach or repudiation of this contract by Seller, Buyer shall not be entitled to any consequential damages in excess of $1000. This limitation shall not apply, however, to damages for injury to the person if the goods are consumer goods.

§ 4.3.4. Dispute resolution.

In addition to these limitations on the monetary amount of damages, recall from the Second Pass: Explication that contracts frequently contain boilerplate terms governing dispute resolution. Examine these terms to determine whether there are terms that may affect the procedure for obtaining remedies, such as provisions governing arbitration, choice of law, choice of forum, or attorneys' fees.

Having finished our information-gathering passes, we now turn to the Fifth Pass: Evaluation.

Fifth Pass: Evaluation

In the Evaluation pass, you will make normative judgments about the terms of the agreement. You might find weaknesses in language, terms that are too harsh, terms that are missing, or terms that may be negotiated.

Up to this point, you have largely been an investigator, seeking information about the contract, but where you found problems you have put aside your judgments. In this pass, you will:

- Assemble your concerns
- Check the contract for completeness
- Detect weaknesses with language
- Explore opportunities to gain greater expertise

§ 5.1. Assemble your concerns.

In the previous passes, you may have detected some concerns that you want the contract to address. You have practiced preventive law, "what-iffing" the contract, trying to determine what might happen, and determining whether the contract addresses the alternatives. For example, you may have noted either on the Outline or on the contract:

- Omitted terms
- Terms that were stated
- The consequences of breach
- Boilerplate terms

§ 5.1.1. Should you expressly state omitted terms?

You may have noted that some terms you expected to find were omitted. If they were not included because the default rule is clear, you may not wish to express them. But if you have some concern about what the default rule would be, you might want to express them. Other terms that were omitted may include implied promises and implied conditions. Do you want to state some of them expressly in the agreement?

§ 5.1.2. Do you understand and agree with all the stated terms?

With regard to the terms that were stated in the contract, were risks shifted to you? Were there terms that seemed onerous or conditions that gave a party an out? If you noted that you are not sure of the significance of a provision, ask how it fits in with the parties' goals: Why would a party want this term in the contract?

§ 5.1.3. Do you understand and agree with the consequences of breach?

The consequences of breach may not have been spelled out in the contract. Do you want to make these consequences clear? For example, in the process of "what-iffing" the contract, did you detect a term that you want to be material in the event of breach, or one that you do not want to be material, or do you want to set a standard for what is material?

§ 5.1.4. Do you wish to alter any boilerplate terms?

Recall the boilerplate provisions that you set aside. Do you want to adapt any of them for the particular needs of this transaction? For example, a *force majeure* clause may excuse the seller's nonperformance in the event of "revolutions or other disorders, wars, acts of enemies, fires, floods, acts of God" or other events not within the seller's control. As the seller, you "what-if" the provision and determine that you are concerned about a strike at your plant. Rather than argue later about whether that is an excusing event, you might specify that a strike is an excusing event.

§ 5.1.5.   Are there terms you wish to negotiate?

You may have noted on the contract or on the Outline terms that you are unhappy with. These terms may be subject to negotiation. If you are dealing with a contract that cannot be negotiated, determine whether you want to enter the transaction. If risks have been shifted to you, are they worth taking?

§ 5.2.   Check the document for completeness.

Are all blanks and details filled in? Is the contract otherwise complete? Watch out for language that is "incorporated by reference." This means you must find the referenced language and read it in just as if it were expressly stated in the contract. There may also be references to parties who are not parties to the contract. Unless they have signed the contract, they are not bound by its terms. For example, a buyer and seller of real property may provide that a third party escrow will perform certain duties. If the escrow is not a party to the contract, there must be another contract in which the escrow promises to perform those duties. If the contract is only one part of a transaction, you may need to coordinate it with other documents.

§ 5.3.   Detect weaknesses with language.[21]

Does the contract have to be written in its present style? Contracts are often handed down from transaction to transaction, frequently accreting language that is not clear. Language problems include:

- Plain English
- Ambiguity
- Definitions

§ 5.3.1.   Plain English.[22]

If you run a contract through a grammar-checking program, you will usually discover four general problems: long sentences, words of many syllables, the passive voice, and gender-specific language. If you cure those problems, you will find that the contract is now in plain English and is much easier to read. Contracts are rarely written in plain English, although many states require consumer contracts to be written in plain English. Sometimes a contract can be so badly written that translating it into plain English may be necessary to unlock its meaning before you can complete your second pass. Here is an example:

---

[21] *See* Chapter 7.

[22] *See* Chapter 18.

> I agree to pay you _____ percent (_____%) of the selling price as and for your compensation hereunder in the event that you or any broker cooperating with you shall find a buyer ready and willing to enter into a contract for said price and terms, or at such other price and terms as I accept, for the sale or exchange of said real property by you or any other, including myself, while this contract is in force.

This probably means:

> I agree to pay you _____ percent of the selling price (your "commission") if, during the term of this contract, you find a buyer ready and willing to purchase or to enter a contract to purchase the property for the above price and terms. I will pay you the commission if, during the term of this contract, I agree to a sale at any other price or terms, or any other person, including myself, finds a buyer.

You could, of course, let the matter slide. But a preventive approach to problems of language may help avoid conflicts down the road.

§ 5.3.2. Ambiguity.

The preventive approach to contract drafting is particularly helpful when the problem may result in an ambiguity, a word or phrase that can be interpreted more than one way. In "what-iffing" the contract, try to detect whether the meaning of the provision is unclear. Problems with meaning frequently arise because English grammar and usage causes ambiguities. As a reader, you should not feel stupid for puzzling over meaning. In fact, you may prevent a problem from arising later on. For example, assume you are itemizing the subsidiary promises in the agreement and you come across this one:

> Seller shall replace the vehicle if there is a problem with its use and value or safety.

Seller has made a promise here that is subject to a condition. But what is the condition? Is it that there is a problem with

> (use) and (value or safety)

or

> (use and value) or (safety)?

This ambiguity needs to be resolved.

The passive voice may cause ambiguities. For example, in determining the duties of the parties to a residential lease, you find that the contract states:

> The premises shall be kept in good repair.

Does this mean that the landlord shall keep them in good repair or the tenant shall keep them in good repair? By resolving the problem now, you may be preventing a later dispute.

§ 5.3.3. Definitions.

When you need to know the meaning of a word or phrase that appears in the contract, first check to see if there is a definition section of the contract that defines contract terms. If there is, you must use the term as defined in the contract rather than a common sense or dictionary definition. Do not read the definition section until the term appears in a provision of the contract. For example, you are a shareholder and find this provision in your shareholder agreement:

> Shareholders may not transfer any or all of the shares of the Corporation. Exception: Shareholders may transfer any or all of the shares if they comply with the following provisions.

You want to know if you can give a bank a security interest in your shares. It depends on the meaning of the word *transfer*. You find this definition in the definition section of the contract:

> As used in this agreement, *transfer* means to sell, transfer, assign, pledge, encumber or otherwise dispose of or convey (by operation of law or otherwise).

You now replace the defined term in the contract provision with the definition in order to determine the meaning of the provision:

> Shareholders may not sell, transfer, assign, pledge, encumber or otherwise dispose of or convey (by operation of law or otherwise) any or all of the shares of the Corporation.

It is clear that, as defined, a transfer would include granting a security interest.

§ 5.4. Explore opportunities to gain greater expertise.

You will find it easier to read a contract if you have expertise in the substance of the transaction. How can you gain that expertise? You might look to:

- An up-to-date form
- A book or expert on the subject

§ 5.4.1. Find an up-to-date form.

Now that you are an experienced reader of contracts, a good source to improve your knowledge is other contracts used in the area. As you read them, be alert for provisions that address issues that are missing from your contract.

For example, a book publishing contract may contain no term dealing with the publication of an electronic version of the book. Would you know that it would be prudent to address this term? If you did, would you know how to word it? If you have familiarity with modern publishing, the process of "what-iffing" the contract might lead you to ask, "What if the publisher wishes to bring out an electronic version?" You might bring the contract to an expert in the field for review. Or you might contrast your contract with a more up-to-date form and detect that the newer contract contains such a provision.

§ 5.4.2. Find a book or expert on the subject.

You may wish to consult with a book or someone in the business who can identify issues that you missed when "what-iffing" the contract. One reason you read a contract before the fact is to determine what the negotiable terms are. Some are obvious, such as a blank price term that must be filled in by the parties. Other negotiable terms may be found during the course of the analysis you engaged in while reading the contract. For example, you detected risks that were shifted to you, default rules that were changed that disadvantaged you, performances you promised that might have the harsh effect of a condition if not performed, or terms that were omitted. In negotiating, you might identify these areas and negotiate to not take the risk, to return to default rules, to avoid the harsh effect of nonperformance, or to add missing terms.

One thing you may not know as a novice is that there may be certain terms that are customarily negotiable while others are virtually unchangeable. You might consult an expert or a book on the subject to discover the distinction. For example, if you are a first author negotiating a book publishing contract, it is unlikely that you can negotiate the royalty term. You might, however, be able to negotiate such terms as the amount of an advance, the number of complimentary copies, or what happens if the book goes out of print.

Conclusion

As with any "how to" manual, this one will not help you acquire the skill unless you put its teaching into practice. There is undoubtedly a contract in your life that you promised yourself you would read some rainy day. It might be your insurance contract, a lease or mortgage, the warranty you got with your new computer, or the contract you clicked on in order to access an Internet service. Now that you have read *How to Read and Analyze a Contract* through, try reading a contract by following the steps in the Outline. In Appendix A we will work on one together, and in Appendix B you can try it on your own. As with any new skill, the learning curve may initially be steep, but soon you will be an expert contract reader. Achieving a satisfaction similar to solving a difficult puzzle, you will wonder why you have missed the pleasure of contract-reading for so long.

Appendix A
SAMPLE CONTRACT

Here is a sample contract which I will use to demonstrate the application of this method. You might then want to try your hand with the contracts in the Exercises in Appendix B.

Independent Contractor Agreement

Agreement entered into this _____ day of _____, 20____, between Owens Chemical, Inc. (the "Company") of _____, and _____ ("Contractor") of _____.

Recitals

Company operates an industrial chemical business and wishes to hire Contractor as an independent contractor to sell chemicals on behalf of the Company.

Contractor is willing to perform sales services for the Company as an independent contractor.

In consideration of the mutual covenants set forth below, the parties hereby agree as follows:

1. *Description of Work.* Contractor shall devote his full time and use his best efforts to make sales of chemical products to the Company's customers.

2. *Territory.* Contractor shall contact only customers whose principal place of business is located in the following territory.

In case of doubt Contractor shall notify the Company and obtain permission to contact a customer. If Contractor learns of customers in other territories who are interested in purchasing the Company's products, Contractor shall promptly notify the Company of the names of these customers.

3. *Commission.* Company shall pay to Contractor a commission of six percent (6%) of gross sales. Payment shall be made on the 15th of each month for sales made during the previous month.

4. *Relationship of Parties.* The parties intend that an independent contractor-employee relationship will be created by this contract. The Company is interested only in the results to be achieved and the conduct and control of the work will lie solely with the Contractor.

5. *Expenses and Benefits.* Contractor shall be responsible for all expenses involved in performing duties under this agreement and shall not be

entitled to any employee benefits, such as social security, workers' compensation, or insurance.

6. *Liability.* The work to be performed under this contract will be performed entirely at Contractor's risk. For the duration of this contract, Contractor will carry public liability insurance naming Company as an additional insured in the following amount: _____. Contractor agrees to indemnify and hold the company harmless against any liability or loss arising from Contractor's negligence.

7. *Duration and Termination.* This contract shall continue for one year from its execution. It shall be automatically renewed for additional one-year periods unless either party gives written notice of termination at least three (3) months before the anniversary of the execution of this agreement. Provided, however, either party may terminate this agreement at any time for good cause.

8. *Entire Agreement.* This document constitutes the entire agreement between the parties. No agreements between the parties are biding on them unless incorporated in a writing signed by both parties. This agreement may be modified only in writing signed by both parties.

In witness whereof, the parties have executed this agreement on the day and year first above written.

CONTRACTOR: OWENS CHEMICAL, INC.

_____   By:_____
                                     Authorized Agent

First Pass: Orientation

Ascertain the general theme of this contract from the description of the instrument, the caption, and the recitals:

Independent Contractor Agreement

Agreement entered into this _____ day of _____, 20____, between Owens Chemical, Inc. (the "Company") of _____, and _____ ("Contractor") of _____.

Recitals

Company operates an industrial chemical business and wishes to hire Contractor as an independent contractor to sell chemicals on behalf of the Company.

Contractor is willing to perform sales services for the Company as an independent contractor.

The first recital seems to say it all. This is a business that is hiring an individual to sell chemicals for it. A refrain that is expressed a number of times is that the individual is an "independent contractor." We should make a note about that, because it seems to be important.

The primary exchange of promises is found in Paragraphs 1 and 3. What is the relationship between the parties?

1. *Description of Work.* Contractor shall devote his full time and use his best efforts to make sales of chemical products to the Company's customers.

3. *Commission.* Company shall pay to Contractor a commission of six percent (6%) of gross sales. Payment shall be made on the 15th of each month for sales made during the previous month.

The Contractor will work full time for the Company and they will pay him a percentage of his sales. The fact that he is working full time for them seems to suggest he is an employee, but he is not paid a salary. We make note of that.

Looking at the structure of the contract, it appears that no further agreement between the parties is contemplated. As we continue our passes, we will determine whether there are additional terms that might be included.

The parts of the contract. We have already looked at the description of the Instrument and the caption. The closing is properly signed by the Contractor personally and the corporation by an authorized agent:

CONTRACTOR: OWENS CHEMICAL, INC.

_____ By:_____

                       Authorized Agent

There is language of transition preceding the first term and preceding the closing:

In consideration of the mutual covenants set forth below, the parties hereby agree as follows:

In witness whereof, the parties have executed this agreement on the day and year first above written.

There are surprisingly few boilerplate terms in this agreement. Paragraph 8 contains boilerplate that is commonly found in contracts, but the other provisions all seem to be operative terms.

We now look at the transaction against a larger background. What does the company want from the Contractor? Why does it want him to be an independent contractor? What are the goals of an independent contractor, and how do they differ from the goals of an employee?

Because this is a contract for services, it would be governed by the common law. We wonder if there is case law or statutes on point that might govern this relationship, since it seems to be similar to an employment contract, where there is a great deal of public interest.

Second Pass: Explication

Separate out the boilerplate terms. There are surprisingly few boilerplate terms. Paragraph 8 seems to include both a merger clause (*see* § 6.4) and a no oral modification clause (*see* § 11.9):

> 8. *Entire Agreement.* This document constitutes the entire agreement between the parties. No agreements between the parties are binding on them unless incorporated in a writing signed by both parties. This agreement may be modified only in writing signed by both parties.

The balance of the agreement contains the operative terms. What are the promises of each party?

As we have seen, in Paragraph 1, the Contractor promises to work full time and to use his best efforts to sell the Company's products. Contractor might wonder what is the meaning of "full time" and perhaps more importantly, "best efforts"? Is this something more than reasonable efforts? Who is to say how hard he has to work?

In Paragraph 2, there is another promise by Contractor, this one a promise not to do something. He promises to limit himself to customers in a certain geographical area. He should wonder what corresponding rights he has. Is he the only salesperson in this territory or are there others?

In Paragraph 3, as we have seen, Company has the duty to pay Contractor. We see a limitation on Company's duties in Paragraph 5, however, for he has to pay all his expenses and receives no employee benefits. Furthermore, according to Paragraph 6, he has to carry insurance protecting the company in case he is negligent. Notice that he agrees to indemnify the Company against any loss. What if Contractor was required to carry liability insurance in the amount of $500,000, but because of his negligence, the Company became liable to someone in the amount of $750,000. Would he have to pay the Company $250,000 out of his own pocket? This might be a good place to time travel and think about what might happen that would invoke this provision? How might his negligence lead to liability on the part of the Company?

These provisions are all reinforced by Paragraph 4, which yet one more time announces that the contractor is an independent contractor and not an employee.

The duration of the contract is found in Paragraph 8. Contractor should probably put the date 9 months before the first anniversary in his tickler file, for that is when he must give written notice if he wants to terminate the agreement before it renews. Note also that this provision contains a termination agreement allowing either party to terminate at any time for "good cause." What is that? Does this go back to the obligation to "use best efforts" in Paragraph 1? What could Company do that constitutes good cause?

Third Pass: Implication

The only significant condition seems to arise in Paragraph 3, where Contractor must first work and then gets paid for work previously done. This is customary in a work for hire situation.

As we have previously detected, there are a number of provisions that might be clarified by trade usage. What is full time, best efforts, and good cause? We might also want to know what the meaning is of gross sales in Paragraph 3 and expenses in Paragraph 5.

If we did our research on employment law, we would realize that one of the most important default rules of employment is the doctrine of respondeat superior — the employer is liable for the negligence of the employee. If we are cognizant of that rule, we see how Company has tried to contract around it here — if Contractor is an independent contractor rather than an employee, Company is not liable for his negligence. So many of these provisions must be designed to make him an independent contractor.

Fourth Pass: Remediation

What happens if Contractor is not able to perform? As an employee, he might have some protection in the form of sick leave, vacation time, or disability insurance. As an independent contractor, if he is unable to perform, he doesn't get paid. Are there steps he should take to protect himself in that event?

How might Contractor be in breach? He might contact a customer outside his territory. Paragraph 2 seems to anticipate that this could be a problem, but it provides no remedy. Would Contractor be paid for those sales? Would this breach result only in damages, or would it be the kind of "good cause" that could result in termination?

He might be in breach by not purchasing the required liability insurance. Presumably as a named insured, Contractor would be aware if that happened. He might also be in breach by not indemnifying the Company. But as we have seen, a third party would only be able to hold the Company liable in the event of his negligence by proving that the Company was his employer. In that event, would Paragraph 6 be enforceable?

How might Company be in breach? Their principal obligation is to pay him, so he would find out quickly if Company was in breach.

There are no terms that address remedies, so the default rules apply. The agreement would be enforceable in court and each side would pay its own attorneys' fees. However, an exception to that might arise if Contractor were held to be an employee. Both the federal and state governments have wage and hour statutes that protect employees. In the event of breach by Company, or at the termination of his contract, Contractor should consider whether it is in his interest to have his status determined by an appropriate agency.

Fifth Pass: Evaluation

We might want clarification of some of the vague terms in this agreement. Contractor might bargain for exclusive rights within his territory and for elimination of the "hold harmless" clause that appears to make him liable for the Company's loss.

Both sides will want to consult with an expert to determine the extent to which the independent contractor relationship will be honored in the jurisdiction. Contractor will want to know if he may have an opportunity to be treated as an employee when it is in his interest to do so and Company will want an honest evaluation of the risk it is taking and the costs and benefits of the arrangement.

Appendix B

EXERCISES

Use the techniques in *How to Read and Analyze a Contract* to read the following contracts. You may wish to use the Outline to help you organize your thoughts.

Exercise 1.

Agreement for the Sale of Goods

_____ Seller, and _____, Buyer, with addresses as they appear with their names below, agree as follows:

1. Description — Sale of Goods. Seller shall transfer ownership and deliver possession to Buyer, and Buyer shall pay for and accept the following goods: _____.

2. Time of Delivery. Buyer shall have the right to specify the date of delivery, but in no event shall the date specified be before _____, 20___ or after _____, 20___.

3. Delivery in Lots. Buyer shall have the right to demand all of the goods at one time during the period stated in Paragraph 2, or in portions from time to time.

4. Place of Delivery. The goods shall be delivered at Seller's address as it appears below.

5. Method of Tender. Buyer will give notice to the Seller at least 24 hours before Buyer desires to take possession of the goods. Seller agrees that he will furnish the facilities and manpower for loading the goods on trucks furnished by Buyer.

6. Seller to Package Goods. Seller will package goods in accordance with instruction of Buyer provided instructions are furnished in sufficient time to permit Seller to complete the packaging before delivery. Buyer shall pay Seller the reasonable cost of packaging in addition to the price specified in this contract.

7. Identification — Risk of Loss. Identification of the goods under Section 2-501 of the Uniform Commercial Code shall occur at the moment this agreement is signed by the parties. Risk of loss of the goods shall pass to the Buyer upon identification.

8. Title. Title to the goods shall remain with the Seller until Buyer actually receives possession of the goods.

367

9. Disclaimer of Express Warranties. Seller warrants that the goods are as described in this agreement, but no other express warranty is made in respect to the goods.

10. Disclaimer of Implied Warranties. THE GOODS SOLD UNDER THIS CONTRACT ARE PURCHASED BY THE BUYER "AS IS" AND THE SELLER DOES NOT WARRANTY THAT THEY ARE OF MERCHANT-ABLE QUALITY OR THAT THEY CAN BE USED FOR ANY PARTICU-LAR PURPOSE.

11. Amount of Price. The price to be paid by Buyer shall be that contained on the Seller's price list last published before the date of actual delivery of the goods.

12. Time of Payment. Buyer shall pay for the goods at the time and place of delivery.

13. Right of Inspection. Buyer shall have the right to inspect the goods at the time and place of delivery before paying for them or accepting them.

14. Method of Payment. Payment shall be made in cash or by certified check.

15. Remedies. Buyer and Seller shall have all remedies afforded each by the Uniform Commercial Code.

16. Interpretation — Parol Evidence. This writing is intended by the parties as a final expression of their agreement and is intended also as a complete and exclusive statement of the terms of their agreement. [No course of prior dealings between the parties and no usage of the trade shall be relevant to supplement or explain any term used in this agreement.] Acceptance or acquiescence in a course of performance rendered under this agreement shall not be relevant to determine the meaning of this agreement even though the accepting or acquiescing party has knowledge of the nature of the performance and opportunity for objection. Whenever a term defined by the Uniform Commercial Code is used in this agreement the definition contained in the Code is to control.

17. Authority of Seller's Agents. No agent, employee or representative of the Seller has any authority to bind the Seller to any affirmation, representation or warranty concerning the goods sold under this agreement, and unless an affirmation, representation or warranty made by an agent, employee or representative is specifically included within this written agreement, it has not formed a part of the basis of this bargain and shall not in any way be enforceable.

18. Modifications. This agreement can be modified or rescinded only by a writing signed by both the parties or their duly authorized agents.

19. Waiver. No claim or right arising out of a breach of this contract can be discharged in whole or in part by a waiver or renunciation of the claim or right unless the waiver or renunciation is supported by consideration and is in writing signed by the aggrieved party.

20. Assignment — Delegation. No right or interest in this contract shall be assigned by either Buyer or Seller without the written permission of the other party, and no delegation of any obligation owed, or of the performance of any obligation, by either Buyer or Seller shall be made without the written permission of the other party. Any attempted assignment or delegation shall be wholly void and totally ineffective for all purposes unless made in conformity with this paragraph.

21. Time for Bringing Action. Any action for breach of this contract must be commenced within 2 years after the cause of action has accrued.

22. Applicable Law. This agreement shall be governed by the Uniform Commercial Code. Wherever the term "Uniform Commercial Code" is used, it shall be construed as meaning the Uniform Commercial Code as adopted in the State of _____ as effective and in force on the date of this agreement.

23. Arbitration. Any controversy or claim arising out of or relating to this contract, or the breach thereof, shall be settled by arbitration in accordance with the Rules of the American Arbitration Association, and judgment upon the award rendered by the Arbitrator(s) may be entered in any Court having jurisdiction thereof.

SIGNED _____, 20 ____.

Buyer   Seller
Address   Address

Exercise 2.

COMPANY MASTER TERMS

These Company Master Terms ("Master Terms"), made this _____ day of _____, 2002 ("Effective Date"), by and between Company Inc., a Delaware corporation having an address at 555 Madison Avenue, New York, NY ("Company") and The University of Erehwon having an address at #32 Campus Drive, Erehwon ("Customer").

Company offers software and services to scale from course websites, to an entire online campus and that allows institutions to establish and manage accounts for a stored value card system and security access system. Customer wishes to adopt the Company technology to enhance its own educational programs, and Company is willing to provide the Company technology to Customer for this purpose.

Therefore, in consideration of the following mutual covenants and agreements, the parties agree as follows:

1. SCOPE OF AGREEMENT.

1.1 Exhibits and Schedules. These Master Terms describe the general terms by which Customer may license Software (as defined below) and purchase Services (as defined below) and Equipment from Company as set forth in a Schedule. The specific terms related to the license of Software and purchase of Services and/or Equipment are described in the appropriate Software or Service Schedules, and Exhibits thereto (collectively referred to as "Schedules"). Each Schedule and these Master Terms together constitute a separate agreement (the "Agreement") between Company and Customer. Schedules may be added or deleted from time to time by the agreement of the parties, but Customer is only authorized to license Software or purchase Services hereunder to the extent that one or more applicable Schedules is executed and in force.

1.2 Order of Precedence. The provisions of any Schedule will take precedence over these Master Terms, to the extent that they are inconsistent. In the event of any inconsistencies between the terms of these Master Terms and any referenced, attached, or preprinted terms and conditions on the purchase order, these Master Terms shall take precedence.

2. DEFINITIONS

2.1 "Affiliates" means, with respect to any entity, any other entity Controlling, Controlled by or under common Control with such entity, whether directly or indirectly through one or more intermediaries.

2.2 "Available Date" means the date upon which an install copy of the Software and/or the Equipment is made available to Customer. An install copy of the Software or the Equipment is "made available" to the Customer either (i) on the date on which Company has notified Customer that an install copy of the Software is available for download; (ii) on the date Company notifies Customer that the Software may be accessed on the Company ASP server; or (iii) the date on which the Software made available for installation via diagnostic modem; or (iv) on the date Company ships Equipment to Customer. The download site will be made available to Customer for a period of thirty (30) days and Customer MUST download the Software within this thirty day period. A CD containing a backup copy of the Software can be sent to Customer upon Customer's request.

2.3 "Confidential Information" means any non-public information about a party, including, without limitation, the party's business, vendors, customers, products, services, employees, finances, costs, expenses, financial or competitive condition, policies, and practices, computer software programs and programming tools and their respective design, architecture, modules, interfaces, databases and database structures, nonliteral elements, capabilities and functionality, source code and object code, research and development efforts, marketing and distribution efforts, licensing, cross-licensing, marketing and distribution practices; computer software programs and other information licensed or otherwise disclosed to a party in confidence by a third party, and any other non-public information that does or may have economic value by reason of not being generally known.

2.4 "Control" and its derivatives shall mean legal, beneficial or equitable ownership, directly or indirectly, of more than fifty percent (50%) of the outstanding voting capital stock (or other ownership interest, if not a corporation) of an entity, or actual managerial or operational control over such entity.

2.5 "Corrections" shall mean a change (e.g. fixes, workarounds and other modifications) made by or for Company which corrects software errors in the Software, provided in temporary form such as a patch, and later issued in permanent form of an Update.

2.6 "Documentation" means Company's applicable standard end user documentation for the Software and/or Equipment, which may be amended from time to time.

2.7 "Equipment" means the hardware and firmware related to the stored value card system and security access system as identified on Company's then-current price list.

2.8 "Customer Content" means any content (including, but not limited to, course materials and the copyrights, patents, trade secrets and other intellectual property related thereto) provided by or through Customer for use with the Software or the Application Software if applicable.

2.9 "Services" means any consulting, educational, ASP installation, system administration, training or maintenance and support services provided by Company to Customer.

2.10 "Software" means the object code version of the Company software as described on the Software schedule(s), and Supported Interfaces (and any Documentation and help files included within the Software), including any Corrections, Updates and Upgrades provided pursuant to the maintenance and support terms of such schedule.

2.11 "Supported Interfaces" means application-based interfaces (API), network protocols, data formats, database schemas, and file formats used in the Software as described in the Documentation ("Installation Guide").

2.12 "Updates" shall mean the object code versions of the Software that has been developed by Company to correct any software error therein and/or provide additional functionality and that have been commercially released with a version number that differs from that of the prior version in the number to the right of the decimal point (e.g., 2.0 vs. 2.1).

2.13 "Upgrades" shall mean the object code versions of the Software that have been customized, enhanced, or otherwise modified by or on behalf of Company, acting in its sole discretion, to include additional functionality and that have been released with a version number that differs from that of the prior version in the number to the left of the decimal point (e.g., 3.0 vs. 2.0).

3. SOFTWARE AND SERVICES

3.1 Software License/Maintenance and Support Services. Company will provide Customer with Software as well as maintenance and support services set forth on the applicable Software Schedule attached hereto for each annual period that Customer has paid the associated License Fees.

3.2 Sale of Equipment. Company will sell to Customer, and Customer shall purchase from Company, the Equipment pursuant to the terms and conditions in Schedule A. If no Equipment Schedule is attached, Customer acknowledges that Company has no obligation to provide any Equipment to Customer.

3.3 Learning Solutions. Company will provide Customer with the learning solutions set forth on the Learning Solutions Schedule attached hereto. If no Learning Solutions Schedule is attached, Customer acknowledges that Company has no obligation to provide any learning solutions to Customer.

3.4 ASP Services. Company will provide Customer with the ASP services set forth in any ASP Schedule attached hereto. If no ASP Services Schedule is attached, Customer acknowledges that Company has no obligation to provide Customer with any installation, configuration or other professional consulting services.

3.5 Additional Services. Company will provide Customer with any other services that are set forth in a separate schedule attached hereto. If no additional Schedules are attached, Customer acknowledges that Company has no obligation to provide Customer with any additional services.

4. CONFIDENTIALITY

4.1 Nondisclosure and Nonuse. Each party receiving Confidential Information, including but not limited to, materials containing Confidential Information shall (a) disclose such Confidential Information to only those directors, officers, employees and agents of such party (i) whose duties justify their need to know such information and (ii) who have been clearly informed of their obligation to maintain the confidential, proprietary and/or trade secret status of such Confidential Information; and (b) use such Confidential Information only for the purposes set forth in this Agreement. Each party receiving Confidential Information shall treat such information as strictly confidential, and shall use the same care to prevent disclosure of such information as such party uses with respect to its own confidential and proprietary information, which shall not be less than the care a reasonable person would use under similar circumstances. Notwithstanding the foregoing, each party may disclose Confidential Information to the extent necessary pursuant to applicable federal, state or local law, regulation, court order, or other legal process, provided the receiving party has given the disclosing party prior written notice of such required disclosure and, to the extent reasonably possible, has given the disclosing party an opportunity to contest such required disclosure at the disclosing party's expense.

4.2 Notice. The receiving party will notify the disclosing party immediately in the event the receiving party learns of any unauthorized possession, use or knowledge of the Confidential Information and/or Materials containing Confidential Information and will cooperate with the disclosing party in any litigation against any third persons necessary to protect the disclosing party's rights with respect to the Confidential Information and Materials.

4.3 Terms of Agreement. Except as otherwise provided by law, neither party shall disclose the terms of the Agreement to any third party; provided, however, that either party may disclose the terms of this Agreement to its affiliates, attorneys and accountants, or to any potential investor or acquirer of a substantial part of such party's business (whether by merger, sale of assets, sale of stock or otherwise) that is bound by a written agreement to keep such terms confidential, or as may be required by law.

5. TERM; TERMINATION

5.1 Term. These Master Terms and the agreement between the parties shall commence as of the Effective Date and shall continue until the expiration or termination of all Schedules.

5.2 Default. Either party may, at its option, terminate these Master Terms and any or all Schedules if a material default by the other party is not corrected within thirty (30) days after receipt of a written notice of the default.

5.3 Mutual Termination. Either party may terminate these Master Terms and any or all Schedules, immediately by written notice, if the other party breaches any Software Schedule or Section 4 of these Master Terms.

5.4 Effect of Termination. Termination of the Agreement shall not relieve either party of any obligation or liability accrued hereunder prior to such termination, nor affect or impair the rights of either party arising under the Agreement prior to such termination, except as expressly provided herein.

5.5 Survival. The termination or expiration of the Agreement shall not relieve either party of any obligation or liability accrued hereunder prior to or subsequent to such termination, nor affect or impair the rights of either party arising under the Agreement prior to or subsequent to such termination or expiration, except as expressly provided herein.

6. FEES; PAYMENT

6.1 Fees. Customer shall pay Company the fees in US Dollars specified in the Schedules attached as applicable.

6.2 Payment and Late Fees. Customer shall pay Company the Fees in accordance with the applicable Schedules, and in no event later than thirty (30) days of the date of an invoice from Company. Company expressly reserves the right to change the License Fee and Maintenance and Support Fee for any Renewal Term. Any overdue amounts will bear a late fee at the rate of eighteen percent (18%) per annum or the maximum rate permitted by applicable law, whichever is less. All fees are payable in U.S. dollars and shall be sent to the attention of Company's Accounts Receivable Department.

6.3 Audit. For the sole purpose of ensuring compliance with this Agreement, Company shall have the right, at its expense, to audit Customer's use of the Software upon at least seven (7) days advance notice. Any such audit shall be during Customer's normal business hours and shall not be made more frequently than once every twelve months.

6.4 Taxes. The fees hereunder do not include any sales, use, excise, import or export, value-added or similar tax and interest, as well as any costs associated with the collection or withholding thereof, and all government permit fees, license fees and customs and similar fees levied on the delivery of the Software or the performance of Services by Company to Customer. All payments due under this Agreement shall be made without any deduction or withholding, unless such deduction or withholding is required by any applicable law of any relevant governmental revenue authority then in effect. If Customer is required to deduct or withhold, Customer will promptly notify Company of the requirement, pay the required amount to the relevant governmental authority, provide Company with an official receipt or certified copy or other documentation acceptable to Company evidencing payment, and pay to Company, in addition to the payment to which Company is otherwise entitled under this Agreement, such additional amount as is necessary to ensure that the net amount actually received by Company equals the full amount Company would have received had no such deduction or withholding been required.

6.5 Billing Contact. Customer's billing/invoicing point of contact is: [omitted]

7. DISCLAIMERS AND REMEDIES.

7.1 Limited Warranty. Unless otherwise indicated on an attached Schedule, Company warrants to Customer, subject to the remedy limitations set forth herein, that during (i) a period of twelve (12) months from the Available Date of the Equipment manufactured by Company or third-party Equipment sold by Company, unless otherwise specified in the applicable Schedule(s) and (ii) a period of ninety (90) days from License Available Date for the Software manufactured by Company, that such Equipment and Software will substantially conform to the applicable Documentation, provided that Company has received all amounts owed under this Agreement and Customer is not in default of any part of this Agreement. Customer must notify Company in writing of the deficiency within the warranty period and must install any generally-released Corrections, Upgrades and Updates. Company's sole obligation is limited to repair or replacement of the defective Software or Equipment in a timely manner.

7.2 Disclaimer of Warranty. EXCEPT FOR THE LIMITED WARRANTY IN SECTION 7.1 ABOVE AND ANY SPECIFIC WARRANTIES PROVIDED IN AN ATTACHED SCHEDULE(S), THE SOFTWARE, EQUIPMENT AND ALL PORTIONS THEREOF, AND ANY SERVICES ARE PROVIDED "AS IS." TO THE MAXIMUM EXTENT PERMITTED BY LAW, COMPANY AND ITS LICENSORS AND SUPPLIERS DISCLAIM ALL OTHER WARRANTIES OF ANY KIND, EITHER EXPRESS OR IMPLIED, INCLUDING, WITHOUT LIMITATION, IMPLIED WARRANTIES OF MERCHANTABILITY AND FITNESS FOR A PARTICULAR PURPOSE. EXCEPT AS SPECIFICALLY PROVIDED IN AN ATTACHED SCHEDULE(S), NEITHER COMPANY NOR ITS LICENSORS WARRANT THAT THE FUNCTIONS OR INFORMATION CONTAINED IN THE SOFTWARE WILL MEET ANY REQUIREMENTS OR NEEDS CUSTOMER MAY HAVE, OR THAT THE SOFTWARE WILL OPERATE ERROR FREE, OR IN AN UNINTERRUPTED FASHION, OR THAT

ANY DEFECTS OR ERRORS IN THE SOFTWARE WILL BE CORRECTED, OR THAT THE SOFTWARE IS COMPATIBLE WITH ANY PARTICULAR OPERATING SYSTEM. COMPANY AND ITS LICENSORS MAKE NO GUARANTEE OF ACCESS OF ACCURACY OF THE CONTENT CONTAINED ON OR ACCESSED THROUGH THE SOFTWARE.

7.3 Limitations of Liability. TO THE MAXIMUM EXTENT PERMITTED BY LAW, IN NO EVENT WILL COMPANY OR ITS LICENSORS BE LIABLE TO CUSTOMER OR ANY THIRD PARTY FOR ANY INCIDENTAL OR CONSEQUENTIAL DAMAGES (INCLUDING, WITHOUT LIMITATION, INDIRECT, SPECIAL, PUNITIVE, OR EXEMPLARY DAMAGES) ARISING OUT OF THE USE OF OR INABILITY TO USE THE SOFTWARE, EQUIPMENT OR ANY PORTION THEREOF, DEFECTS IN WARRANTY, ANY SERVICES, OR FOR ANY CLAIM BY ANY OTHER PARTY, EVEN IF COMPANY AND/OR ITS LICENSORS HAVE BEEN ADVISED OF THE POSSIBILITY OF SUCH DAMAGES. IN NO EVENT SHALL COMPANY'S LIABILITY EXCEED THE AMOUNT OF FEES PAID FOR THE PARTICULAR SOFTWARE, EQUIPMENT AND/OR SERVICE LICENSED UNDER EACH SCHEDULE HEREUNDER FOR THE CURRENT TWELVE (12) MONTH PERIOD.

8. INDEMNIFICATION

8.1 Company. If Customer receives a claim that the use of the Software or Equipment infringes a patent, copyright or other intellectual property right, Customer must promptly notify Company in writing. Company shall, at its own expense and option: (i) defend and settle such claim, (ii) procure Customer the right to use the Software or Equipment, (iii) modify or replace the Software or Equipment to avoid infringement; or (iv) refund the applicable fee paid for the current term. In the event Company exercises option (i) above, it shall have the sole and exclusive authority to defend and/or settle any such claim or action, provided that Company will keep Customer informed of, and will consult with any independent attorneys appointed by Customer at Customer's own expense regarding the progress of such litigation.

8.2 Exceptions. Company shall have no liability to Customer under Section 8.1 or otherwise for any claim or action alleging infringement based upon (i) any use of the Software or Equipment in a manner other than as specified by Company; (ii) any combination of the Software or Equipment by Customer with other products, equipment, devices, software, systems or data not supplied by Company (including, without limitation, any software produced by Customer for use with the Software) to the extent such claim is directed against such combination; or (iii) any modifications or customization of the Software or Equipment by any person other than Company ("Customer Matter").

8.3 Customer. Customer shall, at its own expense, defend or, at its option, settle any claim, suit or proceeding brought against Company arising out of a Customer Matter and shall pay any damages finally awarded or settlement amounts agreed upon to the extent based upon a Customer

Matter ("Company Claim"); provided that Company provides Customer with (i) prompt written notice of such Company Claim; (ii) control over the defense and settlement of such Company Claim; and (iii) proper and full information and assistance to settle or defend any such Company Claim.

8.4 Exclusive Remedy. THE FOREGOING PROVISIONS OF THIS SECTION 8 STATE THE ENTIRE LIABILITY AND OBLIGATIONS OF EACH PARTY, AND THE EXCLUSIVE REMEDY OF EACH PARTY WITH RESPECT TO ACTUAL OR ALLEGED INFRINGEMENT OF ANY INTELLECTUAL PROPERTY RIGHT.

9. MISCELLANEOUS

9.1 Severability. Should any term or provision of this Agreement be finally determined by a court of competent jurisdiction to be void, invalid, unenforceable or contrary to law or equity, the offending term or provision shall be modified and limited (or if strictly necessary, deleted) only to the extent required to conform to the requirements of law and the remainder of this Agreement (or, as the case may be, the application of such provisions to other circumstances) shall not be affected thereby but rather shall be enforced to the greatest extent permitted by law, and the parties shall use their best efforts to substitute for the offending provision new terms having similar economic effect.

9.2. Conflict Resolution. In the event of a dispute between the Parties relating to the terms and conditions of this Master Terms or any Schedule, or the performance of the Parties hereunder, the Parties shall first attempt to resolve the dispute by internal discussions involving their appointed representatives within thirty (30) days of the dispute arising.

9.3 Arbitration. If any dispute, controversy or claim cannot be resolved to the satisfaction of both Parties pursuant to Section 9.2 above within Section 9.2's thirty (30) day period, either Party may, submit the matter to binding arbitration to be finally settled in accordance with the Commercial Arbitration Rules of the American Arbitration Association (the "AAA") then obtaining, by a panel of three arbitrators; provided, however, that this clause shall not be construed to limit or to preclude either Party from bringing an action in a court of competent jurisdiction for injunctive or other provisional relief as necessary or appropriate. Each Party shall have the right to appoint one arbitrator from the list of arbitrators supplied to the parties by the AAA, and the two arbitrators so appointed shall appoint the third. Any award or determination of the arbitration shall be final, non-appealable, and conclusive and binding upon the parties, and any court of competent jurisdiction thereon may enter judgment. Any award shall include interest from the date of damages incurred for breach or other violation of this Agreement, and from the date of the award until paid in full, at a rate to be fixed by the arbitrators. The prevailing party may recover its costs of arbitration, including reasonable expert witness fee and reasonable attorneys' fees.

9.4 Governing Law. This Agreement shall for all purposes be governed by and interpreted in accordance with the laws of the Commonwealth of Virginia without reference to its conflicts of law provisions. Any legal suit, action or proceeding arising out of or relating to this Agreement shall be commenced in a federal court in the Commonwealth of Virginia, and each party hereto irrevocably submits to the non-exclusive jurisdiction and venue of any such court in any such suit, action or proceeding. The U.N. Convention on Contracts for the International Sale of Goods shall not apply to this Agreement.

9.5 Modification and Waiver. Any modification, amendment, supplement, or other change to this Agreement or any Schedule attached hereto must be in writing and signed by a duly authorized representative of Company and Customer. All waivers must be in writing. The failure of either party to insist upon strict performance of any provision of this Agreement, or to exercise any right provided for herein, shall not be deemed to be a waiver of the future of such provision or right, and no waiver of any provision or right shall affect the right of the waiving party to enforce any other provision or right herein.

9.6 Assignment. No right or obligation of Customer under this Agreement may be assigned, delegated or otherwise transferred, whether by agreement, operation of law or otherwise, without the express prior written consent of Company, and any attempt to assign, delegate or otherwise transfer any of Customer's rights or obligations hereunder, without such consent, shall be void. Subject to the preceding sentence, this Agreement shall bind each party and its permitted successors and assigns.

9.7 Remedies. The parties agree that any breach of this Agreement would cause irreparable injury for which no adequate remedy at law exists; therefore, the parties agree that equitable remedies, including without limitation, injunctive relief and specific performance, are appropriate remedies to redress any breach or threatened breach of this Agreement, in addition to other remedies available to the parties. All rights and remedies hereunder shall be cumulative, may be exercised singularly or concurrently and shall not be deemed exclusive except as provided in Sections 5, 7 and 8. If any legal action is brought to enforce any obligations hereunder, the prevailing party shall be entitled to receive its attorneys' fees, court costs and other collection expenses, in addition to any other relief it may receive.

9.8 Notices. Any notice or communication permitted or required hereunder shall be in writing and shall be delivered in person or by courier, sent by facsimile, or mailed by certified or registered mail, postage prepaid, return receipt requested, and addressed as set forth above or to such other address as shall be given in accordance with this Section 9.8, and shall be effective upon receipt.

9.9 Force Majeure. Except with regard to payment obligations, neither party will be responsible for any failure to fulfill its obligations due to causes beyond its reasonable control, including without limitation, acts or omissions of government or military authority, acts of God, materials shortages, transportation delays, fires, floods, labor disturbances, riots, wars, terrorist acts or inability to obtain any export or import license or other approval of authorization of any government authority.

9.10 U.S. Government Sales. If Customer is a U.S. Government entity, the Software is provided with RESTRICTED RIGHTS. Each of the components that comprise the Software is a "commercial item" as that term is defined at 48 C.F.R. 2.101, consisting of "commercial computer software" and/or "commercial computer software documentation" as such terms are used in 48 C.F.R. 12.212. Consistent with 48 C.F.R. 12.212 and 48 C.F.R. 227.7202-1 through 227.7202-4, all U.S. Government end users acquire the Software with only those rights set forth herein. Contractor/manufacturer is Company Inc., 555 Madison Avenue, New York, NY. All rights not specifically granted in this statement are reserved by Company.

9.11 Export Control. Customer shall not export or allow the export or re-export the Software, any components thereof or any Confidential Information of Company without the express, prior, written consent of Company and except in compliance with all export laws and regulations of the U.S. Department of Commerce and all other U.S. agencies and authorities, including without limitation, the Export Administration Regulations of the U.S. Department of Commerce Bureau of Export Administration (as contained in 15 C.F.R. Parts 730–772), and, if applicable, relevant foreign laws and regulations.

9.12 Relationship. Company and Customer are independent contracting parties. This Agreement shall not constitute the parties as principal and agent, partners, joint venturers, or employer and employee.

9.13 Entire Agreement. An Agreement, which includes these Master Terms, and the applicable Schedule(s) and Exhibit(s), constitute the entire, full and complete Agreement between the parties concerning the subject matter hereof, and they collectively supersede all prior or contemporaneous oral or written communications, proposals, conditions, representations and warranties, and prevails over any conflicting or additional terms of any quote, order, acknowledgment, or other communication between the parties relating to its subject matter.

IN WITNESS WHEREOF, the parties hereto have executed these Master Terms as of the date first written above.

Company	CUSTOMER The University of Erehwon
Signature	Signature
Print Name and Title	Print Name and Title
Date:	Date:

Attachments:

Schedule A-1 Equipment Purchase
Software Schedule B-1Company System Software License
Attachment 1 to Schedule B-1 Online Card Office Specifications
Schedule C Company System Software and Equipment Maintenance and
Basic Support
Exhibit C1.2 Company System Coverage
Exhibit C1.3 List of Equipment
Schedule E-1 Cards and Supplies Purchase
Company Professional Services Agreement

BIBLIOGRAPHY

ANNOTATED BIBLIOGRAPHY

There are a number of works on contract drafting that I come back to time and again. These are the idiosyncratic choices I would place on a drafter's desk:

Robert Dick, LEGAL DRAFTING (Carswell 1972) (2nd ed. 1985). This book applies many of Reed Dickerson's principles to contract drafting. The American reader should not be distracted by its Canadian orientation.

Reed Dickerson, THE FUNDAMENTALS OF LEGAL DRAFTING (Little, Brown 1965) (2nd ed. 1986). Although oriented more toward legislative drafting than contract drafting, this landmark book contains a great deal of fundamental information and many useful suggestions.

Carl Felsenfeld & Alan Siegel, WRITING CONTRACTS IN PLAIN ENGLISH (West 1981). This book looks at Plain English contracts in depth, considering style, substance, and visual aesthetics.

Charles M. Fox, WORKING WITH CONTRACTS: WHAT LAW SCHOOL DOESN'T TEACH YOU (PLI 2002). I'm hopeful that law students who use DRAFTING AND ANALYZING CONTRACTS do get taught something in law school about drafting contracts. Fox's sensible advice is a great advanced course, particularly when applied to sophisticated financing and acquisition agreements.

Frederick M. Hart & William F. Willier, FORMS AND PROCEDURES UNDER THE UNIFORM COMMERCIAL CODE (part of Bender's Uniform Commercial Code Service). This formbook contains a lucid explanation of each Code section and its exemplification as a contract provision, often indicating the legal effect of alternative provisions.

David Mellinkoff, LEGAL WRITING: SENSE AND NONSENSE (West 1982). This book is a valuable manual on the process of drafting with clarity and precision.

Justin Sweet, *The Lawyer's Role in Contract Drafting*, 43 CAL. ST. B.J. 362 (1968). This article sensitively explores the drafting process from the perspective of a practitioner.

Also:

E.L. Piesse, THE ELEMENTS OF DRAFTING (Carswell 9th ed. 1996). This Australian work contains numerous helpful suggestions, often tracing a concept back historically and indicating its appearance in case law.

Louis M. Brown, HOW TO NEGOTIATE A SUCCESSFUL CONTRACT (Prentice-Hall 1955). This excellent (and unfortunately out-of-print) work discusses the substantive purpose of significant terms in many familiar contracts.

Frank E. Cooper, WRITING IN LAW PRACTICE (Michie 1963). This book contains thoughtful chapters on "Law is Language" and "Drafting Contracts." Unfortunately, the author does not discuss the problems presented for discussion and drafting.

Sidney F. Parham, Jr., THE FUNDAMENTALS OF LEGAL WRITING (Michie 1967). This book contains many useful suggestions, but lacks concrete examples.

Peter Nash Swisher, *Techniques of Legal Drafting: A Survival Manual,* 15 U. RICH. L. REV. 873 (1981). This article contains little new information, but synthesizes the available sources in a clear and concise fashion.

Richard Wincor, CONTRACTS IN PLAIN ENGLISH (McGraw-Hill 1976). The title is misleading. This is not a book about the "Plain English" movement. It describes in plain English how lawyers as planners negotiate and draft contracts, with an emphasis on international transactions.

INDEX

[References are to page numbers.]

I–1

[References are to page numbers.]

[References are to page numbers.]

[References are to page numbers.]

[References are to page numbers.]

[References are to page numbers.]

[References are to page numbers.]

R

S

T

U

V

W

[References are to page numbers.]